Essays on Economic Policy

J. Marcus Fleming

ESSAYS
ON
ECONOMIC POLICY

J. Marcus Fleming

NEW YORK   COLUMBIA PRESS   1978

Library of Congress Cataloging in Publication Data

Fleming, John Marcus, 1911–1976.
Essays on economic policy.

Includes bibliographical references and index.
1. Economics—Addresses, essays, lectures.
2. International finance—Addresses, essays, lectures.
3. Economic policy—Addresses, essays, lectures.
I. Title.
HB171.F55 1977   330   77-15991
ISBN 0-231-04366-X

Columbia University Press
New York   Guildford, Surrey
Copyright © 1978 Columbia University Press
Printed in the United States of America

To
Hilary and Alison

CONTENTS

PREFACE

A T THE TIME of his untimely death on February 3, 1976, J. Marcus Fleming left behind a rich collection of papers on economic policy issues written over the course of four decades. A collection of his writings had been published in 1971 under the title *Essays in International Economics*. As the title indicates, the papers contained in that volume dealt with international economic problems. This left his early writings concerned mainly with welfare economics as well as his work on international monetary economics completed since the publication of the 1971 volume scattered over a wide variety of journals. Mr. Fleming had taken the first steps toward the publication of these essays and the selection of articles included in this volume is essentially his own.

The papers are being published with the approval of Mrs. Gloria Hile Fleming. Mr. H. Robert Heller, Chief of the Financial Studies Division in the International Monetary Fund, has been in charge of the preparation of this book.

The Fund appreciates the willingness of Columbia University Press to publish this volume as well as the proceedings of the Conference on *The New International Monetary System*, held in honor of J. Marcus Fleming at the International Monetary Fund (IMF) headquarters on November 11–12, 1976.

May 1977

JACQUES J. POLAK

BIOGRAPHY OF
JOHN MARCUS FLEMING, C.M.G.

BORN IN Bathgate, Scotland on March 13, 1911. Educated at Bathgate Academy and Edinburgh University, where he received the degree of M.A. (honors) in history in 1932 and M.A. (honors) in political economy; the Geneva Institute of International Post Graduate Studies, 1934–35; and the London School of Economics, 1935. He was a Traveling Fellow of the Rockefeller Foundation, 1937–39.

During 1935–37 he served with the Economic Intelligence Section, Financial Department, League of Nations. He held various positions in the U.K. Ministry of Economic Warfare from 1939 until 1942. During 1942–50 he served with the Economic Section, Cabinet Office, rising to the position of Deputy Director of the Section. He was Visiting Professor, Columbia University, New York from 1951 until 1954.

He was also Member, U.K. Delegation to the San Francisco Conference in 1945; Member, Preparatory Commission, United Nations, 1946; Member, International Trade Conference Preparatory Commission, 1947; U.K. Representative, Economic and Employment Commission, United Nations, 1950.

He joined the International Monetary Fund in 1954 as Chief of the Special Studies Division of the Research Department. In 1959 he became Advisor, Research Department and in 1964 Deputy Director, Research Department.

He is survived by his widow, Mrs. Gloria Hile Fleming, and two daughters by a previous marriage, Mrs. Hilary Knatz and Mrs. Alison Hay, as well as two grandchildren.

COMMEMORATIONS

GOTTFRIED HABERLER

JOHN MARCUS FLEMING, born March 13, 1911, had his earliest economic education at the University of Edinburgh. In 1932 he received an M.A. (with honors) in history, and in 1934 received an M.A. (with first-class honors) in political economy. His fellow student and lifelong friend was the late Ragnar Nurkse (1907–59). Their economics professor was F. W. Ogilvie, who, according to the reminiscences of both Marcus Fleming and Ragnar Nurkse, must have been a most inspiring teacher.

After receiving his M.A., Marcus was awarded a graduate research fellowship and spent the academic year 1934–35 at the *Institut Universitaire de Hautes Etudes Internationales* in Geneva, where he attended Ludwig von Mises's seminar. He then went to the London School of Economics to study with Friedrich von Hayek and Lionel Robbins for the academic year 1935–36, but at the end of 1935 was offered a job at the Secretariat of the League of Nations in Geneva. The late Alexander Loveday was the head of the Financial Section and Economic Intelligence Service—where the business-cycle research (financed by the Rockefeller Foundation) and most other economic research of the League of Nations took place (although there was a separate Economics Section). Ragnar Nurkse, who had joined the League in 1934, brought Marcus Fleming to the attention of both Loveday and myself. It was then that I met Marcus, and his first assignment with the League of Nations was to assist me in writing *Prosperity and Depression: A Theoretical Analysis of Cyclical Movements* (first published by the League in 1937).

We worked closely together for nine months or so until I left the League, in September 1936, for Harvard University. Marcus stayed on to work with Jan Tinbergen, who continued the business-cycle research. In the summer of 1937 I returned to Geneva for several weeks to start work on a revised and enlarged edition of *Prosperity and Depression* (which appeared in 1939). In this endeavor I again had the enormous benefit of Marcus's help. (The second edition took full account of Keynes's *General Theory*. The manuscript of the first edition had been substantially completed before the *General Theory* appeared, although it had been possible to refer to Keynes's work in footnotes.)

The collaboration between Marcus and myself was very close and very stimulating. His sharp mind prevented many slips, and his contribution to the long chapter entitled "The International Aspects of the Business Cycle" was especially great. I regretted that the strict rules of the British civil service, which applied at the Secretariat of the League of Nations, prohibited the mentioning of collaborators and assistants. (Most League of Nations publications appeared as official documents without crediting the author, but the business-cycle work, financed by a Rockefeller Foundation grant, was an exception in that the author's name was given.)

Marcus Fleming was a first-rate theoretical economist. As this collection of his papers shows, his theoretical interests covered a much larger area than the international economic and monetary problems that were his primary concern after he joined the staff of the International Monetary Fund in 1954. His study of history, which preceded his study of economics, gave his work a broader perspective than is generally found among the present generation of economists, and his interests also extended into social philosophy. D. H. Robertson referred to him on one occasion as "that Scottish metaphysician." (The term "metaphysics" did not then have the slightly derogatory connotation that it now has in some circles. Perhaps it would be better rendered today as "philosophy.")

Marcus Fleming was one of those rare persons who combine theoretical acumen and wide factual knowledge—embracing both historical and contemporary statistical—with practical political judgment. He was equally effective and equally at home in academic circles and in meetings with central bankers and policy makers.

His many friends knew his warm personality and his wonderful sense of humor. His untimely death is a grievous loss to all of us and to the science of economics.

LORD ROBBINS

I FIRST met Marcus Fleming in London, where he stayed for a while to attend seminars in the Economics Department of the London School of Economics. He was *en route* from Edinburgh, where he had taken his first degree, to Geneva, where he was to study for a time at the *Institut des Hautes Etudes Internationale*—Rappard's Institute as we used to call it. It was at once clear that here was a young man of unusual intellect and character and, although there could be no questioning his intention to widen his horizon by travel abroad, he was certainly marked out in my mind as someone to watch and perhaps entrap in an academic relationship. This impression was confirmed when, a short time afterward, I met him again in Geneva when he had become outstanding as a member of the Mises seminar at the Institute, a pretty sure test of quality in that inspiring and exacting atmosphere.

It was during the war, however, that our acquaintanceship ripened into close collaboration and warm friendship. As a migrant from Geneva expert circles, he was a welcome recruit to the Economic Section of the War Cabinet Office; and as colleagues in that body we worked together until the end of hostilities. Marcus's special assignment was liaison with the shipping committee, a task he performed with exemplary thoroughness. However, major questions of policy were discussed in common in the Economic Section, and it was not long before Marcus became one of the outstanding participants in our deliberations. As might be expected from his subsequent career, his influence was exercised especially in relation to international economic relations, conspicuously the discussions of postwar policy, which arose from the famous clause VII of the Lend Lease Agreement. The main responsibility in this field lay with James Meade, whose shining achievements in that connection have become well known, but there were no important developments that did not come under Marcus's penetrating scrutiny and comment.

In those days the Economic Section was a small organization of some half dozen professional economists with appropriate secretarial assistance. We were left to do our work in our own way, apart from attendance at interdepartmental committees and the preparation of briefs and memoranda for the chairman of the weekly Lord President's Committee that was in effect the committee chiefly responsible (subject to the Cabinet) for major decisions of economic policy. There were no stipulated regularities in the way we lived. Sleeping accommodation was provided in allegedly bomb-proof cellars, and the tension of war evoked unquestioning work to full capacity from all of our members. But the hours in which this was deployed varied with individual members. Marcus was essentially a nightbird in the sense that his more serious efforts took place in the small hours of the morning. He would sleep very late, devote normal working hours to more or less routine business, and then, as evening or night came, settle down to what he regarded as more important work. If I, as chairman of the section, wished to have effective contact with Marcus, I would seek him out shortly before midnight when, surrounded by what seemed to be—but was not—an intolerable chaos of papers, he would be prepared to suspend his labors and settle down to serious talk. And how serious it was. Marcus would take nothing for granted. Each problem that presented itself was examined, not merely in regard to the needs of the fleeting moment but also *sub specie aeternitalis*. How much one learned from a mind of such quality!

Intellectually and in regard to his ambitions, Marcus was a complex character. It goes without saying that academically he was first-rate, a truly profound thinker. At the same time there was a side of him that was fascinated by the administrative process. After the war academic advancement lay open; I myself can testify on two occasions to sounding his willingness to be considered for important chairs that eventually, after much hesitation, he declined; and I have little doubt that there were other approaches with a similar outcome. In this I suspect he was at least partly influenced by an overly optimistic estimate of the capacity of the intellectual in a democracy in peace time to have a clear cut and sensible influence on policy. Doubtless in this respect, he had his moments of disillusionment. But his fundamental spiritual equilibrium was not easily shaken, and in the high position that he eventually achieved in the Research Division of the IMF I fancy he found a congenial compromise between his various impulses, at once not too far removed from action and reality, yet permitting the exercise of that speculative disposition on the products of which, I fancy, his lasting reputation will probably rest.

JAMES E. MEADE

MARCUS FLEMING, the economist, had a rare combination of qualities: a fastidious intellectual integrity, a basic interest in the meaning of economics and its relation with ethics, great powers of economic analysis, a determination not to leave a problem unsolved—a battery of qualities that he directed persistently at devising economic policies for the betterment of the human condition. Practically all of his working life was spent in national or international public service practicing the art of the application of relevant basic economic analysis to the current affairs of the real world.

How well and with what affection one remembers his ways in the practice of this art! When as a colleague in Whitehall one accompanied him to a meeting at which some important decision on policy was to be taken, how one became quite anxious, as the committee seemed on the point of reaching the desired conclusion, that no ill-informed member would support the right conclusion for the wrong reason, for Marcus could not suffer the correct policy to be supported with incorrect analysis. The decision on policy would be postponed to enable him to clarify the issue by explaining just why the policy that we advocated did not possess the virtue just claimed for it.

Nor can I forget Marcus's reaction when I urged him to remain on with me as a colleague in Whitehall after the war instead of accepting the offer of an important academic chair. He sat down with me, produced a long foolscap sheet of paper, drew a long line down the middle, wrote down all of the arguments for staying in the left-hand column and the arguments for going in the right-hand column, and proceeded to give marks to each argument. With some difficulty we managed to adjust the numbers so that the left-hand column won by one util.

Economic debate with Marcus was always greatly repaying, and this memory of an old friend gives me opportunity to record my own indebtedness. In particular, his article entitled "On Making the Best of Balance of Payments Restrictions on Imports"* stimulated me completely to recast the draft of my book, "Trade and Welfare," and was in

---

* Published in the earlier collection of his papers, *Essays in International Economics*, Allen and Unwin, 1971.

my mind the begetter of the analysis of the second best. Many other economists must in similar manner, directly or indirectly, owe much to his fertile and persistent mind.

R. A. MUNDELL

J•MARCUS FLEMING'S contribution to theoretical economics and international monetary policy spanned four decades from his service in academe, government, and the International Monetary Fund. His own collected essays, represented by a previous work, have already illustrated his range and style, and Columbia University's publication of the present volume as well as the forthcoming proceedings of the Columbia-IMF conference memorial volume fittingly pay tribute to both his academic interests when he was a member of Columbia's economics department and his position of influence at the IMF.

My first meeting with Marcus was at the IMF in 1961 when our relationship was quite close for two years, and later at many meetings of the Bellagio Study Group on international reform. As the IMF observer he was actually a full participant quite capable (when he did not have on his IMF cap) of debating issues roaming outside the scope of what was then the Fund orthodoxy of fixed exchange rates and balanced budgets. In fact Marcus was not an orthodox thinker. He had an independent view of the world based on a curious blend of cynical realism and compassionate idealism.

He was a Keynesian to the very roots of his economic training, though not an anti-monetarist Keynesian. (How could any Fund member be anti-monetary?) I once heard him claim there were only two Keynesians left at the Fund—himself and the Managing Director (Per Jacobsson)! This was despite his immersion in Austrian doctrines at the feet of von Mises in Geneva in the days when Rappard, Mises, Röpke, Meade, Loveday, Tinbergen, Polak, and Haberler made Geneva an exciting, intellectual milieu. He seemed to relish taking the unconventional side against the tide, although he was never so presumptuous or obstinate as to think he could do much to control big swings in world events and would wisely reconcile his policy thinking to political realities whenever events proved irresistible, though not without muttering some Celtic lament.

In 1961 the Fund was running out of convertible currencies to lend and the GAB (General Arrangements to Borrow) was set up at the Vienna meetings. But the talk of Washington in that first Kennedy year was the monetary–fiscal policy mix. It was the year of the Twist, the economic manifestation of which was the ill-fated attempt to raise short-term interest rates to protect the balance of payments and lower long-term interest rates to arouse investment. Marcus that year was active in the theater (literature, drama, and history were old avocations) but nevertheless managed to write a paper on the monetary–fiscal policy mix that built upon the subject I had worked on, and he produced a paper that is still worth reading today by students.

I should mention that despite the great differences in our approaches to economics we did manage to collaborate on a paper, "Intervention in the Forward Exchange Market," although it turned out to be, for me at least, a precedent I had no wish to repeat! Marcus could be exasperating. We seemed to spend more time than should have been necessary arguing whether our two-country world consisted of countries A and B, or countries A and non-A. Marcus's style won out but only because he had the last draft!

Marcus was an internationalist, and he made an interesting contribution to tariff theory (written when he was at Columbia) by extending the optimal tariff literature to include the change in welfare in his "non-A." He was also a European by the depth of his culture, yet not sufficiently so to allow his Scottish soul to greet with pleasure the prospect of Britain joining the Common Market. In 1961–63 he tried to persuade Britain to stay out. An Appolonian by instinct, I suspect his years in Geneva had taught him to fear the Dionysian monster he could see or imagine still slumbering in the heart of Europe. He had a touch of genius, disciplined enough to protect itself from mere flights of fancy. In one sense he seemed out of place in economics, manifested in a taste for the esoteric. However, his mastery of some aspects of theory, but especially esoteric theory, was superb. I think he never fully integrated the theory he knew with his knowledge of reality and economic practice. Or perhaps the theory he often worked on (such as ethics) was an escape from the everyday world, and was therefore a recreation from the frustrations of trying to get fellow practitioners to follow policies (as Meade points out) for the *right* reasons. He touched on very diverse aspects of economics and had interesting insights in each field he studied. But he would frequently not follow up his own insights sufficiently to drive home his point. He was something of an aesthete in a muddy universe, a problem no doubt thrust on him because of the trying times in which he lived.

He told me shortly before he died how much he was looking forward to getting back to serious intellectual pursuits in his retirement in Edinburgh—the contemplation of the "just price" and other matters of values and ethics in which he was also a pioneer. Perhaps he was a misplaced medievalist. He will be deeply missed by his friends and colleagues, and some of the ideas he sprinkled about will find fuller expression in another generation or a better world.

JACQUES J. POLAK*

TOGETHER with the earlier *Essays in International Economics*, published in 1971, the reprints of papers by J. Marcus Fleming presented in this book make the bulk of Fleming's published work readily available. But these many articles of rigid and often dry economic reasoning do not portray much of a picture of Fleming, the man.

Not much more can be gleaned from his contributions to Fund doctrine and policy—the many anonymous Fund reports in which it is sometimes difficult to recognize the original contributions from the surrounding compromises necessary for their acceptance. Among these documents should be mentioned the Fund's *Annual Reports*, the First and Second Amendments to the Articles of Agreement, and a number of more specific reports. Of these, Fleming's contributions are the most direct and obvious in the two Reports on Compensatory Financing of Export Fluctuations (1963 and 1966) and in the Guidelines for Floating Exchange Rates (1974).

However, much more of Fleming's personality comes through—to the extent that the carefully written word is allowed to reveal the personality of the writer—in the voluminous notes and memoranda prepared during his tenure at the IMF. Rereading many of these written during the last several years brings back a vivid picture of Fleming as his colleagues knew him.

* I am greatly indebted to Herbert K. Zassenhaus for his help in the preparation of these notes.

An analyst far more than an operator, he was a major figure in the senior staff of the Research Department of the Fund, and as such carried on a continual, relentless, and often sharply dialectic interchange of professional ideas with his colleagues. An astonishing volume of memoranda remains as the sediment of this interchange, to supplement personal memories of his personality. Fleming was to an exceptional extent a man of the written word, even in his daily contacts. Casual technical conversation is recorded in carefully constructed memoranda, painstakingly correct in grammar and elegant in vocabulary, although their content was often complex and occasionally less than pellucid. There was a certain formality to his communication, whether addressed to a young economist or to the Managing Director.

These memoranda show Marcus Fleming as an international civil servant *par excellence*, with a fierce loyalty to service of the community of nations, nourished from deep moral conviction. He applied his powerful and systematic intellect to the complex mechanism of international financial and economic transactions and to the search for improvements in this mechanism. He preferred the closeness to action in an official international organization to the perhaps larger freedom of a teacher or an academician. Thus, for the last twenty-two years of his life, he served the IMF while remaining in close touch with, and continuing to contribute to, academic thought. At the same time, he had a keen interest in the arts and read extensively in many fields, such as philosophy and history.

Fleming's thoughts and writings bear a distinctly academic hue, and it was indeed his typical role to develop theoretical analysis relevant to the guiding of IMF operations, rather than himself to engage in them. To gauge the parts he played, it is perhaps well to record once again a few elements of his thought that recur repeatedly in debates with Fund colleagues, though less in his published work.

There is a pervasive emphasis on applied welfare economics, that is, on values more moral and social than analytic and economic, in Fleming's discussions of the interactions between international transactions and their control and on the domestic employment, income distribution (within and between countries), and development goals. This emphasis carries over into his choice of policy priorities and policy recommendations. It explains his preference for measures other than demand management as remedies for balance of payments deficits wherever there is evidence of less than full employment. He thus tended to favor exchange rate changes and, to a lesser extent, incomes policies for purposes of external adjustment. Furthermore, he was strongly inclined to the use of incomes policies in the area of domestic stabilization, and he established a group in the IMF to do more research on the possibilities and limitations of such policies. As an economist, he had no love for trade or payments restrictions, and he went far in exploring the possibilities of multiple exchange rates for capital transactions as a substitute for much more restrictive regimes for capital transactions at a unitary rate, but he could not stomach a dogmatic position that accepted deflationary policies as a means to avoid restrictions. The concern for full employment is so strongly felt that it surfaces in some rare emotional notes among his otherwise strictly professional communications. In one of these notes, he warns against what he termed the "sadism" of "IMF orthodoxy" in the design of domestic financial-policy conditions for the use of IMF resources. In a comment on the conclusions of a draft consultation report with one country, he expressed his amazement at the ease with which IMF officials, secure in their own jobs, made policy suggestions that would involve an increase of unemployment in the countries with which they consulted: "I never cease to marvel at the insouciance with which Fund staff members, most of whom have never had a day's unemployment in their lives—except perhaps in their youth when their parents were supporting them—recommend in almost all circumstances increases on unemployment for other people as a way of checking prices that are rising uncomfortably fast. Under any normal value system or welfare function an unemployment rate of 6 percent would be reckoned a far worse evil than the price inflation of 4 to 5 per annum now prevailing in . . . ."

These convictions and ideas gave to many of Fleming's writings, throughout his IMF career, a flavor of free-thinking critique—indeed, of heterodoxy and sometimes even of contrariness. Since he commanded the intellectual respect of colleagues, even when his positions were considered "academic" or impractical, he contributed intellectual discipline to internal IMF deliberations—a discipline from which no one probably benefited more than this writer. Although Fleming changed his mind very infrequently, his critical reasoning only rarely lost its force by being taken as a sign of obstinacy.

Fleming was a perfectionist, intolerant of bad economics, superficiality, and lack of form. And he made as little allowance for human weakness in others as in himself. His caustic criticism produced, on occasion, feelings of hurt and resentment. But these feelings were rarely personal and never lasting. One note expressing pique on the part of a colleague was promptly returned with a scribbled answer, "I was brought up on the controversial style of the Cambridge Economics Department. In words once used by GBS to an indignant Scotsman: 'Hoots toots awa' man. Dinna tak offence whaur nane's meant!'" With all his insistence on rigorous analysis as an economist, he also showed, at critical moments, considerable flexibility in his capacity as an international civil servant; witness the ultimate success of his long struggle for the Executive Board to reach agreement on a set of IMF guidelines for floating.

Substantively, Fleming's turn of mind led him to early attempts at expanding the possibilities for IMF-created international liquidity; thus, he developed the scheme of compensatory export financing, made innumerable contributions to the design of the special drawing rights (SDR) system, and later supported the "link" between SDR creation and development assistance. And he had always been in favor of floating rates. (Occasionally, his request for permission to publish a paper on some of these subjects would put IMF policy on publication by staff members—liberal as it was and still is—to a rather severe test.) Characteristically, though, his support of floating was not of the "benign neglect" variety. On the contrary, a large part of his final five years in the IMF was devoted—with his usual driving energy and unflagging attention to analytical detail—to the design of guidelines for managed floating, including asset settlement and "guided multicurrency intervention" (his phrase). This advocacy of combining free-floating market operation with institutional guidance was fully consistent with his general principles.

Fleming's singular contribution to the IMF left its mark on the design of schemes and on methods of analysis more than on the operations of IMF policy. What perhaps mitigated against the full effectiveness of his policy ideas, particularly in the short run, was his drive for precision in detail, sometimes at the expense of practicality. Some might notice this feature in one of his last efforts, the proposal for guided multicurrency intervention. This, however, is in any event not a proposal that could be put into practice in the near future. And it bore the unmistakable stamp of Marcus Fleming, an indefatigable perfectionist of exceptional moral and intellectual caliber who kept up a flow of new ideas and incisive critique from which the Fund drew so much benefit in the many years he served it.

FRITZ MACHLUP

THERE have been two Bellagio Groups on International Monetary Reform. The first consisted of thirty-two academic economists who met, twice at Princeton and twice in Bellagio and, in the summer of 1964, completed a report on *International Monetary Arrangements: The Problem of Choice* (Princeton, 1964). The second Bellagio Group was organized in the autumn of 1964 as the "Joint Conference of Officials and Academics on International Monetary Reform." Its first meeting was held in Bellagio in December 1964, and there have been seventeen meetings until now. Marcus Fleming missed only one of the seventeen.

The composition of the group was subject to change. The academic members came from a pool of eighteen economists, of whom an average of twelve was in attendance. The officials came from the national monetary authorities of the countries that made up the Group of Ten and from international agencies. There was an unchanging nucleus of officials over the years: Emminger, Ossola, Rickett, Van Lennep, and Fleming. Fleming was the most regular participant of all the officials; perhaps we should say that he was a hybrid—a professional official or official academic.

Perhaps I should briefly mention, in order to avoid confusion, that there was much overlap between the Bellagio Group and the Bürgenstock Group. The latter contained a contingent of practitioners from multinational business and finance. Its sole concern was the problem of greater flexibility of exchange rates. In two of the four meetings of this group, held in 1970 and 1971, officials joined with the practitioners and academics. Marcus Fleming attended both of these meetings.

I have avoided mentioning that the national and international monetary authorities were "represented" by the officials participating in our conferences. The officials represented only themselves and spoke in the capacity of specialists, not as spokesmen for their governments or agencies. This, indeed, was the great advantage of our conferences over the inter-governmental meetings, in which some of the most important issues were "out of bounds" or "off limits." The officials were not supposed to discuss certain questions "officially," but they could discuss them as members of a "seminar" chaired by an academic economist responsible to no one. The number of officials participating in these meetings grew too large for the capacity of the Villa Serbelloni in Bellagio. There had been seven officials at the first joint conference in Bellagio in 1964; there were thirteen in Zürich in January 1966, fifteen in Bologna in May 1968, sixteen in Princeton in September 1968, seventeen in Lugano in March 1969, fifteen in Torremolinos in March 1970, twenty-three in Taormina in January 1971, twenty-one in Cascais in March 1972, and twenty-six in Vienna in January 1973. I have deliberately listed only some of the more glamorous meeting places.

The contributions Marcus Fleming made to our conferences were immensely valuable. He was a model of concise exposition; he would present twenty-five minutes worth of talk in five minutes, in contrast to some who might take seven minutes to say what could be said in two. (Long speeches were taboo in our discussions; we had sometimes as many as fifty-five interventions in a three-hour session.) Marcus' interventions were always to the point, without unnecessary padding or trimmings; they were methodically organized and contained the right mixture of theoretical and institutional intelligence. No one, I am sure, will blame me for indiscretion or breach of confidentiality if I refer here to some of the things Marcus said in our discussions.

In the first meeting of the Joint Conference in Bellagio I asked all participants to state their preferences concerning the agenda. Marcus suggested that we discuss the probable conflicts between the goals of stability and growth and the need for flexibility in monetary arrangements. When we talked about the techniques of controlling the growth of international liquidity—please bear in mind that this was in December 1964—and of supplementing gold and currency reserves by creating new reserve assets, Marcus intervened seven times in the discussion. In his very first intervention on this subject he focused on the idea that the less developed countries ought to get some of the new reserves; and in his second intervention he elaborated on his view that too little aid was being given to the less developed countries. (Again, this was more than two years before the conception of the SDR.) At the same meeting, in the discussion on adjustment, Marcus spoke of the notion of an optimum speed of adjustment and about the role of exchange-rate changes in the process.

At the Zürich meeting in January 1966, Marcus broke a lance for exchange-rate adjustment in cases where the Phillips curves and the relative tolerances for unemployment and price increases varied with each country. He was more explicit on this point in these discussions than in his 1968 Princeton essay, "Guidelines for Balance-of-Payments Adjustment under the Par-Value System." Incidentally, in this essay, he made it clear that his guidelines would not fit "a system of floating exchange rates" (p.21).

When we were preparing for the meeting in Vienna in January 1973 and I circulated a terribly long list of issues that had been proposed for inclusion in the agenda, Marcus wrote in a brief letter to me, "In present circumstances almost everything in connection with the monetary reform is in the 'most urgent' category." At the end of the meeting the group was virtually unanimous that a general resort to floating was unavoidable and imminent; Marcus, although joining in this prognosis, expressed the hope that the floating would be only temporary, that governments would agree on a symmetrical intervention system, and that they would be more cautious regarding the introduction or maintenance of dual markets.

At his last meeting of the Bellagio Group, in Basle at the end of January 1975, Marcus intervened several times on the need and possibility of "an agreed regime for floaters" and opened the discussion on control of total monetary reserves. He was in splendid form.

For eleven years the members of the Bellagio Group have appreciated and profited from the "Sayings of Marcus Fleming." His contribution was unique. What were the qualities that made Marcus Fleming such a valuable member of the Bellagio Group, and probably to all other groups or teams with which he was associated? It was the rare combination of a mastery of economic theory, an understanding of empirical data, a concurrent interest in pure analysis and historical and institutional knowledge, a firm conviction in the need to improve the arrangements under which the economies operate, a quick and flexible mind, and, last not least, an integrity of character and warmth of personality. This mix is hard to find.

Essays on Economic Policy

1

DETERMINATION OF
THE RATE OF INTEREST

M R. KEYNES and his critics have this in common, that they all
look upon the interest rate as being determined by a system of
what might be styled "macroeconomic" equations. Their curves describe
relationships existing between social aggregates—collective categories
such as "total money" and "total supply of loanable funds"—quantities
that are arrived at by adding together the corresponding items appertain-
ing to the various individuals who make up the economic community.
For purposes calling for estimates of quantitative importance such as
statistical testing, forecast, or the framing of policy, and even for purposes
of exposition, it is necessary to express the economic system in terms of
such aggregates. But no one doubts that a more exact understanding of
the underlying relationships can be obtained by "atomic" or "microeconomic" analysis—direct examination of the behavior of the individuals
and institutions who produce, consume, own and administer wealth.
When rival "macroeconomic" theories are put forward, and still more,
when it is asserted that there is no real difference between them, there
should be some recourse to the basic explanation in terms of individual
behavior, from which such theories are, or should be, derived.

First published in *Economica* (August 1938), pp. 333–41. Reprinted by permission of the
London School of Economics and Political Science. This note relates to a controversy to
which contributions included Keynes' "Alternative Theories of the Rate of Interest," *The
Economic Journal* (June 1937), 47:241–52; the three rejoinders by Bertil Ohlin, Dennis
Robertson, and Hawtrey in *The Economic Journal* (September 1937), 47:423–27; and
Abba P. Lerner, "Alternative Formulations of the Theory of Interest," *The Economic
Journal* (June 1938), 48:211–30.

According to Mr. Keynes, the rate of interest is the "price" that equili-
brates the desire to hold wealth in the form of cash with the available
quantity of cash.[1] That is to say, it is determined by the facts that the
demand for cash (or money), and possibly the supply also, are dependent
on the rate of interest, and that demand must equal supply. Professor
Ohlin, on the other hand, prefers the formulation that the interest rate is
determined by the intersection of the demand and supply curves for claims
(credit), though he adds that these curves themselves depend on the
quantity of cash and of assets.[2] He accuses the Keynesian formulation
relating the interest rate and the demand for money of being incomplete.
Mr. Robertson also prefers the "demand-and-supply for credit" theory—
for we can identify his "loanable funds" with Professor Ohlin's "credit"—
but he holds the two methods to be merely "alternative pieces of
machinery"[3] that arrive at the same results in practice. Mr. Hicks believes
the choice between "the ordinary method of economic theory"—which
regards the rate of interest as determined by the demand-and-supply for
loans—and the Keynesian method to be "purely a matter of convenience";
from this point of view, however, the liquidity-preference approach offers
great advantages.[4] Mr. Keynes, for his part, will have none of this indifference—for him the theories are "radically opposed to one another."

The argument put forward in the present note is based on the contention of Professor Ohlin that the rate of interest must be determined within
the framework of "the system of mutually interdependent prices and
quantities."[5] From this point of view both the Keynesian method and
what Mr. Hicks calls the "ordinary method of economic theory"[6] are
inadequate. When the relationships involved are more fully expressed,
the "demand-and-supply for money" and "demand-and-supply for credit"
theories become alternative explanations, but only in the sense that
either, *combined with still other demand and supply equations,* can be used
to determine the rate of interest. Finally, it will be argued that the

---

[1] John M. Keynes, *General Theory of Employment, Interest, and Money* (London:
Macmillan, 1936), p. 167.

[2] Bertil Ohlin, rejoinder, *The Economic Journal* (September 1937), 47:427.

[3] Dennis Robertson, rejoinder, *The Economic Journal* (September 1937), 47:432.

[4] John Hicks, "Mr. Keynes' Theory of Employment," *The Economic Journal* (June 1936),
46:246.

[5] Bertil Ohlin, "Some Notes on the Stockholm Theory of Savings and Investment,"
The Economic Journal (June 1937), 47:227.

[6] I do not mean to quarrel with Mr. Hicks' own formulation of the problem, to which,
indeed, this note owes much. See Hicks, "Mr. Keynes' Theory of Employment," pp. 241, 246.

"liquidity-preference" method when thus amplified is likely for practical purposes to be a more serviceable instrument than the other.

Let us imagine the simplest possible economic system, which will contain all of the elements we require. Suppose there are only three kinds of property, goods (real capital), claims to fixed future money payments (say, "bonds"), and money. Money consisting of banks' demand liabilities is the standard of value and of deferred payments, the medium of exchange, the most liquid asset, and so on. One's stock of bonds may be positive or negative according as one is a net lender or borrower. If one is a bank one's stock of money may be—will be—negative. Some wealth administrators may have a property holding whose net value, at current prices, is negative. Since there are only three kinds of property, there are only two prices, "*p*," the price of goods, and "*i*," the price of bonds. The price of bonds is, of course, a simple function of the rate of interest and statements made of the one hold also of the other, though with a change of sign.

We wish to examine the price-fixing process as it takes place on any given "day"—a period so short that all transactions may be looked upon as taking place at a unique set of prices prevailing during that day. Each wealth-holder starts the day with a certain inventory of the three sorts of property, which may be regarded as a "legacy" from the operations of the previous day. In addition, he produces and consumes goods during the day—the difference representing his real saving or "dis-saving." The amount of this "real saving" we may take for the moment as a datum. He is confronted with the market prices *i* and *p*, and he proceeds to buy and sell, lend and borrow (and, if he is a bank, issue and withdraw) money, until he has arrived at what, at the end of the day, he conceives to be the best possible arrangement of his property. Since there are three kinds of property, three conditions suffice to determine this optimum arrangement. First, he receives by exchange the same value as he gives. The aggregate value of his property at the end of the day is the same as it was at the beginning plus the value of his real saving. The other two conditions are that, at the given prices of goods and of bonds, respectively, he has at the end of the day no further desire to buy or sell goods, or to exchange his holding of claims (or debts) against money.

So far we have taken *p* and *i* for granted. But wealth-holders can only exchange with each other. This implies a "market equation" for each type of property. Aggregate purchases of goods equal aggregate sales.

Aggregate increases of bond holdings plus reductions of bonded debt equal aggregate reductions of bond holdings plus increases of debt. Aggregate increase of money holdings plus reductions in banks' demand liabilities equal aggregate reductions in money holdings plus increases in banks' demand liabilities. For practical purposes, and also for purposes of comparison with current theories, it is best to throw these equations into the form of "gross" instead of "net" demand-and-supply equations.[7] Since the increase in an individual's holding of goods equals his real saving plus what he buys and minus what he sells, the first market equation can take the form that the aggregate holding of goods (demand) equals the aggregate "legacy" of goods plus the aggregate real saving (supply). Similarly, but bearing in mind that the legacy of debts equals the legacy of bond holdings, the quantity of bonds held (demand) equals the quantity of debts (supply). Finally, the quantity of money held (demand) equals the quantity that banks issue (supply).

The question is what, if any, arrangement of p and i will satisfy the market equations and so ensure that the exchanges can be carried out as desired. Now, whatever the prices, as we saw, the individual receives by exchange the same value as he gives. Throw this into the "gross" form and aggregate for all individuals, and you have the condition that the aggregate value of property at the end of the "day" must equal the aggregate value of the "legacies" plus the aggregate value of real saving. This being so, it may be seen that any two of our market equations imply the third, so that it is only necessary to satisfy two of them to satisfy them all.

We remember that for each individual, given his legacy and his real saving, given the prices p and i, and given his scale of preferences (at the end of the "day") for all conceivable combinations of the different kinds of property, his holding of each class of property was determined. Thus his holding—positive or negative—of each class of property may be regarded in general as a function of p and i, the shape of the function depending on his "legacy," and his preference scale, which for the moment we can accept as independent. The market equations—which are "macro-economic" in character—are formed by the aggregation of the demands

<hr />

[7] See the distinction made by Professor Ohlin: "Some Notes on the Stockholm Theory of Savings and Investment," pp. 224–25.

and supplies of individuals. Thus the demand for goods, the demand for and supply of loans, and the demand for and supply of money, are all in general functions of p and i—of the price of goods and the rate of interest. Each market equation defines a relationship between p and i, which will ensure that demand and supply balance on the market. Consequently, any two market equations—those for goods and money, those for goods and bonds, or those for bonds and money—will suffice to determine those values of p and i that will secure equality of demand and supply in those two markets, and, as was explained above, in the third market as well.[8]

Although each wealth-holder is, in principle, liable to hold varying quantities of all of the three types of property, it is always possible that his particular scale of preferences may restrict his choice to two types or even only one. For example, banks may be supposed to deal only in bonds and (negative) money—not at all in goods. Here the individual gross demands for claims and gross supplies of money are functions of i alone. Since the aggregate supply of money is attributed entirely to banks, it is dependent only on i and not on p. The same thing may be true of other demands and supplies, but, of course, in each case there must be some special reason, relating to individual preference scales, why one of the prices can be regarded as irrelevant. If, for example, it could be shown that p has no influence on anyone's demand for money, then the Keynesian liquidity-preference theory of the rate of interest would be at least formally correct, since i could be determined by the market equation for money alone.

We may exclude from consideration wealth-holders whose money stocks are invariable whatever the price structure. If other money holders either never held goods or never varied their holdings of goods, then it might be that the demand for money would be quite inelastic with respect to p. But if, as is surely the typical case, an individual or firm holds, and is willing to vary, all three classes of property, he must be willing to exchange goods for money when p changes, or at least to exchange bonds

---

[8] If we choose to complicate our idyllic economic system by introducing debts of various sorts and maturities, and also ordinary and preference shares, we shall thereby introduce an equal number of new prices and new market equations, but no new points of principle. We shall always have an equation to spare, and we shall always include all of the prices— failing some special reason to the contrary, as explained below—in each of the equations.

for money when, (p/i) and p having altered,[9] he exchanges bonds for goods. For as a business man, when p and (p/i) fall, sells bonds, or increases his indebtedness in order to purchase goods, the special advantages offered by holding bonds become scarcer to him, or the special disadvantages of being in debt become more irksome with the increase of indebtedness, and he is likely, interest rate remaining the same, to draw on his cash balance in order to increase his holding of bonds or to reduce his indebtedness.

At this stage it may be opportune to introduce the possibility that the production, the consumption, and hence the real saving of such wealth-holders, should be regarded as dependent on the price of goods. Suppose that a rise in p evokes an expansion of production accompanied by a lesser expansion in consumption, that is, that it leads to increased saving. What would be the consequence of this increase in saving resulting from a hypothetical rise in p? It would mean an increase in the supply of goods-to-hold without necessarily involving an equivalent increase in the demand. The savers would probably seek to utilize part of their increase in wealth to increase their holdings of money and bonds to reduce their indebtedness. Others would, as previously explained, be moved to similar action by the mere fact that goods cost more. But if this is so, demand for money depends on both i and p, and interest cannot be determined by the market equations for money alone. Probably no one would seriously maintain that interest could be determined by the market equation for bonds alone. The supply curve of bonds with respect to i is usually regarded as itself dependent on p. Sometimes it is not made evident that the demand curve is similarly dependent. Is it not, in any case, somewhat misleading to use the Marshallian apparatus of partial demand-and-supply curves in cases where the variable in question is as much influenced by some price that is excluded from the picture as by the price against which it is plotted to form the curve?

Granted, then, that we have to determine i and p simultaneously and that we have to use two market equations for the purpose, which two is it most suitable to employ? No one has suggested neglecting the market equations for goods, and it would certainly be unwise to do so, chiefly

---

[9] The expression (p/i) is, of course, the market value of goods in terms of bonds, and is directly relevant to the choice between holding goods and bonds.

because when we relax our assumptions about the quantity of goods being fixed and the scales of preferences being given, the important influences of changes in the quantity of goods and in the attractiveness of investment are best illustrated from this equation. This leaves us with the alternative of using the market equation for bonds, or that for money—not to determine the rate of interest but to complete the system whereby interest and the price of goods are simultaneously determined.

Our choice will depend on the applications that we intend to make of our theoretical scheme. If our aim is to explain the movements of i over a period of time, then we shall have to try to set up relationships that will be fairly constant, not only on any given "day," but over a succession of "days." Here we must remember that underlying our various equations for the given "day" was the datum of the "legacy" of the different sorts of property left over to the different wealth-holders from the previous "day." Over a succession of "days," of course, the "legacy" cannot be taken as a constant. Its amount and its distribution vary from day to day as a result of the exchanges of property, and the savings and "dissavings" of the various individuals. The total value of the "legacy" is the same thing as the total value of the quantity of goods in existence. It is easy to include this[10] as an independent variable in our equations—though of course it is dependent on the course of *previous* development—but there is no way of introducing into "macroeconomic" equations the influence of the interpersonal distribution of the "legacy." It will be an advantage, therefore, to use equations that will not seriously be harmed by the neglect of this factor. This might perhaps safely be said of all our market equations insofar as their outcome is concerned. But it would seem likely that changes in distribution of property, while not greatly affecting the relationship between i and p established by the market equation for bonds, might often shift demand and supply both in the same direction. More generally—that is, taking account of the factors underlying the preference scales—the difficulty of making use of the market equation for bonds is that both demand and supply react to the same influences, though, of course, in different degrees and in the opposite directions. Thus if multiple correlation analysis is used to provide a quantitative expression for the theory, it becomes practically impossible

---

[10] Or rather, since this is a multiple of p, simply the quantity of goods.

to distinguish thereby two separate functions, for supply and for demand. From the practical viewpoint, therefore, it seems preferable to work with the market equation for money.

It might be objected to this reasoning that, in any case, any hopes of constructing demand-and-supply functions, whether for money or for goods, which would be valid for a series of "days," are chimerical. The influence of the changing "legacies" might, à la rigueur, be represented by the magnitude of the stock of goods—but what of the scales of preference that, given for the "day," may vary considerably from day to day? We must deal with this problem by seeking to dig out the principal factors underlying the scales of preference, to find magnitudes capable of standing for these underlying factors—whose inner nature may not be properly quantitative at all—and to include these magnitudes as variables helping to determine the demand or supply in question. Let us deal shortly with this matter as it affects the demand for money (the supply is more straightforward).

Mr. Keynes has familiarized us with three motives for holding money—the "transaction motive," the "precautionary motive," and the "speculative motive." The first two relate to the special advantages that money possesses with respect to liquidity and security; the last refers to the anticipated profitability—positive or negative—involved in holding bonds rather than money. But just as we found it to be necessary to include p with i as influencing the demand for money, so now we must take into account the anticipated profitability of holding goods (i.e., of industry and commerce) as well as that of holding bonds. It is surely impossible to contest the importance of the consideration, such as in determining the size of a firm's idle balances.

Factors affecting preference scales can then be classified in the following, somewhat artificial, manner: changes in the relative advantages of money and bonds with respect to (a) liquidity and (b) profitability; changes in the relative advantages of money and goods under the same heads; and changes in the relative attractiveness of liquidity and profit. Changes in the liquidity-yield of the different types of assets are perhaps not normally of great importance for the demand for money. In any case it would be difficult to find a quantitative expression for this factor. On the other hand, changes in the anticipated money return on holding goods and bonds, respectively, (including in this term both yield and capital appreciation) are of first importance. In the case of goods, particularly for long-term movements, it is doubtful whether we should regard anticipations of higher yields as altering the scales of preference, it might be more significant to regard them as reducing the unit of measurement of goods to which the preference scales relate. To state the same concept in a different way, it might be better when comparing preference scales for goods, claims and money at different time points to think of "goods" not as physical magnitudes but as sources of money-yield of a given time-shape and a given probable magnitude.[11] p then becomes a simple function of the rate of yield on investment. Obviously, it is difficult to find a satisfactory magnitude, chosen from current or previous economic events, to stand for *anticipated* capital appreciation on goods. A similar difficulty, and a more serious one (if money is more substitutable vis-à-vis claims than vis-à-vis goods) confronts us when we attempt to measure the anticipated appreciation on bonds. In these cases we must seek to discover whether the rates of change of the prices of bonds and goods cannot be made to provide working approximations for anticipations.

As to the changes in the relative "needs" for liquidity-return and for the special kinds of money-returns obtainable on claims and goods, respectively, the dominant factor here seems to be the variation in the demand for liquid assets arising out of the changes in the flow of money-payments. Probably, from time to time changes in attitude occur that cannot be explained in terms of economic magnitudes, and can in some cases defy rational explanation of any sort. Nevertheless, before the case is given up as hopeless, the attempt should be made to see whether the more measurable and systematic factors do not between them account for the known movements in the quantity of money that people have in the past been willing to hold.

---

[11] The object in changing the unit of measurement is to obtain greater stability in the scales of preference through time. A further step to this end would be to vary the unit of money in accordance with a price index. Preference scales would then relate to "real" balances, and the quantity of bonds and goods-to-hold would be measured in terms of anticipated "real" yield.

2

PRICE AND OUTPUT POLICY
OF STATE ENTERPRISE

1. IN ORDER TO achieve the use of the community's resources that is both the most efficient and the most in conformity with consumers' wishes, they should be distributed among the various uses in such a way that the value of the marginal product of a given factor is the same in every occupation. Insofar as the reward paid to any factor is the same in every occupation, this rule means that the value of the marginal product of a factor should, in every occupation, bear a constant ratio to the price of that factor.

2. The principle that the value of the marginal product of a factor should be equal to the price of that factor is a special case of this general rule, but it is a special case which, for labor, at least, has a great deal to commend it. If labor is paid everywhere a reward that is not merely in a constant ratio to, but actually equal to, the value of its marginal product, two additional advantages may be achieved:

a. A larger proportion of the total national income will accrue labor than if labor is paid everywhere at a wage lower, by a constant proportion, than the value of its marginal product. This will probably serve to improve the distribution of the national income.

b. Labor has the option of earning more income or enjoying more leisure. The more nearly the reward for an additional unit of work approaches the value of the marginal product of labor, the greater—

First published in *The Economic Journal* (December 1944), 54:321–39. Reprinted by permission of Professor James E. Meade and Cambridge University Press.

it may be presumed—will be the welfare achieved by means of a proper balance between work and leisure.[1]

3. How can the principle of equality between the value of the marginal product of a factor and its price best be achieved? Where competition is technically possible, by vigorous and unimpeded competition.[2] Much might be done by the State to promote such competition by removing legal enactments that positively promote monopolization, by reform of the patent law and of company law with this end in view, and by the outlawing of certain forms of business practices that are primarily designed to restrict competition. But there are many cases where monopoly is inevitable. When the scale of production necessary to take advantage of technical economies is large in relation to the market to be served, "trust-busting" must either be ineffective or lead to technical inefficiency. The outstanding examples of such cases are, of course, the public utilities. Where a community needs only one gas-works, or electricity station, or railway network, monopoly must obviously exist. In these cases, socialization in one form or another, of the industries concerned, is the only radical cure to ensure that they are run in such a way as to equate marginal costs to prices of the product produced (or the prices of the factors of production to the value of their marginal products) rather than to make a profit.

4. Recent work by economists[3] has served to make it clear on what principles the output and use of factors by the managers of a socialized plant should be determined:

a. Output should be increased so long as the price of the product exceeds the marginal (not the average) cost of production.

b. One factor should be substituted for another so long as that quantity of the factor taken on, which is required to replace the production of a unit of the factor released, has a lower market price than the unit price of the factor released.

---

[1] See ch. 2 of part 4 of my *Introduction to Economic Analysis and Policy* (London: Oxford University Press, 1937).

[2] With, of course, certain measures of State regulation to deal with divergences between private and social net products of a kind that are compatible with perfect competition.

[3] See, in particular, Oskar Lange, *On the Economic Theory of Socialism* (Minneapolis: University of Minnesota Press, 1938).

c. Rules (a) and (b) can sometimes most conveniently be stated as above, and sometimes most conveniently combined into the single rule that each factor should be taken on in greater quantity so long as the value of its marginal product is greater than its market price.

d. Thus, as a practical set of rules for the operation of a particular firm, it may often be best to state: (i) that more should be produced with a given plant and equipment, so long as the price of the product exceeds the marginal prime cost of production and (ii) that a greater amount of fixed capital should be invested so long as the annual interest on the capital plus the annual cost of repair, depreciation, and so on, is less than the price of any additional output expected from the investment plus the price of any existing prime factors that it is expected to save, minus the price of any additional prime factor it is expected to take on as a result of the investment.

e. It is taken for granted, of course, that maximum efficiency will be an objective throughout, in the sense that the maximum amount technically possible will always be produced from any given collection of factors of production.

5. The fundamental difficulty of supervising State production is to determine whether managers of State plants are behaving efficiently, (a) technically, in getting the maximum output from any given collection of factors of production, and (b) economically, in combining factors in such proportions and producing output in such amount that the value of the marginal product is in each case brought as near as possible to the market price of the factor. *Ex hypothesi*—since the aim is equality between prices and marginal costs, and not between prices and average costs—the amount of profit or loss made is irrelevant.

6. In those cases in which there are a large number of plants under different managers, producing the same product,[4] it may be possible, by collecting data from every plant for every period, to construct production functions expressing output as a function of the collection of factors used. Any manager who was exceptionally inefficient or exceptionally efficient

---

[4] It might, at first sight, appear inconsistent with the argument to assume that there could be a large number of socialized plants producing the same product, since the argument for socialization rests upon the necessity of monopoly for technical reasons. There is, however, no contradiction. Because of the costs of transport of the product, there may need to be local monopolies, but the conditions of production in the various localities may be sufficiently similar to make comparisons of costs, etc., useful. Thus, for example, cost and output data might be compared for a large number of local gasworks.

technically would then probably stand out, since his output would not correspond to that derived from the production function based on average experience. Moreover, by working out from the production function partial derivatives of output in respect of each factor for different amounts and combinations of factors employed, some basis might be obtained for checking the marginal product of different factors in different plants. It is difficult to suggest any comparable procedure where only one or two plants exist; but, in such cases, it is doubtful whether the profit motive under private monopoly deals adequately with the problem.

7. It is, however, worth pointing out one advantage that State production will have over private production in this respect. The task of the manager of a State plant is in two respects simpler than that of a manager of a private plant. The object of the former is to equate the price of the product to the cost of the marginal factors involved in its production, while that of the latter is to equate the marginal revenue derived from the product with the marginal cost of its production. The State manager need not consider the market questions—how much his extra sales will depress the price of his product and how much his extra purchase of factors will raise their prices; the private manager has to consider both of these market questions in addition to all the other questions that the State manager must take into account. Thus:

a. Both managers must consider their technical efficiency, that is, methods of producing the maximum amount from any given collection of factors.

b. Both managers must consider the marginal productivity of the various factors, the additional output to be obtained from the use of an additional unit of the factor.

c. The State manager's job is then done, since he has now only to compare the market price of this additional output with the market price of the additional factors.

d. However, the private manager must proceed next to consider the marginal revenue to be derived from the sale of the additional product, which depends upon the effect his additional sales will have in depressing the market.

e. He must also consider the effect his additional purchase of the factor may have in hardening the market against him, before he is ready to compare marginal revenue with marginal cost.

8. The rules mentioned in the preceding paragraphs would probably serve adequately to cover all the main problems except that of a large new investment either for the production of a completely new product, or for the production of an old product in a new area (e.g., a new electrical generating plant), or—possibly—for a very large new investment increasing very substantially the total output of an existing product. In such cases, however, we cannot make the "atomistic" assumption that we have to deal only with changes at the margin where (a) the effect upon the total output of the product in question is not appreciable, and (b) the effect upon the total amount of factors left for employment in any other particular alternative occupation is not appreciable. The former condition would justify the assumption that the price of the product measures the addition to utility due to its production, and the latter the assumption that the price of the factor concerned measures the loss of utility due to the contraction of output in the industries from which it is withdrawn.

9. In the exceptional cases, however, one cannot afford to neglect the consumers' surplus involved in the additional product. To evaluate the gain to consumers of the additional product, one needs to integrate the area under the relevant range of the demand curve for the product in question. This needs to be compared with the value to consumers of the output that is sacrificed in the alternative occupations open to the factors involved. If these factors can be abstracted at the margin from a number of different alternative uses, it will be sufficient to compare the area under the demand curve in the new industry with the price of the factors involved. If, however, it involves the abstraction of factors in a lump, on a substantial scale, from some other particular industry, it becomes necessary to compare the area under the demand curve in the new industry with the area under the relevant range of the demand curve in the industry or industries from which the factors are to be abstracted.

10. Unfortunately, all of this must remain a matter of considerable numerical imprecision. While the rules for determining relatively small variations in output may be made sufficiently precise to use as actual working rules, the decision as to whether to make a large new investment must be based upon rules that, though logically watertight, are of extreme difficulty to apply accurately in practice. One thing, however, is clear. The issue does not depend on whether the new plant has a prospect of making a profit or avoiding a loss. In other words, it has nothing to do

with the question whether at any output of the new plant the consumers will offer a price which covers the average cost of production. It depends, on the contrary, on whether the total area under the consumers' demand curve in the new plant exceeds the total areas under the relevant portions of the demand curves for the various goods, from the production of which the necessary factors of production are to be abstracted.

11. These rules for the operation of socialized industries are by now more or less generally accepted by technical economists. But certain results of these rules are less familiar. Their budgetary implications are most striking. The principle is to socialize just those industries in which considerable economies of large-scale production may be enjoyed (i.e., precisely those industries in which the marginal cost is below the average cost) and to operate these industries in such a way that the price charged for the product is equal to its marginal cost (i.e., in such a way that a loss is made). This involves doing away with the principle of "charging what the traffic will bear" in the operation of the railways or in the sale of electric current, and charging only the marginal cost of the provision of these services. The previous owners, having presumably been fully compensated, will receive interest on capital now operated in such a way that a considerable loss is made upon it.

12. Nor is it possible to take comfort in the belief that these losses will necessarily be exceptional. I have argued at length elsewhere[5] that if a community's population is of the size that maximizes income per head, the value of the marginal product of labor over the whole range of industries and occupations will be equal to the average product of labor, and in this case the payment of a wage equal to the marginal product of labor would absorb the whole of the national income. In terms of our present problem this would mean that the actual losses made in the socialized "increasing returns" industries, due to charging a price for the product no greater than its marginal cost of production, would just be covered by what profits were still made in socialized industries where "increasing returns" were less marked or in competitive industries in which "increasing returns" did not play an appreciable part and in which a full return on land and capital was accordingly still being earned.

[5] See chapter 2 of part 4 of my *Introduction to Economic Analysis and Policy*.

13. The rules for operating socialized industries *may* thus involve losses commensurate with the total income earned on property in other sectors of the economy.[6] To raise taxation on a scale that will cover defense, social security, and the normal expenses of government as well as the losses to be contemplated in socialized industries, would involve "announcement" effects that even the most sanguine might hesitate to neglect. Even if the necessary funds could be raised by, for example, a proportionate income tax, the rate of tax might well be high enough seriously to interfere with the achievement of the best balance between work and leisure, to which reference has been made in paragraph 2 (b) above.

14. The socialization of "increasing returns" industries is, for these reasons, best accompanied by some measure of public ownership of property. A capital levy, or similar measure, that transfers property to State ownership permits either the cancellation of debt (regardless of whether it has occurred in the past purchase of socialized industries) or State investment of funds in privately operated concerns. In the former case, it removes a current interest charge from the State's expenditure, and in the latter it provides for the State a current income without the unfavorable announcement effects of high rates of taxation. In a community that starts with a large national debt, such a principle can, in fact, be carried a long way before it raises any problems associated with State ownership of privately operated capital. But in such a community *State operation* of "increasing returns" industries may, through the excessive charge that it would impose on the tax revenue, do more harm than good unless it is accompanied by some extension of the principle of *State ownership* of property.

15. There are two incidental advantages to be derived from the socialization of "increasing returns" industries and their operation on the above-mentioned principles.

16. First, it would open up a large new range for capital investment, and this, in an economy otherwise threatened with large-scale unemploy-

[6] This has not always been fully realized by writers on this subject. Thus Lange, *Economic Theory of Socialism* (pp. 74–75, 84) discusses the way in which the income earned in socialized industries may be distributed among consumers or used for corporate savings without recognizing that, far from any net profit being realized, the net losses made in socialized industries might even absorb all profits made in competitive industries, where he allows (*Ibid.*, pp. 120, 125) private enterprise and private property to continue.

ment, might appreciably aid in the maintenance of economic activity. In a socialized plant new investment will be undertaken so long as the price of the additional output (and not the marginal revenue derived from it) represents a return on the cost of the investment greater than the ruling rate of interest. Moreover, in determining whether an entirely new plant should be set up, criteria should be observed (as is argued in paragraphs 8 to 10 above) that, in many cases, will justify the investment, although a loss is bound to be realized on it. For both these reasons, the application of the current principles of pricing to socialized industries should justify much economically productive capital investment that private enterprise could never undertake.

17. Secondly, these principles of pricing in socialized industries involve a shift of income from profits to wages—a shift that, in the case of an optimum population, would involve the distribution of the whole national income in wages. Such a shift will be brought about by bringing down to the marginal cost of production the prices charged for the products of the socialized industries, without reducing money wages at the same time. Such a shift of income from profits to wages would probably lead to a more equal distribution as between persons.

J. E. Meade

London

COMMENT

1. Mr. Meade's statement of the principles that should govern the price and output policy of a state-controlled enterprise, though possibly a little oversimplified, is not, I think, open to serious objection. Indeed, one only wishes that they commanded a wider measure of understanding and acceptance outside the narrow ranks of the economists. Where I differ from him, however, is in attaching greater importance to the administrative, and less to the financial difficulties involved in applying these principles.

2. In paragraph 4 of his article, Mr. Meade formulates acceptably the conditions for "optimizing" inputs and outputs where the associated variations of input and/or output can be made very small by comparison

with the total turnover in the factor- and product-markets concerned.[7] Where, however, by reason of the indivisibility of the units of input and/or output, relatively large associated variations of input and/or output have to be considered, one can no longer determine optimal behavior by simply comparing marginal rates of substitution with relative prices.

3. For example, if the problem is to determine whether a public undertaking should expand output by an amount significantly large in relation either to product- or to factor-markets, it will be impossible to apply the criterion that the marginal cost must not exceed product price, that is, that the factor cost per unit of additional output must not exceed the unit price of the product relative to the unit price of the factors. If the managers of the undertaking apply this criterion in terms of the prices existing prior to the contemplated expansion of output, they will be unduly predisposed to expand output. If they calculate in terms of the less favorable prices expected to exist after the contemplated change, they will be unduly biased against expansion. The right course is to value the increment of output at the price expected to prevail after the change *plus* the surplus accruing from the fall in product prices to consumers of the increment of output and to value the increment of factor cost at the factor prices prevailing after the change *less* the surplus accruing from the rise in factor prices to the owners of the additional factors required to produce the increment of output.

4. In paragraphs 8 to 10, Mr. Meade gives some attention to this case, but he neglects the producers' surpluses (which may often be more important than the consumers' surpluses), and he greatly exaggerates the exceptional character of the circumstances in which such surpluses would have to be taken into account. He says that the ordinary "marginal" rules would "probably serve adequately to cover all the main problems except that of a large new investment either for the production of a

---

[7] Even in these cases the principles have to be applied with certain commonsense modifications to maintain a measure of price stability. A strict application would lead to an intolerable fluctuation of prices. For example, unless one were a season-ticket holder, one might not know how much one had to pay for one's ticket in a train or tram until one got to the station! It is worthwhile, in order to facilitate the planning of expenditure by one's customers, to introduce some stability into selling prices, even at the cost of maintaining them a little above the optimal level, and even at the cost of a little surplus capacity. Similarly, it is better to pay wages that are slightly too low than wages that fluctuate like a fever chart.

completely new product, or for the production of an old product in a new area (e.g., a new electric generator plant) or—possibly—for a very large new investment increasing very substantially the total output of an existing product." This is surely wrong. Almost every enterprise socialized on the grounds advocated by Mr. Meade will find the ordinary rules inapplicable to certain of its large inputs. The question of socialization in order to secure proper pricing and output policy will only arise in cases where the size of the optimal plant in relation to markets is such that there is a significant difference between profit at optimal output and that same profit *plus all consumers and producers surpluses*. It is only because there is such a significant difference that there is an opportunity of making monopoly profits by restricting output, and that the enterprise or industry cannot be left in private hands. Therefore, in all such cases, the question of setting up a new plant, or even of substantially extending an old plant, will necessitate taking account of such surpluses.

5. Having agreed—for Mr. Meade would probably not dispute the foregoing propositions—on the abstract criteria of price- and output-policy appropriate to a public enterprise, let us consider some of the practical difficulties and implications, beginning with those to which Mr. Meade attaches the greatest importance—viz., the budgetary implications. It is clear that if enterprises which have previously been run on monopolistic lines, with a view to making the maximal profit, are taken over by public authorities and run on the lines advocated by Mr. Meade, the profit earned will diminish, and, if full compensation has been paid to the previous owners, the difference will have to be met from the public purse. This will happen whether increasing, constant, or diminishing returns prevail in the undertakings in question.

6. Mr. Meade, however, seems to regard it as a circumstance particularly unpropitious from the financial point of view that undertakings socialized in order to secure optimal behavior will, as he asserts, operate under conditions of increasing returns (in the sense of diminishing factor cost per unit of output). I doubt whether this assertion is either true or relevant.

7. Socialization, of the type Mr. Meade is considering, comes into question only when it is impossible to secure genuine competition between units of optimal size. This will occur when the production units are so large, relative to the product and factor markets concerned, that

it would be impossible, by trust-busting, etc., to create a sufficient number of firms to secure competition without making production units too small. Under such conditions it will probably be the case that to set up, and operate in optimal fashion a single additional plant, will so depress product prices and enhance factor prices as substantially to reduce the profit earned by the additional plant below the level which it would have attained if prices had been unaffected. We saw, in paragraphs 3 and 4, that in such circumstances it may be right to build an additional plant if the profit at "previous" prices is substantially in excess of the capital cost, even if profit at "subsequent" prices fails to cover the cost. In this case, the additional plant (and all similar plants in the same industry) will work under conditions of increasing returns or diminishing average cost.[8] But is not another outcome equally possible? It may be right to *refrain* from building an additional plant if the prospective profit at "subsequent" prices is substantially below the capital cost, even though prospective profit at "previous" prices somewhat exceeds the capital cost. In this case the remaining plants in the industry, of a type similar to the additional plant which is just not worth while building, will work under conditions of diminishing returns, and will therefore make large profits. *Prima facie*, therefore, in the absence of precise knowledge regarding the demand and cost conditions in the actual industries and undertakings ripe for socialization, it appears just as likely that socialized undertakings will work under diminishing as under increasing returns. On the average, therefore, they will probably make much the same rate of profits (abstracting from considerations of risk, etc.) as prevails in the competitive sector of private industry, where, of course, constant returns is the rule.

8. Even if Mr. Meade were justified in assuming that his socialized undertakings would operate under increasing returns, the bearing of this on the financial problem of socialization would be at best very indirect. It is true that in such circumstances the undertakings would have to be run at a loss (in the sense of failing to cover their capital cost, failing to make a normal profit). What matters, however, in the present context is

---

[8]   Profit < capital cost
  $\therefore$ revenue < total cost
  $\therefore$ product price < average cost
  $\therefore$ marginal cost < average cost
  $\therefore$ average cost is declining.

not the level of profits after socialization, but the decline in profits as compared with the previous level. This, however, is affected not by the slope of the *average* cost curve, but by the slope of the *marginal* cost curve over the range of output extending between monopoly output and optimal output. It can be shown that the more negatively inclined the marginal cost curve over this range of output the greater will be the disparity between monopoly profits and optimal profits.[9] I would not, of

---

[9] Take the case where the demand curve is linear, and the supply curve of the factors is infinitely elastic.

Then, if R = revenue,

O = output,

C = cost (at constant factor prices),

X = the loss involved in moving from the maximal profit position to the optimal position,

a, b, α, β, S, are constants,

and if the values of the variables at the maximal profit position, and the optimal position, are indicated by suffixes m and o respectively;

Let
$$R = aO - bO^2.$$

Then marginal revenue $= \dfrac{dR}{dO} = a - 2bO$ and product price $= \dfrac{R}{O} = a - bO.$

Let
$$C = S + \alpha(O - O_m) + \beta(O - O_m)^2 \text{ where } O \text{ is not } < O_m.$$

Then
$$\text{marginal cost} = \frac{dC}{dO} = \alpha + 2\beta(O - O_m).$$

At the maximal profit position,
$$\frac{dR_m}{dO_m} = \frac{dC_m}{dO_m}$$

$$\therefore \quad O_m = \frac{a - \alpha}{2b}.$$

At the optimal position,
$$\frac{R_o}{O_o} = \frac{dC_o}{dO_o}$$

$$\therefore \quad O_o = \frac{a - \alpha + 2\beta O_m}{b + 2\beta}.$$

Substituting for $a - \alpha$
$$O_o = \frac{2O_m(b + \beta)}{b + 2\beta}.$$

[Since $O_o - O_m = (bO_m/b + 2\beta) = $ a quantity that is positive for positive values of O_m, it is legitimate to determine optimal output with the aid of a cost equation applicable only to outputs in excess of O_m.]

course, deny that there is a certain correlation between the slope of the *marginal* cost curve between monopoly and optimal output and the slope of the *average* cost curve at optimal output, and that if one were assured that, in socialized undertakings, average cost at optimal output was always declining, one would expect the disparity between monopoly profit and optimal profit to be greater than if increasing average cost had been the rule. But the connection is indirect and uncertain. In any event, there is, as we have seen, no particular reason to expect the average cost curve in socialized undertakings to be falling rather than rising, nor is there any particular reason why the slope of the marginal cost curve in such undertakings should as a rule be less positive than in other undertakings.

9. Whatever bearing the shape of the cost curves may have on the magnitude of the disparity between monopoly profits and optimum profits, it is indisputable that some disparity will exist and will constitute a burden on the Exchequer. The seriousness of a financial burden of this sort consists in the adverse effects on productive incentives and on the distribution of income to which it may give rise. What these effects are will depend on how the money to meet the deficit is raised. In the present case it appears likely that if the most appropriate method of financing the loss arising out of socialization is followed, the effect will be to annul some, but not all, of the benefits that, as Mr. Meade explains in paragraphs 1 to 4 of his article, would otherwise result from the policy of socialization.

Now the loss involved in moving from the maximal profit position to the optimal position $= X$

$$= R_m - R_0 - C_m + C_0$$
$$= aO_m - bO_m^2 - aO_0 + bO_0^2 + \alpha(O_0 - O_m) + \beta(O_0 - O_m)^2$$

$$= \frac{(a - \alpha)^2(b + \beta)}{4(b + 2\beta)^2}.$$

Now, suppose that β varies (O_m remaining constant, of course). When $\beta = \infty$, $X =$ zero. As β falls, X rises, until, as $\beta \to -\frac{1}{2}b$, $X \to \infty$. (β can never fall below $-\frac{1}{2}b$.) In words, the loss involved in moving from the maximal profit position to the optimal position varies inversely with the slope of the marginal cost curve for outputs exceeding monopoly output.

Similarly, it can be shown that, when the supply curve of a factor is linear, the demand curve of the product infinitely elastic, and the supply curves of any other factors also infinitely elastic, the loss involved in moving from the maximal profit position to the optimal position varies directly with the slope of the marginal product curve for inputs exceeding monopsony input.

10. Suppose, first, that the loss is financed out of a tax levied on the product of the socialized undertakings. The effect in this case is entirely to annul the benefits of socialization. The undertaking on being socialized will be run at the same output as formerly; what was previously a disparity between price and marginal cost will now be called a tax, and what was formerly monopoly profit will accrue to the Exchequer as the proceeds of the tax and will be used to pay compensation to the former owners for the loss of their monopoly revenue.

11. Suppose next that the tax, instead of being levied on the produce of the socialized undertakings, is levied *ad valorem* on output generally. The effect of this change will be to restore one of the most important— in fact, *the* most important—of the benefits for which the socialization was undertaken, in that it will correct the maldistribution of resources as between the different branches of industry that resulted from the inequality in the ratio of marginal cost to price in the different branches. The other benefits, however, that socialization was expected to bring— the increase in the proportion of national income accruing to labor, the raising of the incentive to work to its appropriate level—will be annulled, for the reason that, on the average of all industries, the gap between marginal cost and price will remain as great as ever.

12. There are many other ways in which the loss could be financed, by measures such as an increased income tax, or death duty, by a tax on capital, by a reduction in public expenditure. This is not the place to inquire into their relative merits or demerits in respect of effect on income distribution, on incentive to invest, on propensity to consume, or on incentive to work. One general observation can, however, be made on each and every one of them regarded as an alternative to a general indirect tax. If it is right, after the socialization, to finance the losses resulting from the socialization by method x rather than by a general indirect tax, it would have been right before the socialization to raise money by method x in order to finance a general subsidy on output. The only benefit, therefore, that is properly attributable to the socialization is that of an improved interindustrial distribution of resources. Any other benefits which may accrue from the fact that the socialization is financed by some other way than by a general indirect tax, could have been obtained by appropriate fiscal measures, without the socialization.

13. It might perhaps be surmised that a similar objection could be advanced against the sole remaining virtue which, in paragraph 11 above,

is still attributed to socialization—namely, that it enables the maldistribution of resources between different industries to be corrected. Could not the same result be equally well achieved without socialization by a combination of a subsidy on goods produced under monopolistic conditions and a tax on goods produced under competitive conditions? The answer is that once the monopolistic industries have been socialized and are being managed according to correct principles, it becomes possible to reduce the "tax" formerly imposed on their products by the monopolist owners and to increase the tax on products produced by private enterprise under competitive conditions, without untoward effects on the distribution of income. Whereas a policy of subsidizing goods produced by private monopolies and taxing other goods would have the effect of expanding the share of monopoly profits in the national income. In addition, of course, it would provide a very undesirable incentive to adopt monopolistic practices.

14. It follows from what has been said in the foregoing paragraphs that Mr. Meade is mistaken in believing that socialization, with its concomitant increase in taxation, provides any additional argument for the State's taking heroic steps to reduce its indebtedness or acquire property. No doubt it would be very gratifying if the State could painlessly acquire a property income which could then be used to relieve taxation. But this cannot be done except by achieving a budget surplus, which is never a painless procedure. If a large surplus is aimed at, such as would probably be required in order to offset the capitalized value of the losses involved in socializing a substantial sector of industry, it could probably only be achieved by resort to a capital tax or levy. But such a levy, particularly if it is expected to be repeated at irregular intervals, has many unfortunate effects on incentive and the distribution of income. In order to decide whether it is worth while, it is necessary to balance the marginal disadvantages of a levy on capital now against the marginal advantages of the permanent reduction in general taxation which would thereby be made possible. Now, a combination of socialization of the type under discussion *plus* a general indirect tax on output has, as we have seen, no net effect on incentive or income distribution, favorable or unfavorable, except that of removing barriers to an optimum interindustrial distribution of resources. The marginal disadvantages of a capital levy are in no wise diminished, nor are the marginal disadvantages of current taxation

in any way increased. The desirability of socialization to eliminate monopoly has therefore no bearing on the case for or against a capital levy, or (more generally) for or against budgeting for a surplus.

15. While I am less impressed than Mr. Meade by the financial difficulties involved in the application of criteria of optimal production and pricing by public undertakings, I am more impressed than he is by the difficulty of securing efficient management under these conditions. In the first place, I do not agree that, given good-will, the task of a manager of a State plant run on the optimal principles is significantly simpler than that of the manager of a private plant or of a State plant run on the lines of a private monopoly. Mr. Meade says that the State manager, unlike the private manager, is dispensed from considering how much extra output would depress the price of his product and raise the price of his factors. But this is only true if the State manager sets out to find his optimal position by a process of random trial and error. If he tries to cut short this process—and since, in reality, the optimal position is always changing, he ought to try to cut it short—he must guess how much a given expansion of output will affect product and factor prices, since he has to equate marginal factor cost with the ratio of product to factor prices. Much the same is true of the private manager. He can find the output corresponding to maximum profit by trial and error, but if he wishes to cut short the process, he must guess at the relationship between output and prices. Whatever may be the relative difficulty of the problems confronting State and private managers in deciding on the scale of operation of existing plants, it is clear, from what has been said in paragraph 4, that when it comes to deciding whether or not to set up an additional plant there is nothing to choose between the difficulties confronting State and private enterprise, respectively.

16. Second, and more important, the application of the principles of optimization will make it more difficult to weed out the inefficient managers than it is when the enterprises are run for profit. Admittedly, it is just as difficult for an outsider to estimate the precise efficiency of the management in the one case as in the other. But in the latter case the level of profits is at any rate a rough-and-ready index of managerial efficiency, whereas in the former case it is no guide at all. This for two reasons. A lowering of the cost curve, reflecting technical efficiency of management, will raise monopoly profits by much more than profits at

optimal output. The latter, indeed, may not be affected at all. In the second place, the manager of a plant that purports to be run on optimal lines can easily cover up any shortfall of profits due to his technical inefficiency by slightly restricting output.

17. Mr. Meade suggests that it would be possible for someone at the center to obtain, by means of comparative statistics, an accurate and up-to-date idea of the technical production functions of the various plants in a socialized industry. If this were possible, it would certainly facilitate the task of weeding out inefficient managers. But, of course, the same methods of control would be applicable to a socialized industry run for profit, so that the relative advantage of running such an industry on the maximal profit principle rather than the optimal principle, in respect of the elimination of inefficient managers (though it would be reduced to vanishing point) would, at any rate, not be reversed.[10] In most cases, however, these methods of central control by statistics would prove themselves to be unsatisfactory. It is just because different plants have different production functions ("special circumstances") that cannot be fully comprehended at the center, that it is necessary for private combines (and will probably be necessary for socialized industries) to devolve a good deal of initiative on the managers of individual plants.

18. More serious than the difficulty of weeding out inefficient managers is that of providing managers, so long as they are maintained in their functions with an adequate incentive to effort and efficiency. Where the enterprise is run for profit, such an incentive can be provided partly by the fear of being replaced and partly by making managerial remuneration vary with profits of the firm. Now the first incentive will, as we have seen, apply somewhat less effectively to the manager of an enterprise run on the optimal principles than to the manager of one run for profit. In any case, dismissal is a drastic and exceptional remedy for inefficiency. The lack of a gentler but more persistent and finely modulated pressure in the direction of efficient management is, therefore, a serious drawback.

19. What is the upshot of the argument? We have found that the socialization of monopolistic or oligopolistic undertakings, accompanied by compensation, and followed by the application of the accepted criteria

---

[10] Mr. Meade's point may count as an argument for the superior efficiency of public over private enterprise as such, when both are conducted according to the same principles. But this is a question with which we are (happily) not concerned here.

of optimal output and price policy, will result in an improvement in the interindustrial distribution of resources, but it is also likely to result in a lower technical efficiency of production in the industries directly affected than could have been attained had the undertakings been run for profit. From this two consequences follow: (a) Where there is a choice between securing the application of the desired criteria by direct instructions to the managers or by the restoration of competitive conditions, the latter policy should have a measure of preference even at the cost of *some* reduction in the unit of management below the optimal size. This implies giving a measure of preference to "trust-busting" and other antirestrictionist measures over socialization as a means of coping with monopoly, unless there is reason to believe public enterprise more efficient than private, even where an industry is competitive. (Incidently, if antimonopoly measures of the trust-busting type can be carried through without the payment of compensation to the monopolists, additional advantages arise, particularly an improvement in the incentive to work.) (b) Even where the restoration of competition is impossible, industries should be managed in accordance with the principles of optimal production only in cases where the avoidance of monopolistic restriction of output with a given technique is more important than the preservation of the maximum incentive to maintain technical efficiency and progress.

J. M. Fleming

London

REJOINDER

1. Mr. Fleming doubts whether the assertion that financial losses will be made in socialized industries is either true or relevant. As to its truth, he argues that the average cost in socialized industries is just as likely to be rising as falling. His argument is based upon considerations of the discontinuity of cost curves of which I had failed to take account. There is, however, still, in my opinion, a presumption that decreasing costs will be more frequent than rising costs. A large number of cases probably exist (e.g., transport, public utilities, and industries where the cost of transport of the product from one local market to another is high) where there is room only for a single plant in a local market. In these cases, decreasing costs alone will operate up to the optimum output of such a single plant.

Between this output and the output of many plants of optimum size—
in spite of intermediate ups and downs at the points at which new plant
is introduced—there will be no net change in average cost, unless there
are economies of large-scale production external to the individual plant.
Over this range, there is no net rise or fall in average cost, while up to
this point there will be only falling costs. As Mr. Fleming has pointed out
to me, this is not conclusive proof that falling costs (and losses) are more
probable than rising costs (and profits) at the points of intersection of the
demand curve and the marginal cost curve. But to me, at least, it suggests
a strong probability that on further examination this will be found to be
the case.

2. The probability of decreasing costs is reinforced if allowance is
made—as it should be made—for economies of large-scale production
external to the individual plant. In this case, the average cost of the
optimum output from a plant of optimum size will be lower when there
is a large number of such plants than when there is only one. This is a
second reason for expecting socialized industries to be operating under
decreasing rather than increasing costs.

3. As Mr. Fleming himself points out, even when plants are operating
under increasing average cost, optimal profits will be less than monopoly
profits, so that even in these cases the financial problem exists if full compensation has been paid to the owners when the industry was socialized.

4. As to the relevance of the financial consideration, Mr. Fleming
points out that my argument for the State ownership of property was not
properly grounded. Without the further extension of State ownership of
property, the financing of losses in socialized industries will not necessarily worsen the distribution of income and the incentive to work, since
such losses could be financed by indirect taxation without any net adverse
effects in these respects. State ownership of property should rather be
regarded as a means (which could be adopted independently of the
socialization of "increasing returns" industries) for positively improving
the distribution of income and the incentive to work. Mr. Fleming's
criticism is correct, but I remain unrepentant in my conclusion, since I
am prepared to kill more than one bird with a single stone. The socialization of "increasing returns" industries can improve the interindustrial
distribution of resources without further State ownership of property, but
the full improvements that it might also bring to the distribution of

income and the incentive to work cannot, I still maintain, be enjoyed without such extension of State ownership.

5. Finally, in paragraph 15 of his comment, Mr. Fleming has overlooked the central point that it was my intention to make. Given that State managers and private enterprise managers both know (a) the prices of the factors, (b) the prices of the products, and (c) the marginal physical products of the factors, then the State manager will, and the private enterprise manager will not, know whether more or less of any factor should be employed. True, the State manager will not yet know how much more or less to employ, but—unlike the private enterprise manager—he will at least know in which direction he should move.

J. E. Meade

London

3

A CARDINAL CONCEPT
OF WELFARE

I HOPE to show that, given any ethical system that conforms to certain conditions (of a sort to which many ethical systems do in fact conform), it is in principle possible to assign numbers to the different degrees of general welfare obtaining in different hypothetical situations, and to the different degrees of well-being experienced by the several individuals in these situations, in such a manner as to ensure that welfare is the sum of individual well-beings. The indicators of welfare and individual well-being that permit of this additive relationship are unique: the numbers assigned to the different degrees of welfare and well-being may all be altered by a common proportion but in no other way. Ethical systems that meet the prescribed conditions yield a concept of welfare as an extensive or additive magnitude, susceptible of fundamental measurement.

By this I do not mean that these ethical systems necessarily postulate a concept of welfare based on some other property (e.g., happiness) that is independently and empirically measurable. I mean that they themselves provide a way of measuring welfare through the process of ethical evaluation. All reasoning that presupposes an ethical system of this type may legitimately speak of welfare as in the fullest sense a cardinal magnitude. This applies, for example, to any brand of welfare economics that may be based on an ethical system of this type. And it can, I believe, be shown that to be able to treat welfare as cardinal is, if not a necessity, at least a considerable convenience for any such welfare economics. At the end

First published in the *Quarterly Journal of Economics*, August 1952. Reprinted by permission of Harvard University Press.

of this paper I briefly indicate the directions in which I believe this convenience to lie.

What do we mean when we dispute whether any property (e.g., welfare, utility, happiness) is ordinal or cardinal? The contrast is less sharp than is sometimes supposed. In order to be cardinal, or in the fullest sense measurable, a property has to be able to meet a certain number of requirements. Some properties satisfy some of these requirements and fail to satisfy others.[1]

Consider the property "blankness." The first requirement of cardinality is that the property arise out of ordinal relations between pairs of "objects" (or however one may term that to which the property applies) so that one can say "*A* is blanker than *B* (*B* is less blank than *A*)." Secondly, this relationship must be asymmetrical, so that if *A* is blanker than *B*, *B* is not blanker than *A*. Thirdly, the relationship must be transitive, so that, if *A* is blanker than *B* and *B* is blanker than *C*, *A* is blanker than *C*. Fourthly, if *A* and *B* are of the same degree of blankness (if neither is *A* blanker than *B* nor *B* blanker than *A*) and if *A* is blanker than *C*, *B* must be blanker than *C*. It follows that if *A* is as blank as *B* and *B* as blank as *C*, *A* is as blank as *C*.

If all of these requirements are met, we may speak of blankness as an ordinal magnitude, different degrees of which may be distinguished, occupying different positions in a linear order. Numbers can then be assigned to the degrees of blankness possessed respectively by different objects, in such a way that the same number will be assigned to objects of the same degree of blankness, and that the blanker of two objects will always be assigned the higher number. Such numbers may be regarded as particular values, corresponding to particular degrees of blankness, of a continuous function, or indicator providing a cardinal representation of the property "blankness."

Any property meeting only those requirements discussed above, and fails to meet those discussed below, can, however, be represented by any one of a family of indicators whose only connection is that they are

---

[1] The following five paragraphs are much influenced by N. R. Campbell, *Account of the Principles of Measurement and Calculation* (New York, Longmans, 1928), and M. R. Cohen and E. Nagel, *Introduction to Logic and Scientific Method* (New York, Harcourt Brace, 1934), ch. 15. The idea of "mutual measurement," however, is, so far as I know, my own.

increasing functions one of another throughout their entire range. Such numerical indication falls short of measurement. If k_1, k_2, k_3, and k_4, are descending degrees of blankness it is meaningless to compare the "distance" between k_1 and k_2, with that between k_2 and k_3. Still the "distance" between k_1 and k_4 may be considered as "greater than" that between k_2 and k_3, in the sense that, whatever indicator may be used to represent blankness, k_1 *minus* k_4 will exceed k_2 *minus* k_3.

The fifth requirement of cardinality is that it should be possible to limit the range of admissible indicators of blankness so that any admissible indicator differs from another only with respect to origin or zero-point, and proportionate scale. The criterion of an admissible indicator is that it should simplify the mathematical expression of the relationship between blankness and other properties (magnitudes). That is, it should enable this relationship to be expressed in the form of a simple numerical equation (law). Where the class of admissible indicators is thus limited blankness may be said to be a measurable magnitude, though possibly only an intensive one. Where the other magnitudes in question are themselves measured by an independent process, the measurement of blankness may be said to be "derived." It is possible, however, that the criterion of mathematical simplicity may enable suitably limited classes of indicators to be selected simultaneously for a number of magnitudes not otherwise measurable. This I would call "mutual measurement."

The sixth and final requirement for a cardinal blankness is that (a) among the objects to which blankness appertains there should be some that, if only by convention, can be regarded as collections or combinations of parts which are themselves capable of existence as independent objects and (b) a process of mutual measurement is possible whereby the blankness of the complex objects can be expressed as the sum of the blanknesses of their parts. If blankness meets this requirement also it is measurable by the fundamental process and may be regarded as a truly extensive or cardinal magnitude. We can say "A is three times as blank as B," meaning that A is as blank as a complex object C that is composed of objects D, E, and F, each of which is as blank as B.

The property whose cardinality is in question may be either one believed to manifest itself in the world of experience or one implicit in a conceptual scheme or theory. In the former case all of the requirements of cardinality have to be fulfilled empirically. For example, the numerical equation referred to above has to be a scientific law. In the latter case, on the other hand, the various requirements have to be shown by deductive reasoning to be implicit in the postulated conceptual scheme or theory. An example of a cardinal magnitude of the first kind would be length as found in nature. An example of a cardinal magnitude of the second kind would be length as defined in certain geometries.

My cardinalization of welfare is of the second type. It is my contention that all ethical systems that obey certain not very exacting conditions— and not only, as is frequently assumed, those explicitly based on some property, such as "pleasure," believed to be measurable in an empirical sense—yield a concept of welfare that fulfills all six requirements of cardinality discussed above.

Although I regard welfare as an ethical concept and its cardinality as dependent on ethical presuppositions, I hope that this cardinality may prove useful for the purpose of welfare economics. This does not mean that I wish to bring value judgments into economics—quite the contrary. Though no ethical relativist, I think economic science had better be *wertfrei*. But welfare economics is inevitably concerned with values in the sense that it represents the application of economic science, in itself *wertfrei*, to the service of a *postulated* set of ethical ends. There are, in principle, as many systems of welfare economics as there are systems of ethical ends. But economic analysis is more serviceable to certain systems of ends than to others (e.g., to those emphasizing individual happiness rather than those emphasizing moral righteousness), and my contention is that if an ethical system permits of a cardinal concept of welfare, that fact is likely to make economic analysis still more serviceable to it.

The ethical postulates set forth below do not purport to constitute a complete ethical system. They do not even define the minimum conditions that any ethical system must meet if welfare is to be measurable. All they do is to give an example of a set of propositions which, if included explicitly or implicitly in any ethical system, will suffice to ensure that the welfare concept characteristic of that ethical system will be susceptible of fundamental measurement. I choose this particular set of sufficient conditions partly because they can be expressed in terms analogous to those with which economists are familiar, and partly because they appear to be satisfied by most of the ethical systems that I personally regard as intellectually respectable!

I. BASIC ETHICAL POSTULATES

Postulate A. Let us mean by a "situation" a hypothetical past and future of the universe. Then *behavior should be determined, at least in part, by expectations as to the situations that would result, respectively, from the adoption of each of the various alternative courses of action.* Let us mean by the statement *"A is more desirable than B"* that, to the (not negligible) extent that behavior should be determined by consequences, a course of action resulting with certainty in situation *A* should be preferred to one resulting with certainty in situation *B.* Then we can formulate postulate A as: *the relation "more desirable than" exists in some instances as between situations.* From its definition, this relation must be asymmetrical, thus fulfilling the first requirement of cardinality.

Postulate B. The ethic is self-consistent. *If A is more desirable than B and B is more desirable than C, then A is more desirable than C.* This fulfills the second requirement of cardinality.

Postulate C. In principle (i.e., given certain knowledge) there is no indeterminacy as to the relative desirability of situations. *If A is as desirable as B* (neither more nor less desirable than *B*) *and B is as desirable as C, then A is as desirable as C.* This fulfills the third requirement of cardinality. It follows from postulates A, B, and C that situations are arranged, with respect to their relative desirability, in a linear order of precedence. Desirability or welfare (see below) may thus be considered an ordinal magnitude.

Postulate D. (What follows is rather long and complicated but is best treated as a single postulate since the rejection of its initial steps would entail its rejection as a whole. On the other hand, ethical systems to which this postulate is repugnant may nevertheless be compatible with some other postulate that, because of its formal analogy with this, will serve the same purpose so far as the measurement of welfare is concerned, and may be substituted at this point.)

Let us define a "mental state" as "the experience of a sentient being or individual over a moment of time, that is, over a period of time short enough for any such experience to be homogeneous." In considering situations as ends of moral action, attention must be paid (according to this postulate) not to the external or physical aspects of the situations but to the mental states that they contain or engender. In assessing the relative desirability of the various possible situations one is really evaluating the various possible mental states in their various possible combinations.

Let us define an "elementary" situation as one in which only a single mental state exists or in which no mental state exists. Then the same properties, whatever they are, that render the elementary situation associated with some particular mental state a relatively desirable one will tend to enhance the desirability of any situation of which that mental state forms a part.

Let us define "welfare (in any situation A)" as "the desirability of situation A." And let us define "the well-being of individual x at moment t (in situation A)" as "the desirability of a hypothetical elementary situation containing a mental state identical with that existing (as part of situation A) in individual x at moment t." Postulate D then affirms that if (a) each individual at each moment of time has the same degree of well-being in situation A as in situation B, the two situations have the same degree of welfare and (b) all individual-moments save one have the same degree of well-being in situation A as in situation B, and if that one has a higher degree of well-being in situation A than in situation B, then situation A will have a higher degree of welfare than situation B. More briefly, *welfare is an increasing function of the well-being of each individual at each moment of time*. If D is any indicator of welfare and x, y, $z \cdots$ are any indicators of individual-momentary well-beings, then $D = D(x, y, z \cdots)$,[2] and $D'_r > 0$, when $r = x$, y, $z \cdots$ and D'_r is the partial derivative of D with respect to r.[3]

I have identified well-being with the welfare of elementary situations. What the above equation does is to describe a certain internal relationship that is posited to exist within the welfare ordering of situations, according to which the welfare-rating of complex situations depends on that of elementary situations. All this may seem a little abstract, for I

---

[2] From our method of deriving well-being from the welfare of elementary situations, it might reasonably be assumed that the choice of an indicator for welfare would *ipso facto* determine the indicators of the various well-beings and establish a relationship between them which would not exist if the well-beings had been independently derived. In order to make our argument cover interpretations of the welfare function using an independent concept of well-being, it is assumed in the subsequent treatment that separate indicators are initially chosen, independently, and arbitrarily, for each of the several well-beings and for welfare.

[3] There seems to be no justification for treating welfare as a function of well-beings which is not at the same time a justification for treating it as an *increasing* function of well-beings. It was, however, not strictly necessary to introduce the latter assumption explicitly at this point since it could have been deduced as a corollary of postulate E.

have said nothing about what determines the welfare-rating of elementary situations, and hence the various well-beings. That depends on the particular ethical system that one assumes. In one system well-being may be correlated with "happiness" (whether conceived as an ordinal or cardinal property of states of mind), in another with "righteousness" somehow conceived, in another with "knowledge," or with "intensity of consciousness"—these being different ways of conceiving goodness-as-an-end. Or there might be no single mental property with which well-being is correlated. A man may be quite unable to say what makes him regard one mental state as better (as an end) than another. From the standpoint of the measurability of welfare and well-being, it does not in the least matter what a man's conception of well-being is so long as his ordering of situations with respect to desirability depends on his ordering of states of mind in the manner described in postulates D and E.

I spoke of the possibility of substituting for postulate D some analogous postulate. An ethical system might base its ordering of alternative courses of action not on the nature of the mental states that are expected to result from the respective courses of action, but on the orderings of these courses of action by a (somehow selected) set of individuals. These individual orderings might themselves have an ethical or a nonethical character. If by welfare we now mean the position of a course of action in the general ordering, and by well-being the position of the same course of action in an individual ordering, we can then formulate the analog of postulate D in almost the same language, namely, that welfare should be an increasing function of individual well-beings. Although the underlying meaning has changed substantially, it is still quite plausible that ethical systems of this type would conform to this analog of postulate D.[4] They are perhaps less likely to take the next hurdle, postulate E.

Postulate E. In assessing the relative desirability or welfare of any two situations no account need be taken of states of mind common to both situations. If situations A and B are identical with respect to the states of mind of certain individual-moments and different with respect to the states of mind of other individual-moments, and if A' and B' are identical with situations A and B, respectively, except that they do not contain the

---

[4] Professor Abram Bergson constructs his welfare function on this assumption; see "A Reformulation of Certain Aspects of Welfare Economics," *Quarterly Journal of Economics* (February 1938), 52:310–34.

states of mind common to A and B (because the individuals who experience the same states of mind in A as in B are nonexistent at the moments in question both in A' and in B'), then A will be more, equally, or less desirable than B according as A' is more, equally, or less desirable than B'.

I would maintain that, in practice, everyone who seeks to assess the desirability of "situations" at all (i.e., everyone whose ethic requires him to take account of the results of alternative courses of action) does and must accept this postulate implicitly. For example, we all exclude the past from our ethical calculations. I am sure that most readers' eyebrows were raised when I defined a situation, for the purpose of ethical evaluation, as including the past as well as the future. I entirely agree that the past is irrelevant in this context. But the only justification for excluding it from our consideration is that past states of mind are there for good and all and cannot be affected by what we may now decide. Again, in considering policies affecting the inhabitants of this planet we do not feel hampered by our ignorance regarding states of mind that prevail among the inhabitants of Mars. And in cases where a course of action can be presumed to exhaust its effects within a short period of time, we normally refrain from speculation as to the condition of mankind in some remote future. There is, however, no logical stopping place in this process. If we are content to ignore individual-moments that are past, or remote in time and space, because they are unaffected by our decisions, we must be prepared to ignore individual-moments in all cases in which they are unaffected by our decisions.

It was assumed in postulate D that situational changes that leave unaffected the well-being of each individual-moment have no effect on welfare. From this, and from the last paragraph but one, it follows that, in comparing two situations for welfare, not only can those individual-moments whose states of mind are the same in both situations be left out of account but also those whose states of mind, though they may be different in one situation from what they are in the other, are of the same well-being in the two situations. *The desirability of any situational change (the sign of the change in welfare) depends on the levels of well-being, in the two situations, of those individual-moments whose well-beings are affected by the change.* Symbolically we may express this as follows:

$$\text{Sign } dD = f(dx, dy \cdots : x, y \cdots) \qquad \begin{array}{l} dx \neq 0 \\ dy \neq 0 \end{array}$$

It should be noted that the above proposition does not imply that the well-being of any individual at any time may not be psychologically affected by what he believes the states of mind and well-beings of other people to be, or by what he remembers of his own past states of mind. What we are concerned with here is the ethical evaluation of a situational change after all psychological as well as physical interconnections have been taken into account.

As already observed for postulate D, it makes no difference as regards conformity to postulate E what the substantive content of well-being is deemed to be. If well-being is correlated with happiness, then postulate E requires that all those whose happiness is unaffected by any situational change should be ignored in the evaluation of that change. If well-being depends on loving-kindness, those whose level of loving-kindness is left unchanged should be ignored.

Let us revert for a moment to the subsidiary line of thought developed earlier in which welfare relates to a general ordering not of "situations" but of courses of action, and in which well-being relates not to a general ordering of individual states of mind (or rather of the associated elementary situations) but to individual orderings of courses of action. In such a conceptual scheme the analog of postulate E would be a requirement that whether one course of action is deemed more or less desirable than another should depend solely on the respective ratings given to the two courses of action in the orderings of those individuals who are not indifferent as between the two. This seems to me a fairly plausible condition to which many systems of general ordering based on individual orderings may conform. But it cannot claim support from what I regard as the compelling arguments of the last paragraph but three, which relate to a different class of ethical systems.

The list of ethical postulates is now complete. My impression is that in the case of ethical systems that evaluate situations on the basis of the states of mind they contain, the only postulate that is at all likely to give trouble is postulate D, which may be repugnant to systems attaching importance to the *pattern* or combination of states of mind within a situation as well as to the states of mind themselves. In the case of systems of general ordering based on individual orderings or preferences the stumbling block, if any, is more likely to be postulate E.

Corollary to Postulate E. Consider situational changes that leave unaffected the well-beings of all individual-moments save two. Let x and y be the two well-beings affected by the changes, while z represents all the unaffected well-beings. We know from postulate D that if there is some situational change that raises x-well-being from a specific level x_1 to another x_2 and leaves welfare unaffected, it must reduce the level of y-well-being. We also know from the same postulate that if there is some situational change that raises x-well-being from x_1 to x_2 and reduces y-well-being from y_1 to y_2 and leaves welfare unaffected, any other change at the same level of z-well-being that raises x from x_1 to x_2, starts from y_1, and leaves welfare unaffected, must reduce y to y_2. So that, with respect to the assumed level of z-well-being, the increase in x-well-being from x_1 to x_2 may be deemed equal in its effect on welfare to the increase of y-well-being from y_2 to y_1. Moreover, from postulate E we know that if a situational change that raises x from x_1 to x_2 and lowers y from y_1 to y_2, leaves welfare unaffected *at a given level of z-well-being*, then a change with the same effect on x and y, *at a different level of z-well-being*, will also leave welfare unaffected. So that the increase in x from x_1 to x_2 is equal, in its effect on welfare, to the increase in y from y_2 to y_1 irrespective of the level of z-well-being.

If numerical indicators are selected at random for x, y, and z, the amount of the fall in y that will offset, in its effect on welfare, a unit increase in x will vary with the initial levels of x and y but will be independent of z. For infinitesimal changes the rate at which y must fall as x rises in order to keep welfare constant will be equal to the ratio between the partial derivative of welfare with respect to x and the partial derivative of welfare with respect to y. By analogy with the marginal utility of commodities we might term this ratio that of the "marginal welfare of x-well-being" to the "marginal welfare of y-well-being." Using "a well-being" to mean "the well-being of an individual-moment," we conclude that *the ratio of the marginal welfares of any two well-beings depends solely on the amounts of the two well-beings in question and is independent of the amount of any other well-being.* In symbols:

$$\frac{\partial\left(\dfrac{D'_x}{D'_y}\right)}{\partial z} = \frac{\partial\left(\dfrac{D'_y}{D'_z}\right)}{\partial x} = \frac{\partial\left(\dfrac{D'_z}{D'_x}\right)}{\partial y} = 0.$$

While the above equations will hold true irrespective of the choice of indicators for the various well-beings, any alteration in the indicators will alter the numerical values of the marginal welfare ratios as well as of the well-beings themselves.

II. MUTUAL MEASUREMENT OF WELFARE AND WELL-BEINGS

The next step is to show that, for any ethical system compatible with postulates A to E, it is possible so to measure (i.e., assign indicators to) welfare and individual-momentary well-beings that welfare is the sum of well-beings, and that the measurements so arrived at are unique save for proportionate scale.

We have seen that, where D is any cardinal indicator of welfare and x, y, z, any cardinal indicators of individual-momentary well-beings,

$$D = D(x, y, z) \qquad (1)$$

$$D'_r > 0 \qquad (r = x, y, z) \qquad (2)$$

$$\frac{\partial\left(\dfrac{D'_x}{D'_y}\right)}{\partial z} = \frac{\partial\left(\dfrac{D'_y}{D'_z}\right)}{\partial x} = \frac{\partial\left(\dfrac{D'_z}{D'_x}\right)}{\partial y} = 0. \qquad (3)$$

We want to find new indicators of welfare and well-beings, W, d, e, f, which are increasing functions of D, x, y, $z \cdots$ respectively, and such that

$$W(D) = d(x) + e(y) + f(z). \qquad (4)$$

Now, it is easy to show that equations (1) to (3) must be satisfied if equation (4) is satisfied.[5] What we have to show, however, is that if

[5]

$$D = f(W) = f(d + e + f) = D(x, y, z) \qquad (1)$$

$$D'_x = \frac{dD}{dW} W'_x = \frac{dD}{dW} \cdot \frac{dd}{dx},$$

and since

$$\frac{dD}{dW} > 0, \quad \text{and} \quad \frac{dd}{dx} > 0, \quad \therefore D'_x > 0 \qquad (2)$$

$$\frac{\partial\left(\dfrac{D'_x}{D'_y}\right)}{\partial z} = \frac{\partial\left(\dfrac{dD}{dW} \cdot \dfrac{dd}{dx} \div \dfrac{dD}{dW} \cdot \dfrac{de}{dy}\right)}{\partial z} = 0. \qquad (3)$$

equations (1) to (3) are satisfied, equation (4) must be satisfied. This can be proved by demonstrating the actual process whereby, starting from indicators D, x, y, z, which satisfy equations (1) to (3) one can arrive at indicators W, d, e, f, satisfying equation (4).

The essence of the procedure adopted is to take a specific infinitesimal change in the well-being of some particular individual-moment (such as would result from a specific situation change) and to use this as a yard-stick for measuring out units of well-being for all individual-moments. All increments in well-being that have an effect on welfare equivalent to that of the yardstick are regarded as numerically equal.

Operation 1. Starting from a particular level of z-well-being, $z = m$, consider an increment in z-well-being amounting to one (infinitesimal) unit as measured by the original arbitrary scale of z-well-being. This is the yardstick.

Operation 2. Starting from the arbitrary zero-point $y = 0$, mark out on the original arbitrary scale of y-well-being successive infinitesimal positive increments, dy, such that the effect on welfare of a y-increment is equal to the effect of a unit increment of z at $z = m$. Since these increments are infinitesimal, the effect on welfare of any such increment dy will be equal to dy times the marginal welfare of y at the point in question D'_y, and this will be equal to the marginal welfare of z at the point $z = m$, $D'_{z=m}$. It follows that dy, in terms of the original y-scale, will be equal to the ratio of the marginal welfare of z at $z = m$ to the marginal welfare of y (i.e., $dy = (D'_{z=m}/D'_y)$). From the corollary to postulate E we know that this ratio is a function of y alone and is independent of x. There is therefore no ambiguity about the amounts of the successive increments dy as we move up the y-scale.

Coming back to $y = 0$, mark off negative increments on the y-scale each of which is equal, in its effect on welfare, to the negative of a unit increment of z at $z = m$.

Construct a new indicator of y-well-being called b in which each of the dy increments, marked off according to the process described above, will correspond to a unit increment in b; b will have the same zero-point as y and will be a monotone increasing function of y. Since the units of b have been so chosen that a unit increment of b at any level will have the same effect on welfare as a unit increment of z at $z = m$, and since all of these unit increments are infinitesimal it follows that the marginal welfare of b, D'_b, will be equal, for all values of b and of x, to the marginal welfare of z at $z = m$, $D'_{z=m}$.

Operation 2 is not complete when it has been performed on y-well-being alone. The same kind of transformation has to be applied to the original indicators of all well-beings other than that of z, a unit increment of z from the point $z = m$ always being used as the yardstick. Thus in the case of indicator x we mark out successive increments each equal to the ratio $(D'_{z=m}/D'_x)$ and constitute these the units of a new indicator a, which is an increasing function of x with the same zero-point, and with D'_a equal to $D'_{z=m}$ for all values of a and b.

Operation 3. We now apply operation 2 in reverse. Take as yardstick a unit increment on the b-scale of y-well-being, starting from any arbitary level, $b = n$. Then, in precisely the same manner as before, transform the original indicator z into a new indicator c having the property that, for all levels of c and a, the marginal welfare of c, D'_c, is equal to the marginal welfare of b at the point $b = n$, viz., $D'_{b=n}$. Let t be the level of c corresponding to our original starting point $z = m$. This, of course, will be the one level of z-well-being at which marginal welfare is unaffected by the transformation of z into c (i.e., $D'_{c=t} = D'_{z=m}$).

It can easily be shown that, for all values of a, b, and c (i.e., for all situations), the marginal welfare of a is equal to that of b which is equal to that of c. $D'_a \equiv D'_b \equiv D'_c$.[6]

Operation 4. We are now in a position to transform the initial welfare indicator, D, into a new indicator which will be equal to the sum of the well-beings, a, b, and c *plus* an arbitrary constant. Start from the level of welfare at which $D = 0$. Since, as we have seen, the marginal welfares, of a, b, and c, are equal whatever the values of a, b, and c, the increase in D that would result from raising a by one unit will be the same as that resulting from raising b, or c, by one unit. Mark off such an increment on the D-scale, and continue up the scale marking off adjacent intervals, each of which represents the effect of increasing the level of a (or of b, or

---

[6] a. When $c = t$, $D'_a = D'_b = D'_c = t$ for all values of a and b. But (D'_a/D'_b) is independent of c. Therefore $D'_a \equiv D'_b$ for all values of a, b, and c.

b. When $b = n$, $D'_c = D'_b = n$ for all values of a and c. Also, since, as we have seen, $D'_a \equiv D'_b$, it follows that when $b = n$, $D'_a = D'_b = n = D'_c$ for all values of a and c. But (D'_a/D'_c) is independent of b. Therefore $D'_a \equiv D'_c$ for all values of a, b, and c.

c. Since $D'_a \equiv D'_b$ and $D'_a \equiv D'_c$, therefore $D'_b \equiv D'_c$ for all values of a, b, and c.

of c) by a single unit. Going back to $D = 0$, mark off, in an analogous manner, adjacent reductions in D, each of which represents the effect of reducing the level of a (or of b, or of c) by a single unit.

We can now establish a new indicator of welfare, U, with the same zero-point as D, and having the property that each of the intervals marked out in the D indicator, in the manner described above, corresponds to a single unit of U. Then the marginal welfare of a (or of b, or of c) in terms of the new indicator will always be unity, for all values of a, b, and c. $U'_a = U'_b = U'_c = 1$. And this means that U is a linear function of a, b, and c. $U = a + b + c + K$, a constant.

The final step is to eliminate the constant K by adjusting the zero-points of the welfare and well-being indicators while keeping the unit-intervals unchanged. Fortunately this can be done in a way that will give the new zero-points a definite significance. From Postulate E it can be deduced that if, in any situation R, each of the elementary situations that correspond respectively to the various well-beings has the same welfare as a situation S in which no mental state exists, then situation R will have the same welfare as situation S. Let us now (a) assign a zero value to any well-being of which the associated elementary situation has the same welfare as situation S, (b) assign a zero value to the level of welfare of situation S and (c) adjust the existing welfare and well-being indicators U, a, b, c, by subtracting from each the values previously assigned to the new zero points. We then find that in the case of situation R, (zero) welfare will equal the sum of (zero) well-beings, so that the new constant replacing K must be zero. If W is the new indicator of welfare obtained by adjusting U in this way, and if d, e, and f are the new indictators of well-being obtained by adjusting a, b, and c, respectively, we can now represent welfare simply as the sum of the individual-momentary well-beings. $W = d + e + f$.[7]

Starting with an arbitrary set of indicators of welfare and well-beings, and using as a yardstick an arbitrary increment in one of the well-beings, we have arrived at a particular set of indicators that meet our requirement

---

[7] On the alternative interpretation of the welfare function in which welfare represents a general ordering and well-being an individual ordering of courses of action there seems to be no particularly "natural" basis for choosing zero points. The constant K can be eliminated by taking any particular course of action and regarding as zero both its position in the general ordering and its position in each of the individual orderings.

that the relation between welfare and well-beings should be additive. Using a different yardstick we would have arrived at a different set of indicators. But the class of admissible indicators is limited. They may differ only in respect of proportionate scale in the sense that if the measurement of some particular level of some particular well-being is altered by x percent, all the measurements of all the well-beings and of welfare must also be altered by x percent.[8]

III. FUNDAMENTAL MEASUREMENT OF WELFARE

We have arrived at a simple additive relationship between welfare and well-beings. Welfare relates to situations, well-being to individual-moments. But the well-being of an individual-moment has been defined as the welfare of an elementary situation containing a single state of mind. Now by a not very strained convention, complex situations containing several states of mind can be regarded as combinations of elementary situations each containing one of the states of mind. Thus our additive relationship between the welfare of any complex situation and that of the elementary situations of which it is composed is in effect an additive relationship between the welfare of a whole and that of its parts. This is sufficient to constitute welfare a fundamentally measurable magnitude. It is legitimate to say that the welfare of situation A is three times that of

---

[8] Let there be two sets of welfare and well-being orderings, W, d, e, f, and V, p, q, r, respectively, such that

$$W = d + e + f \quad \text{and}$$

$$V(W) = p(d) + q(e) + r(f)$$

where $\qquad\qquad V'(W) > 0, \quad p'(d) > 0, \quad q'(e) > 0, \quad r'(f) > 0$

then $\qquad\qquad V'(W) = p'(d) = q'(e) = r'(f) = k$

but $\qquad\qquad \dfrac{\partial q'(e)}{\partial d} = 0$

$\therefore\ p''(d) = q''(e) = r''(f) = 0$ (i.e., k is constant).
And since the two sets of indicators have identical zero points,

$$\frac{V}{W} = \frac{p}{d} = \frac{q}{e} = \frac{r}{f} = k.$$

situation *B*. What this means is that if each of the states of mind existing in situation *B* were available in triplicate and all were combined in a single situation *B*, then *B* would have the same welfare as situation *A*.

On the alternative mode of interpreting the welfare function in which welfare measures the degree of preference given to a particular course of action in a general or social ordering, while well-being measures the preference given to it by some individual, it is not clear to me that fundamental measurement is possible. The property measured relates to courses of action that are not divisible or combinable in any significant sense within the conceptual framework. For purposes of application, however (see section VI), measurement of welfare by the "mutual" process as described in the preceding section appears to serve as well as fundamental measurement.

IV. OTHER WAYS OF MEASURING WELFARE

I have nowhere claimed that postulates A to E are necessary conditions for measuring welfare. It appears likely, however, that something analogous to them must be found if the criterion for the true measurement of welfare is to be such that it enables welfare to be regarded as the sum of well-being. Equations (1) to (3) are, as we have seen, necessary conditions for this. Of course, a wide variety of interpretations can be given to "welfare" and "well-being."

It seems fairly clear, on the analogy of the Neuman-Morgenstern cardinalization of utility, that welfare could be measured on the basis of certain postulates regarding ethical behavior with respect to uncertainty. Let us define a prospect as a probability distribution of a certain variety of outcomes, and the welfare of an outcome as the desirability of a prospect containing a 100 percent probability of a particular outcome. The criterion of "true" measurement both of prospect-desirability and of welfare would then be that prospect-desirability should equal the sum of the welfares of the different possible outcomes weighted by their respective probabilities. While the criterion is rather more complicated than that used in this paper it seems to me likely, though I have not gone into the matter, that the necessary conditions for this type of cardinalization would be somewhat analogous, at least, to those discussed in this paper.

V. THE RELATION OF CARDINAL WELFARE
TO CARDINAL UTILITY

It is important to distinguish the question of the measurability of welfare from that, more discussed in economic literature, of the measurability of utility. "Utility" is an ambiguous concept. It is sometimes used to mean welfare or "desirability," sometimes "desiredness" (ophelimity), and sometimes a vague intermediate category—"that which it would be rational to desire." Taking utility in the sense of "desiredness," the measurement of utility can be achieved only if some restrictive assumptions can be made regarding the preferences, as manifested by the behavior, of individuals acting on the market, just as measurement of welfare is only possible if some restrictive assumptions can be made regarding ethical judgments.

One way of measuring utility to an individual implies that the marginal rate at which he would be willing to substitute the consumption of any one commodity for that of any other is independent of the amounts of the remaining commodities that he consumes. Another method implies that the marginal rate at which the individual would be prepared to substitute consumption at one time-point for consumption at another, is independent of his consumption at the remaining time-points. A third method implies that the individual chooses between uncertain prospects as if he had a cardinal scale of utility applicable to various possible outcomes and as if he were trying to maximize the mathematical expectation of this utility.

Such assumptions are, of course, open to empirical verification. I doubt whether anyone would claim for them more than an approximate validity, which implies that at best, utility could only be regarded as "more or less" cardinal. Where more than this is claimed it is because people have in mind not actual but some sort of ideal behavior.

As is evident from the argument presented in this paper, the measurability of welfare depends on the characteristics of the ethical system in question and not on the validity of behavioristic assumptions such as would enable us to derive a measurement for individual utility, in the sense of "desiredness." Nevertheless, empirically measurable individual utilities might be of assistance in the application of an ethic. For example, suppose that through a scrutiny of an individual's behavior in choosing between different combinations of present and future income, his utility could be expressed as the sum of magnitudes, each of which is a function of the income of a different future period. Then *if* the individual can be assumed to choose as the ethic would have him choose, save in his neglect of effects on the well-beings of others, increments in his utility might reasonably be assumed to be proportional to increments in the sum of his true momentary well-beings.[9] Assuming no significant external economies or diseconomies of consumption,[10] this would serve to indicate the slope of the marginal welfare of the individual's income at various points of time, though it would still shed no light on the relative marginal welfare of the incomes of different individuals.

VI. USES OF A CARDINAL WELFARE

Granted that welfare can meaningfully be regarded as cardinal, the question remains whether any practical advantage is to be reaped by so regarding it. For my own part I should not have thought it worthwhile to engage in a cardinalization of welfare as a pure exercise in moral philosophy if it had not seemed to me to serve a useful purpose in relation to welfare economics. In effect, certain of the rules of prescriptive economics can be more clearly and helpfully formulated if it is permissible to refer to welfare as measurable. Admittedly, some of the operations for which a cardinal welfare appears to me useful would be considered by the purists to be outside the scope of welfare economics proper. Others could scarcely be excluded by the strictest canon. An adequate treatment of these questions must be reserved for a separate paper. For the present the following brief indications must suffice.

The concepts of welfare and well-being as discussed thus far in this paper could not, as they stand, be made the basis of any type of welfare economics. For that they would have to acquire additional substantive

[9] In the assumed circumstances the individual's utility must be an increasing function of the sum of his true momentary well-beings. The only alternative to assuming that increments in his utility are proportionate to increments in the sum of his well-beings is to assume that any increment to his income at any given time-point effects a uniform proportionate increase or reduction in the marginal well-beings of his income at all other time-points. This seems implausible.

[10] In the sense that the consumption of one person has no significant direct effect on the welfare of another. Much recent work, e.g., James S. Duesenberry, *Income, Saving, and Theory of Consumer Behavior* (Cambridge: Harvard University Press, 1949), emphasizing the influence exercised by the consumption of one person on the consumption behavior of another makes any such assumption extremely questionable.

content. Moreover, unless this content is such as to permit of some correlation between well-being and individual preference, it is unlikely that economic theory as we know it would have much to contribute to the attainment of the welfare in question. An extreme example of such a correlation would be to postulate a perfect correspondence between individual well-being and individual preference. A truer conception (in my opinion), though a more old-fashioned one, is to regard individual-momentary well-being as an increasing function of happiness, so that a situational change will enhance the well-being of an individual at a moment of time if it makes him happier at that moment. On this view we may still assume some correspondence between individual well-being and individual preference, though only an approximate one.

Let us decompose situational changes, as has been customary in welfare economics, into (a) a productional component, which either shifts everyone to a more preferred position or everyone to a less preferred position, and (b) a distributional component, which "improves" the position of some and "worsens" that of others. Then the first and most obvious application of a cardinal welfare concept is in the evaluation of distributional components. It is difficult to see how else one could set about assessing the merits of a distributional change than by imagining the effects of the change on the various individuals or classes of individuals concerned, measuring them by the yardstick of some specific well-being difference, probably drawn from one's own remembered experience, and adding the results. The process of measuring the effect on any individual consists essentially in estimating how many intermediate degrees of well-being, such that the difference between each degree of well-being and the next is ethically equivalent to the yardstick, could be interposed between the pre- and the post-change levels of well-being of the individual in question. This is a purely subjective process, and a difficult one, but it will be rendered less arduous if the evaluator is not hampered by doubts as to its legitimacy.

Another application of cardinal welfare is in correcting the bias of individual choice in respect of time-preference. I think it difficult to handle the question of optimal saving, for example, without assuming a specific indicator of welfare.

Finally—and this brings us into the indubitable sphere of welfare-economics—reference to a specific indicator of welfare appears to be necessary in evaluating the productional component of certain types of large situational changes. What I have in mind is something akin to Marshall's use of producers' and consumers' surpluses in the evaluation of the productional component of sizable changes such as the building of a bridge or the imposition of a tax. When such changes are in question the least unsatisfactory test of productional desirability is one that has reference to the areas (over the relevant intervals) of product-demand curves and factor-supply curves drawn on specific assumptions. But this test can be justified only if one can assume that the marginal welfare-yield of money to the average spender is constant over the relevant intervals of these demand and supply curves.

Admittedly, Professor Hicks has shown[11] that even without invoking a cardinal welfare, one can have a satisfactory measure of the productional component and can employ a test of the type discussed above, provided that income effects can be assumed to be virtually absent with respect to those products and factors whose prices change substantially. But I would contend (a) that even where the Hicksian solution is applicable, the conception of constancy in the marginal utility (welfare) of money, if conceptually admissible as we have argued, is preferable because simpler than that of absence of income effects, and (b) that there are cases where it is not permissible to assume absence of income-effects but where it may nevertheless be permissible to assume constancy of marginal utility (welfare) of money to the average individual. Such cases—which arise when the distributional elements in the change predominate over the productional elements, so that it is precisely those products and factors most susceptible to income effects whose prices are most affected— can, I think, be handled only with the aid of a cardinal concept of welfare.

[11] In a series of articles in the *Review of Economic Studies*, vols. 8, 9, 11, and 13.

4

CARDINAL WELFARE AND INDIVIDUALISTIC ETHICS: A COMMENT

MOST OF Dr. Harsanyi's paper "Cardinal Welfare, Individualistic Ethics, and Interpersonal Comparisons of Utility,"[1] I find very convincing. I fear, however, that his claim that one of the postulates he uses to establish an additive cardinal social welfare function is "weaker" (less restrictive) than those employed for the same purpose in my paper, "A Cardinal Concept of Welfare,"[2] may lead some readers to assume that, taken as a whole, his postulates are weaker than mine. On the contrary, Harsanyi's postulates, though personally I find them unobjectionable, are in combination somewhat more restrictive than my own.

In the paper in question I sought to show (roughly speaking) that all ethical systems that (a) permit social welfare to be expressed as a single-valued increasing function of (arbitrarily chosen) indicators of individual utility and (b) conform to the postulate described below will permit social welfare to be expressed as the sum of (suitably adjusted) indicators of individual utility.

The crucial postulate—my so-called postulate E—I will express, as does Harsanyi, in the form of finite differences rather than, as in my original paper, in the form of infinitesimals.

First published in *The Journal of Political Economy* (August 1957), 65:355–7. Copyright ⓒ 1957, The University of Chicago. Reprinted by permission of the University of Chicago Press.
    [1] John C. Harsanyi, "Cardinal Welfare, Individualistic Ethics, and Interpersonal Comparisons of Utility," *The Journal of Political Economy* (August 1955), 63:309–21.
    [2] J. Marcus Fleming, "A Cardinal Concept of Welfare," *Quarterly Journal of Economics* (August 1952), 26:366–84.

Postulate E. There are at least three individuals. Then suppose that individual A's utility is the same in situation X as in situation X' and is the same in situation Y as in situation Y' but is higher in X or X' than in Y or Y'. Suppose further that individual B's utility also is the same in X as in X' and is the same in Y as in Y' but is higher in Y or Y' than in X or X'. Suppose also that all other individuals have the same utility in X as in Y and the same utility in X' as in Y'. (This situation is illustrated in Figure 1 for the three-person case of individuals A, B, and C, where

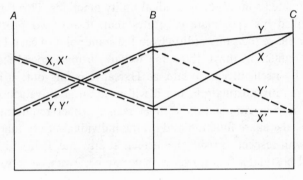

Figure 1

the vertical lines represent the respective utility indicators and the lines linking them represent the different "situations.") Then, if social welfare is the same in X as in Y, it must be the same in X' as in Y'. In other words, whether one man's utility loss is deemed to outweigh another man's utility gain depends solely on these gains and losses themselves and not at all on the level of utility enjoyed by other men whose utility is unaffected.

All of the foregoing discussion relates to the welfare evaluation of "situations" or sure prospects. Harsanyi's social-welfare function, however, includes not only such sure prospects but also "uncertain prospects," provided that these can be expressed as probability distributions of attaining different "situations." Now, it has been shown[3] that any (social

---

[3] See the references to the work of Von Neumann and Morgenstern and of Marschak in Harsanyi, "Cardinal Welfare, Individualistic Ethics, and Interpersonal Comparisons of Utility," p. 312, *n.*10.

or individual) ordering of such prospects that is rational with respect to risk[4] can be represented by a unique cardinal indicator such that the value of each uncertain prospect is the sum of the values of its possible outcomes weighted according to their respective probabilities.

Harsanyi shows that if (a) cardinal indicators with those properties have been established both for social-welfare and for the utility of each individual and if (b) the zero point of the social welfare function is appropriately chosen, then the addition of one further condition of an ethical nature will suffice to ensure that the social-welfare function must be the weighted sum of the individual utility functions. This further condition, called his "postulate c," states that, if any two prospects are indifferent (have the same utility) from the standpoint of each individual, they are indifferent (have the same welfare) from a social standpoint.

Taken by itself, this postulate, as Harsanyi points out, is no doubt weaker than my postulate E, but it will yield an additive social-welfare function only in conjunction with Harsanyi's other requirements that (a) the social-welfare function and (b) the individual-utility functions are rational with respect to risk. The former, at any rate, I should regard as an ethical postulate. But, however that may be, it can be shown that in combination Harsanyi's postulates are not only not weaker than postulate E but actually entail that postulate and, indeed, go beyond it to impose further restrictions on the social-welfare function.

That this must be so can be proved quite simply, if indirectly, from the fact that postulate E is a *necessary* condition for the existence of a linear relationship between social welfare and the utilities of individuals.[5] If $W = aU_1 + bU_2 + cU_3 + d$ (where a, b, c, and d are constants), the change in U_2 required to offset the effect on W of a given change in U_1 (i.e., ΔU_1) will be—$(a/b)\Delta U_1$, a quantity entirely independent of the magnitude of U_3. But if postulate E is necessary to the existence of such a linear welfare function, it must be implicit in the postulates by which

[4] Such an ordering may be said to be rational with respect to risk if it fulfills a number of conditions, of which the crucial one is that, if any two prospects X and Y offer identical probability distributions of obtaining subprospects, such that each subprospect of X, taken by itself, ranks equal to the corresponding subprospect of Y, then X ranks equal to Y.

[5] What my paper sought to prove was not this simple proposition that postulate E was *necessary* to the existence of a cardinal concept of welfare as the sum of individual utilities but that—in conjunction with the other postulate listed by me—it was *sufficient* to permit the construction of such a function.

Harsanyi constructs his social-welfare function. Those postulates therefore cannot be less restrictive than postulate E.

This proof, however cogent, is indirect and somewhat unsatisfactory. It shows that Harsanyi's postulates *must* imply postulate E but does not show *how* they do so. A more direct proof is offered below.

Let Figure 1 illustrate the values assigned to situations X, Y, X', and Y' respectively on the utility indicators of individuals A, B, and C when these indicators are constructed on the basis of Harsanyi's assumptions. Suppose, further, that situations X and Y are equivalent from the standpoint of a social-welfare function constructed on Harsanyi's principles. If we can prove that situations X' and Y' must also be equivalent from the standpoint of the social-welfare function, we shall have proved that my postulate E is implicit in his assumptions.

Let there be (a) a prospect P that consists in a fifty-fifty chance of attaining situations Y and X' respectively and (b) a prospect P' that consists in a fifty-fifty chance of attaining situations X and Y' respectively. Since, for both individuals A and B, the utility of X is equal to that of X' and the utility of Y is equal to that of Y', it follows from the principle of rationality with respect to risk that prospect P must be equivalent to P' from the standpoint both of A-utility and of B-utility. Again, since for individual C the utility of Y is equal to that of X and the utility of Y' is equal to that of X', it follows from the same principle that P is equivalent to P' from the standpoint of C-utility also.

Now from Harsanyi's postulate c, since P and P' are equivalent from the standpoint of each individual, they must also be equivalent from the standpoint of social welfare. Moreover, since Harsanyi's welfare-function values prospects on an actuarial basis, the welfare value of P must be halfway between that of Y and that of X', and the welfare value of P' must be halfway between that of X and that of Y'. It follows that, if the welfare value of X equals that of Y and the welfare value of P' equals that of P, the welfare value of Y' must equal that of X'.

To posit, as Harsanyi does, that all indicators of individual utility and of social welfare should evaluate risk on an actuarial basis in fact imposes restrictions on the social-welfare function over and above those imposed by postulate E. Any individual's preference ordering of situations can in principle be represented by an infinite set of cardinal indicators, having in common only that each of them increases, to a greater or lesser extent, as the individual moves to a preferred situation. But the proviso about the actuarial evaluation of risk in effect confines the range of admissible cardinal indicators for each individual's utility to a set that is unique up to a linear transformation. That is, while alternative indicators may vary as to proportionate scale and zero point, in all of them the utility difference between any situations S_1 and S_2 must bear the same numerical ratio to the utility difference between any situations S_3 and S_4.

Under these conditions the only freedom left to whoever is setting up an additive welfare function is that of determining what weight per unit to attach to each individual's pre-established utility scale. A "welfare adjudicator" who is free from this proviso with respect to the evaluation of risk, and whose only obligation is to observe my postulate E, is free to determine not only the relative weights per unit to be attached to one individual's utility as against another's, but also the relative weights to be attached to one specific increase of preference as against another at different points on the same individual's preference scale. As I showed in my earlier article,[6] even ethical evaluations that do not have any predetermined cardinal scales of individual utility to start from can establish welfare as the sum of individual utility by using the process of interpersonal comparison itself to determine the appropriate indicators of individual utility.

I conclude that Harsanyi has in effect demonstrated, from a novel and surprising angle, just how plausible and unrestrictive my postulate E is.

---

[6] Fleming, "A Cardinal Concept of Welfare."

5

OPTIMAL PRODUCTION WITH FIXED PROFITS[1]

1. IN A previous article I compared the "marginal-cost" rule of optimal production with the "average-cost" rule.[2] There I made the point that whatever might be the complications and difficulties in applying the former rule, any attempt to apply the average-cost rule to multiproduct, multifactor production in such a way as to maintain a proper balance between the different types of output and input would run into complications and practical difficulties of a still more serious kind.

2. This, as we shall see, is only too true. Rightly or wrongly, however, nationalized industries in Great Britain are required by statute so to conduct their operations that their receipts will at least cover their expenditures on revenue account, and they would probably regard themselves as being as much precluded from making large profits as from making losses. They are also, all of them, multiproduct as well as multifactor concerns, especially since we must regard goods or services produced at different plants or locations as separate products. It is, therefore,

First published in *Economica*, August 1953. Reprinted by permission of the London School of Economics and Political Science.

[1] This paper owes much to F. P. Ramsay's elegant mathematical treatment of an analogous problem in "Contribution to the Theory of Taxation," *The Economic Journal* (March 1937). My results also agree with those of A. S. Manne's interesting "Multi-Purpose Public Enterprise—Criteria for Pricing," *Economica* (August 1952), which appeared only after this article had already gone to press. The present paper may, however, retain some interest in that it deals with "optimal" factor-input and plant expansion, as well as "optimal" output, and considers some problems of application.

[2] "Production and Price Policy in Public Enterprise," *Economica* (February 1950).

of some interest to enquire what the market tests would be of "optimal" production and "desirable" productional adjustment for an undertaking (using a variety of factors to produce a variety of products) that aims at making, or is required to make, its aggregate receipts equal to its aggregate expenses. Or, more generally, what the market tests are for such an undertaking that aims at making, or is required to make, a fixed profit or fixed surplus (positive, zero, or negative) of aggregate receipts over aggregate expenses. It is to be expected that the "optimal" situation attainable subject to such a fixed net revenue requirement will be, in general, "inferior" to the "optimum" that would have been attainable in the absence of the limiting condition.

ASSUMPTIONS AND CONVENTIONS

3. a. Let the economic system contain two classes of participants: "individuals," who are purchasers of final products and suppliers of original factors of production; and "undertakings," which are purchasers of factors of production, whether original factors or intermediate goods, and sellers of products, whether final products or intermediate goods.

b. Let "economic welfare"—hereafter referred to as "welfare"— be a (cardinal) magnitude varying directly with the wellbeing of each individual.[3]

c. Let each individual's "wellbeing" be a (cardinal) magnitude varying directly with the amount of each final product consumed, and inversely with the amount of each original factor supplied by the individual.

d. Let each individual operate under conditions of perfect competition, whether as consumer or as factor supplier.

e. Let each undertaking, other than the (public) undertaking whose production policy is in question, operate under conditions of perfect competition, whether as buyer or seller.

---

[3] By a cardinal magnitude I mean an ordinal magnitude to which it is possible to assign, on significant criteria, a numerical indicator which is unique save for proportionate scale and (possibly) point of origin. As I have shown elsewhere [see J. Marcus Fleming, "A Cardinal Concept of Welfare," *Quarterly Journal of Economics* (August 1952), 26:366–84], the welfare concept derivable from a wide class of ethical systems can legitimately be regarded as cardinal or measurable in a fundamental sense.

f. Any infinitesimal situational change can be regarded, from the standpoint of its effect on welfare, as a combination of (i) a "distributional component" representing the change in the quantities of final products consumed and original factors supplied by each individual that would result from a money transfer, at current prices, between individuals and (ii) a "productional component" representing a residual change in the quantities of final products consumed and original factors supplied, of such a character as to be uniformly beneficial or uniformly detrimental to all individuals, in the sense that it is equivalent, in its effect on wellbeings, to an increase, or a reduction in money incomes, equally spread over all individuals.

g. Let the (subjective) "real income change" associated with an infinitesimal situational change signify the change in welfare resulting from the productional component of that change.

h. In the case of any "large" or noninfinitesimal situational change let a notional "path," consisting of infinitesimal "steps," be traced, with respect to product and factor quantities and prices, between the initial and final situations. Let this path be so far realistic as to be consistent with the psychological preferences of individuals, and with the production functions of all undertakings other than the (public) undertaking whose production policy is in question. Finally, let the path be consistent with the assumption that the factor-inputs and product-outputs of the public undertaking in question vary gradually in some particular mutual relationship—which need not be realistic— over the interval between the initial and final situations.

i. Let the real income change associated with any large situational change signify the sum of the real income changes associated with the infinitesimal situational changes occurring at each step of such a path.

MARKET TEST OF
PRODUCTIONAL IMPROVEMENT

4. It follows from all of these definitions and assumptions that, in the case of an infinitesimal change, resulting from a change in the operations of the public undertaking, the real income change can be deduced to be positive or negative according as the value, at current prices, of the increments in the product-output of the public undertaking exceeds or falls short of that of the increments in its factor-input. In the case of a large situational change initiated by the public undertaking the real income

change can again be deduced to be positive or negative according as
the value of the increments in the product-output of the public undertaking exceeds or falls short of that of the increments in its factor-input,
provided that:

> a. Each output—and input—increment is valued at the price of
> the product or factor in question averaged over the interval between
> the initial and the final situation along a path constructed in the
> manner described in paragraph 3h.
> b. The marginal welfare yield of money to the average individual
> is the same at each step of the prescribed path.[4]

FIRST CONDITION OF "OPTIMIZATION"

5. A situation no feasible departure from which will result in a real
income increase may be regarded as a productional optimum, subject to
the possibilities of the model. Assuming that such an "optimal" situation
exists, and can be approached gradually, by infinitesimal adjustments,
any infinitesimal departure from this "optimum" that may be initiated by
our public undertaking must be such as to entail a zero real income
change. This is the first condition of "optimization."

6. In a model containing no fixed net revenue requirement, or other
artificial constraints, the condition will be satisfied generally if it is satisfied for all variations affecting two elements (e.g., one factor and one
product), both of which must relate to the same plant (i.e., be linked by
the same continuous production function). This brings us to the well-
known rules equating price ratios with marginal rates of substitution, for
example, that the price of each product must equal the value of the
marginal factor cost in terms of each factor.

7. With the introduction of the requirement that a given net revenue
be earned it ceases to be possible in general to vary two elements only
while keeping the others constant. On the other hand, unless the required
net revenue is so high as to be unattainable or attainable only in a single
input–output situation, it should in general be possible to vary any three

---

[4] This is not the place to elaborate the proof of this proposition or to justify the welfare-
economic approach adopted, but I hope to do this eslewhere.

elements at a single plant, or any four elements consisting of one pair in each of any two plants, in such a way as to keep net revenue constant at the required level. If the first condition of "optimization" is satisfied for all input–output variations of these kinds it will be satisfied for all possible input–output variations compatible with the fixed net revenue requirement.

8. In seeking to establish a market test for the satisfaction of the "first condition" in such cases it is convenient to begin by considering a variation consisting in an expansion of output q_1 and input f_1 in plant I, combined with a change (say, a contraction) in output q_2 and input f_2 in plant II.

9. This adjustment is to leave the net revenue of the undertaking unchanged. It follows that the effect on this net revenue of the expansion in q_1 and the associated expansion in f_1 must be equal and of opposite sign to the effect of the contraction in q_2 and the associated contraction in f_2. Let us define the "joint marginal revenue," $R_{q(f)}$, of any product q with respect to any factor f as the rate at which any increase in the output of q augments net revenue both directly and indirectly by way of its effect on the input of f, all other outputs and inputs remaining unchanged. Then the rate at which the output of q_2 falls as that of q_1 rises must equal the ratio of the joint marginal net revenue of $q_1(f_1)$ to the joint marginal net revenue of $q_2(f_2)$.

10. It follows from paragraph 4 that the market test of a zero real income change, in the case of an infinitesimal output–input adjustment, is that the value, at current prices, of increments to output should equal the value of increments to input. Thus the value of the increase in the output of q_1 *less* that of the associated increase in the input of f_1 must equal the value of the decrease in the output of q_2 *less* that of the associated decrease in the input of f_2. Let us define the "joint quasitax," $T_{q(f)}$, on any product q with respect to any factor f as the margin between the price of q and the value of the marginal factor cost of q in terms of factor f, so that the value of the increase in q_1 *less* that of the associated increase in f_1 is given by the increment in q_1 *times* the joint quasitax on $q_1(f_1)$. Then the rate at which the output of q_2 falls as that of q_1 rises must equal the ratio between the joint quasitax on $q_1(f_1)$ and the joint quasitax on $q_2(f_2)$.

11. From the last two paragraphs it follows that

$$\frac{T_{q_1(f_1)}}{R_{q_1(f_1)}} = \frac{T_{q_2(f_2)}}{R_{q_2(f_2)}}$$

12. Generalizing this result we conclude that *the first condition of 'optimization'* (viz., that infinitesimal adjustments of input and output should entail zero real income changes) *will be satisfied only by situations in which the ratio of joint quasitax to joint marginal revenue is the same for all product-factor pairs.* The fact that the ratio is the same for all pairs, when each pair is in a different plant, implies that it is also the same for all product-factor pairs in the same plant.

13. Moreover, the pairs for which the (T/R) ratio is equal may not be completely separate. They may have a product or factor in common. Thus the ratio $(T_{q(f)}/R_{q(f)})$ will be the same for $q_1(f_1)$, for $q_2(f_1)$, and for $q_1(f_2)$, where q_1 and q_2 are any two products and f_1 and f_2 any two factors in the same plant. This result, which is here derived as a corollary from a proposition established by considering adjustments affecting product-factor pairs in different plants, could have been more directly established from a consideration of adjustments involving two products and one factor, or two factors and one product, drawn from the same plant.[5]

14. The criterion of "optimal" production set forth in paragraph 12 might have been expressed in terms of product–product pairs, or of factor–factor pairs instead of in terms of product–factor pairs. The formulation adopted, however, seems to be the simplest and the most easily remembered.

15. Let us look a little more closely at the concept of "joint marginal revenue" of product q with respect to factor f. This can be regarded as falling into two parts: (a) that derived from the increase in the quantities of q and f at constant prices and (b) that derived from the change in the prices of all the undertaking's products and factors, at constant output (and input) quantities—both parts being expressed as rates of change with respect to q. Part (a) is simply $T_{q(f)}$, the joint quasitax on q with respect to f. Part (b) might perhaps be termed the "joint marginal transfer effect" of product q with respect to factor f, $D_{q(f)}$, since it measures the

---

[5] It is only where the undertaking consists of no more than a single plant that this proposition requires to be directly established. See Appendix, note 1.

rate at which income is transferred, through price changes, from consumers and factor suppliers to the undertaking, as q increases (with f).[6]

16. Since, as we have seen from paragraph 12, the ratio

$$\frac{T_{q(f)}}{R_{q(f)}}\left(=\frac{T_{q(f)}}{T_{q(f)}+D_{q(f)}}\right)$$

must be the same, at the optimal position, for all product–factor pairs, it follows that $(T_{q(f)}/D_{q(f)})$, the ratio of joint quasitax to joint marginal transfer effect, must also be the same for all product–factor pairs.

17. Now the joint marginal transfer effect of any product q with respect to any factor f, $D_{q(f)}$, can be split up into (a) the marginal transfer effect of product q taken by itself, D_q, and (b) the marginal transfer effect of factor f taken by itself, D_f, *times* the marginal factor cost of q in terms of f.[7] Both of these elements (a) and (b) are virtually certain to be negative. An increase in the output of q, taken by itself, would bring down the price of q and also the average price of the products of the undertaking as a whole, and would have little if any effect on factor prices. An increase in the input of f, taken by itself, would raise the price of f, and also the average price of the factors of the undertaking as a whole, and would have little if any effect on product prices. It can therefore safely be assumed that the joint marginal transfer effect, combining the two elements, will be negative for all product–factor pairs.

18. Since $D_{q(f)}$ is negative for all q and all f, and since $(T_{q(f)}/D_{q(f)})$ is the same for all q and all f, $T_{q(f)}$ must be either positive for all q and all f, or negative for all q and all f. *Joint quasitaxes should be either positive for all product-factor pairs or negative for all product-factor pairs.* Another inference from the negativeness of $D_{q(f)}$ is that, if joint quasitaxes are negative, joint marginal net revenues, $R_{q(f)}$, must also be negative. All situations satisfying the first condition of "optimization" must therefore fall into one of the following three classes, namely, those in which $T_{q(f)}$ is (a) positive and $R_{q(f)}$ negative for all product-factor pairs, (b) negative and $R_{q(f)}$ negative for all product-factor pairs, and (c) positive and $R_{q(f)}$ positive for all product-factor pairs.

[6] See Appendix, note 2.
[7] The marginal transfer effect of a product is the rate at which the net revenue of the undertaking increases, *by reason of price repercussions*, as the output of the product in question expands, *all other outputs, and all inputs, being assumed to remain unchanged.* The marginal transfer effect of a factor is analogously defined. For formula, see Appendix, note 2.

19. It would make for simplicity if it were possible to resolve the joint quasitaxes, $T_{q(f)}$, on product-factor pairs into simple quasitaxes, one for each product, T_q, and one for each factor, T, such that (a) any given product (factor) would have the same quasitax with whichever factor (product) it was paired and (b) the undertaking, when behaving "optimally," would act like a competitive firm subject to product- and factor-taxes. This would imply that it would bring the price of each product *less* product quasitax into equality with the marginal cost in terms of each factor, valued at the appropriate factor price *plus* factor quasitax.

20. There are several—indeed an infinite number of—ways of resolving joint quasitaxes on product-factor pairs into simple product and factor quasitaxes of this sort. Perhaps the most convenient way is to make the quasitaxes both for products and for factors proportionate to the marginal transfer effects of the respective products and factors. If this is done the joint quasitaxes on all product-factor pairs will likewise be proportional to the respective joint marginal transfer effects, thus satisfying the first condition of "optimization." Indeed, the (T/D) ratio will be the same for product-factor pairs as for products and factors taken separately.

$$\frac{T_{q(f)}}{D_{q(f)}} = \frac{T_q}{D_q} = \frac{T_f^{\,8}}{D_f}$$

21. Since all D_q and all D_f are of the same sign, namely, negative, all T_q and all T_f will be of the same sign. We can now formulate our rule of "optimization" as follows: *In the "optimal" position all quasitaxes, whether on products or on factors, will be of the same sign and will bear the same proportion to the marginal transfer effects of the respective products or factors.*

22. It is noteworthy that the same market characteristics (a large negative D_q or D_f) that condemn a product or factor to bear a relatively high quasitax when all quasitaxes are positive entitle it to a relatively high quasisubsidy (as it might be called) when all quasitaxes are negative. The size of the relative marginal transfer effects serves only to determine the *relative* quasitaxes or subsidies. The size of the *absolute* quasitaxes and subsidies will depend on how far the net revenue that the under-

---

[8] See Apendix, note 3.

taking is required to earn exceeds or falls short respectively of the net revenue that it could earn with zero quasitaxes (i.e., with prices kept equal to marginal cost).

23. The marginal transfer effect for any product or any factor depends on the demand conditions of *all* products of the undertaking and the supply conditions of *all* factors of the undertaking. Broadly speaking, D_q will be (negatively) high if the product q, and other of the undertaking's products that are highly substitutable for it, are *not* easily substitutable for products produced outside the undertaking. And D_f will be relatively high (negatively) if the factor f, and other of the factors employed by the undertaking which are highly substitutable for it, are not easily substitutable by factors employed outside the undertaking.

24. In the special case in which a variation in the output of a product leaves unaffected the prices of all the other products and factors of the undertaking the negative of the marginal transfer effect of that product when expressed as a proportion of its price, $-(D_q/P_q)$, will reduce to the reciprocal of the elasticity of demand for that product. In the analogous case affecting a factor the negative of the marginal transfer effect of that factor, when expressed as a proportion of its price, $-(D_f/P_f)$, will reduce to the reciprocal of the elasticity of supply of that factor. If such market independence should prevail for all products and factors of the undertaking, the "optimal" *ad valorem* quasitaxes on all products and factors will be proportional to the reciprocals of the corresponding elasticities.

SECOND CONDITION OF "OPTIMIZATION"

25. A situation may satisfy the first condition of "optimization" (i.e., be a position of stationary real income)[9] without necessarily being an "optimum." It may equally well be a "pessimum" or point of inflection. For the second, and sufficient, condition of "optimization" to be fulfilled, the following requirement must be met, at the stationary real income position, with respect to any infinitesimal output–input variation affecting three variables (outputs or inputs) at a single plant, or any four variables consisting of one pair at each of two plants: the rate at which real income rises as any one of these variables increases or decreases must itself be

---

[9] "Real income" is used here to signify "cumulation of (subjective) real income changes along a path of variation." It has no true zero.

falling. This ensures that a continuance of the variation past the stationary real income point would begin to entail a decline in real income.

26. As will be seen from the Appendix,[10] the outcome depends on the way in which the ratios of joint quasitax to joint marginal transfer effect vary with the expansion of the respective product–factor pairs. Under normal market conditions the second condition of optimization will *not* be satisfied for stationary real income points in which joint marginal revenues are positive. Situations falling within class (c) of paragraph 18 will normally be "pessima." That is, production should be expanded beyond the monopoly, or maximum net revenue, position, to a point at which joint marginal revenues are negative for all product–factor pairs.

27. Where marginal net revenues are negative, there is normally but one constant real income position, and that an "optimum," so long as the net revenue requirement is such as to call for quasitaxes that are positive or only moderately negative. But if the net revenue requirement should necessitate large quasisubsidies a multiplicity of constant real income positions may emerge, of which some are local "optima" and some "pessima." These local "optima" will be characterized by a tendency to concentrate quasisubsidies on some particular product or factor—a different one in the case of each local "optimum," leaving other quasisubsidies relatively moderate.

TEST OF "IMPROVEMENT" FOR SMALL ADJUSTMENTS

28. Local "optimal" positions are arrived at by effecting all improvements attainable by infinitesimal adjustments. A first formulation of the test for "improvement" for small adjustments can be derived directly from paragraph 4. Let the undertaking's "net quantum change at current prices" signify the aggregate value of its increments of output *less* increments of input at current prices. Then *any infinitesimal adjustment will constitute an "improvement" if, while keeping net revenue unchanged, it results in a positive net quantum change at current prices.*

29. Let the undertaking's "net price change at current quantities" signify the aggregate value of its increments in product prices *less* in-

---

[10] See Appendix, note 4.

crements in factor prices, at current output- and input-quantities. This, combined with the net quantum change, makes up the increment in the undertaking's net revenue, which must be zero. Hence *any infinitesimal adjustment will constitute an "improvement" if, while keeping net revenue constant, it results in a negative net price change at current quantities.*

30. In the case of small adjustments affecting two product-factor pairs it will constitute an "improvement" to expand that pair for which the (T/D) ratio is the more negative. This result will be achieved if quasi-taxes (subsidies) on individual products or factors are always altered in the direction of making relative quasitaxes (subsidies) on the different products and factors more nearly proportional to the relative marginal transfer effects.

TEST OF "IMPROVEMENTS"
FOR LARGE ADJUSTMENTS

31. In the absence of a net revenue requirement the only necessity for formulating a special test of "improvement" for large adjustments on the part of an undertaking is provided by the existence of indivisibilities in production. As a result of such indivisibilities, as the output of the under-taking expands, a phase of "disimprovement" in which the value of marginal factor cost exceeds that of marginal output may be followed by a phase of "improvement" in which the opposite is true. And the real income losses of the former phase may be outweighted by the real income gains of the latter, so that a large expansion in production embracing both phases is "justified." The principal examples of such large-scale input–output adjustments arise in connection with investment; for in-stance the introduction of a new type of product or the installation of a new plant.

32. The introduction of a net revenue requirement gives rise to a number of additional reasons why large adjustments may have to be considered, quite apart from physical indivisibility, though that doubtless remains the principal reason. It has already been indicated that, when quasisubsidies are high, a variety of local "optima" may emerge. Again, even where quasitaxes or moderate quasisubsidies prevail, the existence of unusual market conditions, for example, demand elasticities which

over a phase increase markedly with increasing output, may give rise to such a proliferation of local optima. The choice between such local "optima" can only be made on the basis of a test of "improvement" for large adjustments.

33. As can be seen from paragraph 4, the rule for testing the "desirability" of a large adjustment differs from that for testing a small adjustment only in the fact that the increments of output and input are valued, not at current prices, but at the *average* prices prevailing over the interval over which outputs and inputs are varied, such variation being assumed to take place along a given notional "path" as described in paragraph 3 (h). This involves measuring the areas under the relevant product-demand and factor-supply curves, over the relevant interval. The first formulation of the test of "improvement" for large adjustments therefore runs as follows: *Any large adjustment will constitute an "improvement" if, while keeping net revenue constant, it results in a positive net quantum change at average prices* (along the chosen path over the relevant interval of variation).

34. There is also a second formulation of this rule, analogous to the second formulation of the rule for infinitesimal adjustments. Bearing in mind that the (zero) change in net revenue resulting from the large adjustment can be regarded as the sum of a series of infinitesimal changes occurring along the "path" of variation, and that each such infinitesimal change in net revenue can be broken down into a quantum component and a price component, we can reformulate our rule as follows: *Any large adjustment will constitute an "improvement" if while keeping net revenue constant it results in a negative net price change at average output- and input-quantities* (along the chosen path over the relevant interval of variation). This implies that any adjustment that is in the general direction of *expanding* outputs and inputs and that leaves net revenue unchanged will be likely to constitute an "improvement."

35. The following are some examples of how these market tests work out in particular cases:

a. If, in the initial or preadjustment situation, quasisubsidies are in operation for all products and factors, the setting up of a new plant may be worthwhile even if the net quantum change *at that plant* is somewhat negative so that in the absence of a net revenue requirement the installation would not have been worthwhile. The reason is that, in order to counteract the negative effect on net revenue of the setting up of the new plant on the net revenue of the undertaking as a whole, production at the old plants will have to be contracted, which, in the assumed circumstances, will entail a positive net quantum change at the old plants.

b. If, in the initial situation, positive quasitaxes prevail for all products and factors, the setting up of a new plant may not be worthwhile even if the net quantum change at the new plant is positive, if the effect on net revenue of the undertaking as a whole is too negative. For then the contraction of output at the old plants required to restore net revenue to its original level will entail a negative net quantum change at these plants that may exceed the positive change at the new plant.

c. If the setting up of a new plant should tend to increase the net revenue of the undertaking it will always be "worthwhile." This will be true even if, in the initial situation, quasisubsidies prevail, so that production at the old plants has to be increased with adverse effects on real income. For whereas, in the new plant, the net quantum increase will be larger than the positive effect on the net revenue of the undertaking, in the old plants the net quantum decline will be less than the negative effect on the net revenue.

d. If we define a "technological improvement" as an adjustment whereby it becomes possible to reduce the input of some or all factors without raising the input of any factors and without reducing the output of any products, then technological improvements are almost (but not quite) certain to be "desirable" even when quasisubsidies prevail initially. We may divide the adjustment into two "stages": (i) a reduction in factor-inputs keeping all outputs constant and (ii) a subsequent all-around expansion of production designed to bring net revenue down to the original level. In stage (i), unlike the case discussed under (c) above, the effect on net revenue will be greater than the net quantum change, by reason of the fall in price of the factors affected. Still, the beneficial effect of stage (i) should outweigh the detrimental effect of stage (ii) as long as the factors whose use is economized in stage (i) have supply conditions similar to those whose input is expanded in stage (ii).

PRICE DISCRIMINATION

36. We have defined the "optimal" behavior of the undertaking, under our assumed conditions, in terms of the quantities and prices of its various products and factors, and their interrelations. But what, in this context,

is a "product" or a "factor"? How should input and output items be classified? This, too, is a problem of "optimization." The most general answer is that only those items should be classed together that would properly be given identical treatment even if initially classed as separate commodities. The precise answer will depend on the restrictions placed on the process of "optimization." Thus, in the absence of a fixed net revenue requirement products completely interchangeable in consumption and in production should be classified together, as should factors interchangeable in factor supply and in utilization for productive purposes. Even if, by artificial product differentiation different prices could be charged for a physically identical product, this should not be done since it would violate the rule that price should be brought into equality with the value of marginal factor cost. Products (or factors) classified in this principle will differ as a rule, either in physical quality, or geographic location.

37. Given an obligation to earn a given net revenue, however, a public undertaking ought to treat output (or input) items differently not only if they differ in physical characteristics but also if they differ with respect to marginal net revenue. For example, if certain output items that, though physically identical and interchangeable in production, can somehow without cost be differentiated into two classes, or conventional "products," having different rates of marginal net revenue, it will be possible, without altering net revenue, to effect a positive real income change by expanding the output of one of these conventional "products" and contracting that of the other. If quasitaxes prevail, the "product" having more negative marginal transfer effect (e.g., the product with the more inelastic demand) should be contracted, and the other expanded. If quasisubsidies prevail, the opposite course should be followed. In the former case output as a whole will tend to expand, in the latter case to contract, but in both cases the net quantum change will be positive.

38. Of course, product differentiation is never quite costless. Thus there will be cases in which output (or input) items should be classed together even though the class is not entirely homogeneous with respect to marginal transfer effect. The question, how far the costs of product differentiation should be incurred, and how far product differentiation should be carried, is one to be decided on the same principles as apply to any large input–output adjustment—the principles discussed in the preceding section. This is so without qualification in cases in which the

products are differentiated by making minor changes in their appearance or other physical qualities, consumers being left free to choose between the varieties of product thus created. The situation is a little more complicated in cases in which the undertaking, in order to be able to charge one class of consumers a higher price than another class for an identical product, introduces restrictions in the resale of its product by the latter to the former class, or in which, to permit charging of different prices for the same product in different uses, it prohibits the diversion of the product to a use other than that for which it has been sold. Even in such cases the market test of "improvement" set forth in paragraph 33 will apply, with one gloss and one qualification.

39. The gloss is that, in computing the net quantum change, the costs of organizing and enforcing the product-differentiation must be included as a negative item. The qualification relates to the possibility that there may be marginal evasion of the restrictive regulations laid down by the undertaking in order to implement its product differentiation, that is, there may be an increased "leakage" of products from the low-priced to the high-priced markets as the price discrepancies increase. If evaders reap any net gain from such marginal evasion, this will not be taken into account by our market tests, which will therefore be unduly discouraging to product differentiation and price discrimination.

40. Yet another type of discrimination is possible whereby the price charged any consumer will vary according to the amount he consumes. This, too, can be conceived in terms of product differentiation. Thus all xth units of product consumed per unit of time by each of the various consumers could be regarded as one "product," all yth units as another "product," and so on. Essentially the same rules of "optimal" production and "improvement" apply to these rather queer "products" as to the relatively ordinary types of products considered so far, and they determine the extent to which product differentiation is desirable, and the extent to which different (marginal) prices should be charged for the first, second (etc.) units consumed. It is clear that *some* degree of multipart pricing will in general be desirable—unless its enforcement is too costly—but the familiar test of "optimization" is scarcely helpful in deciding how far this form of discrimination should be carried, since it is difficult to asign a simple meaning to "marginal transfer effect" in the case of "products" thus defined.

PROBLEMS OF APPLICATION

41. Considerations of space do not permit me to enlarge on the problem of how far and by what means the market tests discussed in this paper could be applied by public undertakings in practice, and I must confine myself to summary indications on this (all-important) point. Let us consider in turn (a) decisions regarding current production, and (b) largish investment decisions.

Current Production

42. I assume it desirable, in the interests of efficiency, that marginal adjustments to current production be carried out by managers of individual plants in the light of principles or incentives supplied by the central administration of the undertaking. Thus the central administration would lay down the rates of quasitax or subsidy for each product and each factor and the local managers would arrange production in the light of postquasitax prices.

43. Just how this would be done raises the same problems as in the case of straightforward "optimization" without a net revenue requirement. The local managers might be instructed to seek to maximize the profits of their respective plants in free competition with each other, subject to the actual payment of product and factor taxes to—or receipt of subsidies from—the central administration; or the central administration might (a) fix prices as well as quasitaxes, (b) instruct the managers, on the basis of these prices, to produce in amounts that will maximize their respective profits after payment of quasitax, and (c) adjust the prices in the light of the demand-supply situation (e.g., by raising prices when order books fill up, and lowering them when stocks accumulate). Or the managers might be instructed to strive to meet the full demand at the going prices, which would be altered from time to time so as to equate product-price *less* product-quasitax with the value, at factor-price *plus* factor-quasitax of marginal factor cost.

44. Whichever method is adopted, the task facing the local managers is neither less difficult, nor significantly more difficult, than that which would face them in the absence of a net revenue requirement, in other words, if all quasitaxes were zero.

45. On the other hand, the central direction of the undertaking has its task considerably complicated by the existence of a net revenue re-

quirement in that it has the responsibility of determining the appropriate quasitaxes. It must ensure that (a) the quasitaxes are either all positive or all negative, (b) that they are adequate to ensure the earning of no more and no less than the required net revenue, (c) that they are at the lowest level compatible with earning the required net revenue, and (d) that they are proportionate to the respective marginal transfer effects of the products and factors in question. Conditions (a) and (b) are fairly straightforward operations; (c) is a matter of ensuring that the undertaking is producing more and not less than if it were attempting to maximize its profits: it should not be too difficult to decide on which side of the maximum profit watershed the undertaking lies at any one time, unless the required net revenue happens to be rather near to the maximum attainable. Operation (d), however, is a very tricky affair. It cannot be accurately performed, and indeed cannot be performed at all adequately, without a combination of market research and informed guesswork of a high order.

46. It may be objected that those economists who, in a spirit of hearty academic common sense, advocate the average cost rule, have in mind something simpler, if also vaguer, than the formulas that have been developed in this paper. But they seldom make clear which of the infinite number of ways of covering average cost they have in mind. There are some ways of covering average cost that are very wasteful indeed. For example, the idea frequently propounded or implied that not only should each nationalized industry cover its costs, but each plant and section with it should be made to do so also, would multiply the "diseconomies" inherent in the imposition of a net revenue requirement. The more efficient plants would have to be worked to excess in order to get their costs up to the required extent, or else would have to sell at an artificially low price, thus giving rise to faulty product allocation.

47. Let us consider, however, whether any "working rules" could be devised which, though less accurate than the criteria developed in this paper, would have sufficient advantages in respect of simplicity and applicability to offset its theoretical imperfections.

48. The most promising "rough-and-ready" rule would probably be to impose on all production a uniform *ad valorem* quasitax or subsidy. Whether it was nominally imposed on products or on factors would be in principle a matter of indifference. The point is that in allocating the tax no account would be taken of differences in marginal transfer effects (expressed as a proportion of the prices of the respective products or

factors). This, as previously pointed out, would relieve the undertaking's central administration of a difficult problem. It might also afford a slight simplification of the task of the local managers in applying the quasitaxes. The rule could probably be adopted without serious disadvantages in cases where product-differentiation according to product use or according to classes of consumers is for some reason impracticable and where the various products of the undertaking are of the same general sort and are closely substitutable.

49. There are, however, cases, such as in transportation and provision of power, in which price discrimination is possible and in which there may be considerable diversity of marginal transfer effects (elasticities of demand, etc.) as between different classes of consumers, different traffics, different uses of the service. In such cases even a bad guess at relative marginal transfer effects of the different products would almost certainly be less wasteful than a wooden application of the uniform *ad valorem* rule. I would envisage that the relative marginal transfer effects, and hence the relative quasitaxes (subsidies), once calculated, would remain un-revised for some considerable time, while the absolute quasitaxes might have to be altered (to keep net revenue constant) much more frequently.

Investment Decisions

50. I assume that, in any public undertaking, large investment decisions such as the introduction of a new product, the installation of a new plant, or the substantial extension of an existing plant, will be reserved to a central authority and not decided by local managers. Critics of the "marginal-cost principle" have often objected to the "orthodox" market test for such large adjustments, in the absence of a fixed net revenue re-quirement, that it entails attempting to calculate consumers' and pro-ducers' surpluses by measuring the areas under the product–demand curves, and marginal cost curves (or factor-supply curves) over the relevant intervals of variation. And it is deemed one of the "honest-to-goodness" advantages of the average-cost principle of pricing that it avoids such difficulties. Now we can see, from paragraph 32, that if the average-cost principle (which is simply a special case of a fixed net revenue requirement) is to be applied in the least harmful way it will involve even more of this "measuring areas under curves." For these areas will have to be measured, not only with respect to the primary variation itself

(the bulky investment and the product-factor changes directly associated with it), but also with respect to the complementary adjustments that the undertaking is obliged to make in other plants in order to prevent a change in net revenue.

51. Nor does the alternative formulation of the rule, in paragraph 34, offer any escape from this difficulty since in order to apply it exactly it is necessary to measure areas not, this time, *under* but rather *to the left of* demand-and-supply curves over the relevant intervals.

52. But perhaps there are, with regard to investment, as with regard to current production, some possible approximate working rules that, at some sacrifice in theoretical perfection, would spare us these complications? An obvious candidate, at any rate in the case of a public undertaking which has to meet a zero net revenue requirement (i.e., to make receipts cover costs), is the rule whereby a new plant should be set up when, but only when, it is expected to earn enough to cover its own costs. This test, however, will be either too stringent or too lax according to whether the undertaking is operating under conditions of quasisubsidies or quasitaxes. The main reason for this lies in the contraction of output at preexisting plants that the installation of a new plant—unless highly efficient and obviously worth having—is likely to necessitate in order to maintain the net revenue of the undertaking. As has been already pointed out in paragraph 35, if quasisubsidies prevail the new plant may be worth installing even if the net quantum change at the new plant itself is negative—and in this case the net revenue at the new plant is likely to be even more negative than the net quantum change. On the other hand, if positive quasisubsidies prevail the new plant may not be worth installing even if the net quantum change at the new plant is positive—and in this case the net revenue at the new plant *may* be even more positive than the net quantum change.[11]

53. In practice the test would be likely to lead either to extreme over-investment or to extreme under-investment. For example, if the capital costs at old plants are calculated on a replacement basis, new plants,

[11] The net revenue at the new plant will be less positive or more negative than the net quantum change at that plant insofar as its installation tends to bring down the prices of its products and raise the prices of its factors. If the new plant is noncompetitive with the old plants, this will always be the case. If however, it is completely competitive with the old plants, it will be the case only if the installation results in a positive net quantum change—and a negative net price change—for the undertaking as a whole.

being technically more efficient than old, should normally be able to earn a profit so long as the undertaking as a whole is able to cover its costs. Thus, even if we start from a position in which quasisubsidies are paid, and the test is therefore too severe, expansion will be deemed desirable. As expansion goes on, quasitaxes will take the place of quasisubsidies and the test, instead of being too severe, will become lax. Nevertheless, the expansion will continue, far past the optimal point, until a saturation point is reached at which any further investment would make it impossible for the undertaking as a whole to cover its costs.

54. If, on the other hand, the capital costs of old plants are calculated on an "original-cost" basis, an inflationary trend may artificially reduce the average costs of the old plants so that in conditions under which the old plants can only just pay their way, new plants may find it impossible to cover costs. Heavy quasisubsidies will prevail, and the test will be unduly restrictive of investment.

55. A more promising working rule is that suggested by Professor A. M. Henderson to the effect that new investment should be undertaken whenever this can be done without either reducing the undertaking's net revenue or raising product prices.[12] The implications of this rule are best seen by comparing it with the alternative formulation of the "improvement" test put forward in paragraph 34—a formulation itself in part inspired by consideration of Professor Henderson's rule. The two theoretical shortcomings of Professor Henderson's rule are that it (a) fails to take account of changes in factor prices, and may therefore unduly favor investments that exploit factor-suppliers and (b) is unclear as to the manner of measuring product price changes. If these are measured on the basis of prechange output quantities the test will be unduly restrictive of investment, if on the basis of postchange qualities, unduly encouraging. If *average* quantities are chosen as the base we are faced with the difficulties mentioned in paragraph 50.

56. My own view is that the only simplification of the tests set out in paragraphs 33 and 34, respectively, that does not involve a disproportionate loss in accuracy is that of assuming linear product-demand and factor-supply curves over the relevant intervals of variation. This would enable us to evaluate the net quantum change in terms of an

[12] *Review of Economic Studies* (1948–49), no. 39.

arithmetic mean of prechange and postchange prices, or a net price change in terms of an arithmetic mean of prechange and postchange quantities.

57. So far as the operation of the central direction of the undertaking is concerned, it would seem preferable to use the quantum-test rather than the price-test, as affording a more direct measurement of real income change. The main virture of the price-test formulation is to enable those outside the undertaking to apply a rough check of the operations of the management, since prices are perhaps more quickly and easily ascertained from outside than quantities.

CONCLUSION

58. In this paper I have considered the problem of the "optimal" behavior of an undertaking that, in a competitive environment, is placed under the obligation of earning a net revenue (profit) of fixed amount. I conclude that:

a. ideally such an undertaking should so regulate its current production—its output of divisible products and input of divisible factors—that product price equals marginal cost, subject to the application of "quasitaxes," positive or negative, on all products and all factors;

b. these quasitaxes should all be of the same sign and as low as is compatible with earning the required net revenue;

c. relative quasitaxes should be determined in a special way with reference to the "marginal transfer effects" of the products and factors in question;

d. large adjustments (e.g., investments) should be undertaken only if they give rise to a positive "net quantum change" while leaving net revenue unchanged;

e. these rules imply the desirability of a measure of price discrimination, product differentiation, and multipart pricing; and

f. no very great simplification of these rules is possible without a disproportionate loss in accuracy.

59. If these conclusions are correct, the complications that are inevitably created by any attempt to apply the average cost (or zero net revenue) principle with any sort of regard to economy surely constitute

a powerful argument against applying that principle at all, and in favor of leaving public undertakings free from any obligation to earn a given net revenue.

60. If, however, for political or pseudoethical reasons, it is deemed indispensable that nationalized industries "cover their costs," it should be realised that there will be very little hope of having such industries run on any sort of approximation to correct economic principles unless trained economists are employed to advise not only on the principles themselves but in the detail of their application to output, investment, and pricing policies. No business manager, administrator, or accountant, lacking familiarity with applied welfare economics, could be expected to devise those working rules and compromises that represent the best practicable adaptation of general principles of the sort discussed in this paper to the concrete circumstances of particular industries and plants at particular times.

APPENDIX

Note 1

Consider a one-plant undertaking whose production function is

$$K(a_1 \cdots a_n, b_1 \cdots b_m) = 0$$

where a_1 (etc.) stands for the output of product q_1 (etc.) and b_1 (etc.) stands for the input of factor f_1 (etc.) so that

$$\sum_{r=1}^{n} K'_{a_r} \, da_r + K'_{b_1} \, db_1 + \sum_{s=2}^{m} K'_{b_s} \, db_s = 0 \qquad (1)$$

From the first condition of "optimization," where P stands for "price,"

$$\sum_{r=1}^{n} P_{q_r} \, da_r - P_{f_1} \, db_1 - \sum_{s=2}^{m} P_{f_s} \, db_s = 0 \qquad (2)$$

From (1) and (2)

$$\sum_{r=1}^{n} da_r \left\{ P_{q_r} + P_{f_1} \left(\frac{K'_{a_r}}{K'_{b_1}} \right) \right\} = \sum_{s=2}^{m} db_s \left\{ P_{f_s} - P_{f_1} \left(\frac{K'_{b_s}}{K'_{b_1}} \right) \right\}$$

If we define the joint quasi-tax $T_{q_r(f_1)}$ as $P_{q_r} + P_{f_1}(K'_{a_r}/K'_{b_1})$, then, if all outputs and inputs are constant save for a_1, a_2, and b_1,

$$T_{q_1(f_1)} \, da_1 = -T_{q_2(f_1)} \, da_2 \qquad (3)$$

Then if $N(a_1 \cdots a_n, b_1 \cdots b_m)$ stands for the net revenue of the undertaking, from the requirement that net revenue should remain constant,

$$N'_{a_1} \, da_1 + N'_{a_2} \, da_2 + N'_{b_1} \, db_1 = 0$$

in other words, if $R_{q_r(f_1)}$ signifies $N'_{a_r} - N'_{b_1}(K'_{a_r}/K'_{b_1})$,

$$R_{q_1(f_1)} \, da_1 = -R_{q_2(f_1)} \, da_2 \tag{4}$$

Then, from (3) and (4)

$$\frac{T_{q_1(f_1)}}{R_{q_1(f_1)}} = \frac{T_{q_2(f_1)}}{R_{q_2(f_1)}}$$

Note 2

Let x and g be two of the n products, and y and h two of the m factors, of the undertaking, x and y being in the same plant. Let $R_{x(y)}$ signify the joint marginal revenue of x with respect to y, $D_{x(y)}$ the joint marginal transfer effect of x with respect to y, D_x the simple marginal transfer effect of x, and D_y the simple marginal transfer effect of y. The notation is in other respects analogous to that of note 1, a signifying output, b, input, and P, price. Then

$$R_{x(y)} = N'_{a_x} - \left(\frac{K'_{a_x}}{K'_{b_y}}\right) N'_{b_y}$$

where

$$N'_{a_x} = P_x + \sum_{g=1}^{n} a_g \frac{\partial P_g}{\partial a_x} - \sum_{h=1}^{m} b_h \frac{\partial P_h}{\partial a_x}$$

and

$$N'_{b_y} = -P_y + \sum_{g=1}^{n} a_g \frac{\partial P_g}{\partial b_y} - \sum_{h=1}^{m} b_h \frac{\partial P_h}{\partial b_y}$$

Thus, if

$$R_{x(y)} = T_{x(y)} + D_{x(y)} \qquad \text{(cf. para. 15)}$$

where

$$T_{x(y)} = P_x + \left(\frac{K'_{a_x}}{K'_{b_y}}\right) P_y,$$

then

$$D_{x(y)} = D_x - \left(\frac{K'_{a_x}}{K'_{b_y}}\right) D_y \qquad \text{(cf. para. 17)}$$

where

$$D_x = N'_{a_x} - P_x = \sum_{g=1}^{n} a_g \frac{\partial P_g}{\partial a_x} - \sum_{h=1}^{m} b_h \frac{\partial P_h}{\partial a_x}$$

and

$$D_y = N'_{b_y} + P_y = \sum_{g=1}^{n} a_g \frac{\partial P_g}{\partial b_y} - \sum_{h=1}^{m} b_h \frac{\partial P_h}{\partial b_y}$$

Note 3

Let q be any product and f any factor in the same plant.
Let a be the output of q and b the input of f

Let

$$\frac{T_q}{D_q} = \frac{T_f}{D_f} = z$$

Then, by definition in paragraph 19,

$$T_{q(f)} = P_q + \left(\frac{K'_a}{K'_b}\right) P_f = T_q - \left(\frac{K'_a}{K'_b}\right) T_f$$

$$= z\left\{D_q - \left(\frac{K'_a}{K'_b}\right) D_f\right\} \quad \text{(cf. para. 17)}$$

$$= z\, D_{q(f)}$$

Note 4

Consider an infinitesimal product-factor adjustment affecting two product-factor pairs q_1, f_1, and q_2, f_2, each pair being at a different plant. (The analysis is also applicable to an adjustment affecting two products and one factor at the same plant. In this case f_1 and f_2 must be assumed identical.)

Let (dW/da_1) signify the rate at which, as the adjustment proceeds, real income rises as a_1 (the output of q_1) increases. Indicate $T_{q_1(f_1)}$ by T_1, and $T_{q_2(f_2)}$ by T_2, and analogously for R and D. Then

$$\frac{dW}{da_1} = T_1 + \frac{da_2}{da_1} T_2$$

$$= T_1 - \left(\frac{R_1}{R_2}\right) T_2 \tag{1}$$

The second condition of "optimization" will be fulfilled only if

$$\frac{d^2 W}{da_1^2} > 0$$

that is, differentiating (1) and bearing in mind that $R_1 \equiv T_1 + D_1$, if

$$\frac{D_2}{R_2}\left(\frac{dT_1}{da_1} + \frac{R_1^2}{R_2^2}\cdot\frac{dT_2}{da_2}\right) < \frac{T_2}{R_2}\left(\frac{dD}{da_1} + \frac{R_1^2}{R_2^2}\cdot\frac{dD_2}{da_2}\right)$$

that is, at the stationary real income position, where $\dfrac{T_1}{D_1} = \dfrac{T_2}{D_2}$, if

$$\frac{(dT_1/da_1)}{T_1} - \frac{(dD_1/da_1)}{D_1} \gtrless -\frac{R_1}{R_2}\left\{\frac{(dT_2/da_2)}{T_2} - \frac{(dD_2/da_2)}{D_2}\right\} \quad \text{as} \quad \frac{T_2}{R_2} \gtrless 0 \quad (2)$$

In other words,

$$\left\{\frac{d(T_1/D_1)}{da_1} \div \frac{T_1}{D_1}\right\} \gtrless -\frac{R_1}{R_2}\left\{\frac{d(T_2/D_2)}{da_2} \div \frac{T_2}{D_2}\right\} \quad \text{as} \quad \frac{T_2}{R_2} \gtrless 0 \quad (3)$$

Now

$$\frac{d(T_1/D_1)}{da_1} = \frac{d(T_1/P_1) \div (D_1/P_1)}{da_1}$$

$$= \left\{\frac{D_1}{P_1}\cdot\frac{d(T_1/P_1)}{da_1} - \frac{T_1}{P_1}\cdot\frac{d(D_1/P_1)}{da_1}\right\} \div \left(\frac{D_1}{P_1}\right)^2$$

and under normal market conditions (e.g., with demand and supply elasticities constant or declining) one would expect that

$$\frac{d(D_1/P_1)}{da_1} \gtreqless 0.$$

We can now distinguish three cases—

a. If quasitaxes and joint marginal revenues (T_1, T_2, R_1, R_2) are all > 0,

$$\frac{d(T_1/P_1)}{da_1} < 0, \therefore \frac{d(T_1/D_1)}{da_1} > 0,$$

$$\therefore \text{ left-hand side (LHS) of (3)} > 0.$$

For analogous incomes

$$\text{right-hand side (RHS) of (3)} > 0.$$

$$\therefore \text{ LHS} < \text{RHS}$$

And since $(T_2/R_2) > 0$, inequality (3) embodying the second condition of "optimization" will *not* be fulfilled.

b. If quasi-taxes (T_1, T_2) are >0, while joint marginal revenues (R_1, R_2) are <0 as before, LHS $<$ RHS.
But now $(T_2/R_2) < 0$ so that inequality (3) *will* be fulfilled.
c. If quasitaxes and joint marginal revenues are all <0,

$$\frac{d(T_1/P_1)}{da_1} < 0$$

$$\frac{d(T_1/D_1)}{da_1} \text{ and LHS may be either} \gtrless 0$$

As

$$T_1 \to 0, \frac{d(T_1/P_1)}{da_1} \to -\infty$$

$$\therefore \frac{d(T_1/D_1)}{da_1} \to \infty \quad \text{and} \quad \text{LHS} \to \infty.$$

Similarly, as
$$T_2 \to 0, \text{RHS} \to -\infty.$$
Since

$$\frac{T_2}{R_2} > 0,$$

inequality (3) will be fulfilled if *either* T_1 or T_2 are sufficiently near to zero. As

$$T_1 \to -\infty,$$

$$\frac{(dT_1/da_1)}{T_1} \to 0$$

Therefore from inequality (2),

$$\text{LHS} \to -\frac{(dD_1/da_1)}{D_1} \quad \text{which is probably} <0.$$

There is probably a critical value of T_1 below which LHS is <0 and a critical value of T_2 below which RHS is >0. Inequality (3) cannot be fulfilled if T_1 and T_2 are *both* below these critical values.

6

EXTERNAL ECONOMIES AND THE DOCTRINE OF BALANCED GROWTH

THE OBJECT of this paper is to examine an argument advanced by some of the most distinguished writers on the theory of economic development, to consider to what extent and under what conditions it is valid, and to point to some of its implications.

The argument in question runs roughly as follows. In underdeveloped countries there is little incentive to invest capital in the introduction of modern efficient methods of large-scale production in individual industries producing goods for domestic consumption because the markets for the respective industries are too small. Since, however, the adoption of such methods in any one such industry would increase the demand for the products of the other industries, the incentive would be much greater if investments in a wide range of consumer-goods industries were undertaken, or at least considered, in conjunction. The adoption of investment projects which, though unprofitable individually, would be profitable collectively would, it is implied, be a good thing. This argument is frequently referred to as the "doctrine of balanced growth."

Certain elements in the doctrine are adumbrated in Allyn Young's celebrated article, "Increasing Returns and Economic Progress."[1] The

First published in *The Economic Journal* (June 1955), 65:241–56. Reprinted by permission of Cambridge University Press.

[1] Allyn Young, "Increasing Returns and Economic Progress," *The Economic Journal* (December 1928), 38:527–42.

doctrine itself is set forth briefly in Professor Rosenstein-Rodan's "Problems of Industrialisation of Eastern and South Eastern Europe,"[2] and more fully in chapter 1 of Professor R. Nurkse's *Problems of Capital Formation in Underdeveloped Countries*. The argument as presented in the present paper, however, does not purport to reproduce exactly the views of any of these writers. In the first place, they differ to some extent among themselves, and secondly, my presentation is either, as outlined above, too rough and ready, or else, as expounded below, too pedantically precise, to mirror faithfully the explicit thought of any one of them. What I have tried to do is to reconstruct the logical presuppositions of a doctrine that, with certain variations noted below, is common to Rosenstein-Rodan and to Nurkse.

We must now attempt to analyze the argument under discussion into its explicit and implicit elements. These are as follows:

1. The installation in any one of a wide range of home market industries in an underdeveloped country or region of a new plant capable of operating at a unit cost lower than that of existing production in the industry might be financially unprofitable because of the smallness and inelasticity of the market for the industry within the country or region in question.[3]

2. If demand for the product of such an industry were increased the installation of the new plant would become more profitable or less unprofitable.

3. Any increase in output, involving a reduction in unit cost of production, in a typical consumer-goods industry will tend to increase real income and hence real demand for the products of most other consumer-goods industries and thus to increase the profitability of installing more efficient plants in the latter provided, however, that interest rates do not rise too much.[4]

---

[2] Paul N. Rosenstein-Rodan, "Problems of Industrialisation of Eastern and South Eastern Europe," *The Economic Journal* (June–September 1943), 53:202–11.

[3] ". . . the small size of a country's market can discourage or even prohibit the profitable application of modern capital equipment by any individual entrepreneur in any particular industry." R. Nurkse, *Problems of Capital Formation in Underdeveloped Countries* (Oxford: B. Blackwell, 1953), p. 7.

[4] "Although the initial displacement may be considerable and the repercussions upon particular industries unfavorable, the enlarging of the market for any one commodity produced under conditions of increasing returns generally has the net effect . . . of enlarging the market for other commodities." Allyn Young, "Increasing Returns," p. 537. "The industries producing wage goods can thus be said to be complementary." Rosenstein-Rodan,

4. It follows that the installation of more efficient plants of the type described in each of a wide range of consumer-goods industries, though unprofitable if undertaken separately, might be profitable if undertaken jointly.

Moreover:

5. The joint installation of such plants, if profitable, would be desirable (i.e., would tend to increase real national income).

6. Because of its effects on the incentive to install efficient new plants in other industries the installation of a single plant, though unprofitable, might tend to raise real national income.

The rather odd-sounding proviso about interest rates at the end of step (3) in the argument has to be introduced into my scheme to take account of the fact that Rosenstein-Rodan and Nurkse usually describe the inter-industry relationships dealt with under 3 and 4 above as affecting not the profitability—net of interest—of installing efficient new plants but the "inducement to invest" or "marginal efficiency of investment," that is, the return on the capital invested in such new plants, including interest as well as profits. Now anything which enhances the rate of return on a new plant will enhance its profitability also, provided that the relevant interest rate does not rise "too much," that is, provided that the supply of capital is not "too inelastic."

Let us now consider various steps in the argument in greater detail. Step 1 is clearly valid. In a country of low *per capita* income and/or scattered population and/or poor communications the demand in a given region for the output of even a generally consumed manufactured product may be so small that the output (at minimum unit cost) of a single modern plant whose installation is under consideration would exceed the total previous output of the product in that region. The particular demand curve for the output of the projected new plant, though elastic over the

---

"Problems of Industrialisation," p. 206. "Where any single enterprise might appear quite inauspicious and impracticable a wide range of projects in different industries may succeed because they will all support each other in the sense that the people engaged in each project now working with more real capital per head and with greater efficiency in terms of output per man hour will provide an enlarged market for the products of the new enterprise in the other industries." R. Nurkse, *Problems of Capital Formation*, p. 13.

Our authors would not confine the scope of this interaction to consumer-goods industries. They do, however, emphasize its applicability as between such industries, and as we shall see, it is on this particularly vulnerable application that I wish to focus my criticism.

range of output for which it is displacing previous production, might be highly inelastic and steeply downward sloping for higher outputs. The unit cost curve of the new plant, even though it lies, for larger outputs, below the unit cost of preexisting production, may lie, for smaller outputs, above that unit cost, and for all outputs may lie above the demand curve for the plant. Under these conditions it would not be profitable to install the new plant.

Step 2 in the argument is likewise a valid one. If the particular demand curve for such a plant as has been described should be raised, *while cost conditions remain unchanged*, the effect would obviously be to reduce the loss associated with its operation, possibly to turn the loss into a profit.

The qualification is, however, all important. If the raising of the demand curve were to be accompanied by a raising of the unit-cost curve, the outcome might well be different. For a rise in the cost curve, taken by itself, would tend to reduce the profits, or increase the losses, of operating the plant, would reduce the scale of the plant's output if it were in operation and might make it unprofitable to install the plant at all.

We come now to the central question, with which step 3 in the argument is concerned, as to the circumstances in which the installation of a low unit-cost plant in one industry will increase the profitability of a similar installation in another industry.

In a closed economy any increase in the supply of any consumer good A, the supply of other such goods remaining unchanged, will tend to increase the prices of each of the latter products relative to that of A, though in the case of close substitutes the increase will be small. The increase in real income associated with the expansion in output of A will normally lead to some increases in the demand for non-A commodities as well as for A, and, in order that the increase in demand should be confined to A, the price of non-A commodities must rise relative to that of A; in other words, there will be an increase in the real price of the average non-A commodity.[5]

This increase in the real price of non-A commodities, provided that it is associated with no change in real factor prices, will tend to cause the output of non-A commodities, taken as a group, to expand even under

[5] In other words, an increase in the average price of non-A commodities relative to the average price of all commodities including A.

existing methods of production, and may make it profitable to install new large-scale plants. The extent to which this will occur will be greater: (a) the lower the income elasticity of demand for A, (b) the less the elasticity of substitution between A and non-A, and (c) the greater the elasticity of supply in non-A. But there will always be *some* positive reaction so long as the income elasticity of demand for A is less than unity, and the elasticity of substitution between A and B less than infinite, and so long as there is a positive elasticity of supply for non-A.

Step 4 in the argument follows directly from the previous steps.

Steps 5 and 6 are of a different character from the others in that they entail welfare-economic considerations. It is convenient to consider them in terms of a conceptual scheme that distinguishes in the case of any change in the output of a plant, between: (a) the increment in profits (IP), net of return on capital, (b) the increment in direct (social) net product (IDNP), and (c) the increment in real national income (IRNI). The IP corresponds to the Pigovian marginal (or additional) private net product and the IRNI to the Pigovian marginal social net product. The IDNP consists of the sum of the IP and the net benefits in the form of real income transferred from the firm operating the plant to its consumers, workers, suppliers, and others, as a result of the price changes resulting from the change in production. The IDNP is measured by the value of the additional output less the value of additional factor input, output and input being valued at the average prices prevailing over the relevant intervals of the corresponding product-demand and factor-supply curves. That the IDNP should be positive is the well-known Dupuit test of desirability of a finite change in production. The IRNI exceeds the IDNP to the extent that the change in production gives rise to economies outside the plant in question. An analysis of such external economies, given in the appendix, shows them to include such items as changes in net product in other plants, changes in factor supply and changes in the national terms of trade.

Returning to point 5 in the argument, the introduction of large-scale plants in a variety of increasing return industries will tend to reduce product prices (without reducing factor prices) in those industries, and will thus confer transfer benefits on the rest of the community. If the net profit of the new plants in positive, therefore, the increment in direct net product resulting from their introduction will be still more positive.

Unless, as is improbable, the new plants reduce aggregate factor supplies, bring about a deterioration in terms of trade or otherwise give rise to diseconomies outside the industries in question, their introduction is bound to enhance national real income.

As regards point 6, for reasons analogous to those just discussed, not only any introduction of new plants but also any increased output in existing plants which it profitable under imperfect competition is likely to have a positive direct net product and make a positive contribution to national income. Consequently if expansion in industry A renders profitable the expansion of imperfectly competitive industry B the total contribution to national income of the former expansion will include, not only the transfer benefits that it itself confers, but also the economies to which it gives rise in industry B. Even if the expansion at A is unprofitable, its total contribution may be positive, thanks to these transfer benefits and external economies.

A further point, which our authors might have made, but did not, is that the expansion of demand for an industry will increase not only the profit but also the direct net product involved in introducing a new plant there. Consequently, if conditions are such that the joint introduction of plants in a variety of industries may be profitable, though the plants are individually unprofitable, they will also be such that the plants would jointly yield a positive net product, even though individually none of them would do so.

As we have seen, the validity of step 3 depends on the assumption that real factor prices will not be affected when the supply of A is increased and that of non-A goods remains unchanged. This, however, could happen only in a limiting case. Normally real factor prices will be raised or lowered, or some raised and others lowered. There is, therefore, a possibility that the real prices of the factors entering into the operation of modern plants in non-A industries may rise to such an extent as to outweigh the rise in the real prices of non-A products, and thus to induce a contraction rather than an expansion in output and investment in non-A industries.

In conformity with what appears to be the intention of the balance-growth doctrine, in what follows we shall assume that the influence exercised by an increase in the supply of A on the real demand for other products is randomly distributed among non-A industries with respect to the possibilities for obtaining economies from increased output and investment in such industries. In other words, those industries of a critical size in this respect are not, on the average, either specially complementary to, or competitive with, industry A.

Suppose, now, there is only one stage of production and only one homogeneous factor of production, "labor," which is available in fixed supply. Under these conditions the installation of the new plant[6] at A will increase the incentive to install efficient new plants in non-A industries provided that the wage-rate does not rise so far as to prevent an expansion of output in the average non-A industry. And output in the average non-A industry will expand only if labor-input in non-A industries as a whole expands. Since the supply of labor is fixed, this can happen only if the input of labor at A contracts, that is, if the employment of labor at the new plant is less than the amount of labor released from the other production units in the industry.

Clearly the employment of labor at A cannot contract if A is a completely new industry at which there has been no previous production. Even, however, if there has been some previous production, it is probable in an underdeveloped country that this will be carried on in small units under conditions of constant (long-term) real unit cost. In this case if the new plant is unprofitable it is impossible that the employment of labor in the industry should decline.

For since the preexisting production units operate at constant labor cost, the price of the product in terms of wage units will remain constant so long as any of the preexisting units continue to operate. Aggregate demand for the product will also remain constant, so that the output of the new plant will at first merely replace output of preexisting units. If, at the point at which the new plant is itself producing practically the entire previous output of the industry it is still not profitable, though the product price in terms of wage units is almost at the level that made preexisting production units profitable, the aggregate labor-cost—and employment—of the new plant must be higher than that of the entire industry prior to its installation. If the output of the new plant is further increased, though its *average* labor cost may fall, its *aggregate* employment of labor must be still further increased.

---

[6] A "plant," in this model, may be conceived as a group of workers cooperating in some process that requires a minimum number of workers to achieve any output at all.

It would appear, therefore, that where there is a single factor of production in fixed supply the installation of an unprofitable new plant in industry A, even though its unit cost, at the least unprofitable output, is below that of preexisting production, is likely[7] to induce contraction rather than expansion in other consumer-goods industries, to yield external *dis*economies rather than external economies. The installation, over a wide range of such industries, of a set of unprofitable large-scale plants would render them not less but more unprofitable than if they had been installed singly. It would, moreover, tend to reduce the real national product. At first sight, this might appear to be contrary to common sense, since the new plants were described as being more efficient and working at lower unit cost than preexisting production in their respective industries. But this is only true of plants which are installed singly. If all of the plants are installed together the rise in wages will force the typical new plant to operate at a level that keeps the labor requirement of its industry approximately what it was under preexisting methods of production, and at this level, as we have seen, the unit costs of the new plants will be greater than those of preexisting production.

The situation might be roughly expressed by saying that, whereas the balanced-growth doctrine assumes that the relationship between industries is for the most part complementary, the limitation of factor supply ensures that that relationship is for the most part competitive.

Taking account of the multiplicity of factors of production introduces certain complications and qualifications into the argument without greatly altering its conclusions. Each industry and method of production is likely to have factors that are more or less specific to it. Thus when the new plant is introduced at A there is likely to be some fall in the price of factors specific to the old-fashioned methods of production in the industry. As output in the old sector of the industry is curtailed there will be a decline in product price, and a corresponding decline in marginal cost in the form of nonspecific factors released to other industries, so that the aggregate receipts of the new plant will fall short of the value of factors released from the older sector of the industry and the plant

---

[7] This conclusion would be certain but for the possibility that this output from preexisting production units might operate under conditions of diminishing returns. This, however, it more likely to occur where several factors of production exist, and is considered below.

may be unprofitable even though it employs fewer resources than those released from the older sector. This creates a possibility, though by no means a certainty, that an unprofitable plant, with a positive direct net product, may effect a net release of factors from the industry and thus create external economies.[8]

Another probable consequence of the multiplicity of factors of production is that the weighting or "mix" of factors used in running the new modern plant at A may resemble more closely the factor mix employed in running actual or potential modern plants in other industries than the combination of factors employed in production outside A taken as a whole. In this case it is possible that even if the plant installation at A on balance increases the supply of factors to non-A industries it will so raise the prices of those factors which are particularly in demand for the running of modern plants that the net effect on the installation of such plants will be discouraging.

It would appear therefore that, so long as factors of production are in fixed supply, the introduction of large-scale production units in consumer industries is likely to give rise not to economies but to diseconomies in other industries competing for the consumer market unless the former industries are already big enough for the introduction of the new plant to make possible a net reduction in the resources employed there: that this is unlikely to occur where the new unit is unprofitable, and cannot occur unless it passes the Dupuit test of the desirability of a "large" investment, that is, unless it has a positive direct net product.

It is noteworthy that the introduction of more efficient production methods in a large competitive industry such as agriculture is not only certain to be profitable but likely to release factors to other industries so long as the elasticity of demand for the industry as a whole is less than unity. This suggests that if underdeveloped countries were to press ahead with improvements of a financially profitable character in agriculture they might do more to make profitable large-scale efficient production

---

[8] If the direct net product is negative, the new plant cannot possibly create external economies. For the direct net product of the new plant is measured by its price integral *less* its marginal-cost integral. And the net release of resources from the industry is measured by that part of its output that is curtailed, less the marginal-cost integral of the new plant. And the price integral of the new plant cannot possibly fall short of the marginal-cost integral on the curtailed output of the older sector of the industry. So that the direct net product of the new plant must always exceed the net release of resources from the industry.

in other industries, such as manufacturing, which are in a phase of increasing returns, than by trying to develop simultaneously a wide range of such manufacturing industries.

Thus far we have assumed a closed economy. The introduction of foreign trade makes little difference to the argument. Indirectly, through the various mechanisms whereby external equilibrium is maintained, the demand for exports varies with the demand for imports. If the scope for economies of scale is equal in export and in home-market industries it makes no difference which gains at the expense of the other. It will still be true that the expansion of industry A will create a balance of economies or diseconomies elsewhere, according as A absorbs less or more factors than before. It is, however, sometimes argued that in underdeveloped countries the export trades sell on more perfect markets than do the domestic trades, so that fewer unexploited opportunities for economies of scale remain in the former. If so, the expansion at A will be more likely to generate external economies of scale than the previous argument would imply if, as is often the case, the industry A happens to be one which is more competitive in product markets with imports, and/or more competitive in factor markets with exports, than it is, in the respective markets, with purely domestic industries.

In order to really salvage the doctrine of external economies under examination, however, it is necessary to drop the assumption that the supply of factors of production is fixed in favor of the assumption that the supply varies positively with real factor prices. For then, in order that an expansion in A should increase the profitability of additional output and the installation of new plants in industries producing other consumer goods, thus generating economies, it is no longer necessary that the employment of factors in A should actually decline as output increases, but merely that factor employment there should not rise more than the increased factor supply evoked by the rise in real factor prices. As we have seen, of our authors, only Rosenstein-Rodan explicitly assumes an elastic supply of labor in his illustration of the doctrine, though Nurkse, in arguing in terms of the inducement to invest, is in effect assuming some elasticity in the supply of capital.

It should be noted that the possibility of expanding the supply of labor at a given money wage by increasing the level of money demand would not constitute factor elasticity in the sense relevant here, since the whole argument is concerned with "real" demand, and full employment is assumed from the start. There are, however, a number of *prima facie* reasons why the supply of factors in an underdeveloped country or region may show a measure of elasticity of a sort relevant to the present argument. Not all of them, however, are very conclusive. For example:

1. The supply of labor from individual workers may increase when real wages increase, because the workers are better able and more willing to work. But the opposite result is at least as likely to happen because the worker wishes to take out part of his real income in leisure, and "absenteeism."

2. Higher real wages may attract workers on the margin of the labor force into employment, and higher rents may make it profitable to bring poorer qualities of land into cultivation. On the other hand, higher family incomes may lead to a withdrawal of marginal women, children and older workers from the labor force.

3. Higher real rewards may tempt workers and capitalists to migrate into the country or region in question, thus increasing the supply of factors there. Economies facilitated by this means in the area of immigration, however, may be balanced by diseconomies in the area of emigration.

4. Higher real wages in a country at an early stage of demographic development may bring about an expansion of population that will entail an expansion in the labor force a couple of decades later. At a later stage of demographic evolution, however, higher real wages may have a zero or a negative effect on population growth.

For the purpose in hand the main potential sources of elasticity in the supply of factors of production are the three listed below, which will be discussed at greater length.

5. Insofar as factors of production are themselves products of an earlier stage of production—and here we depart from the assumption that there is only one stage of production—an increase in the real prices of those product-factors may bring about an increase in their supply and in the aggregate amount of factors supplied to subsequent stages of production.

6. A rise in the demand for factory labor may attract workers from employments, such as agriculture, where their productivity is very low, and thus give rise to a virtual increase in the supply of labor or at least an increase in its supply to that sector of industry in which economies of large-scale operation are to be obtained.

7. Higher interest rates may increase the supply of capital, especially from abroad.

First, let us take account of the "vertical disintegration" of production—the fact that industries buy the products of other industries, as well as original factors of production, and that some industries are predominantly suppliers of other industries rather than of final consumers. Thus far we have considered industries as acting on each other "horizontally," through the interrelated markets that they serve or the interrelated factors they buy. But industries also affect each other in greater or lesser degree in a more direct manner, or, "vertically," as suppliers or customers. We are concerned with the effect of this "vertical" connection on the "horizontal" one, to which the balanced-growth doctrine, as expounded by Rosenstein-Rodan and Nurkse, primarily refers.

The introduction, in industries serving final consumers, of more efficient large-scale methods of production may encourage increased output in factor-producing industries if it tends to raise the prices of produced factors (intermediate products) more, or reduce them less, than the prices of the original factors of production used by the latter group of industries. Now, as a matter of fact, the type of technical changes associated with the substitution of large-scale for smaller-scale production not only tend to raise the demand for capital relative to labor but also to raise the demand for intermediate products as compared with original factors as a whole.

We may assume that, in an underdeveloped country, the industries producing factors of production—especially those producing power, transportation, minerals, and capital goods—will, like the consumer-goods industries, frequently operate under conditions of imperfect competition, where efficient production is hampered by the smallness of the market. The stimulus given by the installation of large-scale production in consumer-goods industries to profitability, production, and investment in the supplying industries will therefore give rise to an increase in the net product of the latter. This means that the increased use, if any, of original factors in expanding the factor-producing industries will permit a more than equivalent increase in the supply of produced factors, so that the industries producing for final consumption will secure a net increase in the supply of the two sorts of factors taken together. It follows from this that the installation of modern large-scale production in one consumer-goods industry, even though it involves an increased use of factors of production—in both kinds—may nevertheless, in the manner described, leave other consumer-goods industries better supplied with factors than before, thus giving rise to economies there.

It is noteworthy that the chances that the introduction of more efficient large-scale operation in one consumer-goods industry will generate economies in another such industry are here increased only by reason of economies generated at an earlier stage of production. The latter ("vertical") type of external economies will, of course, enhance real national income just as surely as the former or "horizontal" type, and in magnitude are likely to be the more important of the two. Moreover, the "vertical" generation of economies operates not only from later to earlier stages of production, but also with even greater probability, from earlier to later stages. Thus the expansion of output in a producer-goods industry, provided that it involves an increase in net product, will tend to increase the profitability of other industries in general, and will encourage economies in such of those industries as are operating under increasing returns.

There can be little doubt but that the conditions for a "vertical" transmission of external economies—whether forward from supplying industry to using industry, or backward from using industry to supplying industry—are much more favorable than for a "horizontal" transmission between industries at the same stage. There is, therefore, a much stronger case for joint planning of the development of industries at earlier and later stages of the same "line" of production than of industries at the final stage of different "lines." The fact that our authors, other than Allyn Young, seem to lay more emphasis on the "horizontal" rather than the "vertical" variant of the balanced-growth doctrine is probably due to the fact that the external economies underlying the former are less frequently discussed in the literature than those underlying the latter. But the "horizontal" transmission of economies may have been neglected by Marshall and his commentators precisely because, where it exists at all, it is relatively unimportant.

Let us now turn to the possibility, listed in item 6 above, that the enhanced real demand for labor arising in various branches of secondary industry as a result of the expansion and modernization of one such industry may be satisfied by drawing labor away from an overcrowded agriculture where its marginal productivity is negligible or relatively low.

As already mentioned, Rosenstein-Rodan, in expounding his version of the "horizontal" variant of the balanced-growth doctrine, explicitly assumes that the labor supply for industrial expansion is drawn from agriculture where it would otherwise be underemployed.

There can be no doubt of the fact, attested by many observers, that underemployment, in the sense specified above, exists in the agriculture of many underdeveloped countries. There can also be little doubt but that an expansion in the real demand for labor in any particular industrial branch would attract some of the underemployed agricultural labor to secondary industry, and to that extent would improve the prospect of reaping economies of scale in the industrial sector as a whole. The crucial question, however, so far as the creation of external economies is concerned, is whether the expansion of industrial branch A would lead to a transference of labor from agriculture to industry sufficient to permit an expansion of branches of industry *other than* A.

It is by no means clear how this question should be answered. Much will depend on the reasons for the prior existence of the agricultural underemployment. It is assumed that this is no mere case of inadequacy of monetary demand combined with rigidity of money wages in secondary industry. There remain two possible lines of explanation. One is that the underemployment is voluntary in the sense that real rewards for unskilled labor in industry are insufficiently in excess of those in agriculture to attract sufficient labor to equalize marginal productivity in the two sectors. Even though the marginal product of labor in agriculture be far below that in industry, labor may stay on the land partly because of a family system under which the individual worker is paid according to the *average* product of peasant labor rather than its *marginal* product, and partly because of inertia, and lack of enterprise.

In this event, however, it seems unlikely that more workers would be attracted from agriculture than are absorbed by the initial expansion in industry A. For expansion in A, output remaining constant elsewhere, is likely to increase the demand-price for food at least as much as for the products of other secondary industries. Insofar as this expansion entails an increase in real income, it will no doubt tend to raise demand for manufactures in higher proportion than for food; but the increased output of A is likely to be more competitive with other manufactures than with food, and the probable transference of income from taxpayers—or whoever bears the losses of the expansion at A—to peasants and workers will tend to raise demand for food rather than manufactures. For these and other reasons[9] the real demand-schedule for labor in secondary production outside A appears more likely to fall than to rise relative to the schedule of real *per capita* income in agriculture. If the demand for labor A is sufficiently strong to draw labor from agriculture it will be sufficiently strong to draw it from other secondary industries also. The availability of underemployed agricultural labor may enable A's labor force to expand without that of other secondary industries having to contract as much as it otherwise would: it will not permit the latter to expand as well.

A second line of explanation for the initial state of underemployment in agriculture is that workers, while desirous of moving from agriculture to secondary industry, are unable to obtain employment there owing to factors such as the artificially high level of industrial wages maintained by labor unions. In this event much depends on how these wages are determined. It is assumed that as the demand for labor expands in industry A industrial money wages will rise at least as fast as prices in general; otherwise, the agricultural unemployment would be of a type curable by mere monetary expansion—a hypothesis that we have excluded. If, as might well happen, the unions were to take advantage of the increased demand for labor in industry A to prevent any whittling away of the original disparity between industrial wages and agricultural incomes, this would entail a decline in secondary industries other than A unless the prices of non-A manufactures were to rise faster than those of agricultural products, which, as we have seen, is unlikely. Even if the unions were to confine themselves to preventing a decline in industrial real wages, it is quite possible, for the reasons discussed in the foregoing paragraph, that the rise in agricultural prices would so far outstrip the rise in prices of non-A manufactures as to entail a decline in the real demand-schedule for the latter, and hence a decline rather than an expansion of employment in non-A industries.

---

[9] Although any influences transmitted "vertically" to basic industries, or any repercussions on other industries of the economies generated in basic industries, are more likely to favor secondary production than agriculture, on the other hand, the latter is less likely to be affected by scarcity of capital or intermediate products resulting from the initial expansion at A.

In all probability some tendency for industrial wages to be artificially maintained in relation to agricultural incomes is fairly general in under-developed countries. It is obvious that real wages are not in practice raised so fast in response to a rise in the real demand for industrial labor as to prevent all movement from country to town. This, however, does not prove that wages do not rise fast enough to nullify the benefits which the several industries would otherwise derive from *each other's* expansion.

Even if secondary industries other than A do not succeed in adding to or retaining their labor force, they may still expand if other factors of production become more plentiful. But the mere fact that agricultural labor is seriously underemployed provides no guarantee that an expansion in A that absorbs more factors than are created by associated economies in basic industries will draw sufficient labor out of agriculture to permit an increase in output, profits and net product in secondary industries other than A.

Let us now turn to the third main possibility of factor elasticity, men-tioned in item 7, namely, that the supply of capital is to some extent elastic with respect to the rate of interest. This assumption, as we have seen, has from the start been, in effect, woven into the balanced-growth doctrine by Rosenstein-Rodan and by Nurkse insofar as they express that doctrine in terms of the inducement to invest (see footnote 4).

An elastic supply of capital would undoubtedly facilitate the creation of external economies of scale. If capital were in infinitely elastic supply, so that additional capital requirements in any industry had no effect on the cost or availability of capital for the use of other industries, and if all requirements could be met from domestic saving, then any expansion in industry A that did not involve an increased use of factors of production *other than capital* would be fairly certain to generate expansion, and the economies associated therewith, in other industries.

A distinction must be drawn, however, between capital obtained from foreign and from domestic sources, respectively. When development is financed by foreign capital, additional interest or dividends will have to be paid to capitalists resident abroad. In order to transfer these sums the country in which the development occurs will have to generate an export surplus partly by reducing imports and partly by increasing exports. So long as export industries offer the same sort of opportunities for economies of scale as those producing for the domestic market, the increase in exports will have no ill effect. If, on the other hand, no economies of scale are possible in export industries, only that part of the addition to the national factor supply that accrues to home-market industries will generate such economies.[10]

How elastic is the supply of capital in fact likely to be in an underdeveloped country or region? This is a question that cannot be satisfactorily answered, or even formulated, in terms of the comparative static analysis used in this paper—at least so far as capital of domestic origin is concerned. Any increase in real income associated with the expansion of capital and output at A would tend to raise the domestic supply of *saving* and gradually and cumulatively the domestic supply of *capital*. In the very long run the expansion at A might evoke an additional supply of domestic capital large enough to meet its own requirements and leave some over for other industries. Within the sort of time period of interest for the purposes of economic policy, however, capital-expansion in one industry is likely to be at the expense of capital-expansion in other industries, unless additional capital is available from abroad in highly elastic supply.

The transfer of capital from abroad, unlike the increase in supply from home saving, is responsive to the increase of interest rates or profit opportunities rather than to that of real income in the developing country. Although the two types of responsiveness in capital supply resemble each other in operating only over time, the bulk of any additional supply forthcoming from foreign sources in response to the higher interest rates (etc.) is likely to appear much sooner than the bulk of any additional supply accumulated from new domestic savings.

It is impossible to generalize about the elasticity of supply of capital from abroad. In certain cases the supply curve may even be downward-sloping, as when the fact that *some* foreign capital is willing to venture into an underdeveloped country encourages additional supplies at even lower interest rates and lower profit expectations. Or the curve may be highly elastic for moderate amounts and inelastic for large amounts (if the capital is drawn from somewhat restricted circles of investors abroad).

---

[10] The net addition, if any, to the factor supply of home-market industries will be the larger the greater the share of import saving in the aggregate improvement in the real trade balance, and the smaller the proportion of the improvement required to offset deterioration in the terms of trade.

Or it may be elastic for some industries and inelastic for others. (Frequently the industries for which foreign capital supply is inelastic will be precisely the home-market industries where the economies of scale are most to be expected.) Or, in the case of countries having forfeited the confidence of investors, the supply of foreign capital may be highly inelastic all around.

Inelasticity in the supply of capital from abroad tends to render the doctrine of balanced growth not so much invalid as inapplicable. Even where a diversified investment program would yield a higher return on capital invested than would the projects taken individually, the higher cost of capital might make the large-scale program as unprofitable as the piecemeal approach. More fundamental is the criticism already noted that even where capital is available in elastic supply the mere fact that it is obtained from abroad reduces the extent to which it can be used to exploit economies of scale in home-market industries and reduces the chances that the combined investment program will in fact yield a higher return to capital than would the projects taken one by one.

CONCLUSION

This paper has examined the basic assumptions underlying a modern variant of the balanced-growth doctrine, namely, that the introduction of lower (unit) cost methods of production involving expansion in the output of an industry, even if itself unprofitable, will enhance the profitability of other industries not specially related to it as customers or suppliers, and, if these industries are operating under imperfect competition, will promote economies of larger-scale production there.

We have concluded that the argument, as usually presented, overemphasizes the repercussions on the demand for, and ignores repercussions on the costs of, the other industries, and that, in an economy where factors of production are in fixed supply, the introduction of unprofitable though efficient large-scale production in one industry is more likely to reduce than to increase the profitability of other industries.

We have seen, however, that the chances are much better for a "vertical" propagation of external economies, from customer industry to supplying industry, and especially from supplying industry to customer industry, and that developments in industries at different stages in the same "line" of production are more likely to afford each other mutual support than those in different lines of production.

Moreover, the chances that expansion in one industry will generate economies in other industries not "vertically" related to it will be increased if economies are generated "vertically" in factor-producing industries. This has the effect of introducing a measure of elasticity into the supply of factors of production, which is in general favorable to the creation of external economies.

Conditions of elastic supply of labor or capital likewise tend to favor the applicability of the balanced-growth doctrine. The overall elasticity of the labor supply is, however, likely to be low, and the ease with which labor can be transferred from agriculture to nonagricultural industry, where the opportunities for economies of scale are greater, has frequently been exaggerated.

As to capital, the domestic supply is likely to be practically inelastic within any short period of years. Access to imported capital, on the other hand, varies very much from country to country and from time to time; and, in any case, foreign capital is less effective than domestic capital in widening the market and promoting economies of scale.

The chances that diversified development in a variety of industries will play a mutually supporting, mutually validating role, as required by the balanced-growth doctrine, are greatest when the necessary additional capital is obtainable on easy terms, when unions can be prevented from pushing up real wages in industry, when reserves of underemployed agricultural labor are eagerly waiting to obtain industrial employment, when there are opportunities for economies of scale in the basic, factor-producing industries, and when, taken singly, the investments in question are only just not profitable. When too many of these conditions are absent the combined installation over a variety of industries of unprofitable though efficient undertakings may have the effect of rendering each of these undertakings still more unprofitable than if it had been set up by itself.

NOTE ON EXTERNAL ECONOMIES

The term "external economies," since it was introduced by Marshall, has been employed in a variety of senses, often confusing and misleading.

The usage that I consider most convenient for the purpose of welfare economics and that represents a development of that introduced by Professor Kahn in "Some Notes on Ideal Output,"[11] is the following: Let us adopt the following definitions:

1. The *"increment in direct net product"* of a firm is the sum of any net increase in the volume of its sales, *less* any net increase in the volume of its purchases (including purchases of labor and other original factors of production), *plus* any net increase in its real stock of physical assets. This is a sum of physical increments valued at current prices.[12] (The fact that output is netted not only of purchases from other firms but also of purchases from factor-owners makes this a different concept from that of an increase in real "value added.")

2. The *"increment in net factor supply"* of a factor-owner (worker, capitalist, landowner) is the sum of any increases less any reductions in the supply of his factors to different uses. (A transfer of labor to a better-paid use would constitute such an increase, but not, of course, an increase in remuneration for labor in a given use.)

3. The *"increment in tax quantum"* associated with any type of transaction is the increase in the volume of transactions of this type *times* the current tax rate. Subsidies are counted as negative taxes.

4. The *"increment in government services"* consists in the money equivalent of any net increase in government services provided without charge, other than those provided to firms.

5. The *"increment in net psychic income"* of any individual is the money equivalent of all additional advantages less additional disadvantages accruing to him, other than those arising through changes in his money income, or in the nominal purchasing power of that income. This is something of a hold-all residual item, containing, for example, not only all changes in satisfaction associated with a change in occupation as such, but also those associated with changes in the availability of consumer goods at unchanged prices.

---

[11] Richard F. Kahn, "Some Notes on Ideal Output," *The Economic Journal* (March 1935), 45:1–35.

[12] Where adjustments large enough to alter prices are in question the price of each increment will be the average price over the corresponding interval of variation on the relevant product-demand or factor-supply curve. This average price will be a function of the "path" of variation and thus of the convention whereby that path is determined.

Now the sum of all increments of the first three types will together constitute that part of the increment of the real national product which is marketed and is statistically measurable.[13] Inclusion of the increments of types (4) and (5) will add the nonmarketed and the intangible elements in the real national product. In a closed economy this sum will also represent the increment in the real national income. In an economy with foreign trade, however, we must add:

6. The increment, resulting from change in the terms of trade, in the import equivalent of the existing volume of exports.

Now, any increment in one of the above mentioned categories may be termed, if positive, an "economy" and, if negative, a "diseconomy," and any economy of diseconomy that is brought about by the actions of a particular firm, other than a change in its own direct net product, I shall refer to as an "external" economy or diseconomy, respectively, generated by the operations of that firm.

External economies affecting direct net product, factor supply, tax quantum or psychic income can be cross-classified into two main categories:

a. economies that affect production and enjoyment functions in such a way as to increase the outputs of affected firms for given inputs or to increase the satisfaction derived by persons from given employment and consumption patterns; and

b. economies arising out of production adjustments, employment adjustments, or consumption adjustments, undertaken by the affected firms, workers, or consumers in response to changes in the market situation resulting from the initial operation.

Where perfect competition is pervasive only external economies of category a can occur.[14] Economies of category b can occur only in connection with firms, workers, or consumers operating under imperfect competition or price-fixing or subject to indirect taxation. Such economies can accompany infinitesimal adjustments only where production (or employment or consumption as the case may be) has previously been

---

[13] Summation of the first two types of increments alone would have given us a measure of the increment in real national product in which individual products are weighted according to their factor cost—a faulty weighting from a welfare–economic standpoint. Inclusion of type (3) increments alters the basis of weighting to that of market price.

[14] For comparison, see J. E. Meade, "External Economies and Diseconomies in a Competitive Situation," *The Economic Journal* (March 1952), 62:54–67.

uneconomically organized. Thus a small expansion of input and output in a firm resulting from an expansion in product demand can lead to an increase in direct *net* product only when, for reasons of profit-maximization or *force majeure*, product price has previously been in excess of marginal cost. Where *large* individual adjustments are concerned, however, such as installation of new plant, a change in market conditions can make economic an adjustment yielding an increase in direct net product, even though such adjustment was previously uneconomic.

7

REJOINDER TO
PROFESSOR NURKSE

O N THE second page of my paper "External Economies and the Doctrine of Balanced Growth" [*The Economic Journal* (June 1955), 65:242] I mentioned that both Professor Nurkse and Professor Rosentein-Rodan, by speaking in terms of the "inducement to invest," were implicitly assuming some elasticity in the supply of capital, and on p. 248 I stated—rather belatedly, I admit—that Rosenstein-Rodan was explicitly assuming an elastic supply of labor.

It is true that from p. 245 onward, in my critical examination of the balanced-growth doctrine culled from the views of these authors, I treated the doctrine as not in itself entailing any particular assumption about factor supply. I regret that the reader was not reminded sufficiently often that the authors of the doctrine had in fact put it forward under more restrictive assumptions. I regret even more having confused the issue by initially (on p. 242) defining the doctrine in Nurkse's restricted form. What I do not regret, however, is having discussed the doctrine in the unrestricted form in which "it was never put forward," as this was the most convenient way to conduct a systematic examination of the role of factor-supply conditions in determining its validity. Such an examination seemed, and seems, to me desirable because: (a) the vital importance of this role had not been made clear in the literature, and (b) different assumptions about factor supply had in fact been made by Rosenstein-Rodan and Nurkse.

First published in *The Economic Journal* (September 1956), 66:537–39. Reprinted by permission of Cambridge University Press.

In these circumstances it would not be surprising if unwary adherents of the "doctrine" should seek to apply it in conditions in which it was not properly applicable.

I question whether the bearing of factor-supply conditions on the validity of the doctrine is quite so self-obvious as Nurkse indicates. It is not, for example, "intuitively obvious," nor is it indeed the case,[1] that a technically progressive but unprofitable innovation involving an expansion of *output* in a particular industry—which is what I was arguing about—will *necessarily* involve an increased use of factors and hence, in an economy with fixed factor supply, hurt instead of helping the profitability of other industries. Still less is it obvious, or even true, that it will necessarily involve a departure from optimal allocation.

But if Nurkse is a little too hard on the doctrine of balanced growth in conditions of fixed factor supply, he is a good deal too sanguine about it on his implied assumption of elastic capital supply. Even a perfectly elastic supply of capital is *not* sufficient, nor did I grant it to be sufficient,[2] to ensure that investments in different home-market industries will tend to render each other more profitable. In particular, it may make a great deal of difference, as I pointed out, whether the capital is assumed to be raised at home or abroad.

Nurkse makes great play with my "static assumptions," but I am not clear in which respect these are thought to render my argument misleading. The main practical relevance of the balanced-growth doctrine is its bearing on the results of alternative government policies or alternative courses of entrepreneurial action. For example, what difference will it make to the real income of a country if the government (a) takes steps, (b) does not take steps, to encourage the introduction of technically efficient plants involving output expansion in a wide range of industries in circumstances in which the introduction of any such plant in any single industry would be unprofitable? Ideally, this calls for a comparative process analysis covering a period starting at the moment of decision and extending indefinitely into the future. Not only, however, would such a comparative dynamic analysis be excessively complicated, but the characteristic contribution of the "balanced-growth doctrine" to the analysis

[1] As I pointed out in "External Economies and the Doctrine of Balanced Growth," *The Economic Journal* (June 1955), 65:246, n.1.

[2] *Ibid.*, pp. 252–53.

seems to relate, not to the transitional period when the supply of labor or capital is in process of expanding or of being redistributed in response to the decision referred to at (a) above, but to a stabler post-transitional period. Since the static character of my assumptions largely consists in my ignoring this transitional period, I do not think that my conclusions are thereby invalidated.

Allyn Young, in his *Economic Journal* article of December 1928, was discussing a somewhat different sort of question, involving a comparison, not of alternative processes relating to the same time periods, but rather of states of affairs in *different time periods*, that is, periods preceding and following significant changes in factor supply. In discussing this sort of "simple dynamic" or historical question some of my factor-supply schedule analysis may have less relevance than to the "comparative dynamic" question that I was actually discussing. This is why I treated him as a precursor rather than a proponent of the doctrine I was examining.

8

THE BEARING OF NONCOMPETITIVE MARKET CONDITIONS ON THE PROBLEM OF INFLATION

IN RECENT YEARS there has been an increasing tendency in economic writing to distinguish between "demand-induced" and "cost-induced" (or "wage-induced") inflation, and to emphasize the role of "cost-push" as against "demand-pull" in imparting an upward trend to the movement of general prices.

It is true that the prices of most industrial products are largely determined by their costs of production and that any rapid increase in product prices is likely to be associated with a rise in factor costs. This, however, provides no reason to alter the traditional treatment of inflation as a demand-supply phenomenon so long as factor prices, including wages, are themselves determined by supply and (derived) demand on competitive markets. If there is a case for distinguishing any new category of inflation it must rest on the fact that in reality prices of factors and products seldom are determined on perfectly competitive markets.

Thus the present paper examines the effects that noncompetitive pricing of factors and products may have on the rate of growth of the price of final output and on the appropriateness of policies aiming at price stability. The treatment is analytical and can therefore throw but limited light on the strength of the forces at play in any actual instance of

First published in *Oxford Economic Papers*, February 1959. Reprinted by permission of Oxford University Press.

inflation, but may serve to suggest which relationships it would be most useful, if practicable, to establish and quantify by empirical investigation. For simplicity, the analysis is conducted in terms of a closed economy.

After a description of certain aspects of the inflationary process, as it would develop under conditions of perfect competition, it is shown that departures from competitive pricing occurring in the course of inflation are mainly due to the interaction of (a) monopolistic restriction of supply, (b) "stickiness" in money wages and prices, and (c) attempts to maintain stable relationships between prices of different sorts.

A distinction is drawn between "underpricing" and "overpricing"— both being defined in relation to the competitive price of the item in question. The effects on the price of final output of changes in the degree of overpricing or underpricing of labor and of various categories of products, respectively, are then analyzed on the assumption of a given supply of money. While in most cases reduction in underpricing and increase in overpricing are found to increase the velocity of circulation and to raise the price level of final output, the degree and mechanism of the inflationary effect will differ for reduced underpricing and increased overpricing, respectively, and for wages and other prices, respectively.

On the basis of this static analysis a dynamic model of inflation is then described in which provision is made for the influence on price change of (a) the (limited) responsiveness of wages and prices to demand pressures, (b) the adjustment of prices to costs, and (c) the (lagged) influence of cost of living on wage-rates. The inflationary effects of changes in "aggressiveness" on the part of labor and enterprise and of changes in the rate of expansion of the money supply are then explained in terms of the model. It is shown that whereas, except in extreme cases, the inflationary effects of attempts to secure higher real rewards will be of a temporary character, the rate of monetary expansion will in the end determine the rate of price inflation.

Changes in the rate of monetary expansion are shown to affect the level of output and the rate of development, but whereas in the case of "creeping" inflation these effects may be permanent, in the case of stronger inflation they are likely to be of a temporary though not reversible character.

The policy implications of noncompetitive pricing are then considered and it is shown that financial disinflation and antimonopolistic action are not alternative but complementary policies; the application of either makes the other not less but more desirable.

Finally, the bearing of the analysis on the classification of inflations is considered and a distinction is drawn between "cost-determined" and "cost-induced" inflation.

THE INFLATIONARY PROCESS
UNDER PERFECT COMPETITION

In an economy where prices, of products and factors alike, move flexibly in response to demand and supply on competitive markets, labor will be fully employed and productive facilities will be utilized to their full economic capacity. In these circumstances, if product prices in general are rising this is best attributed to the fact that the flow of total money demand is rising faster than the total supply of goods and services, as determined by changes in the working population, in the stock of capital, and in productivity.[1]

The growth in monetary demand may conveniently be regarded as determined, in the first instance, by (a) the growth in the stock of money, and (b) changes in the velocity with which the stock of money circulates.

These in turn are influenced by more ultimate factors. Velocity in particular is likely to be influenced by any important changes in real economic relationships. For example, if the marginal "efficiency" or profitability of new investment should increase, whether because of technical developments, or because savings are too low to enable the growth in the capital stock to keep pace with the growth in the working population, the consequential increase in interest rates will operate to raise the rate of turnover of the money stock and the level of money demand.[2]

---

[1] In an "open" economy changes in the terms of international trade would have to be added to this list.

Inflation of the type described above is sometimes attributed to a persistent excess of aggregate real demand in some sense, over the potential supply of goods and services. This appears to imply that the course of inflation is marked either by a continuous shortage of finished goods or by a continuous excess of expected over realized purchasing power. The former assumption is incompatible with perfect competition; the latter seems unwarranted by the facts.

[2] Savings also may increase but, *ex hypothesi*, not sufficiently to prevent the rise in interest rates and increase in velocity.

Some of these underlying factors act on supply as well as on demand. For example, an intensification in the rate of improvement of productive technique will promote inflation insofar as it raises the profitability of new investment and thus provokes an increase in the velocity of circulation, but it will also dampen inflation insofar as it accelerates the rate of growth of output. Very probably, the initial effect of such a development will be inflationary, the ultimate effect disinflationary.

Factors of the type discussed above, however, are unlikely to bring about a rapid and continued increase in the real marginal productivity of capital and hence, apart from their effect on price anticipations, are unlikely to occasion any rapid and long continued rise in the velocity of circulation and in prices. On the other hand, any acceleration in the rate of increase of prices that lasts long enough to evoke an acceleration in the *anticipated* rate of price increase will raise the profitability of investment in money terms and hence promote an increase in the velocity of circulation. A pure speculative inflation based on velocity, however, cannot long continue on its own momentum. As soon as prices and velocity cease to rise faster and faster they must begin to fall, and a series of fluctuations will ensue.

It seems clear, therefore, that continuous inflation is only possible if the monetary authorities permit a corresponding expansion in the supply of money. A limited rise in the real marginal productivity of capital will lead to a fluctuation in velocity of circulation eventuating in a limited once-and-for-all increase in velocity. An increased rate of expansion in the money stock will also lead to velocity fluctuations eventuating in a once-and-for-all increase in velocity,[3] but after the movements in velocity have died down the rate of price expansion will have risen *pari passu* with the rate of expansion in the money stock.

The various factors that affect the velocity of circulation also affect to some extent the size of the money stock, particularly the part that consists of bank deposits. They do not, however, operate unambiguously in the sense of expansion or contraction. Thus a rise in profit and interest rates, by raising the velocity of circulation of bank money more than of cash, will induce the public to draw cash out of the banks, thus tending

---

[3] The once-and-for-all increase in velocity results from the rise in profit rates and interest rates associated with the permanently enhanced rate of price inflation.

to force the latter to contract the supply of bank money. On the other hand, the same increase in profits and interest will tend to sustain the supply of bank money by inducing the banks to tolerate a lower ratio of reserves to liquid liabilities.

For this reason and in order to avoid considering the repercussions of balance-of-payments developments on the supply of money, it seems best to regard the latter as determined by official policy. Included among the reasons that may motivate governments to permit an excessive expansion of money stock are a desire to maintain a higher real budget deficit than would otherwise be possible, a desire to keep interest rates, especially those paid on public debt, artificially low, and a desire to reduce the real capital value of the national debt.

The most respectable argument for inflationary financial policies is the possibility of utilizing the mechanism of "forced savings" to raise the total level of national savings and investment above what would otherwise be possible. Under competitive conditions, however, the only forced savings that arise in the private sector are those resulting from time-lags between the earning and the receipt of income and between the receipt and the expenditure of income. Owing to these lags, private expenditure on consumption will be related to the income of a previous period and, when prices and incomes are rising, this will artificially reduce the proportion of current income that is currently consumed and increase the proportion that is saved. This type of forced saving is unlikely to persist after people have come to realize that they have for some time been consuming less than corresponded to their true level of real income.

As for the public sector, in countries where indirect taxes are of an *ad valorem* type and direct taxes are progressive while national debt interest and other money transfers constitute a large part of budgetary expenditures, inflation is likely to result for a time in an increase in public savings. This type of forced saving also is likely to dwindle or disappear as political influence gets to work to enforce an increase in public expenditure or reduction in taxation.

The evil effects of inflation in causing a maldistribution of investment, in disrupting the credit system, and in bringing about a violent transfer of wealth and income from creditors to debtors, and transfer of income from pensioners to taxpayers, are well known. Where such inflation occurs in a fully competitive market economy, it can and indubitably should be brought to an end by curtailing the rise in the flow of monetary demand; in the circumstances assumed a disinflationary financial policy could be put into effect without reducing employment or output, and with little, if any, permanent detriment to real investment.

CONDITIONS RESPONSIBLE FOR NONCOMPETITIVE PRICING

Very few goods and services are priced on perfectly competitive markets. An item may be said to be "overpriced" or "underpriced" according to the relation of its actual price to the price it would have if its own market were perfectly competitive but prices and conditions on markets for other items were what they actually are.

Departures from competitive pricing usually arise from either (a) a combination among sellers, (b) the existence of firms sufficiently large relative to the (possibly specialized or localized) markets on which they sell to be able to influence price, or (c) government price control.

In the circumstances described under conditions (a) and (b) it is natural that prices should tend to move toward levels somewhat in excess of the competitive norms. Thus wages will tend toward target levels in which a certain amount of unemployment prevails and product prices toward target levels at which there is a certain degree of underproduction.[4] However, there are a number of reasons why prices that are determined on imperfectly competitive markets do not move in such a way as to maintain a constant degree of unemployment or underproduction.

In the first place, there is a tendency for imperfectly competitive prices, when expressed in money terms, to move only slowly, or only after a lapse of time, in response to the various pressures and motives to which they are subject. Such inertia or "stickiness" is notable with respect to wages and salaries, rents, and the prices of public utility and transport services and of such manufactures as are produced by industries in which

---

[4] There is also likely to be underutilization of productive capacity but where a monopolistically inclined industry can control the entry of new firms, underutilization of capacity may largely be replaced by underinvestment in new capacity.

cartelization or concentration exists. Most of these prices, especially wages, show a greater resistance to downward than to upward movements, but when inflation is in its early stages or is gathering speed, wages and "administered" prices are likely to lag behind the general rise, thus becoming increasingly underpriced, or at least less overpriced than they would otherwise have been. This "stickiness" arises from the slowness with which labor contracts are renegotiated, from a tendency to think in terms of money rather than real rewards, and from a desire not to disturb customer relationships by too frequent changes in prices.

There are other influences affecting price formation that may tend to alter the degree of underpricing or overpricing of certain items. For example, there is probably a tendency for wages of more than the "target" degree of scarcity to rise faster and faster the longer that scarcity is maintained. More important and better established are (a) the tendency to adjust wages, with a longer or shorter time-lag, to compensate for changes in the cost of living, (b) the tendency to maintain customary relativities between the wages earned in different occupations, (c) the tendency to maintain proportionality between the prices of manufactured goods and their variable unit costs, and (d) the tendency to maintain a more or less fixed relationship between farm prices and the prices the farmer pays for industrial goods.

Tendency (a) comes increasingly into operation as inflation proceeds. Its effect, as we shall see, is to reduce any underpricing of labor that may have arisen from the sluggishness previously discussed, and possibly to promote overpricing. Tendency (b) also has the effect of reducing underpricing and promoting overpricing of labor by extending to other types of labor the wage advances granted to those types for which the pressure of demand on supply is greatest. Tendency (c) may operate, as we shall see, according to circumstances in the direction of promoting overpricing or underpricing. Tendency (d), which as a rule depends on the action of the state, is frequently inoperative at early stages of inflation when farm prices are in any case above parity, but may operate to promote overpricing at a time when attempts are being made to restore price stability.

The manner in which these various mechanisms, acting in conjunction with demand pressures, operate on prices can be shown only by the construction of a model such as is discussed in a later section of this paper.

EFFECTS OF CHANGES
IN UNDERPRICING

The following two sections contain an analysis of the effects on the price level of final output of once-and-for-all changes in the degree of underpricing or overpricing of labor and of various categories of products, respectively, on the assumption that the supply of money is given. Alternative assumptions are made regarding the price flexibility of items other than those whose prices are initially affected by the changes under examination. These changes should be thought of as superimposed on a general upward movement of prices and money supply, and when particular prices are said, for short, to be "reduced", "increased," or "held constant," this must be understood not in an absolute sense but relative to the price trend that would otherwise have prevailed. The purpose of this static analysis is to facilitate the understanding of dynamic models—not only that discussed in a later section, but any other that the reader may construct for himself.

Let us first consider the effects of increases in underpricing such as will occur during the early phases of an inflation when prices of certain factors and products lag behind the rise in their competitive market values.

Underpricing of any type of labor or product will usually be associated with a shortage, that is, an excess of demand over supply, in that type of labor or product.[5] The fixing of an artificially low profit margin at any stage of production is likely to lead to underpricing of the product.

Any reduction in wages involving emergence of or increase in labor shortage is likely to reduce the price level of final output, even if all prices other than wages are freely determined on competitive markets. This is not due to any increase in output—which if anything is likely to be adversely affected by the diseconomies resulting from "hoarding" of labor and its misallocation—but rather to a reduction in the velocity of circulation and hence in monetary demand. The increased underpricing of labor will involve a transfer of income from workers to employers, hence from low savers to high savers, which will enhance the aggregate

---

[5] In exceptional cases of underpricing, particularly in public utilities, output may be held at a level sufficient to satisfy the entire, artificially enhanced demand, even though marginal output has to be produced at a loss. This case is not further considered in the present paper.

propensity to save and reduce the propensity to consume. While the profitability of existing capital will be increased, that of new investment is unlikely to be affected.[6] The transfer of income to entrepreneurs will facilitate direct investment and may increase the amount of investment that will be undertaken at a given interest rate, but this increase is unlikely to fully offset the decline in consumption by workers. The net effect of lowering wages will thus probably be to make interest rates, velocity of circulation, level of monetary demand, and price level of final output all lower than they would otherwise have been. The reduction in the price level, however, will be proportionately far less than the reduction in wage rates.[7]

We have been assuming product prices to be competitively determined. If labor is in short supply products cannot be overpriced,[8] but they can be underpriced. If the products at the final stage in production are underpriced (i.e., in short supply) and unaffected by wage movements, a fall in wages will somewhat reduce demand for, and shortage of, the products in question. In the more probable event that product prices are determined by profit margins that are somewhat inflexible in absolute or percentage terms, a fall in wages will automatically be transmitted to the prices of intermediate and finished products and will increase the shortage (underpricing) of these products rather than of labor itself.

Consider now the effect of increased underpricing of particular products, assuming wages and the prices of other products to be competitively determined.

A reduction in the price of intermediate goods[9] involving an increased shortage of such goods will have effects similar to those of a reduction

---

[6] The technical possibilities for substituting capital for labor and the marginal productivity of labor remain the same as before. Assuming no change in the relative prices of investment goods and other goods the relationship between the cost of additional investment goods and the value of the product of labor saved will thus remain unchanged.

[7] The decline in money demand necessary to bring about a fall in the price level proportionate to that in wages is greater than the decline in payrolls. And the actual decline in demand will be considerably less than the decline in payrolls since (a) part of the income transferred from the workers will be spent on consumption and direct investment by entrepreneurs and (b) the decline in interest rates will stimulate investment.

[8] To raise the price of products above the competitive price would reduce demand and output and, with fixed technical coefficients, reduce employment. But if there is unemployment there cannot be shortage of labor.

[9] That is, materials, semimanufactures, and even manufactures before the stage of sale to consumers or investors.

in the price of labor in short supply. Since, however, the transfer of income will be, not from workers in general to employers in general, but from workers and employers in the earlier stages of production to employers at the later stages, the effect of a given transfer in dampening aggregate demand and reducing the price of final output will be even smaller.

A reduction in the price of finished goods in short supply will have little if any effect on income distribution. However, there will be incentive effects on the inducement to invest and propensity to consume, tending to reduce the flow of monetary demand.

If the price of all investment goods is reduced, the demand for and price of consumption goods will decline through the action of the Keynesian "multiplier" to almost the same extent as those of investment goods.

Again, if the prices of all consumer goods are reduced, investment goods prices will tend to decline as well, though to a lesser extent than the prices of consumer goods. The reduction in consumer prices and incomes will reduce quasirents and hence the profit on new investment, and, were interest rates constant, investment goods prices would be reduced in proportion. But the decline in incomes relative to the holding of money balances will bring down interest rates and mitigate the reduction in investment expenditure.

If a certain proportion of final output consists of commodities whose prices are competitively determined and that hence do not participate in the increase in underpricing, its effect on the value of output will be reduced by more than this proportion since at least a part of the expenditure saved on the underpriced goods will be diverted to those that remain subject to competitive pricing.

A reduction in price confined to particular classes of investment goods in short supply is fairly certain to lead to *some* net reduction in investment expenditure and, hence through the action of the "multiplier," in consumption expenditure also. Since expenditure on investment goods in short supply will be reduced by the reduction in their price, overall investment expenditure could only be maintained if expenditure on those investment goods that are competitively priced were to increase to a corresponding extent. This, however, would drive up the prices of the latter and thus reduce the marginal profit rate to be earned through investing in their purchase. To maintain the level of investment expenditure in the face of this decline in the profit rate, it would be necessary to reduce interest rates. This, however, would entail a decline in the velocity of circulation, which is incompatible with the maintenance of investment— and total—expenditure. Investment expenditure must therefore, on balance, be reduced.

An increase in underpricing confined to particular types of consumer goods, on the other hand, is much less likely to effect a significant net decline in expenditure. True, the transfer of expenditure from underpriced consumer goods to those subject to competitive pricing will force up the price of, and reduce the marginal utility of money expenditure on, the latter. But only if, and to the extent that, the reduction in marginal utility of expenditure is expected to be temporary will there be any tendency for total consumption expenditure to decline and only if consumption expenditure is reduced will velocity of circulation, total expenditure, and prices in general fall below what they would otherwise have been.

It has been assumed, thus far, that labor is subject to competitive pricing and that wages will decline[10] *pari passu* with finished goods prices in order to maintain full employment. If, as is in the short run more probable, money wages are unaffected by the decline in product prices, any reduction in price of finished goods will reduce profits and increase the propensity to consume. This will make still smaller the decline in aggregate consumer expenditure associated with any given reduction in price of underpriced finished goods.

The foregoing analysis has run in terms of increases in underpricing. Decreases in underpricing, such as occur in the later stages of inflation, have the opposite results. Increases (relative to trend) in the wages paid to labor in short supply, and to a lesser extent increases in the prices of intermediate products in short supply, lead to inflationary changes in the distribution of income; increases in the prices of investment goods in short supply to increases in the value of investment relative to output; and increases in the prices of consumer goods in short supply to increases (probably slight) in the propensity to consume.

---

[10] The reader may be reminded that this "decline" is conceived not absolutely but relative to the trend that wages would have followed in the absence of the change in underpricing.

EFFECTS OF CHANGES
IN OVERPRICING

Overpricing of any type of labor will usually be associated with un-employment or short time in the occupation in question, but it may also find expression in abnormally low labor productivity or in a diversion of labor to less productive occupations. Overpricing of products may sometimes find expression in the piling up of abnormally high inventories but is more usually associated with restriction of output and an un-economically low utilization of productive equipment, that is, with an output level at which price exceeds marginal cost.

The consequences of changes in overpricing are not closely analogous to those of changes in underpricing. When, in the earlier stages of infla-tion, decreases in overpricing are succeeded by increases in underpricing, a fundamental alteration takes place in the inflationary mechanism, and the same is true in the later stages of inflation when decreases in under-pricing are followed by increases in overpricing. Whereas changes in underpricing predominantly affect money demand, changes in overpricing affect supply as well as demand.

Consider, first, the effects of an increase in wages, involving an increase in the overpricing of labor, on the assumption that all other factors and products are priced on competitive markets. Let us ignore, for the time being, any effect on the flow of monetary demand. Even in those condi-tions the rise in wages will tend to raise the price of finished products by provoking a decline both in the employment of labor and in the volume of production—a mechanism that is absent in the case of a reduction in the underpricing of labor. Another way of putting this is to say that finished goods prices will rise on account of a rise in costs quite apart from any increase in monetary demand.

Since the marginal productivity of labor will increase as employment declines, the rise in finished goods prices, under competitive conditions, will be proportionately less than that of wage rates. Whether finished goods prices will increase or decline relative to wage costs, and whether in consequence the share of wages in the national income will fall or rise, will depend on whether the elasticity of substitution between hired labor and all other factors taken together is above or below unity. In the short run the elasticity of substitution between hired labor and other factors is probably less than unity especially in the vicinity of full employment.

Thus far it has been assumed that the magnitude of the flow of money demand will be unaffected by the rise in wages. In fact demand is almost, though not quite, certain to increase even if the rise in prices is not allowed to evoke any increase in the supply of money.

As employment, output, and real income decline there will be an increase in the ratio of consumption to income, for three reasons: (a) The proportion of his income that the average individual consumes probably increases as his real income declines; (b) The increase in the share of wages in the national income that, as we have seen, is likely to take place, will tend to raise consumption. This, however, is not likely to be very important since the decline in the share of nonwage incomes is likely to fall not so much on the firms employing wage labor as on landholders and agriculturists, whose marginal propensity to consume may be little lower than that of wage earners; (c) The rise in unemployment will involve increased net expenditures by social insurance funds or transfers to the unemployed from taxpayers with a lower marginal propensity to consume.

On the other hand, the fall in output and real income will tend, with interest rates and scarcity of money unchanged, to bring about a reduction in real investment. In the short run, however, investment plans are probably not very sensitive to variations in current output and profits and the tendency to a fall in real investment will probably not go so far as to involve a decline in the ratio of investment to income, still less a decline in that ratio great enough to offset the decline in the savings ratio.[11] It will therefore be necessary for interest rates—and money scarcity in general—to rise in order to curtail investment plans, and such a rise will evoke an increase in the velocity of circulation and hence in the flow of money demand.

There can be little doubt but that a given proportionate rise in wages will effect a bigger increase in product prices if labor is initially overpriced than if it is initially underpriced. In the former case prices rise in response to changes in supply as well as in demand, and if the demand

[11] If investment were more responsive than savings to changes in real output and income, the economic system would be highly unstable since there would be no equilibrium level of output corresponding to a given rate of interest.

effects are smaller in the former than in the latter case this is largely because the distributional changes are less marked. In other words, this occurs because prices *do* rise more nearly in proportion to wages in the former case than in the latter.

The effects of increased overpricing of labor in raising the general price level for finished goods will be somewhat intensified when account is taken of the stickiness of certain nonwage elements in production costs. Profit margins in industry, insofar as they are not determined by competition, are likely to be fixed in percentage terms. This will prevent the share of profits in industrial income from declining as it would otherwise have done with reduced employment and will enhance both the rise in finished goods prices and the fall in employment and output that corresponds to a given rise in wages.

In certain sectors of industry prices might tend to rise even more than wages. For example, in cases where prices are determined on the "full cost" principle, profit margins may be actually increased as output diminishes in order to preserve a given level of real profits. Or again—and this probably affects a wider range of industries—real labor costs per unit of output may increase as output declines, because of the importance of overhead costs, because workers seek to "spread the work" as employment declines, or because employers hang on to labor that is not strictly necessary for production.

In other sectors of industry, imperfection of competition may actually moderate the price rise that would have been occasioned by a wage increase under competitive conditions. This will occur when price margins are "sticky" in absolute rather than percentage terms, and *a fortiori* when firms are reluctant to alter the absolute level of product prices. In this case price margins will decline and wages will rise at the expense of profits. On balance we may conclude that the existence of imperfect competition in various sectors of industry may not greatly alter the overall picture of the effects of wage increases on product prices that has been drawn on the assumption of perfect competition.

More importance probably attaches to the fact that raw-material prices may not be allowed to decline as they would probably tend to do under perfect competition when wages are increased and employment in industry is reduced, while attempts may be made to defend farm price parities by raising agricultural prices *pari passu* with industrial.

These reactions obviously tend to intensify the increase in finished goods prices corresponding to a given increase in wages, and hence to intensify the decline in output that will result from a given wage increase for any given level of money demand. They will probably also tend, on balance, to increase the flow of money demand.

A rise in profit margins involving increased overpricing of products, if applied in an environment in which wages are determined on competitive markets, is likely to *reduce* the prices of finished goods. Wages will decline in such a way as to prevent the emergence of unemployment, and the decline in the ratio of wages to national income will probably reduce conassumption expenditure more than it will raise investment expenditure.[12] Since output will be little affected, any significant fall in expenditure will be likely to involve a fall in the price of final output.

If, however, wage rates are "sticky" in money terms the rise in profit margins is certain to bring about a rise in finished goods prices and, in the absence of any change in the flow of money demand, output and employment will decline. It is impossible in this case to say whether the velocity of circulation, and hence the flow of money demand, will rise or fall. Insofar as the rise in profit margins is confined to industry, the decline in output will tend to induce a fall in raw-material prices, and probably food prices, which will mitigate the rise in the price level.

A rise in price, involving increased overpricing, of farm products will tend to raise the price level of final output through the withholding of farm supplies quite apart from any increase in aggregate demand. If all other goods and services are supplied under competitive conditions their prices will probably fall,[13] thus mitigating the increase in the price level of final output. If, however, wages and industrial prices are resistant to downward pressures, the supply of industrial as well as agricultural goods will probably decline and the price level of final output will rise more than if wages had been flexible.

---

[12] It is, however, not at all certain that raising profit margins, with labor competitively priced, will have a disinflationary effect—much less certain than that reducing wages of labor in short supply, with products competively priced, will have such an effect. In the latter case, as we have seen, the increase in the inducement to invest will be small. In the former case it may be very substantial. Newly invested plant may be able to reap the advantage of the high profit margin by increasing the underutilization of existing plant. This rise in the inducement to invest may even outweigh the fall in the propensity to consume.

[13] This assumes that the elasticity of substitution of farm products and industrial products is less than unity.

Since farmers have a rather high marginal propensity to spend (on consumption and farm investment) the transfer of real income from non-farmers to farmers may have little or no adverse effect on aggregate expenditure, while the reduction in overall real income will tend to raise consumption expenditure in money terms. Velocity of circulation and money expenditure may therefore increase, raising the price level further. If the rise in farm prices is implemented, not by crop restriction or destruction, but by the accumulation of surplus stocks, this will constitute a further, artificially induced, stimulus to investment. In the latter event it is uncertain whether there would be any net decline in industrial output and employment.

INFLATION MODEL WITH NONCOMPETITIVE PRICING

It is useful to construct a simplified dynamic model in order to illustrate some of the possible interactions between demand and cost influences in the inflationary process under noncompetitive conditions.

Suppose that wage changes are determined—after a time-lag required by the process of collective bargaining—by the scarcity of labor and by the trend in the cost of living, or price level of final output. More specifically, let actual wage rates at any time equal "target" wage rates at a previous time, the interval between the two times being referred to as the "adjustment lag." Then let the proportional rate of increase of target wage rates consist of two elements, one of which varies positively with the scarcity of labor,[14] while the other is a fraction of the proportional rate of increase of the price level of final output.

In this model the "aggressiveness" of labor may be measured by the level that the first or "scarcity" element in the rate of increase of target wages attains in a state of optimal labor scarcity, that is, a state of "full" but not "overfull" employment. The flexibility or "demand sensitivity" of wages will be indicated by the extent to which this element in the increase of target wages varies with variations in the degree of labor scarcity. The ratio formed by dividing the second or "cost-of-living" element in the

---

[14] By "scarcity" of labor is meant demand less supply. Scarcity may be positive or negative and is measured when positive by unfilled vacancies and when negative by unemployment or underemployment.

proportional rate of increase of target wages by the proportional rate of increase in the price level of final output indicates the degree to which workers are compensated for changes in the cost of living. This "compensation ratio" will normally be less than unity.

If finished products were competitively priced the ratio of the price level of final output to the level of money wages would vary with the degree of labor scarcity, the variation being slight when unemployment prevails but sharp when labor is in short supply. In the present model, however, it is assumed that this "price/wage ratio" will respond less strongly to changes in labor scarcity than under competitive conditions. At a "normal" level of unemployment profit margins will be above competitive levels and products will be somewhat overpriced. At higher levels of unemployment product overpricing will be still greater, but when labor is in short supply some products will probably be in short supply also. To each degree of labor under- or overpricing will thus correspond to a given degree of under- or overpricing of products.

Now assuming a constant proportional rate of increase in the money stock, and a constant real productivity of investment, there will always be some equilibrium degree of labor scarcity at which both prices and wages rise at constant proportional rates. In such an equilibrium position the proportional rate of increase of target wages will be equal to that of actual wages and equal to the sum of the proportional rates of increase of prices and of productivity, respectively. If the compensation ratio were as high as unity the "cost-of-living" element in the rate of increase of wage rates would alone be equal to the rate of increase of prices, and labor scarcity would therefore have to be such as to make the first element in wage increase equal to the rate of productivity increase. But so long as compensation is only partial the "cost-of-living" element in wage increase will fall short of the rate of price increase, and the "scarcity" element in wage increase must exceed the rate of growth of productivity if prices are to rise. The relationship between the different variables is set forth in the following formulas:

$$\frac{\dot{w}}{w} = \frac{\dot{w}_1}{w} + \frac{\dot{w}_2}{w} \tag{1}$$

when

$$\frac{\dot{w}_1}{w} = \frac{\dot{e}}{e} + \frac{\dot{p}}{p}(1 - c) \tag{2}$$

and

$$\frac{\dot{w}_2}{w} = c\frac{\dot{p}}{p}, \tag{3}$$

where $(\dot{w}_1/w)$ stands for the first or "scarcity" element, and $(\dot{w}_2/w)$ for the second or "cost-of-living" element, in the proportional rate of wage increase, $(\dot{e}/e)$ for the proportional rate of increase in productivity $(\dot{p}/p)$ for the proportional rate of increase in the price of final output, and c for the compensation ratio.

Now, since, in this equilibrium situation, the scarcity of labor and that of products are both constant, and since the anticipated profit rate is also constant,[15] the velocity of circulation of money will be constant and the proportionate rate of price increase will be equal to the proportionate rate of increase of productivity. It follows that wages will rise at the same rate as the stock of money.[16] The various elements in the rate of wage increase will then be determined in accordance with the following formulas:

$$\frac{\dot{w}_1}{w} = c\frac{\dot{e}}{e} + \frac{\dot{m}}{m}(1 - c) \tag{4}$$

and

$$\frac{\dot{w}_2}{w} = c\left(\frac{\dot{m}}{m} - \frac{\dot{e}}{e}\right), \tag{5}$$

where $(\dot{m}/m)$ stands for the proportional rate of increase of the money stock.

It will be observed from these equations that the equilibrium value of each of the elements of the rate of wage increase is determined irrespective of the aggressiveness of labor or the restrictiveness of enterprise. Thus, starting from such a position of dynamic equilibrium, if *an increase* takes place *in the "aggressiveness" of labor*, so that wages tend to rise faster than before, there will be a decline in the scarcity of labor until, at a new equilibrium position, wages are once again rising at the original rate.

The effects of the temporary acceleration of wage inflation can be deduced from what was said in previous sections about the effects of once-over wage increases.

---

[15] This follows from the fact that the real productivity of investment and the anticipated rate of price increase are both constant.

[16] This abstracts from any increase in the size of the working population.

The nature of the transition from the old equilibrium to the new will be somewhat different according as the compensation ratio is or is not negligible. If wages are insensitive to changes in the cost of living (i.e., if $c = 0$), the transition will be a relatively smooth one. There will be an acceleration in the expansion of monetary demand achieved through an increase in circulation velocity but, apart from any stimulus that may be given to the inducement to invest through anticipations of intensified inflation, the intensified expansion of money demand will not suffice to prevent some decline in labor scarcity. The inflation of prices will be intensified, though to a lesser extent than that of wages; in other words, profit margins will decline. If labor is initially underpriced and in short supply the stimulus to price inflation will be relatively slight and will be applied predominantly from the side of demand. If labor is originally overpriced and partly unemployed, the stimulus to price inflation will be about as great as the rise in wage inflation and will be largely applied from the side of cost.

As the scarcity of labor declines the rate of increase of wages will decline. The speed of wage inflation will go on falling until it reaches its initial level, corresponding to the rate of expansion of the money stock. The rate of price inflation will likewise fall to its initial level. At the new point of dynamic equilibrium labor scarcity, and possibly output, will be below their initial levels, as will be also the price–wage ratio; on the other hand, velocity of circulation will be somewhat higher than in the initial position.

The transition to the new equilibrium, however, will not be entirely straightforward. Owing to the adjustment lag of actual wages behind target wages, when labor scarcity has fallen to its new equilibrium level wages will still be rising at a rate appropriate to a somewhat higher level of labor scarcity, that is at a rate higher than the rate of monetary expansion of the money stock. This will force labor scarcity (and possibly output) temporarily below the new equilibrium levels. Labor scarcity and output will settle down at these equilibrium levels only after oscillating around them for a time.

The transitional inflation to which a given increase in labor aggressiveness gives rise will be more severe if wages are at least partially compensated for changes in the cost of living (i.e., if $c > 0$). The enhanced rate of price inflation resulting from the initial acceleration of wage inflation will then provoke a further intensification of wage inflation and so on in a spiral of rising wages and prices. Owing to the adjustment lag the transitional inflation will take time to reach its maximum intensity. As the scarcity of labor declines, however, a point will be reached at which the deceleration of the "scarcity" element in wage increase begins to outweigh the acceleration of the "cost-of-living" element, and the intensity of wage and price inflation will diminish. Finally the original rate of wage and price inflation will be restored at a lower level of labor scarcity, but only after oscillations have taken place in labor scarcity (and possibly in employment and output) more severe than would have occurred in the absence of a link between wages and the cost of living.[17]

Whether or not such a link exists, inflation will be more intense during the transition period following a rise in labor aggressiveness than in either the initial or the new equilibrium position, and this may bring about an increase in the anticipated rate of price inflation and hence in the anticipated rate of profits. In this event the transitional intensification of inflation may for a time result not in a decline but even in an increase in labor scarcity, which will further feed the inflation. Such speculative spurts in inflation, however, based as they are on the elasticity of velocity of circulation, contain, as mentioned earlier, the seeds of their own reversal.

A decline in the rate of productivity growth will, of course, increase the rate of price inflation corresponding to any given rate of wage inflation. The equilibrium rate of wage inflation, being equal to the rate of expansion of the money stock, will not be affected by the change in productivity growth, and the equilibrium rate of price inflation will therefore increase. The rise in productivity growth will also affect the inducement to invest and propensity to consume in the ways already indicated. Apart from the last-mentioned reactions, however, if there is any link between wages and the cost of living a decline in productivity growth will affect the equilibrium level of labor scarcity in the same way as, though to a lesser extent than, an increase in labor aggressiveness. By intensifying the price inflation it will raise the "cost-of-living" element in wage increase and

---

[17] The greater severity of these oscillations around the new equilibrium position is accounted for (a) by the greater violence of the transitional intensification of inflation between the old and the new equilibrium and (b) by the fact that actual wage growth at a given degree of labor scarcity lags by more than a single adjustment period behind the equilibrium rate of wage growth at that degree of scarcity.

hence necessitate a corresponding decline in the "scarcity" element. In addition to the "permanent" increase in price inflation, there will be a transitional intensification of inflation while the scarcity of labor is declining to its new equilibrium position.

An increase in the extent to which wages are compensated for changes in the cost of living will have the same sort of effect as an increase in labor aggressiveness or a decline in productivity growth in giving rise to a transitional intensification of inflation on the way to a new and lower equilibrium level of labor scarcity.

In all three of the contingencies just examined—an increase in labor aggressiveness, a slowing down in productivity growth, and an increase in the compensation ratio—the extent of the decline in labor scarcity that will ensue will depend on the demand-sensitivity of wages, that is, in the extent to which the rate of wage inflation will decline with a given decline in the scarcity of labor.[18] In all probability this sensitivity is quite high when labor is in short supply and profits are abnormally high; it is unlikely to be great when unemployment is moderate and profits still reasonably high; it may again become considerable when there is enough unemployment to undermine the power of the unions.

The following two types of causal factors will cause a temporary spurt followed by a temporary flagging in the process of inflation without permanently affecting the equilibrium rate of inflation or level of labor scarcity.

A shortening in the adjustment lag for wages will have the effect of bringing actual wages closer to "target" wages for any given rate of wage and price inflation. Suppose such a shortening is carried out gradually over a period equal to the adjustment lag itself. In the first period wages and prices will rise at more than the equilibrium rate; velocity of circulation will increase and labor scarcity will decline. In the second period wages and prices will rise less fast than in the first period (a) because of the decline in scarcity and (b) because with a compensation ratio less than unity, the rise in the "cost-of-living" element in wage increase will not be as great as the intensification of wage inflation that occurred in the first

---

[18] The greater the demand-sensitivity of profit margins, that is, the more these margins contract as scarcity of labor and products declines, the *greater* will be the transitional intensification of inflation. The reason for this "perverse" effect of reducing profit margins is discussed later.

period. Although for a time wages and prices may continue to increase faster than the money stock and labor scarcity may continue to decline, a turning-point will occur in both respects. The rate of inflation will fall below the rate of monetary expansion and labor scarcity will rise again. In the end labor scarcity will settle down at its initial level and the initial rate of inflation will be restored. Actual wages and prices will then be the same as they would have been had the inflation gone on at the original rate[19] but "target" wages will have been reduced by the cumulative effect of the temporary reduction of labor scarcity.

Suppose, now, that *an increase* takes place *in percentage profit margins in industry or in the ratio of farm prices to industrial prices*. As in the previous case, price inflation will at first exceed monetary expansion, will then slow down—for the same reason as in the previous case—until it is less than monetary expansion, and will ultimately return to the initial situation of being equal to monetary expansion.[20] Labor scarcity will first decline, then return to the original level. As a result of this excursion into subequilibrium levels of labor scarcity, wages, after equilibrium is restored, will remain somewhat lower than they would have been in the absence of the rise in profit margins or farm prices. Indeed, a rise in profit margins by raising the share of profits in the national income will probably reduce the velocity of circulation and hence effect a permanent reduction, not only in the level of money wages, but even in the level of product prices.[21] Owing to the nature of the distributional changes involved, a rise in the ratio of farm to non-farm prices is far less likely than is a rise in profit margins to involve a decline in the equilibrium level of general product prices. Indeed, if implemented through the accumulation of surplus stocks it is fairly certain to result in a velocity of circulation,

---

[19] This must be so since money supply, output, and velocity will all be the same as if no disturbance had occurred.

[20] If the initial position is one in which many finished goods are in short supply while others are produced under competitive conditions, a rise in margins might give rise to an increase in velocity with little or no decline in real demand for products. The scarcity of labor would then actually *increase* due to the rise in profit margins. As the intensified wage and price inflation reduces the range of products in short supply, however, declines in output will begin to occur that will reduce the scarcity of labor.

[21] If profit margins are raised in a situation in which products are underpriced, a small rise in margins by reducing product shortage may increase velocity of circulation. After a point, however, further increases in margins will tend to reduce velocity for the reason expressed in the text.

and hence a level of prices somewhat higher than in the initial position.

In the three cases just considered, in which a temporary inflationary phase evoking a decline in labor scarcity is followed by a disinflationary phase accompanied by a return to the original equilibrium position, the violence of the inflationary interlude and the extent of the temporary decline in labor scarcity (and possibly employment and output) will both be the greater, the greater is the magnitude of the compensation ratio.

THE ROLE OF OFFICIAL POLICY

We have seen from the preceding section that once-over changes in the pricing policies and attitudes of firms, combines, trade unions, and governments are unlikely to exercise any permanent effect on the rate of price inflation, unless and insofar as they act on the growth of the money supply. Moreover, while in some cases the effects on the velocity of circulation and on the level of employment will be enduring, in other cases these effects also will be temporary. These conclusions are based on the operations of a particular model but are likely to hold true of any model in which wage growth is to any extent sensitive to changes in the scarcity of labor.

A continuing price-inflation, therefore, can only occur if there is a continuing expansion in the stock of money. Conversely, save in the extreme case where interest rates are at those minimum levels at which the willingness to hold additional quantities of money unspent becomes indefinitely great, a continuing expansion in the stock of money, with given pricing practices, will always produce a continuous rise in prices.

It might seem, therefore, that the nature of the conditions governing pricing have little to do with the policies appropriate for the authorities to adopt with respect to inflation, and that in all cases the course appropriate from an economic, though difficult from a political, standpoint is to curtail the expansion in the flow of money demand and in the stock of money.

Insofar as the prevention of inflation is regarded as in all circumstances the overriding objective of policy, this conclusion appears to be correct. The significance of noncompetitive pricing lies in the possibility that in certain circumstances it may render disinflationary financial policies so damaging to savings and investment, or even to employment, output, and consumption, that it becomes doubtful how strongly and how quickly they should be applied and whether they should not be supplemented by other policies designed to act more directly on prices.

In order to evaluate the importance and relevance of this consideration let us examine the effects, under conditions of noncompetitive pricing, of varying the rate of expansion of the money stock.

In terms of the economic model considered in the previous section, any permanent increase in the rate of expansion of the money stock will in the end bring about a corresponding increase in the rate of growth of money wages. To some extent this will be effected through a rise in the "cost-of-living" element in wage growth. But so long as the compensation ratio is less than unity there will also have to be some increase in the "scarcity" element in wage growth,[22] and, consequently, some increase in the scarcity of labor, whether in the form of reduced unemployment or increased shortage. This effect will be the greater (a) the smaller is the compensation ratio and (b) the smaller is the sensitivity of wage growth with respect to changes in labor scarcity. The new and higher equilibrium level of labor scarcity will be associated with a new and higher level of product scarcity also, and with a new and lower equilibrium level of velocity of circulation.

In addition to the permanent increase, there will also be a temporary increase in the scarcity of labor and products, provided that the movement in actual wages lags behind that of target wages. When labor scarcity first attains its new equilibrium level, actual wages and prices will not yet be rising as fast as the money stock. The "scarcity" element in wage increase will reflect the lower level of labor scarcity prevailing one period earlier while the "cost-of-living" element will reflect even lower and earlier levels of scarcity.[23]

In consequence, the scarcity of labor and products will go on increasing and the velocity of circulation will go on declining, past the new equilibrium point, until such time as the decline in the "scarcity" element in wage growth brings about a turn of the tide, and labor scarcity once more declines toward the new equilibrium level. The *permanent* increase

---

[22] See equation (4).

[23] When there is a lag of actual wages behind target wages and actual prices compared to actual wages, the "cost-of-living" element in wage growth approaches its equilibrium relationship to any given value of the "scarcity" element in wage growth only gradually and asymptotically over an indefinite time period.

in labor scarcity that will result from a given increase in the rate of monetary expansion will be the greater the smaller is the extent to which wages are compensated for changes in the cost of living, and the *temporary* increase in labor scarcity will be the greater the longer is the time-lag of actual behind target wages.

Now it is probable that the extent to which wages are adjusted in compensation for price changes, and the time-lag with which wages are so adjusted, are both dependent on the degree of inflation itself. The faster prices rise beyond a very moderate rate of increase, the more fully will wages be compensated for changes in the cost of living, and the faster prices rise beyond a more rapid rate of increase the shorter will be the time-lag of adjustment. It follows from this that whereas a rise in the rate of monetary expansion from a position of price stability may well yield a permanent increase in labor scarcity, a similar intensification of an inflation that is already substantial may yield little or no permanent increase in labor scarcity, while finally an intensification of an inflation that is already rapid may yield little even of a temporary increase in labor scarcity.

The desirability of a given increase in labor scarcity depends very much on whether it takes the form primarily of a decline in overpricing (unemployment) or of an increase in underpricing (labor shortage) and also on the extent to which it is accompanied by increased underpricing (shortage) of products. The only merit of an increase in the shortage of labor lies in the fact that the increase in the proportion of nonwage to wage incomes with which it is associated tends to bring about an increase in the proportionate of national income that is saved and hence makes possible an accelerated rate of development. The importance of this type of "forced saving" no doubt considerably exceeds that resulting from the lag between the earning and the spending of income. As against this advantage of an increase in labor shortage must be set the disadvantages that it will entail, namely, (a) increased inequality in the distribution of income and consumption and (b) increased distortion of economic incentives. When labor and products are in short supply their allocation and utilization are to some extent arbitrary, wasteful, and irrational. Moreover, shortages brought about by an intensification of inflation are likely to be more acute in some sections of the economy than in others—a circumstance that tends to aggravate their disturbing effects. On the other hand, an increase in labor scarcity that takes the form of a decline in unemployment will carry with it the advantages not merely of evoking additional savings and investment but also of permitting an increase in consumption; not only will the national product be increased by absorbing the unemployed, but the utilization of the previously employed manpower will probably improve. In addition, there are intangible but important gains in the form of increased security and increased self-respect among the working people.

The foregoing argument has related to an increase in the rate of expansion of the money stock. A curtailment in the rate of monetary expansion will have the opposite effects. It will tend to bring about (a) a decline in labor (and product) scarcity that will be "permanent" unless it gives rise—as it probably will in the end—to a lossening of the link between wages and the cost of living and (b) an essentially temporary decline in labor (and product) scarcity. The more serious is the initial rate of inflation, the smaller are likely to be both the permanent and the temporary declines in labor scarcity, and the higher the initial degree of labor scarcity the more desirable is any decline that does occur.

Disinflationary financial policies should be continued so long as they do not threaten to give rise to a significant amount of permanent unemployment. They should not be abandoned at the first sign of unemployment, which may well be of a temporary character. However, when conditions in the labor market are such that an excessive degree of price and wage inflation persists despite the fact that substantial unemployment has prevailed for some time, a severe policy dilemma may arise. In this case much depends on the size of the compensation ratio. If the inflation has gone on so long that wage–price links affording a high degree of compensation for cost-of-living changes are widespread, a further reduction in the rate of monetary expansion may be defended as involving little additional unemployment. On the other hand, where cost-of-living compensation plays but a minor role there will be a case for at least postponing the application of a disinflationary policy which could restore price stability only at the cost of a substantial loss in employment and output.

In such circumstances the question arises whether the government should not seek to reconcile the objectives of full employment and price stability by influencing the process of wage and price determination itself. There are various methods that might be adopted to this end.

One method that is frequently resorted to is the subsidization of consumer goods, particularly those consumed by wage earners. If the subsidies are financed in large part by taxation of profits and higher incomes they are quite likely to lead to some decline in the rate of growth of target wages, not only in money but even in real terms, inasmuch as part of the reason why workers demand increased wages is to maintain or improve their position relative to other groups in the community. Nevertheless, to effect a permanent increase in the levels of employment and output that are compatible with price stability would call for a continual increase in such subsidization. The effect of this would be intolerable in the long run, since if financed by taxation it would call for a continual redistribution of income in favor of labor, while if financed by government borrowing it would entail a progressive decline in the proportion of investment to consumption. Therefore, subsidization is of value only as a means of meeting temporary situations, such as adverse shifts in the terms of trade, or else as a means of holding the wage–price spiral in check pending the application of more fundamental measures of control.

The same objection, that its efficacy is merely temporary, is equally applicable to any attempt that may be made, whether through controls or other antimonopolistic policies, to reduce consumer prices or profit margins without recourse to subsidization. Such policies have to be widely applied if they are to be of any use in controlling consumer prices. They can only hold up the wage–price spiral for so long as it is feasible to continue squeezing profit margins, which is probably not for very long. The compression of monopolistic profit margins may, of course, be desirable in itself, quite apart from any disinflationary effect. Moreover, some measure of control over prices and profits may well be indispensable politically as a means of inducing the workers to acquiesce in wage control. But it is the propensity of target real wages to rise excessively that is the key to the difficulty of maintaining full employment without inflation, and it is unlikely that this propensity can be overcome without some direct official intervention in the process of wage determination.

This is not the place to discuss the possibilities and dangers of different forms of wage control. A measure of control may be exercised informally, by remonstrating with the unions, or by stiffening the backs of employers, as well as by the exercise of legal authority. If legal means are applied they may be directed toward lengthening the process of negotiation, or limiting the extent of wage increases that may be granted, or they may go so far as to prescribe the actual wages that are to be paid. In any event the crucial—and most difficult—problem is to limit increases in the generality of wages while allowing for the changes in relative wages that are necessary to attract labor into the proper channels or to satisfy the requirements of equity.

Assuming that it is feasible to so control the process of wage determination as to permit a reconciliation of full employment and price stability, this does not in any way remove the necessity for controlling the rate of expansion of the money stock. In the absence of an appropriate monetary policy prices might rise excessively even if wages did not, or if prices also were controlled product shortages might be intensified. The true relation between monetary policy on the one hand and price and wage policy on the other is complementary, not competitive. There may be occasions where the case for permitting a mild degree of inflation to prevail as a means of increasing the level of economic activity is strengthened by the consideration that if the inflation should tend to get out of hand it can be curbed by an effective wage policy. There may even be occasions where to permit inflation to continue may be the best means of persuading all concerned of the necessity for an effective wage policy. With these qualifications, however, the basic relationship of wage policy to financial policy is that an effective wage policy would tend to remove any objections there might otherwise be to the pursuit of a disinflationary financial policy.

CLASSIFICATION OF INFLATIONS

In the light of the foregoing analysis it is possible to venture certain conclusions as to the feasibility and relevance of classifying inflations with reference to demand and to cost, respectively.

It seems necessary to distinguish two principles of classification. According to the first principle price inflations may be divided into three categories: (a) demand determined, (b) cost determined, and (c) cost-and-demand determined. According to the second principle inflation may be classified as (i) demand induced, and (ii) cost induced.

Inflations that occur at full employment or at a fixed degree of employment of resources, with consumer prices perfectly flexible, may be said to be "*demand determined.*" This will be the case where consumer prices are arrived at by perfect competition and where all factors and intermediate products are either competitively priced or underpriced or, if overpriced, are subject to a constant degree of monopolistic restriction of supply.

Inflations that occur when consumer prices are insensitive to variations in demand may be said to be purely *"cost determined."* This condition is satisfied when, in all branches of production, wages are uninfluenced by the degree of labor scarcity and profit-margins are unaffected by the level of demand or by the degree of underpricing of labor. Inflation would then take place as a result of attempts to secure mutually incompatible levels of real or relative incomes, such as in the form of a wage–price spiral.

All other inflations constitute a mixture of demand-determined and cost-determined inflation, because wages, profit margins, and farm prices, though not entirely flexible, are in some degree influenced by demand. This is, of course, by far the commonest category of inflation.

Demand-determined inflations may also be said to be *"demand induced."* Cost-determined inflations, however, cannot always be said to be *"cost induced,"* or to exemplify a *"cost–push."* Thus it may well happen that though a moderate wage–price spiral is in progress money demand is high enough to keep both labor and consumer goods underpriced (i.e., in short supply) and is expanding as fast as or faster than prices. Then only the fact that the system is cost determined keeps the inflation from being as severe as it would otherwise be.

Among the inflations of mixed determination it is natural to attempt to distinguish those inflations, or phases of inflation, that are predominantly demand induced from those that are predominantly cost induced. The criterion in this case might be the trend in the scarcity of labor and of products. Inflationary phases associated with growing overpricing (or declining underpricing[24]) would be deemed cost induced, while those associated with declining overpricing (or growing underpricing)[24] would be deemed demand induced.

---

[24] Only changes in the underpricing of finished goods are relevant here and even in the case of finished goods a decline in underpricing involves not only a rise in costs but also an equivalent expansion—or liberation—of demand. But the expansion of demand as well as the rise in prices may be regarded as induced by the rise in costs.

First published in International Monetary Fund, *Staff Papers* (November 1963). This paper is an expanded version of a lecture delivered on March 18, 1963 to the Graduate Seminar in International Economics, University of Michigan, Ann Arbor, Michigan.

If this conventional criterion is adopted, however, it is necessary to bear in mind that either type of inflation may mask a potentiality for the other. A slackening in the growth of money demand may reveal the underlying upward pressure of costs and initiate a phase of cost-induced inflation. Conversely, the cessation of an increase in overpricing may reveal an underlying pressure of demand that will perpetuate the inflation though at a lower rate. It follows from our analysis that cost-induced inflation is of an essentially temporary character. Even without any change in psychological attributes or institutional arrangements the increase in unemployment to which it leads will itself suffice to bring it to an end.

On the other hand, not only does increased overpricing tend to speed up the turnover of money and flow of demand but in many cases that, on our definition, lie on the borderline between demand-induced and cost-induced inflation, the expansion in demand is motivated by the desire on the part of monetary authorities to defeat or offset tendencies to overpricing and the associated unemployment and underproduction.

The distinction between demand-induced and cost-induced inflation is frequently held to entail important consequences for policy, to the effect that while it is appropriate to deal with a demand-induced inflation by curtailing the expansion of money demand, a cost-induced inflation should be dealt with by other action bearing more directly on costs and prices. As we have seen in the previous section, however, it is not so much the trend in the scarcity of labor and products that is important from the standpoint of policy as the absolute level of that scarcity, and specifically the level of actual and potential unemployment.

9

DEVELOPMENTS IN THE
INTERNATIONAL
PAYMENTS SYSTEM

I WOULD LIKE to discuss the way in which views regarding an appropriate system of adjustment for international disequilibria have developed in the postwar period and may develop in the future. In particular, I shall inquire how these views are likely to respond to recent developments in the international economic environment. However, a brief outline of the major system of thought that prevailed on these matters at the end of World War II will provide a useful backdrop to our discussion. In what I have to say, I shall be concerned primarily with the means of dealing with disequilibria between industrial countries; a separate lecture would be required to consider the special problems of the less developed parts of the world.

THE POSTWAR ORTHODOXY

In the later years of the war, and in the early postwar years, there prevailed a novel orthodoxy regarding the type of international payments arrangement that should obtain after a transition period of postwar relief and reconstruction—an orthodoxy squarely opposed to the old faith in the gold standard that had determined international financial policy after

First published in International Monetary Fund, *Staff Papers* (November 1963). This paper is an expanded version of a lecture delivered on March 18, 1963 to the Graduate Seminar in International Economics, University of Michigan, Ann Arbor, Michigan.

World War I. This new orthodoxy, largely the work of Maynard Keynes, was incorporated, with some admixture of U.S. views not entirely compatible with it, into the Articles of Agreement of the IMF and the General Agreement on Tariffs and Trade (GATT).

The essential presupposition of the new doctrine was that national authorities were to be free to direct their monetary and fiscal policies toward purely domestic objectives which, it was hoped, would be those of maintaining full employment without price inflation. The maintenance of external equilibrium was to be entrusted, after the transitional period, to three or four main instruments: (a) exchange-rate adjustment, (b) the use of gold and foreign exchange reserves and other forms of compensatory official financing, including drawings on the IMF, (c) restriction of capital outflow, and (d) restriction of imports. There were, however, to be no exchange restrictions that would impede multilateral settlement of current transactions.

Of these instruments of adjustment, only capital restriction was to be applied entirely at the discretion of national governments. Exchange rates were to be altered on the initiative of the government concerned, but only with the consent of the international community as expressed through the IMF, and only for the purpose of correcting a fundamental disequilibrium. Temporary disequilibria were to be met by the use of external liquidity— that is to say, by drawing on national reserves and, within prescribed limits, on the resources of the IMF. Import restriction was to be applied only to the extent that was allowed by the contracting parties to the GATT, with the advice of the IMF, to be necessary to safeguard the balance of payments, or more precisely, to defend the reserves, of the restricting country. Save during the postwar transitional period, any restrictions on imports were to be on a nondiscriminatory basis.

The general aim of this system was to adjust payments disequilibria with the least possible impairment of full employment, of freedom of international trade, and, in a sense, of exchange stability. It was designed to avoid the faults alike of the gold standard, of Schachtianism, and of the currency chaos of the 1930s. The system was remarkable for simplicity and, up to a point, for logical consistency. However, not only was it admittedly unsuitable to the circumstances of the postwar reconstruction period—so that provision had to be made for a special and much more permissive regime during that period—but even for application to more normal times it had grave weaknesses, some of which were visible from the start.

In the first place, although the system was intended, among other things, to promote exchange stability and to minimize restrictions on international trade, it imposed no specific obligation on countries to refrain from inflationary domestic policies that might necessitate undue resort to devaluation and/or import restriction. The IMF could protest to members about their monetary and economic policies. It could deny the use of its resources to countries that might be held to be using them in a manner contrary to IMF purposes, in that they were *not* using them to avoid policies destructive of national or international prosperity. But inflation was never mentioned in set terms.

A second weakness lay in the provisions regarding exchange-rate adjustment, which could take place only on the initiative of the member and with the concurrence of the IMF. This arrangement, while admittedly designed to prevent competitive devaluations of the sort that had occurred during the 1930s, was held by some British critics to be too rigid to enable exchange rates to play the role that properly belonged to them in a system in which monetary policies were directed single-mindedly toward the maintenance of domestic full employment. True, the IMF was obliged to agree to any changes in rates that might be required to correct a fundamental disequilibrium, even if that disequilibrium had been brought about by perverse domestic policies, such as inflation. But, in the first place, "fundamental disequilibrium" is a fuzzy and ambiguous concept. To an economist, an equilibrium rate of exchange, even a long-term equilibrium rate, is something that is liable to change, gradually but continuously, with changing international relationships with respect to productivity, wage levels, normal capital exports, normal degree of employment, and so on. Such a gradual slipping away from fundamental equilibrium is particularly likely to ensue if monetary and fiscal policies are determined without regard to the balance of payments situation. However, all architects of the IMF agreement, including the British, were clearly of opinion that par values of currencies, once established, should stay put for longish periods of time, and be changed only at infrequent intervals—that is to say, when fundamental disequilibrium in the economist's sense has become substantial. As Professor Meade, among others, has pointed out,[1] this system of the "adjustable peg," as he calls it, invites disequilibrating speculative capital movements at periods when a fundamental disequilibrium appears to be developing but has not yet reached a point at which an exchange adjustment will be made to correct it. However, in the early postwar period, when capital controls were widely and vigorously applied, this danger did not, perhaps, appear to be too serious.

A more important defect of the system of exchange-rate adjustment, as soon appeared, was the fact that countries might not wish to devalue their currencies, even when—perhaps as a result of inflationary pressure— these had clearly got out of line. Since overvaluation, by creating payments difficulties, entitled deficit countries to impose import restrictions against surplus countries without fear of retaliation, thereby permitting them to maintain relatively favorable terms of trade, the incentive to devalue, at any rate in a world in which the unemployment problem had been overcome, might be unduly weak.

In these circumstances, the system was likely to tolerate the perpetuation of disequilibria, and thus to put an undue strain on the remaining instruments of adjustment, the use of liquidity or compensatory official financing, and the application of import restrictions on balance of payments grounds.

Owing to U.S. influence, the role of international liquidity in the postwar adjustment mechanism as actually established was much more modest than had been envisaged by Keynes in his Clearing Union plan. Not only were IMF quotas smaller than those of the Clearing Union but there was very soon established an interpretation of the Articles of Agreement of the IMF under which the use of these quotas was considerably less automatic than many countries—though not the U.S. delegation— thought had been agreed at Bretton Woods. On the other hand, the stock of "two-way" liquidity, in the form of gold, foreign exchange reserves, and IMF drawing rights, was supplemented, to meet the special needs of the reconstruction period, by "one-way" facilities for official compensatory financing in the form of long-term U.S. loans to the United Kingdom, France, and other countries, and, later, in the form of Marshall

---

[1] J. E. Meade, "The Case for Variable Exchange Rates," *The Three Banks Review* (September 1955) no. 27, pp. 3–27.

Plan aid. (I call these "one-way" facilities because their use did not give rise to liquid claims in the hands of the lending country.) Whether there was too much or too little international liquidity of all sorts in the early postwar years is impossible to say; the relevant criteria point in opposite directions. For the purpose of minimizing the need for payments restrictions on imports, there was too little liquidity; for the purpose of discouraging inflationary policies and promoting adequate adjustment of exchange rates or relative cost levels, there was too much. Given the somewhat perverse attitudes of governments toward the remaining instruments for adjusting payments disequilibria, and given the overpermissive character of the transitional period arrangements, of which I speak later, no satisfactory treatment of the problem of international liquidity was then possible.

The outcome of these various weaknesses, in the early postwar years, was an excessive reliance on restriction of imports and restriction of capital outflows as a means of keeping external payments and external receipts in balance. This tendency was encouraged by the special circumstances of those years: the urgent need to rebuild the war-shattered economies; the fervor with which full employment policies were pursued, especially in the northern European countries; the existence of a functioning apparatus of controls over trade and payments, backed up by a system of rationing of consumer goods and allocation of raw materials; and, finally, the existence, under the IMF and GATT agreements of a transitional period regime, especially permissive of restrictions and discriminations of all sorts. Even in its posttransitional aspect, however, the IMF-cum-GATT system would have encouraged this tendency by permitting capital controls unconditionally, and by authorizing countries whose reserves were low or falling to impose import restrictions for an indefinite period without much fear of retaliation from surplus countries. It is also cause for regret that the type of import limitation for which the greatest facilities were given, namely, quantitative restriction on imports, was precisely that which was least amenable to a market test, and hence most arbitrary in its incidence. Had special import surcharges or special import exchange rates been substituted for quantitative restrictions as the preferred instrument for dealing with temporary payments difficulties, it would have been easier to distribute scarce foreign exchange among the different types of imports in a rational way, easier to avoid meaningless discrimination, and, with the revenue that would have accrued to the authorities, easier to counteract inflationary pressures. But balance of payments import duties were regarded with aversion by ministries of commerce and were not permitted by the GATT, while multiple exchange rates were condemned by monetary authorities, both national and international, with even more severity than were quantitative restrictions.

THE TRANSITIONAL PERIOD REGIME

I do not wish to dwell on the arrangements for international payments adjustment that prevailed during the so-called postwar transitional period. As far as practically all the industrial countries are concerned, these arrangements have lapsed with the restoration of convertibility and are— one hopes—not very relevant to the problems of the future. The essence of the transitional system[2] was that countries were allowed to retain, and even adapt to changing circumstances, restrictions on imports, restrictions on payment for imports—including, naturally, restrictions on the transfer of import proceeds to third country accounts—and hence the whole network of trade and payments agreements based on the principle of bilateral or regional balancing.

One point about this system, or lack of system, is not always realized, namely, that even if it had not already come into existence before the IMF and GATT started their operations, its emergence was inevitable once it was granted that import restriction was an appropriate means of meeting the widespread payments difficulties that resulted from a combination of heavy demand pressures, unevenly distributed as between Europe and America, and a distorted structure of initial par values.

Briefly, the connection is this. If many countries are simultaneously applying import restrictions on payments grounds, and if they seek to apply these restrictions in a nondiscriminatory fashion, they will find that they are restricting imports from each other and thus worsening each other's payments problems. To provide each other with an incentive to liberalize their mutual trade, it was natural for pairs of such countries in the early postwar years to set up financial arrangements under which the proceeds of exports from one partner to the other could not be converted into hard currency but had to be used for payment of imports from the other, or else allowed to accumulate. The distortion of trade involved in

---

[2] As sanctioned under IMF, Article XIV and GATT, Article XIV.

such bilateral balancing was, of course, considerable, but it was deemed preferable to the curtailment involved in putting all trade on a "hard-currency" basis. The existence of currency inconvertibility was often invoked as a justification for trade discrimination. The true relation was the contrary; inconvertibility could be justified, if at all, only as providing a financial climate propitious to trade discrimination.

The basic trouble, as I said, was that of differential inflation and distorted exchange rates. A number of tendencies in the early postwar years induced industrial countries other than the United States to maintain exchange rates that were overvalued relative to the dollar. On the one hand, the reconstruction effort in Europe naturally tended to generate inflationary pressures. On the other hand, special circumstances rendered devaluation temporarily unattractive. In the first place, given the prevalence of underpricing and associated supply shortages, little expansion in export volumes could be expected from devaluation to offset its adverse influence on the terms of trade.[3] Again, overvaluation and the balance of payments difficulties resulting therefrom not only entitled a country to impose discriminatory import restrictions without fear of retaliation from the hard currency countries but even tended to enhance its claim to aid in the form of grants and loans. It is no wonder that the transitional period arrangements gradually withered away only in the mid-1950s and were still technically applicable to European countries fifteen years after the end of World War II.

These arrangements might have continued to be effective in practice even longer than they actually did but for a chance combination of circumstances. The existence of the sterling area meant that a large part of the world could finance its payments deficits by converting balances held in the United Kingdom. A drain of this sort, together with the United Kingdom's own deficit, drove that country to devalue in 1949, during the recession of that year, when it seemed that the period of postwar inflation and shortage might be coming to an end, and an adjustment of exchange rates might therefore be of value in promoting exports. Sterling devaluation, in its turn, brought about devaluation on the part of continental countries. Had all of these countries been able to foresee the great expan-

---

[3] This was one of the considerations that led the IMF to agree to many initial par values that it recognized as unlikely to be realistic in the long run.

sion in U.S. demand caused by the Korean conflict, they would probably have postponed their devaluations. However that may be, the adjustment of relative costs then brought about, reinforced by the fact that productivity in Europe tended to grow faster than in the United States, bore fruit in the middle 1950s, when improving payments situations made it possible for European countries to gradually free their imports from restrictions imposed on payments grounds.

I do not wish to dwell on the process of liberalization and restoration of convertibility, which began by being confined to the transactions of European countries with each other and with other soft currency areas and was later extended to their transactions with the dollar area.

THE REVIVAL OF FINANCIAL METHODS
OF ADJUSTMENT

As the opportunity arose to get rid of restrictions on trade and payments, the European countries were glad to take advantage of it. The technique of restriction had become unpopular. Controls over external transactions were difficult to administer without matching controls over domestic transactions that, having become even more unpopular, were everywhere disappearing. It became generally recognized that the whole system of controls was not only arbitrary in its application but also a drag on efficiency and progress. And as the restrictions were progressively relaxed, the bureaucratic apparatus that had administered them was dismantled and it became more and more difficult to contemplate their reintroduction.

This, however, would have created a gap in the armory of weapons for dealing with payments disequilibrium, had not something been found to take the place of import restriction as a means of dealing with temporary deficits in the balance of payments. Although the reserves of European countries were increasing, international liquidity by itself was certainly not sufficient to accommodate all disequilibria other than those deemed suitable for correction by exchange-rate adjustment. The gap was filled by a revival of the use of financial policy—particularly monetary policy—for the purpose of influencing the external as well as the internal situation of a country. Originally, while it was recognized that the prevention by each country of domestic inflation would help to avoid the generation of unnecessary external disequilibria, it had not been part of the doctrine underlying the postwar institutional setup in the international economic field that, merely in order to correct a payments deficit, disinflation should be carried further than might be necessary for the preservation of internal stability. Now the conviction grew that monetary policy could be used, not merely to check short-term disequilibria arising from capital movements, overstocking, and the like, but also to influence the rate of increase of money costs and thus check at an early stage emergent tendencies toward a fundamental disequilibrium—and this without more than transitory repercussions on employment and output.

The spread of optimism in this regard was encouraged by the special circumstances prevailing during the 1940s and 1950s. Throughout those years, despite occasional slight recessions in the United States, a condition of high demand pressure prevailed almost continuously in industrial countries outside the Western Hemisphere. In such an environment, a country experiencing temporary payments difficulties could generally restore external equilibrium by disinflationary measures, the adverse effects of which on its employment, production, or economic growth were relatively slight and short-lived. Even countries that have tended to get into fundamental disequilibrium—whether, like the United Kingdom, because wages tended to rise too rapidly relative to the rate of productivity growth, or, like the United States, for more complicated reasons—have been able to prevent too serious a deterioration in their basic balance of payments at the cost of a degree of underemployment and underutilization of capacity that has not until recently been considered excessive.

In these circumstances, the view that external as well as internal equilibrium is a legitimate object of financial and, particularly, monetary policy gained increasing acceptance in official quarters and among economists.[4] The early postwar examples provided by Belgium and Italy of the

---

[4] The new attitude toward mechanisms of international adjustment engendered by this experience of the effectiveness of financial policy, combined with the growing conviction, of which I have spoken previously, of the harmfulness of quantitative restriction, received expression as early as 1951 in a noteworthy article by O. Emminger, "Wandlungen der Zahlungsbilanzpolitik" in *Wirtschaftstheorie und Wirtschaftspolitik*, a volume in honor of Adolf Weber. It is interesting to compare this paper with the early postwar articles by Ragnar Nurkse, such as *Conditions of International Monetary Equilibrium* (Princeton University, Essays in International Finance, no. 4, 1945) and "Domestic and International Equilibrium," in *The New Economics*, Seymour E. Harris, ed. (New York: Knopf, 1947), pp. 264–92, which provided classic expositions of the then orthodox position on the international adjustment mechanism.

effectiveness of financial restraint in producing a strong balance of payments had been associated with levels of unemployment generally considered to be excessive. More convincing were the examples provided by the Federal Republic of Germany in 1950, by Japan on various occasions, and by France in 1958—albeit that, in the last case, the adoption of a program of financial restraint was accompanied by devaluation.

The growth of confidence in the possibility of using financial instruments to prevent long-term disequilibria from getting out of hand without undue repercussions on domestic prosperity led logically to a declining emphasis on currency devaluation as an instrument of adjustment, and an increased tendency to interpret the Bretton Woods Agreement in the sense of a virtual fixity of exchange rates, save in the most exceptional circumstances. The acceptance of this point of view was furthered by the fact that the long persistence of inflationary tendencies, and the repeated failure of heralded recessionary tendencies to appear, naturally strengthened the influence in each country of the monetary authorities, whose aversion both to devaluation and to inflation has always been particularly marked.

The proposition that the inflationary pressures of the postwar period caused a trend toward greater exchange stability and greater reliance on financial policies as means of equilibrating international payments naturally holds primarily for deficit countries, where the policies to be applied were those of monetary restraint. Surplus countries have generally been almost as reluctant as they were during the interwar period to have deliberate resort to expansionary policies for the sake of correcting their payments imbalances. Indeed, at times, rather than import inflationary pressures from abroad, countries have contemplated, or actually embarked upon, currency revaluations. Thus in the immediate post-Korean inflation of 1950–51, some European countries were thought to be considering such a step, while Canada allowed her currency to appreciate rather than endure the inflationary pressures resulting from the great influx of capital. Finally, in 1961, Germany and the Netherlands carried out a slight revaluation in their currencies rather than make the relative cost adjustments, which their chronic surpluses appeared to require, entirely by upward movements in wages and prices. However, it is noteworthy that both these countries, in 1961 and 1962, in the interest of restoring the fundamental position of the U.S. dollar, showed a willingness to facilitate increases in wages and prices that must have been unwelcome from a purely domestic standpoint. Moreover, while generally reluctant to follow the "rules of the gold standard game," most creditor countries have shown considerable willingness to provide financial assistance, accelerate debt repayment, and promote outward capital movements by various means, including low discount rates, to the extent that this could be done without creating too much inflationary pressure at home.

RECENT CHANGES IN THE INTERNATIONAL ECONOMIC ENVIRONMENT

In recent years, a number of tendencies that have, or might have, important implications for the international payments system have been at work in economic life. In the first place, there has been a considerable increase in the international mobility of capital. This is connected, no doubt, with the relaxation of capital controls in European countries and with the improvement in facilities for covering exchange risks. It is also a result of the fact that U.S. capital, which was always free to leave the country, has in the last few years been attracted by the relatively high rates of profit prevailing in European countries and by the increased relative strength of European currencies.

Other developments of importance are the slowing down in the growth of international reserves and the increased precariousness of the international reserve structure that has resulted from the decline in the strength of the U.S. dollar, relative to the currencies of other main industrial countries. Up to a point, deficits in the United States and the United Kingdom tend to increase the level of world reserves because of the propensity of other countries to hold part of their marginal reserves in the currencies of these two countries. But beyond that point, the underlying weakness of these currencies has tended to check the growth of foreign exchange holdings, and to create a problem of inducing other countries to hold on to the exchange holdings that they already have.

Another factor is the growing appreciation of the importance of "cost-push" elements in the determination of price levels. Prices can rise uncomfortably rapidly at a time when there is slack and underemployment in the economy. And wages may react not only to the state of the labor market, but also to other factors more or less independent therefrom, such as the cost of living as affected by import prices, or the general state of political or industrial sentiment.

Finally, we come to a development that looks as though it were taking place but which may or may not prove permanent, namely, the ending of the period of high demand pressure that followed World War II. This period of pressure has been longer since World War II than it was after World War I, perhaps because of such factors as a more plentiful supply of international liquidity, a higher level of public expenditure, especially for defense, the absence of a precarious structure of international short-term indebtedness, more skillful and determined full employment policies, and a more expansionary demographic development. But it has been weakening for some years and, unless there is an exacerbation of the "cold war," seems unlikely to recover its former strength. Up to now, this weakening has been marked only in the United States, Canada, and the United Kingdom, while several continental countries continue to be concerned about rising prices. But this price inflation is largely of a wage–cost character, and, though demand continues to be buoyant in Europe and Japan, the countries in which it is flagging are responsible for a large proportion of world industrial output. If the payments disequilibrium between the two halves of the industrial world were rectified, the existence of a general easing of demand pressures might become patent to all.

INCREASED INTERNATIONAL MOBILITY
OF CAPITAL

The enhanced international mobility of capital has three main immediate consequences. In the first place, it adds to the instability of the balance of payments as a whole by introducing an element that is itself inherently less stable than most of the other items in the international accounts. Second, it expands the volume of interest arbitrage, or, more generally, the volume of capital that moves in response to international discrepancies in interest or profit rates. Finally, it increases the magnitude of the flows of hot money that occur when changes in exchange rates are believed to be imminent.

Owing to the second and third of these consequences, capital mobility tends to intensify certain types of payments disequilibria while mitigating others, and has an important bearing on the relative effectiveness of alternative adjustment policies.

Thus, suppose that a short-term change in world market conditions affects a country's balance of trade, and thereby threatens to disturb the country's internal equilibrium between total demand and total supply. In the absence of capital mobility, it might be possible to offset the external balance of payments effects by the use of reserves, while offsetting the internal overall demand effects by credit policy. With high capital mobility, however, credit policy, as an instrument for maintaining internal equilibrium, is undermined. Any attempt that a deficit country may make, by lowering interest rates, to prevent a decline in its exports from leading to domestic recession will induce an outflow of funds, which may exhaust its reserves; while a surplus country that wants to avoid "importing inflation" may, at least, have technical difficulties in reducing the money supply and raising interest rates. Moreover, if the large reserve movements that are apt to result from an attempt to apply offsetting credit policies in the situation described give rise to fears of devaluation (or revaluation), the disequilibrating flow of interest-motivated funds will be reinforced by a flow of speculative funds in the same direction.

Consider, now, a different kind of disequilibrium, brought about, say, by a temporary recession that occurs in some countries but not in others. In the absence of capital mobility, the countries experiencing the recession would tend to develop a payments surplus—thus relieving their own deflationary pressure by visiting on other countries both deflationary pressure and payments difficulties. With high capital mobility, however, though the deflationary pressure will still be exported, the payments surplus of the recession countries will be reduced by an outflow of capital resulting from the fall in interest rates there. With very great capital mobility, the balance of payments of the recession countries may even deteriorate. The enhanced capital mobility, while it will not necessarily mitigate the payments disequilibria arising out of recessions, will always make it easier for other countries to maintain prosperity.

By and large, however, there is little doubt that the enhanced international mobility and volatility of capital, though it occasionally acts as a stabilizing force, more often aggravates the difficulties of countries that are trying to combine internal stability and high employment with external equilibrium. One way of dealing with the most disturbing type of capital movement, namely, speculative movements, is to try to influence the exchange rate anticipations that give rise to them. For example, contractionary monetary and budgetary policies may be applied to restore "confidence" in a currency. Such policies may be justified, even if their ultimate effect on output and employment, if persisted in, would be bad, provided that they act so quickly on the flow of capital that they can be speedily terminated or reversed.

More generally, the moral that some experts and monetary authorities tend to draw from the enhanced mobility of capital is that exchange rates should be fixed even more firmly and irrevocably than under the par value system. If all possibility of exchange-rate alteration could be removed, at least among a limited group of countries—for example, by the adoption of a common monetary unit—currency confidence would be complete, the volume of funds responsive to interest differentials would increase still further, and the balance of payments could easily be kept in line through interest policy. However, it is not clear how, under this system, internal financial stability would be maintained; and it would seem impossible to correct serious disequilibria in the basic balance of payments without doing undue damage to output and employment in deficit countries.

Quite opposite conclusions are drawn from the same factual premises by many of the most distinguished academic economists, who advocate the adoption of flexible or floating exchange rates more or less tempered by national intervention on foreign exchange markets. Experience, both in Europe in the 1920s and in Canada in the 1950s, suggests that, if appropriate policies to maintain internal stability are pursued, the floating rate system does tend to elicit equilibrating rather than disequilibrating exchange speculation. Moreover, floating rates may be applied, as they were by Canada in the 1950s, to mitigate the inflationary or deflationary pressures that would otherwise arise from capital flows that, though non-speculative, are essentially irregular or nonrecurrent. However, there is some danger that an outward movement of capital, by depressing the exchange rate and raising the cost of imports, might, in the absence of suitable countermeasures, set off a wage–price spiral. Again, it is difficult to see how, under this system, the danger against which the par value system was devised (viz., that of competitive exchange depreciation) could be properly guarded against. Professor Meade's suggestion[5] for an

[5] James E. Meade, "The Future of International Payments," in *Factors Affecting the United States Balance of Payments*, a compilation of studies prepared for the Subcommittee on International Exchange and Payments of the Joint Economic Committee, U.S. Congress (Washington, D.C., 1962), pp. 241–52.

international fund actively intervening in exchange markets to minimize undesirable fluctuations, while undoubtedly attractive, seems to me Utopian. Governments do not, unfortunately, trust international officials that much! In the unlikely event of the floating rate system being adopted by industrial countries generally, the best way of preserving the element of international control would probably be to retain par values and the requirement of international consent for any change in these values; to permit actual rates to deviate from par values by rather wide margins— 5 percent or so; and to lay down rules limiting the right of national authorities to intervene within the margins. The hope would be that equilibrating capital movements would generally keep actual rates from fluctuating to the full permitted extent.

Apart from schemes such as these, a principal purpose of which would be to alter the psychological climate in which certain types of speculative movement take place, other devices have recently been applied or advocated to obviate the adverse effects that capital movements of various kinds may have on the maintenance of internal and external stability. One school of thought would like to return to the technique envisaged at Bretton Woods for dealing with the problem of speculative or other unwelcome capital movements, namely, the application of restrictions enforced by exchange controls. This, however, is probably against the trend of the times.[6] Monetary authorities are frequently unable or unwilling to apply such restrictions effectively. In any event, capital restrictions are just as crude and arbitrary in their incidence as quantitative restrictions on imports; the most noxious types of capital movement are frequently the most difficult to control.

A somewhat more promising approach, which has recently been developed both theoretically[7] and practically, is that of distinguishing between the various instruments and applications of financial policy, and directing some instruments and applications primarily to external, others primarily to internal, ends. Thus, a country suffering simultaneously from payments difficulties and an unduly low level of demand and em-

---

[6] Since these words were written, a tax restraint on selected types of capital export, the Interest Equalization Tax, has been proposed by the U.S. Administration—without exchange controls.

[7] See Robert A. Mundell, "The Appropriate Use of Monetary and Fiscal Policy for Internal and External Stability," *Staff Papers* (1962), 9:70–79.

ployment could seek to reflate by reducing taxes or increasing public expenditures while raising interest rates so as to attract funds from abroad. Or, within the field of monetary and debt management policy, it could seek to lower long-term interest rates to stimulate investment while raising short-term rates to attract funds from abroad. By such means, the enhanced mobility of capital might be made to serve, instead of frustrate, the aim of simultaneously maintaining internal and external equilibrium.

These techniques, however, have serious limitations. Interrelationships between the long and the short ends of the capital market set limits to the power of the authorities to determine short-term interest rates without reference to long-term rates, and vice versa. Again, the device of directing interest policy toward the achievement of external, and budgetary policy toward that of internal, equilibrium is not only subject to practical difficulties but also open to objections of principle. Thus, in many, perhaps most, countries the budget is too inflexible to be relied upon as the sole means of maintaining internal stability. Again, even where there is sufficient fiscal flexibility to make the policy-mix a technically feasible one, it may be disadvantageous, from a national standpoint, to rely upon it exclusively, and it will be disadvantageous, from a general standpoint, to apply it on a purely national basis.

Thus, if a country's cost level is out of line with those of its competitors, any attempt to maintain full employment by fiscal means alone is likely to result in a chronic budget deficit and a persistently low level of national savings and growth, unless factors are at work, or other policies are applied, which will ultimately restore the country's competitiveness. Again, even if no fundamental international disequilibrium exists, the combination of policies under discussion is one which, if adopted as a general rule by all countries, clearly could not work satisfactorily without a measure of international coordination. If each country were to determine its interest rate with reference to its balance of payments, taking as given the interest rates prevailing in other countries, the rates in the world as a whole would be indeterminate, and there is no guarantee that they would suitably reflect propensities to save and invest. Thus, there might be a situation in which interest rates were everywhere unnecessarily high, and governments were generally forced to run budget deficits to maintain full employment. To avoid such situations, the best method would be to regulate the geographical structure of interest rates through cooperative international action. The aim of such regulation would be to obtain an average level of rates of rates in industrial countries appropriate to the state of demand pressure in the world as a whole, and rate differentials between countries that would provide the necessary assistance to those with weak reserve positions.

Another device for dealing with international capital movements that has become more widely used in recent years is official intervention in the forward exchange market. By supporting its own forward exchange rate, that is, by speculating in favor of its own currency, a central bank or Treasury can attract short-term funds from abroad. This instrument is particularly appropriate as a means of countering adverse currency speculation on private account. Its scope is, however, limited, since it can influence only such short-term funds as are sensitive to the forward exchange rate, that is, mainly covered interest arbitrage funds.

In an ideal world, all undesirable movements in private capital would be countered by officially sponsored movements in the opposite direction, that is, by compensatory official financing. This, of course, includes the use of gold and foreign exchange reserves as well as official borrowing from international institutions, other governments, or private lenders. It is only when, and to the extent that, deficit countries are unable without undue risk to defend their currencies by compensatory official financing that it may become desirable for them to apply such mixed financial policies as I have just described. Both types of policy aim to affect net capital flows, but the mixed financial policies make it necessary, if suitable levels of over-all demand are to be preserved, to adopt budgetary policies not otherwise desirable, while compensatory official financing has no such disturbing side effects. However, there may not be sufficient external liquidity in the world, or it may not be possible to create enough to meet the needs of deficit countries without giving rise to too much inflation in the world as a whole. One way of circumventing the latter difficulty is to provide liquidity in a form in which it will be available only in certain circumstances—for example, when required to meet payments disturbances of external origin—or under certain policy conditions—for example, avoidance of inflation. At present, the IMF is the principal source of such "conditional" liquidity in the world.

THE GOLD EXCHANGE STANDARD
AND INTERNATIONAL LIQUIDITY

In addition to the enhanced danger of erratic capital movements, other factors are making for an increased need for international liquidity. These include two of the four main developments in the international economic environment that I mentioned earlier, namely, the faltering of the gold exchange standard and the dwindling of inflationary forces in the world. It is easy to see how a need for more international liquidity might arise from the increase in the international mobility of capital and from the slowing down in the expansion of international reserves. The change in the inflationary climate has, as will appear, a rather more complex bearing on the subject. One aspect, however, is fairly obvious. Among the objections to increasing external liquidity is that it may encourage countries to give too slack a rein to expansionary financial policies and thus cause too much inflation in the world. A dwindling of inflation on other grounds, obviously weakens the force of this objection.

Liquidity, as I have pointed out, may be available in unconditional form, or in a form the use of which is conditional on the observance of certain policies. This distinction does not necessarily correspond, but in actual fact often does correspond, in a rough way, to the distinction between liquidity derived from a country's own liquid assets or reserves and that derived from borrowing facilities.

Proposals for controlling and expanding the level of international liquidity pursue either the institutional approach or the intercentral bank approach. The first approach is in a sense multilateral; the second is usually bilateral. The first is governed by rules and regulations; the second is much more ad hoc. According to the institutional approach, the necessary international liquidity would be built up in the form of claims on an international institution, such as the IMF, and in the form of facilities for borrowing from—or drawing on—this institution. Some advocates, such as Professor Triffin, lay major emphasis on the creation of liquid claims, or deposits, with the institution;[8] others, such as Dr. Bernstein, lay more emphasis on the power to borrow from or through

---

[8] See Robert Triffin, *Gold and the Dollar Crisis* (New Haven: Yale University Press, 1960).

it.[9] The recent extension of the resources of the IMF through the establishment of lines of credit with ten major industrial countries[10] has the object of safeguarding its ability to provide the second sort of liquidity, but would, incidentally, permit the creation of liquidity of the first or reserve type, since the lending countries would acquire highly liquid claims on the IMF. The intercentral bank approach is itself, as it were, a two-lane highway, one lane being concerned with the practice of holding reserves in the form of foreign exchange, and the other with the provision of short- or medium-term intercentral bank credits. Ideas on the systematization of the gold exchange standard on a reciprocal basis, with many reserve centers, have been studied by Professor Posthuma. More immediately practical, but tentative, steps in the construction of a network of credit arrangements have been pursued on the initiative of the U.S. monetary authorities, while the British have made suggestions designed to make these arrangements operate in a more multilateral way. The question of international liquidity is a vast and complex one, about which I cannot hope to say anything worthwhile within the scope of an already overcharged lecture. I shall therefore pass on, having simply indicated the place it occupies within the framework of the general payments problem.

GROWING IMPORTANCE OF COST-PUSH FACTORS

In regard to the third development of which I spoke earlier, namely, the growing prominence of cost-inflationary, as distinct—but not separate—from demand-inflationary factors, it is not possible to speak with much confidence about the bearing of these factors on the effectiveness of mechanisms of international adjustment. Clearly, any tendency of wages or other cost elements to move erratically without close relation to market factors is apt to give rise to international disequilibria of a "fundamental" sort. Moreover, any decline in the sensitivity of wage

---

[9] See E. M. Bernstein, "The Problem of International Monetary Reserves," in *International Payments Imbalances and Need for Strengthening International Financial Arrangements*, Hearings Before and Subcommittee on International Exchange and Payments of the Joint Economic Committee, U.S. Congress (Washington, D.C., 1961), pp. 107–13.

[10] See International Monetary Fund, *Annual Report*, 1963 (Washington, D.C., 1963), pp. 28–29.

movements to the demand–supply situation in the labor market increases the difficulty of using financial policies to correct incipient disequilibria in international payments without undue damage to employment and output. To this extent, cost-inflationary factors make it more difficult to avoid resort to exchange depreciation. On the other hand, cost-inflationary mechanisms have a bearing, though an uncertain one, on the effectiveness of exchange depreciation itself as an instrument of international adjustment. One result of the existence of monopolistic elements in the labor market is that money wages tend to be responsive, not only to demand and supply conditions in that market but also to movements in the cost of living. Now, insofar as devaluation tends to raise the cost of living, it may tend to react on wage rates, so that a bigger devaluation than would otherwise be necessary is required to do the job. However, this may be outweighed by another consideration. Trade unions in industrial countries are amenable to fears of inflation, and generally dislike devaluation almost as much as central banks. They may therefore be particularly responsive to calls for restraint in situations in which devaluation becomes necessary. It is interesting to note that in Britain the greatest restraint in the postwar period was in fact shown just after the devaluation of 1949. Contrariwise, it was after the revaluations of the deutsche mark and the guilder in 1961 that German and Dutch wage rates showed their biggest increases.

The challenge provided by the growing recognition of cost-inflationary mechanisms has begun, in most industrial countries, to evoke a response in the form of what are euphemistically termed incomes policies, but are really attempts on the part of the authorities to influence the formation of wage rates and, occasionally, profit margins. Save in prewar Germany and postwar Netherlands, peacetime attempts in this direction have been highly tentative. Contrary to what is often asserted, no issue of individual liberty would seem to be involved in the strictest wage and price control as such. The extent to which democratic authorities will be able to enforce such controls, or even influence the general rate of growth of wages and administered prices, is still doubtful, however. It is also doubtful whether authorities of whatever stamp, if they were in a position to determine relative wages and prices, would pay enough attention to market considerations to avoid the emergence of serious distortions and diseconomies. If governments ever do succeed in gaining control over general

wage and price levels, the problem of international adjustment of fundamental disequilibria will, of course, be completely transformed.[11] That
day, however, is still to come.

DWINDLING PRESSURE OF TOTAL DEMAND

We come now to the fourth of our environmental developments, namely,
a possibly increasing difficulty, at least among industrial countries, in
maintaining an adequate pressure of aggregate demand and in avoiding
excess capacity and unemployment. If this should in fact emerge, countries disfavored by international demand conditions, or less successful
in maintaining competitiveness, will no longer be able to count on getting
back in line simply by holding inflationary pressures in check for a time;
rather, they may find it necessary to curtail employment and output to
an extent that will be unwelcome. Surplus countries will, no doubt, be
more willing to expand demand in order to eliminate disequilibrium
under the assumed conditions than they have been under conditions of
general excess demand, but some of them may find it technically difficult
to do so.

Under these conditions we may, I think, expect to find countries
becoming more anxious to correct their payments disequilibria by measures that involve an improvement in their balances of payments on
current account, that is, by exchange rate adjustment, by curtailing
imports, whether through licensing or through special import duties,
and by tying aid and capital outflows to national exports.

In other words, we may at last see the emergence of an economic
environment closer than was the economic environment of the 1950s
to what the founding fathers of Bretton Woods expected after the postwar
transitional period. And it is important that the broad objectives they
sought to achieve in those circumstances be adhered to. The use of

---

[11] It is worthy of remark, however, that even complete governmental control over the
domestic price level, though it would eliminate the need for exchange rate adjustment,
would not necessarily make desirable a return to the gold standard system, under which
financial policy was directed toward the maintenance of external equilibrium, while prices
adjusted themselves to maintain internal equilibrium. It would probably still be preferable,
from an international standpoint, that financial policy be primarily directed toward the
maintenance of internal equilibrium while prices and wages are adjusted in the interests of
external equilibrium.

techniques, such as import restriction, that are destructive of international trade should be minimized or, if possible, prevented altogether among the developed countries. The tying of aid and of capital outflows is, like outright dumping of exports, a trade-distorting device, and can be justified, if at all, only insofar as it leads to an increased flow of financial assistance to underdeveloped countries. Exchange-rate adjustment, though admitted as legitimate, should continue to be subjected to international control with a view to preventing its abuse as a weapon for gaining undue competitive advantages and exporting unemployment.

It is also important—for we cannot afford to dispense entirely with any of the instruments of adjustment—that countries remain willing to allow a moderate divergence from the degree of overall demand pressure that would be ideal from the standpoint of internal equilibrium, for the sake of correcting tendencies to fundamental disequilibria in external payments. In a generally deflationary environment, this would be particularly incumbent on surplus countries, as, in an inflationary environment, it is on deficit countries.

However, even assuming that resort to exchange depreciation would be kept under due international control by the IMF, the advent of a situation in which unemployment and stagnation, rather than inflation, were feared would be fairly certain to lead to an increase in the frequency of devaluations. This fact, with the consequential effect on expectations, would be likely to increase the danger of speculative capital movements and thus still further to increase the need for international liquidity, both of the conditional and of the unconditional sort. In the circumstances we are assuming, any effect that an increase in the supply of such liquidity might have in encouraging expansionary policies in industrial countries would, of course, be welcome.

CONCLUSION

Looking at the situation as it is affected by all the developments we have been discussing, one might believe that we are entering a new phase in the postwar history of the international monetary system, a phase that to some extent represents a return to the sort of situation envisaged in the Bretton Woods Agreement. However, the international mobility of capital and the autonomous cost-push elements in price formation will probably continue to bulk larger in reality than they did in the minds of the architects of Bretton Woods; and the lessons of the transitional period as to the frustrations of restrictionism and the importance of avoiding excess demand are unlikely to be wholly forgotten.

Under these conditions, the mechanism of international adjustment may develop in any of a number of possible directions. Indeed, different solutions to the problems set by the environment may be adopted in different parts of the industrial world.

Thus, for example, groups of industrial countries that are closely knit, such as that formed by the present members of the European Economic Community (EEC), may tend toward the kind of solution envisaged by the EEC Commission,[12] in which their mutual exchange rate would be more irrevocably fixed than under the par value system or, for that matter, the gold standard. Under this regime, hot money flows between the members of the group would disappear, and funds would move very readily in response to slight interest differentials. Such a system, however, could hardly hope to ensure full employment to all the countries of the group unless the members were prepared to submit to a thoroughgoing coordination not only of monetary, but also of fiscal and possibly wage, policies; unless they were imbued with a solidarity sufficient to induce those with favorable balances of payments to endure some degree of inflationary pressure for the sake of the others; and unless a high degree of mobility of labor prevailed within the group. Here, the maintenance of employment and activity would become, in effect, a collective, rather than a national, function.

As between countries in which the maintenance of activity remains a national function—including as a single "country" any groups such as those described above—the mechanism of adjustment might develop in a different way. In view of the increasing mobility of capital, monetary policies, here too, are likely to be more closely coordinated by central bank cooperation in the interest of international equilibrium and common prosperity, although it is to be hoped that reserves would be sufficiently plentiful to permit a measure of national independence even with respect to monetary policy. However, the responsibility for maintaining adequate

---

[12] In *Action Programme of the Community for the Second Stage* (Brussels, October 24, 1962).

levels of demand and employment would tend to devolve, at least in the medium term, on budgetary policy, nationally applied. Any need for a country to maintain indefinitely a larger budget deficit, on income account, than other countries would, like a chronic payments deficit, or a chronically depressed state of employment, be among the signs of an overvalued currency. Unless there is a resumption of strong demand pressures in the world, or unless incomes policies become much more effective than they have been to date, exchange-rate adjustments are likely to be necessary rather more frequently than in the past, but the par value system would presumably be adhered to. Under such a system, large speculative capital movements would have to be expected from time to time. Large counterflows of compensatory financing would, therefore, have to be reliably available. This need, together with those arising out of the secular growth in the value of international transactions, and in the probable magnitude of payments deficits, would probably call for a strengthening and expansion of organized arrangements for the provision of international liquidity, whether through central bank cooperation or, as I would hope, through the IMF, or both.

Some may feel that the systems of adjustment we have been discussing—which by no means exhaust the possibilities—are messy and confusing by comparison with the good old-fashioned gold standard. However, what these modern systems are attempting, under conditions much more difficult than in the heyday of the gold standard, is something far more ambitious, both as to ends and as to means, than was ever attempted then. The conditions are more difficult, in that wages and other prices (e.g., farm prices) are far less responsive to demand and supply than they used to be, and much more responsive to other factors. The aims are more ambitious in that we are now concerned, much more than in the past, with full employment and stable growth. The means also are more ambitious in that we are now trying to achieve results not, as in the time of the gold standard, through independent national action, limited only by custom and convention, but through conscious international cooperation, expressed in agreements ranging from informal understandings to legally binding treaties.

10

TARGETS AND INSTRUMENTS

IT HAS BECOME a common practice to present the problems of economic policy in terms of a dichotomy of targets and instruments. That is, it is assumed to be the first step in policy formation to assign desired values to certain economic variables (target variables) and the second step to contrive methods of influencing the values of other variables (instrument variables) in such a way as to ensure, so far as possible, the attainment of the desired values of the former. This practice, which is usually exemplified in macroeconomic analysis, may perhaps have originated in the discussion of the Keynesian problem of reconciling internal and external equilibrium in an open economy,[1] but was first systematically developed by the econometricians for the purpose of providing quantitative advice about economic policy, and is associated in particular with the name Tinbergen.[2] More recently, however, as we shall see, the econometricians, including Tinbergen himself, have tended to move away from this approach, or at least to give it a more sophisticated twist, just at the time when it is becoming more fashionable for literary economists, or even official committees, to apply it, or at least to employ its terminology.

A target variable may be a price (e.g., an exchange rate), a price index (e.g., cost of living), a rate of change of prices, a quantity index (e.g., real gross national product), real wages, real consumption, or the amount

First published in International Monetary Fund, *Staff Papers*, November 1968.
[1] As set forth, for example, in J. E. Meade, *The Theory of International Economic Policy, Volume I: The Balance of Payments* (London: Oxford University Press, 1951).
[2] J. Tinbergen, *On the Theory of Economic Policy* (Amsterdam: North-Holland, 1952), and *Economic Policy: Principles and Design* (Amsterdam: North Holland, 1956).

of some category of real expenditure, a rate of change of quantities (e.g., a growth target), a net value aggregate (e.g., the balance of payments, or a budget surplus), a value ratio (e.g., the share of wages in the national income, the ratio of savings or domestic investment to GNP), or an amount or ratio of excess demand or supply (e.g., unemployment). What makes a variable a target variable is the fact that some policymaker wants it to have a particular value either as an end in itself or as a means whose influence on ultimate ends is exercised outside the system of economic relationships explicitly assumed. Instruments are variables which the policymaker is in a position to influence, either directly or through channels that lie outside the system of relationships explicitly assumed, for the attainment of his desired objectives. Instrument variables acquire that status from their association with various types of policies: government expenditures and tax rates from fiscal policy; interest rates, the quantity of money, and the amount of credit extended by banks from monetary policy; prices and wages from policies of wage or price control; and amounts of raw materials and consumer goods demanded from policies of allocation and rationing, respectively.

It is a central deliverance of the targets-instruments approach that the number of instruments must be at least equal to the number of targets. In making this count, any variables that necessarily vary in a fixed relation to each other—though together they may be adjusted by policy decision—or any variables whose *relative* marginal influence with respect to each target variable is the same should be considered as a single instrument. On the other hand, variables that in all circumstances compatible with the prevailing economic relationships remain at desired levels should not be reckoned as target variables, though in other conditions—for example, if some change occurred in the economic structure or some new policy instrument were introduced—they might become such. It is not difficult to understand the truth of the proposition. If we start from a position in which there are no targets and in which potential instrument variables are set at a given level, it is clear that there must be at least as many dependent variables as there are independent equations describing structural relationships. Otherwise, the equations will not, in general, be compatible with one another. To set a target value for a dependent variable (one that may differ from the actual value of that variable) is equivalent to turning a dependent into an independent variable; this cannot be done in general unless some other variable is changed from an independent into a dependent one, or unless some structural relationship is altered by the introduction of a new dependent variable. These conditions, however, are fulfilled when some policy instrument, previously exogenously determined, is allowed to be determined by the system, including the desired values of the targets, or some new policy instrument is activated and allowed to be similarly determined.

If all the structural equations are linear and all instruments are independently and indefinitely variable, then the number of instruments need be no more than equal to the number of targets. But if the authorities are unable or unwilling to vary the value of instrument variables beyond certain limits (boundary conditions), or if they cannot vary some instruments without affecting others, or if the structural equations are nonlinear (e.g., if the influence of instruments on targets is subject to diminishing returns), it may be necessary to have more instruments than targets.

The targets–instruments approach has some advantages. Given its basic assumption—the legitimacy of posing the problem of policy formation in terms of the attainment of predetermined values for a limited number of target variables—the propositions of the theory are true and useful. And, in spite of what is said below, some of the most important macro-objectives of economic policy can be legitimately expressed in terms of targets that are approximately fixed—near-zero unemployment, near-zero rates of change of domestic price levels, and near-zero imbalance in international payments. Moreover, the approach in question explicitly favors a number of healthy tendencies, for instance, restraint on the tendency of noneconomists to multiply economic targets by attributing intrinsic importance to variables whose significance is purely instrumental, ingenuity in the search for novel instruments of policy, and boldness in overcoming irrational inhibitions against the use of familiar instruments. For example, the growing recognition of the difficulties of reconciling the three targets mentioned above has induced the economic profession to mount an attack on the inflexibility of the exchange rate instrument while pursuing with increased urgency the search for new instruments such as wage policy, or the more conscious use, as separate instruments, not only of monetary policy and fiscal policy, as such, but also particular categories of operations within these broad fields. Above all, the targets–instruments approach, by facilitating the application of statistical and econometric techniques, has helped to put an end to the gross errors that at times characterized the qualitative or rule-of-thumb approach to economic policy formation.

However, progress in the arts is generally bought at a price, normally in the form of a loss of older skills, and in the present instance progress in the quantification of macroeconomic policy has tended to involve an undue sacrifice of the insights of microeconomic welfare theory.

The inadequacy of the targets-instruments approach is often at its most marked where any weakness is most important, namely, in the choice of the target variables and in the determination of their target levels. The old-fashioned welfare economist derives all his intermediate objectives from two ultimate criteria, of which the first—the maximization of real income—is determined, apart from such allowances as may be made for market imperfections, externalities, and errors of anticipation, by the preferences, expectations, and decisions of individuals, while only the second—the distribution of real income—is inevitably a matter for central evaluation. And even here the welfare economist will tend to guide the policymaker toward a rational evaluation by presenting the problem in terms of the effects of income redistribution on the welfare of classes of individuals. The targets–instruments economist, on the other hand, is apt to regard all of his specific targets as data, more or less arbitrarily handed down by the policymaker. It is perhaps an acknowledgment of the arbitrary character of targets arrived at in this way that Tinbergen will casually suggest dropping a target when there are too few instruments to permit all targets to be fully attained.

Often it is the national government or political party that appears to be regarded as the appropriate chooser of targets. Such humility on the part of economists is out of place. Left to themselves, governments are likely to choose target values that, in view of the constraints of the system and the shortage of effective instruments, are incompatible— sometimes rather directly incompatible, as in price stability and a predetermined rate of growth of real income. Moreover, they are very apt to assign end value to variables that have no direct connection with ultimate human needs but are believed, on the strength of some dubious but probably quite complex economic theory, to exercise an influence on economic welfare. For this reason, variables, such as exchange rates, interest rates, or budget balances, that ought to be either treated as primarily instrumental or else left to the determination of the market will be regarded as targets and thereby removed from the category of instruments, or irrational limitations will be put upon their use.

Admittedly, one of the main objects of a quantitative confrontation of targets and instruments is to bring home to the policymaker the fact that his chosen target values are mutually incompatible, given the existing constraints, and to get him to give up some of his target variables, to alter his target values, or to overcome his inhibitions regarding the use of certain instruments. However, such a trial-and-error process is unlikely to be the quickest way of reaching a set of realistic objectives, and the objectives ultimately arrived at by this route, even though mutually compatible, are likely to be less closely related to any rational concept of economic welfare than if the economist had from the start advised his government about its proximate economic goals and policies on the basis of an economic welfare function.

Of course, governments, since they have the power and the votes, must—and should—have the last word in determining objectives. But there is some reason to think that they are sometimes stimulated by the prevailing fashion among econometricians and economists into unnecessary targetry.

Lethargy will often prevent governments from choosing targets unless they are provoked into doing so, and some of the targets they entertain they do not pursue with any seriousness. Unfortunately, however, although the explicit message of the targets–instruments approach is to limit the number of targets, its psychological impact—its demonstration effect—is to make government officials target conscious—to convince them that they are sinning against the light if they do not quantify their national economic goals in as much detail as possible. For example, in the domestic sphere many governments are induced to aim not merely at overall high employment and price stability but at such in every major industry and region of the country. The politician cannot be expected to realize, if the economist does not explain to him, that these aims, however desirable in themselves, cannot easily be realized without impairing the capacity of the economy to adapt to changing needs.

In the international sphere, similar excesses in targetry are not lacking. For example, the otherwise cautious report on the adjustment process by the Organization for Economic Cooperation and Development (OECD)[3] encourages countries to quantify their ambitions with respect not merely to their overall balances of payments but also to their current and capital accounts taken individually. The national targets would then be reconciled by a process of mutual confrontation. This procedure would be unexceptionable if each country were to fix the target level for its current account balance of payments in relation to estimates of what the medium-term trend of its capital account would be at full employment in the absence of capital restrictions. Even then, it would be necessary to (a) coordinate national targets for the over-all balance of payments so as to fit into the expected growth in world reserves and (b) coordinate national estimates as regards the trends in capital movements. What the OECD Working Party seems to have in mind, however, is for each country to prepare a target for its capital account (and hence its current account) reflecting national preferences. The criteria underlying these national preferences being unspecified, it is difficult to guess on what basis the international coordination or mutual adjustment of national targets could take place. And even if countries were able to agree on adjusted targets, one could be fairly certain that if the targets were achievable at all it could only be by methods contrary to an optimal distribution of capital resources.

While the multiplication of unnecessary targets may be said to represent a popular misapplication of the targets–instruments approach, a number of other weaknesses are inherent in the approach itself. Their root cause lies in the essential characteristics of the approach, namely, (a) the representation of social preference by fixed predetermined values of the target variables rather than by a function of such variables. From this follows (b) the attribution of end value to too few of the variables of the system of relationships under examination, and in particular (c) neglect of the end value inherent in the instrument variables themselves. A further consequence is (d) failure to appreciate that the object of policy

---

[3] *The Balance of Payments Adjustment Process*, A Report by Working Party No. 3 of the Economic Policy Committee of the Organization for Economic Cooperation and Development (Paris, August 1966).

is to achieve the best compromise among objectives and not to maximize the number of objectives that are fully attained. Finally, there is a weakness flowing partly from the method as such—in which context it is particularly related to (c) above—and partly from the oversimplified macroeconomic character of the economic models to which the method is applied, namely, (e) an undue neglect of the evils of misallocation, as distinct from unemployment, of resources.

Any rational policymaker who is guided by considerations of social welfare must be able to rank the alternative situations that might *conceivably* result from the application of different policies in order of preference. Among these conceivable situations some will turn out to be feasible. The object of the exercise is to arrive at the most preferred of these feasible situations.

If the welfare significance of all alternative situations that could result from different values of the instrument variables of a given economic model are regarded as determined by the values, in these situations, of certain of the variables of the model (target variables), then, since there is a vast number of possible combinations of instrument values, there will be a vast number of possible situations to be put in order of preference. Moreover, since no two situations are likely to be characterized by the same values of all of the target variables, it is reasonable to assume that no two situations will be graded precisely alike from a welfare standpoint. Such an ordering can conveniently be represented by a continuous function of which the target variables are the arguments.

Tinbergen's fixed targets do not fit into this picture. The welfare ordering that they imply is one in which each possible situation is ranked according to the number and identity of *target variables having prescribed values* (i.e., fixed targets) which it contains. Of these possible situations, there is (given the instruments) a subset of feasible situations, each containing a different set (though possibly the same number) of target variables and hence of fixed targets. Of these, the situation with the preferred fixed targets is to be chosen.

Clearly no one would believe in the validity of such an odd type of preference function in and for itself. If Tinbergen uses it, it may be to some extent because politicians, not being particularly rational, like having fixed targets, but primarily because, given the possible sets of fixed targets and the empirical relationships connecting the variables, it is relatively simple to demonstrate mathematically whether and at what values of the instrument variables each set of targets is feasible.

As is indicated below, the econometricians have found it possible to work with welfare functions of a much more rational type. In any event, literary economists who do not aspire to arrive at the optimal value of instrument variables at one blow through the solution of a set of simultaneous equations do not have the same excuse for adopting a fixed-targets approach.

When the problem of policy is regarded as one of maximizing a welfare function of which certain economic variables (which we may continue to call target variables) are the arguments, rather than one of attaining the maximum number of the most preferred fixed targets, it no longer becomes necessary to limit the number of target variables in relation to the number and nature of the instrument variables that are available. All the variables appearing in the model that either effect welfare directly or influence the value of variables outside the model that in their turn affect welfare directly can be included as arguments in the welfare function. It will not be possible to attain predetermined values for these variables, nor yet to attain the values for each of these variables that would be optimal if they could be varied freely without affecting or being affected by the other variables in the model. But it will be possible to find values for all of them which, given the constraints of the model and the available instruments, are the best that can be attained.

Since most of the variables in any simple macroeconomic model will have repercussions on variables outside the model, most of them should probably be included as arguments in the welfare function, though the weights that should be attached to them will, of course, vary. Among these variables are likely to be found at least some of the instrument variables. In the fixed-targets approach, there has to be a complete dichotomy between targets and instruments. Since the values of the target variables are fixed in advance while the values of the instrument variables must be free to vary, at least to some extent, the latter can never be included among the former. With the welfare-function approach the necessity for such segregation disappears.

One reason for including instrument variables among the arguments of the welfare function is that their manipulation frequently (a) absorbs resources and (b) distorts or (more rarely) improves their allocation, in ways that are rarely taken explicitly into account in simple macro-economic models. For example, a tax imposed for the purpose of checking price inflation is likely, even if it takes the form of a perfectly general tax on consumption, to create some disincentive to effort and enterprise, and, in a national tax, to encourage outward and discourage inward tourism. If it is an expenditure tax that affects investment, or if it is an income tax, it will, in addition, unduly discourage saving and further penalize enterprise. If, as is more likely, it is an indirect tax of restricted application, it will direct resources unduly to untaxed activities. On the other hand, it may sometimes be possible, given the prior existence of price rigidities and market imperfections, to impose a tax, say for anti-inflationary purposes, that will at the same time *improve* the allocation of scarce commodities. In either event, unless—as is rare—measures of misallocation are themselves included as variables in the model, it will be desirable to include the instrument variable as one of the arguments of the welfare function.

Almost any imaginable economic model contains more variables, including instrument variables, that should in terms of any reasonable welfare function be classified as target variables than it contains instrument variables. For this and other reasons already discussed, it will be impossible, even where the target variables—apart from the constraints of the model—have finite optimal values, fully to attain the optimal values of all target variables.

In the case of a complete micromodel, this is very obvious. Even if all prices were fully flexible, and fully competitive conditions prevailed throughout the economy, the attainment of an equitable income distribution would necessitate a system of budgetary transfers that would be bound to distort incentives to work, to save, and probably also to carry on particular productive activities. The same results will ensue from efforts to meet through the budget collective needs of various kinds, to promote an adequate scale of activity in industries of increasing return, or to adjust incentives to take account of the various sorts of externalities. Where wage and price rigidities and other distortions are introduced into the working of the competitive system by the action of economic entities that are large in relation to the relevant markets and that the state cannot or will not control directly, it will be still more difficult to bring target variables, which in this case might take the form of price-cost relationships and relative personal incomes, into the vicinity of their optimal values.

Even in macromodels, however, full attainment of targets is likely to be impossible. In this event, the best feasible result, given the constraints of the model, will be one in which all target variables continue to be treated as such (i.e., none are discarded) and in which a compromise is achieved between the various targets—few, if any, being fully attained. This is particularly true of target variables whose optimal value is not at some natural limit of variation and whose marginal utility in the vicinity of the optimum is, therefore, very low. For example, in the sphere of public finance it is better to compromise between the objective of equalizing the utility of the marginal dollar spent on public services and on private consumption and the objective of avoiding the disincentive effects of taxation rather than to give one objective absolute priority over the other. Again, in the sphere of demand policy it is better to compromise between full employment and avoidance of inflation rather than to give one objective complete priority over the other.[4]

Some target variables, such as the quantity of consumption in general, have no finite optimum value, apart from the constraints of the system, and full attainment of the target in such cases is obviously impossible. Nevertheless, they have constrained optima. These lie at the point at which the marginal utility of increasing the variable in question is equal to the marginal cost in terms of loss of utility from reducing other target variables of a similar character or of removing other target variables having a finite optimum further from their optimal levels.

To a devotee of welfare economics, the most striking inadequacy of the fixed-targets approach lies in its handling of questions relating to the allocation of resources. Admittedly, many of the problems of allocation arise in the microeconomic sphere with which the macroeconomic models, to which the targets–instruments approach is usually applied,

---

[4] For employment, it may be argued that the unconstrained optimum—apart from the links between employment and inflation—is at the natural limit of full employment. However, the fact that full employment brings with it the diseconomies of labor shortage—probably not included as a separate target variable—may mean that the optimum is somewhat short of absolutely full employment, or at least that the marginal utility of employment declines in the vicinity of full employment. Even if this were not so, the marginal diseconomies of inflation at full employment might be so great that a compromise between the two objectives was desirable.

do not and need not deal, since the problems in question can in principle be dealt with by instruments other than those that enter into the macroeconomic models. However, a number of allocation problems concerned, for example, with the degree of restriction or encouragement to be applied to international transactions, the disincentive efforts to taxes, the appropriate levels of public savings, consumption, and investment, or the diseconomies of inflation do arise in a macroeconomic context—very often, as already indicated, in connection with instrument variables. It is much more difficult to devise plausible fixed targets for desiderata in this sphere than in, say, the degree of employment or the balance of payments where, under any reasonable welfare function, the optimal values of the variables in question would lie within a narrow range. It is where variables affecting the allocation of resources are concerned that the constraints of the system call most clearly for compromise solutions and where the necessity, under the fixed-target approach, either of adopting arbitrary target values or of ignoring the significance of variables is most blatant. Thus, in some policy models import restrictions may be banned entirely while in others their undesirable effects are ignored. In sbme models, budget imbalances are banned while in others their implications for national savings and for the balance between private and public consumption are ignored. And in many cases arbitrary boundary conditions are put on the use of instruments while diseconomies of use within these limits are ignored.

The flexible-targets approach, principally developed by Professor Theil[5] but also discussed at an early date by Tinbergen, side by side with the fixed-targets approach,[6] though deriving from the fixed-targets approach

---

[5] H. Theil, "Econometric Models and Welfare Maximization," *Weltwirtschaftliches Archiv* (1954), 72:60–81; *Economic Forecasts and Policy* (2d ed.; Amsterdam: North Holland, 1961); *Optimal Decision Rules for Government and Industry* (Amsterdam: North-Holland, 1964); "Linear Decision Rules for Macrodynamic Policy Problems," *Quantitative Planning of Economic Policy*, Bert G. Hickman, ed. (Washington: The Brookings Institution, 1965), pp. 18–37.

[6] Tinbergen says that "this somewhat more general treatment was suggested to me by Professor Dr. D. B. J. Schouten and Professor Dr. H. Theil," *Centralization and Decentralization in Economic Policy* (Amsterdam: North Holland, 1954), p. 7. See also J. Tinbergen, *Economic Policy: Principles and Design*, and the chapter on "The Theory of the Optimum Regime" in *Jan Tinbergen: Selected Papers*, L. H. Klaassen, L. M. Koyck, and H. J. Witteveen, eds. (Amsterdam: North-Holland 1959), pp. 264–304.

and bearing traces of its parentage, represents a considerable improvement on the latter, and is free from a number of the objections to it that have been made above. This serves as an encouraging demonstration that the weaknesses that have been pointed out are not inevitable features of quantitative treatment of economic policy problems.

The flexible-targets approach treats social welfare explicitly as a continuous function that is to be maximized subject to the constraints of the model. Instrument variables are included among the variables that are the arguments of this function, and it is emphasized that there is no need for the number of instruments to equal the number of target variables, and that the best feasible situation may be one in which none of the target variables is dropped and none attains its optimal value. This approach is, therefore, free of objections (a), (b), (c), and (d) leveled at the fixed-targets approach described earlier.

It is greatly to be regretted that though the econometricians had introduced this approach, and contrasted it with the fixed-targets approach, almost as early as they introduced the latter,[7] literary economists who talk about targets and instruments have usually interpreted targets in the sense of fixed targets, as can be seen in the emphasis they lay on comparing the respective numbers of the two classes of variables.

Even in its flexible form, however, the approach of the Netherlands school of econometricians to the problem of optimal policy formation retains several of the characteristic weaknesses of the fixed-targets method. This is true despite the great sophistication of Theil's work. Here, once more, the root of the trouble lies in the form of the social welfare function that is generally adopted, namely, a particular type of quadratic function. Welfare is regarded as the negative of a weighted sum of squares of the values of the target variables, when these are measured as deviations from their optimal values. Maximum feasible welfare is attained when the weighted sum of squared deviations is minimized, subject to the constraints of the model. Both the optimal values and the weights are fixed in advance. This implies that each target variable has a predetermined optimal value such that (given the values of other variables) any deviation from that value will reduce welfare, that it is a matter of indifference whether that deviation be positive or negative, and that as the optimal

---

[7] Possibly even earlier. A flexible approach is implicit in linear programing as applied to a whole economy.

value is approached the marginal gain to welfare from a further approximation to the optimum declines.

Now, as was pointed out by Tinbergen himself in his original treatment of flexible targets,[8] a distinction has to be drawn between those target variables such as income ratios among classes of income receivers, production ratios among commodities, payments balances, employment ratios, or, one might add, rates of price inflation, where a finite optimum value is relevant, and those, such as real per capita income, where there is no finite saturation point. Predetermined fixed optimal values cannot possibly apply to the latter. Theil, however, gaily sets optimal values for such variables as the levels of consumption and of investment which are clearly of the insatiable type.[9] He is, of course, well aware of the obvious objections, but thinks that if his optimal values are chosen with sufficient art (in relation to what is feasible, given the constraints) his preference function will approximate true preferences well enough, over the relevant range. What this appears to mean is that the relative optimal values of different target variables must be set *before* the calculation is made sufficiently, but not too much, in excess of what the best feasible values will be *after* the calculation is made to ensure that the (a) absolute marginal utilities of such variables are all positive and (b) relative marginal utilities are what they ought to be. This procedure seems to me so circular as to be valueless except as a first step in a (hopefully convergent) process of mutual adjustment of optimal and best feasible values.

A less serious difficulty arises where, as in the employment ratio, for example, the target variable has a finite optimum that lies at or near the limit of variation. In such a case, if the best feasible level tends to exceed the optimum, the target variable can be replaced by a fixed target.

Parenthetically, it may be observed that whether a variable has or has not a finite optimum will depend not only on the nature of the variable but on the presence or absence of other variables in the system. For example, if only one form of resource use appears among the variables in the equations describing the system—whether it be the amount of income going to one sector of the community, or the amount of output of some particular commodity—there will be some finite optimal level

[8] J. Tinbergen, *Centralization and Decentralization in Economic Policy*, p. 52.
[9] H. Theil, *Optimal Decision Rules for Government and Industry*, p. 80.

of that use; but if all of the competing uses of resources appear as variables in the system, the optimal level for any one use will be infinity. One might go further and say that wherever target variables with finite optima appear in a system they are proxies for other variables of the insatiable type, which, for good or bad reasons, do not appear in the system. Thus, for example, the employment ratio is a proxy for output and, at a further remove, for real income. Rate of price inflation and the savings ratio derive their importance from their presumed effects on future real income, though the chain of causation, particularly in the first case, may be so complex and uncertain that a complete model into which all of these relationships would enter explicitly is impracticable.

Even where the target variable is such as to admit of some finite optimum level that is not at the limit of possible variation, it will seldom be precisely a matter of indifference whether the value of the variable exceeds or falls short of its optimal level by a given amount. This is clearly true, for example, of the unemployment ratio, or of the balance of payments.

The least-squares welfare function is open to the further objection that the predetermined optimal values of its target variables and the fixed coefficients by which deviations from these optima are weighted imply that the marginal welfare curves of each of the target variables are independent of the actual values of the other variables. Now this would clearly not hold, for example, in a microsystem in which the supplies of all final products appeared explicitly as arguments of the welfare function; on the contrary, the marginal welfare yield of each product would be a function of the supply of all the others, particularly of substitutes and complements. In some macroeconomic models the value interrelationships between target variables may be less important, though it has to be remembered that such *factual* interactions as may exist between target variables other than those arising from the explicit constraints of the model should be allowed for in the welfare function. Take, for example, a model in which the target variables are unemployment and import restrictions (expressed in terms of an equivalent *ad valorem* tariff), and in which optimal unemployment (taking account of its effect on the trend of prices) is positive, and optimal import restriction is zero. In this instance, the optimal level of either target variable will be virtually independent of the actual level of the other. Moreover, the weight to be assigned to deviations from optimal unemployment depends on the interindustrial distribution of unemployment and is probably not greatly influenced by the degree of import restriction. However, the weight to be assigned to deviations from zero import restriction depends primarily on the elasticity of demand for imports, which probably does depend significantly on the degree of unemployment.

There seem to be two main reasons why the least-squares welfare function, in spite of its many and obvious faults, has been used by Theil and other econometricians in their work on economic policy. The first is connected with the fact that the constraints of the system, representing the factual relationships between economic variables, are of a stochastic character. They can only be established, by econometric methods, with some degree of uncertainty, which is expressed by the inclusion of a random variable. Now the least-squares welfare function is one of a class of quadratic welfare functions, the expectations of which will be maximized (thus arriving at the probably best feasible outcome) when the stochastic linear equations of the system are replaced by nonstochastic linear equations having the same coefficients, in which the random variables are replaced by their expectations or most probable values. More rational welfare functions would probably not have this convenient property.

This, however, appears to be a case of the metric tail wagging the economic dog. Whatever errors might be introduced into the maximization of the expectation of any given welfare function by taking the random variables in the constraints at their most probable values would surely be small by comparison with the errors that would result from treating the random variables in this way and, to quiet one's statistical conscience, altering the welfare function that one is setting out to maximize.

Another probable reason for adopting the least-squares type of welfare function, however, is that it retains the notion of predetermined quantitative targets which the policymaker can be persuaded to choose, or led to believe that he has chosen. In fact, this impression is even more illusory for flexible than for fixed targets since the best feasible values of the target variables—which is what matters in the end—will depend to a considerable extent on the weighting system adopted in the welfare function—a system the implications of which the policymaker may find difficult to comprehend. Moreover, as we have seen in the case of variables without a true finite optimum, the choosing of optimal values—

in the light of preconceptions as to what is feasible—calls for an art which the policymaker is unlikely to possess.

It is, of course, much easier to point out the faults in any given social welfare function—such as the least-squares function—than to suggest a satisfactory alternative. If the target variables, as in a micromodel, were all of the kind that have no finite optima, a welfare function of the Cobb-Douglas type might be appropriate, and would have the advantage of not assuming independent utilities. In most models, however, some of the target variables, at any rate, would have finite optima, and the required conditions for the use of such a function would not be fulfilled.

It may be possible for the mathematicians to devise types of welfare functions that could be used to accommodate target variables, some of which have, while others have not, a finite optimum. The writer is in no position to offer suggestions in this regard; and, doubtless, even the form of the function should vary with the nature of the problem—the particular economic model—under examination. What seems to him desirable is that any welfare function should be derived, by however intuitive a procedure, from estimates of the probable effects of variations in the target variables on real income, appropriately discounted for futurity and corrected, if alternative policy mixes are likely to have substantially different relative effects on particular groups in the community, for differences in the marginal utilities of income of the groups in question.

It is not, however, the ambition of this paper to enter at all deeply into the problems of the quantitative global planner. The concern of the writer is much more with the impact of the targets–instruments conceptual scheme on the work of the economic advisor who is concerned with the relative merits of alternative policies for effecting an improvement in—rather than an optimization of—the economic situation. From this standpoint, the criticisms of the flexible-targets approach offered in the immediately preceding pages are really much less important than those advanced in earlier pages against the fixed-targets system, for the simple reason that it is the concepts of the latter rather than of the former that have seeped down from the econometric stratosphere to the less rarified atmosphere in which most workaday economists draw breath.

To these the message of this paper is as follows: (1) Keep your eye at all times on the probable effects of different policies on real income (corrected where necessary for distributional effect); (2) Do not multiply proximate targets without need but, equally, do not drop legitimate objectives simply because you do not have sufficiently numerous or sufficiently effective policy instruments to attain them all; (3). In particular, do not be hypnotized by the alleged importance of attaining a few fixed targets, often of a macroeconomic character, into forgetting the real income effects of misallocations of resources and distortions of demand; (4). Realize the inevitability of second-best or compromise solutions to policy problems.

It may be worthwhile adding a postscript on the question of the appropriate number of instruments that the policymaker should seek to use. Both the fixed-targets approach and the welfare-economics approach tend to favor a multiplication of policy instruments, the former so as to increase the number of targets that can be attained and the latter so as to permit all objectives to be more closely approximated. Since, as we have seen, it will in general not be feasible to attain the optimal values of such of the target variables as have finite optima, and since some of the target variables may be insatiable, having no finite optima, it follows that, if no costs were involved in the use of instruments, *all* potential instrument variables should be used to some extent. This looks like a charter for interventionism, but the qualification is important. In fact, all instruments involve some costs in use. These costs are of two kinds— costs in terms of labor and capital, and costs in terms of policy management. The latter are analogous to those costs that, after a point, give rise to diminishing returns to scale in an individual enterprise. It is necessary that policies be centrally coordinated, and in each country there is a limit to the number of policies that can be successfully coordinated by the political and administrative machine. For this reason, the costs of applying any given policy instrument will depend not only on the degree of its use but on the number and nature of the instruments already in use. The existence of both of these kinds of cost, and particularly the latter, will set a limit on the number of policy instruments that can appropriately be brought into operation.

11

RESERVE CREATION
AND REAL RESERVES

WHEREAS a rise in the rate of monetary expansion in a single country, even if it is a closed economy, will normally tend, in the long run, to reduce the level of real balances in that country, a rise in the rate of expansion of nominal reserves in the world will not necessarily tend, even in the long run, to reduce the level of real reserves. Indeed, it will tend to raise real reserves, unless the desired rate of increase of real reserves is more sensitive to the yield on reserves, compared with other assets, or unless the rate of inflation that governments will tolerate is more sensitive to increases in the excess of the actual over the desired rate of increase in real reserves, than appears, prima facie, likely to be the case.

An increase in the rate of interest paid on reserve holdings will normally increase the level of real reserves in the long run.

If the liberalization of trade proximately depends on the stock and rate of growth of real reserves and on the yield on reserves, respectively, in the same manner and relative degree as does the rate of price inflation in the world, it will always be promoted by an expansion in the rate of growth of nominal reserves.

If, however, liberalization depends almost entirely on the stock and rate of growth of real reserves and not at all on the yield on reserves, compared with other assets, it will be promoted by an increase in the

First published in International Monetary Fund, *International Reserves: Needs and Availability*, Washington D.C., 1970.

rate of growth of nominal reserves only if such growth results in an increase in real reserves, whereas it will always be promoted by a rise in the interest paid on reserves, since the latter always results in an increase in real reserves.

If the second hypothesis, or some intermediate hypothesis, is valid, it is conceivable that a suitable mix of policies with respect to the creation of reserves and the interest paid on reserves, respectively, would permit a closer approach to world objectives for price inflation and liberalization than would either policy taken by itself.

THE PARALLEL BETWEEN RESERVES AND MONEY

It would probably be granted by the adherents of any school of monetary theory that in a closed economy under conditions of full employment any increase in the rate of growth of the money supply is fairly certain, if continued long enough, to reduce the real stock of money below what it would have been had the original rate of growth continued and hence to reduce the benefits and conveniences that flow from the existence of such a stock. Starting from an equilibrium position in which money, prices, and expected prices are all rising at the same rate, assume a rise in the rate of growth of the money stock. At first, the rate of increase of prices will rise no more than that of money—possibly even less for a while—but, as expected price growth rises in the wake of the rise in actual price growth, the demand for real balances will fall, thus intensifying the price inflation. If the relationships involved are such as to enable real balances to gravitate toward a new long-term equilibrium level, that level will necessarily be lower than would have prevailed at the original rate of money growth since the expected rate of increase of prices, to which the demand for real balances is negatively related, will have risen to the same extent as the actual rate of price increase, and hence to the same extent as the rate of growth of money. In a Keynesian model, the rise in expected price growth will exercise its effect on the demand for real balances exclusively through the intermediary of the marginal efficiency of capital and the rate of interest. In a monetarist model the effect could be more direct. The outcome in either case will be the same.

The question arises as to whether anything comparable occurs when the rate of growth of international reserves is increased, for example, by the issuance of special drawing rights. It is generally agreed that an increase in the degree of reserve ease in the world, as manifested by an increase in the stock, or rate of growth, of real reserves, will have a tendency—though possibly only a weak one—to encourage countries to adopt more expansionary financial policies and hence to promote an accelerated increase of prices; and it is also conceivable that the level of real reserves which countries desire to hold will tend to be lower, the higher is the rate of increase of prices. May it not, therefore, be that any action undertaken to increase the norminal rate of growth of world reserves will, if only in the long run, lead to a reduction in the real level of such reserves, and by so doing intensify reserve shortage, promote the spread of restrictions on international transactions, increase the frequency of currency crises and devaluations, and generally have effects opposite to the ones originally sought by those responsible for speeding up the rate of growth of reserves?

The line of argument set forth above was in fact advanced by two eminent economists at a meeting attended by the writer; and since it has far-reaching implications for the problem of reserve creation, it is important to attempt to establish the extent, if any, to which the analogy between domestic money and international reserves is, in this respect, a valid one.

SOME OBJECTIONS CONSIDERED

It might perhaps be questioned whether any prolonged analysis is required to show that a speeding up in the rate of reserve growth is unlikely to lead to an intensification of balance of payments restrictions, greater frequency of devaluation, and so on. For it might be argued that, if a decline in the relative yield from holding reserves compared with other assets, associated with the acceleration in question, leads countries to tolerate a higher degree of inflation, it must also lead them to a more generous liberalization of trade and a more stubborn adherence to overvalued exchange rates. And, conversely, if an ultimate decline in the magnitude of real reserves drives countries into restrictions and devaluations, it must also tend to check and reverse the inflation that was its cause. This argumentation, though it contains some truth, is not entirely conclusive. Willingness to adopt policies that involve parting with reserves may be a more complex and differentiated affair than is generally assumed. Thus it is not implausible that an increased desire to economize reserves arising from considerations of relative yield on different types of national assets might outweigh a given decline in the real amount of reserves so far as its effect in promoting an expansionary demand policy is concerned, but that the decline in reserves might nevertheless lead to more frequent emergencies in which governments were forced to apply restrictions or to devalue. However this may be, the differences that exist between the relationship of money creation to the holding of real balances, on the one hand, and that of reserve creation to the holding of real reserves, on the other, are sufficiently interesting, apart from their significance for trade and exchange rate policies, to merit consideration on their own account.

Other objections to the proposition under examination suggest themselves at the outset. For example, it might be pointed out that the influence of inflation on the demand for real money balances rests on the fact that assets that rank as money normally carry either no, or at least a relatively low and stable, rate of interest. They therefore become unattractive, when prices are expected to rise, relative to investment goods, or to financial assets whose yield is more closely related to the yield on such goods. On the other hand, the reserves held by monetary authorities, or at least those held in the form of foreign exchange, very often carry a rate of interest that reflects in some measure the prevailing degree of inflation. Despite the popularity of the term "international liquidity" as a synonym for reserves, the decisive characteristic of reserve assets is not so much that they are liquid as that they are under the control of the monetary authorities and can be used to finance payments deficits. Since all of them do not have to be particularly liquid, they can be remunerative, and their yield may be responsive to inflationary influences.

Again, it may be argued that, whereas the influence of inflation on the holding of money balances operates through the opportunities that it offers to individuals to achieve a more advantageous disposition of their own assets and liabilities, any influence of inflation on the holding of reserves would have to operate by affecting the judgment of the authorities as to the most advantageous form in which the country as a whole could hold its wealth—a judgment that might be thought to be somewhat insensitive to yield considerations.

These arguments, also, are inconclusive. There are important types of reserve assets whose attractions, relative to other assets countries might hold, would certainly be weakened by an intensification of price inflation. Moreover, governments, in less developed countries and elsewhere, do take account of the relative advantages for their countries of holding reserves or more directly productive assets. Moreover, the arguments in question, while they may persuade as to the weakness of the influence of price increases on reserve holding, do not prove that an increased growth of normal reserves *may* not result in a reduction in real reserves, nor do they even disprove that it must necessarily do so. In the analogous case of money balances, it is not so much the strength of the influence of inflation on the desire to hold such balances but the absence of opposing forces that is decisive for the sign of the ultimate effect on real balances.

This consideration leads us naturally to what, in my opinion, is the fundamental difference between the relationship of inflation to money balance holding and to reserve holding, respectively. If individuals, owing to intensified inflation, consider it desirable to adjust their portfolios of assets and liabilities in such a way as to reduce their real money balances and increase their real investments, there is nothing to stop them from achieving the first part of their objective though, in a closed economy at any rate, they may be unable to achieve the second. Their efforts to adjust their portfolios will, of course, further intensify price inflation—indeed this is the mechanism through which the decline in real balances is in fact brought about—but they will not be deterred from persisting in the attempt to adjust their portfolios by any consideration of the effect on prices for which, quite rightly, no single individual will feel any responsibility.

The behavior of monetary authorities with respect to international reserves is governed by considerations far more complex than those that determine the behavior of individuals with respect to money balances. Up to a point, the authorities will react to an increase in their reserve ease as individuals would react to an increase in their monetary ease, namely, by taking action intended to reduce the assets in question, reserves and money, respectively. But the authorities will be hampered in so doing by national objectives with respect to internal financial stability, exchange-rate stability, and other factors that have no parallel in the case of individuals.

EFFECTS OF RESERVE INCREASES
ON DEMAND

Suppose that the IMF, by issuing special drawing rights, augments the rate of growth of national reserves in money terms. Countries may then be expected to feel a greater willingness to part with reserves than would otherwise have been the case, and to react in one or another of the following ways: (a) by seeking to invest some of their liquid reserves in foreign assets of a less liquid but more remunerative character; (b) by relaxing restrictions on private capital exports; (c) by relaxing restrictions on imports; (d) by devaluing somewhat later or revaluing somewhat sooner than would otherwise be the case; and (e) by permitting a somewhat higher pressure of demand for homeproduced goods and services.

There are some points of similarity between the reactions described above and the corresponding reactions of individuals to greater monetary ease. Like the latter, they are calculated to undo part of the increase in the rate of growth of reserves and to increase the rate of acquisition of remunerative assets on the part of the nations undertaking them. (Action (e) in addition may be partly intended to increase employment.)

While, however, the corresponding reactions of individuals to increased monetary ease would all be of a demand-enhancing character, some of the reactions described above are of a demand-diverting character and others are likely to be limited in their effect on demand by the attachment either of the countries in question or of other countries to the objective of price stability. Thus (b), (c), and (d) tend to bring about switches in demand between countries, though if these policies are generally adopted the net diversion of demand will be proportionately less than if they had been adopted by a single country. Moreover, the net effects on incomes, both in the countries to which and in the countries from which demand is diverted, are likely to be largely offset by changes in domestic credit and domestic expenditure.[1] Policy (a) may tend to increase demand if it involves a purchase from nonbanks in the country of investment, but is likely to be very largely offset by credit policy in that country. Only reactions of type (e) clearly involve an increase in

---

[1] Policies (b), (c), and (e), by increasing the flow of international transactions, may bring about a once-and-for-all increase in the desired level of real reserves. To take account of this consideration would complicate the analysis at this point, but I revert to it in the postscript. Policy (d) would tend to reduce the rate of increase of real reserves; this effect also is left out of account in what follows.

demand pressure in the world; therefore, in this discussion attention may be safely confined to this item.

Each country may be thought of as having both a desired rate of real reserve growth and a desired degree of internal demand pressure. The desired rate of real reserve growth in any country is the rate at which the authorities of that country would prefer to accumulate real reserves if this could be done by methods having no objectionable side effects on exchange stability, internal demand pressure, and so on, though it would necessarily involve sacrificing an equivalent accumulation of remunerative assets. Other things being equal, this desired rate of real reserve growth will vary inversely with the actual level of real reserves in the country in question.[2] To the desired degree of demand pressure in any country, there corresponds, via the Phillips curve, a certain rate of price inflation, which we may call the preferred rate of price inflation (though, in fact, it may be higher than the rate of inflation that would be desired in the absence of a trade-off between inflation and unemployment).

In a representative country, if the actual rate of real reserve growth equals the desired rate, the authorities will maintain the actual rate of price inflation equal to the preferred rate; the more the rate of real reserve growth exceeds (or falls short of) the desired rate, the more the rate of inflation will exceed (or fall short of) the preferred rate. This conclusion is arrived at as follows. In each country the growth of world (import) prices is taken as given, but the country, by varying domestic demand, can determine the rate of growth of the price of domestic output (together with the level of domestic employment) and believes that it can affect the composition of national investment as between real reserves, on the one hand, and domestic assets, on the other. The latter result is expected to ensue through the effect of demand policy on the balance of payments.

---

[2] As was indicated in my paper, *Toward Assessing the Need for International Reserves*, Princeton University, Essays in International Finance, no. 58 (Princeton, N.J.: Princeton University Press, February 1967), the degree of reserve ease enjoyed by a country may be regarded as a function, in the form of a weighted average, of (a) the level and (b) the rate of growth of real reserves. The level of real reserves should be deflated by a scale factor representing the need for reserves as it changes through time: the growth of real reserves is conveniently expressed as a proportional rate of change. The higher the level of real reserves, the lower will be the rate of reserve growth required to maintain a given degree of reserve ease, and the higher the rate of reserve growth, the lower will be the level of real reserves required to maintain a given degree of reserve ease. In a situation with no growth in the *need* for real reserves, the desired rate of real reserve growth will fall as the level of real reserves rises. The level of real reserves that corresponds to a zero rate of desired real reserve growth may be termed the static target level of real reserves.

In a representative country, just because it is typical, the rate of growth of world (import) prices, though taken as given, will turn out to equal whatever rate of price growth of domestic output that country may choose to set. If prices (including both import and domestic prices) are growing at the preferred rate but real reserve growth exceeds the desired rate, the country will reckon that at some cost in undesired inflation it should, by making its balance of payments more adverse, increase its rate of accumulation of remunerative assets and reduce its accumulation of real reserves; while if real reserve growth falls short of the desired rate, it will reckon that, at some cost in undesired unemployment, it should, by improving its balance of payments, increase its accumulation of real reserves. In neither case, however—and here lies a crucial difference from the behavior of an individual with respect to money—will the country attempt to carry its reaction to the point at which its actual would equal its desired reserve increase, since, after a certain point, the marginal utility that is expected to accrue from approaching closer to the reserve growth target will fall below the increasing marginal disutility of departing further from the internal demand target.

The representative individual, in trying to change the composition of his portfolio as between money balances and other assets by varying his expenditure, will be prevented by price movements from changing his holdings of other assets though the real value of his money balances will change. Similarly, the representative country will be frustrated in any attempt to use the balance of payments as a means for altering the level of its domestic real investment. Changes in incomes and prices at home will be offset, so far as effects on the balance of payments are concerned, by parallel changes in incomes and prices abroad. However, these price changes will produce an effect, in the direction if not in the degree expected, in the rate of growth of real reserves. The fact that both in the case of money and in that of reserves the attempt to change the holding of other assets will be frustrated, while the attempt to alter the holding of money balances or reserves, respectively, will be implemented in some measure but in an unexpected way (i.e., through price repercussions), does not alter the fact that in the second case the attempt itself will be carried less far, being inhibited by considerations of domestic financial stability.

The foregoing—and ensuing—analysis is conducted in terms of a "representative country," that is, a country whose actions are typical of the actions of countries in general weighted according to the importance of their actions, and whose situation, for example, with respect to balance of payments and price growth, is typical of the situation of the world as a whole. No such country may exist, but the methodological fiction enables us to explain with sufficient accuracy for the present purpose what results may be expected from the world as a whole from actions undertaken from motives applicable to individual countries. We do not need to assume that the representative country expects other countries to imitate its behavior, but simply that the other countries do in fact act similarly and that the results of their actions are taken as data by the representative country.

The difference between the demand for money and the demand for reserves can be seen most clearly if we neglect, for the moment, any influence that the rate of inflation (actual or expected) may have on the demand for real money balances and real reserves, respectively. Under this assumption, any increase in the rate of expansion of the nominal stock of money will lead, in a static full employment economy, to an equal proportionate increase in the rate of inflation of prices, the typical individual maintaining his real money balance unchanged. By contrast, any increase in the rate of expansion of reserves in money terms will lead, in the first instance, to a less-than-proportionate increase in prices in the representative country, since only if the rate of increase of real reserves is increased will the authorities permit *any* increase in the rate of inflation. In the long run, to be sure, prices in a static world will probably rise proportionately to the rate of expansion of reserves, but only after an increase has taken place in the stock of real reserves.

We must now take account of the fact that as soon as the acceleration of price inflation affects expectations of further price trends it is likely to have a negative influence not only on the desired real balances of individuals but also on the desired rates of real reserve growth of the representative country corresponding to given levels of its real reserves.[3] The influence, as already indicated, derives in both cases from the fact that prospective inflation enhances the profitability of holding real assets and those monetary claims whose yield is most closely related to that of real assets, as against money on the one hand, and reserves on the other.

---

[3] This is because it will have a negative influence on the country's target level of real reserves as defined in footnote 2. See basic equations below.

When account is taken of this reaction, the resemblance between the individual's demand for money and the government's demand for reserves increases, but the differences remain vital. Briefly, it becomes possible, or at least conceivable, that the end result of speeding up reserve creation will be to reduce the real value of reserves; but it is by no means necessary, as in the case of demand for money, that this should happen, and it is indeed more likely that the real value of reserves will increase. Moreover, it remains true in either event that price inflation in the long run can rise and remain above the level that is preferred in the representative country only if the level of real reserves exceeds the level that is desired.

CHOICE BETWEEN TARGETS

The manner in which the representative country will choose a compromise position as between targets not simultaneously attainable can be set forth mathematically as follows:

All symbols relate to the representative country.

Let p stand for the price of goods and services consumed. Then

$$p = sp_f + (1 - s)p_d$$

where

p_d stands for the price of domestic output,
p_f stands for the price of imports,
s stands for the share of imports in consumption.

Let r stand for the stock of reserves in money units, and let P stand for the preferred rate of increase of the price level (p), and let E stand for the desired rate of increase of real reserves (r/p_f).

Let the country's welfare function take the quadratic form[4]

$$W = T - \left[w \left\{ s\frac{\dot{p}_f}{p_f} + (1 - s)\frac{\dot{p}_d}{p_d} - P \right\}^2 + (1 - w)\left(\frac{\dot{r}}{r} - \frac{\dot{p}_f}{p_f} - E \right)^2 \right]$$

where W stands for welfare, T stands for the level of welfare when the rate of price increase ($\dot{p}/p$) is at its preferred level, and the rate of real reserve increase ($\dot{r}/r$) − ($\dot{p}_f/p_f$) is at its desired level, and w stands for the relative weight attached to the price-change target as compared to the real reserve-change target.

[4] The use of a quadratic welfare function was suggested to me by R. R. Rhomberg.

This implies that the country will attach fixed weights to the disutility of (squared) deviations from its targets for price growth and real reserve growth, respectively.

Now the country will attempt to maximize W, taking T, P, E, and $(\dot{p}_f/p_f)$ (import price change) as given and assuming that

$$\frac{\dot{r}}{r} = K - z\frac{\dot{p}_d}{p_d},$$

where K is a constant.

In other words, if demand is increased in such a way that the inflation of domestic prices increases by 1 percent per annum, the accrual of reserves will decline (or the loss of reserves increase) by z percent of the stock of reserves per annum.

The first order condition for maximizing W as $(\dot{p}_d/p_d)$ is increased is that

$$\frac{dW}{d(\dot{p}_d/p_d)} = 0.$$

This condition will be satisfied if

$$\left\{ s\frac{\dot{p}_f}{p_f} + (1-s)\frac{\dot{p}_d}{p_d} - P \right\} = \frac{(1-w)z}{w(1-s)}\left(\frac{\dot{r}}{r} - \frac{\dot{p}_f}{p_f} - E\right).$$

But in the representative country

$$\frac{\dot{p}_f}{p_f} = \frac{\dot{p}_d}{p_d} = \frac{\dot{p}}{p}.$$

Therefore

$$\left(\frac{\dot{p}}{p} - P\right) = \frac{(1-w)z}{w(1-s)}\left(\frac{\dot{r}}{r} - \frac{\dot{p}}{p} - E\right).$$

BASIC RELATIONSHIPS OF
THE SYSTEM

We are now in a position to demonstrate the effects of increasing the rate of growth of monetary reserves—both the impact effects on the rate of real reserve growth and the long-run effects on the level of real reserves—by setting up a dynamic model of the system of relationships involved. The model is based on the assumption of a demand function for real reserves, which apart from its sensitivity to inflationary expectations, grows at a constant (positive or negative) rate through time.

The basic equations are as follows:

Where p, r, P, and E are defined as above,

> R stands for the static target level of real reserves, that is, the level of real reserves at which $E = 0$;

> $\bar{R}$ stands for the basic target level of real reserves, that is, the value of R when prices are stable;

and a, b, and c are constant coefficients, with $a = \dfrac{(1 - w)z}{w(1 - s)}$,

$$\frac{\dot{p}_t}{p_t} - P = a\left(\frac{\dot{r}_t}{r_t} - \frac{\dot{p}_t}{p_t} - E_t\right). \tag{1}$$

In words, this says that at any point of time the rate of increase of prices will exceed the preferred rate by an amount proportional to the excess of the actual rate of increase of real reserves over the preferred rate.

$$E_t = b\left(\frac{R_t - \dfrac{r_t}{p_t}}{\bar{R}_t}\right) \tag{2}$$

In other words, the preferred rate of increase of real reserves will be proportional to the excess of the static target level over the actual level of real reserves, where this excess is expressed as a proportion of the basic target level of reserves.

$$R_t = \bar{R}_t\left(1 - c\frac{\dot{p}_t}{p_t}\right) \quad \text{or} \quad \frac{R_t - \bar{R}_t}{\bar{R}_t} = -c\frac{\dot{p}_t}{p_t} \tag{3}$$

In other words, the proportional excess of actual over basic target real reserves is negatively proportional to the rate of price increase.

$$\bar{R}_t = \bar{R}_0 e^{kt}, \tag{4}$$

where the basic target level of real reserves grows through time at a constant (positive or negative) rate.

SHORT-TERM EFFECTS OF A CHANGE
IN RESERVE GROWTH

The rate of growth of nominal reserves in the representative country, $(\dot{r}/r)$, will reflect the rate of growth of nominal reserves in the world as a whole, and may be regarded as being determined by a process of international decisionmaking. It is obvious that any increase in $(\dot{r}/r)$ will tend to raise the rate of increase of real reserves, $(\dot{r}/r) - (\dot{p}/p)$, directly.

On the other hand, through equation (1), it also tends to accelerate the rate of price inflation; and this reinforces itself in a self-inflammatory way through the influence of price inflation on the target level of real reserves (equation (3)), hence on the desired rate of expansion of real reserves (equation (2)) and hence on price inflation itself (equation (1)).

Now it turns out that, with this model, the rate of price inflation will be stable in the short run at any point of time only if $abc < 1 + a$, and that any increase in the rate of reserve growth will exercise a positive, nil, or negative influence both on the rate of growth of real reserves at the time when the increase takes place, and on the level of real reserves in the long run according as abc falls short of, equals, or exceeds unity. This second condition is somewhat more stringent than the first; it is possible for the rate of reserve growth to exercise a negative influence on real reserves even though the system is stable in the short run.

So far as the impact effects of speeding up reserve growth are concerned, these propositions may be demonstrated by the following argument. It follows from equation (3) that a primary increase in the rate of price inflation by 1 unit would lead to a decline of $c\bar{R}_t$ in target real reserves. This in turn would give rise (through equation (2)) to a decline of bc in the desired rate of growth of real reserves; and since the unit increase in the rate of price inflation would involve an equal decline in real reserve growth, there would be a rise of $bc - 1$ in the excess of actual over desired real reserve growth. This rise in excess real reserves, finally, would result, through equation (1), in a secondary rise in the rate of price inflation amounting to $abc - a$. If the secondary increase in inflation $(= abc - a)$ exceeds the primary increase $(= 1)$, it will in turn occasion tertiary and further increases of increasing dimensions. Inflation in these conditions for short-run stability is that $abc < 1 + a$.

If this condition is satisfied, we can calculate, as the sum of a geometric series, the total price inflation resulting from a unit primary increase in price inflation. It is $\{1/(1 + a - abc)\}$. In these circumstances a unit increase in the rate of reserve growth will give rise (through equation (I)) to a primary increase in the rate of inflation amounting to a and a total increase in the rate of inflation amounting to $\{a/(1 + a - abc)\}$. The net effect of the increase in the rate of reserve growth $\Delta(\dot{r}/r)$ on the rate of increase in real reserves $\Delta(\dot{r}/r) - \Delta(\dot{p}/p)$ will be positive only if $\Delta(\dot{r}/r) > \Delta(\dot{p}/p)$, that is, if $1 > \{a/(1 + a - abc)\}$. This will be the case only if $abc < 1$.

Whether abc exceeds or falls short of unity it will, in principle, be possible, given the short-term stability of the system, to determine some rate of growth of nominal reserves that will result in a rate of price increase equal to the preferred rate, and a rate of growth in real reserves equal to the desired rate. This rate of growth of nominal reserves depends, *inter alia*, on the level of real reserves relative to the basic static target level of real reserves at the time when the rate of reserve growth is varied.[5] Any other rate of growth of nominal reserves will result in a rate of growth of real reserves which diverges from the desired rate.

What has been said relates to impact effects of changes in $(\dot{r}/r)$.

However, the model used in this paper is not really intended for the analysis of impact effects. If that had been the intention, it would have been necessary to include in equations (1) and (3) time lags that would have reduced virtually to zero the impact effect of changes in reserve growth on price growth, and that of price growth on desired real reserve growth. In the short run, an increase in reserve growth in money terms is virtually certain to increase reserve growth in real terms.

The same might be said of the effect of increases in the growth of money on real money balances. It is in the long run that increases in the rate of expansion of money are likely to reduce real balances, and the purpose of setting up the model in this paper is to see whether the same is true for international reserves. The question is what the amount of real reserves would be in the long run if the rate of reserve growth, which we may term

$$j\left(\equiv \frac{\dot{r}}{r}\right),$$

were raised at a given point of time and maintained indefinitely at the new level, compared with what that amount would have been if the rate

---

[5] The condition is that

$$\frac{\dot{r}}{r} = b\left[\frac{\bar{R} - (r/p)}{\bar{R}}\right] + P(1 - bc).$$

had remained indefinitely at the lower level. Reserves and prices at time zero are taken as given, and no assumptions are made about developments prior to that date.

LONG-TERM EFFECTS OF
A CHANGE IN RESERVE GROWTH

Unfortunately, the argumentation regarding long-term effects is a little complex and has, therefore, been banished to the Mathematical Appendix. The following are the main results:

1. Assuming that the difference between actual and desired real reserve growth has *some* influence on the rate of price increase that governments are willing to promote ($a \neq 0$), the maintenance of a given rate of reserve growth will lead in the long run to one of two possible outcomes. Either the coefficients are such that either:

    a. price inflation ($\dot{p}/p$) tends to approximate a rate equal to the excess of the rate of reserve growth (j) over the rate of growth of basic target real reserves (k), so that real reserves expressed as a proportion of basic target real reserves (what might be termed "normalized" real reserves) tend to converge on a constant positive finite level;

    b. price inflation tends to approximate a rate (dependent on the rate of reserve growth) that exceeds the excess of the rate of reserve growth over the rate of growth of basic target real reserves, so that normalized real reserves tend toward zero.

2. The long-term equilibrium level toward which normalized real reserves tend if outcome (a) applies will not in general correspond to the desired degree of reserve ease. That is, normalized real reserves will not generally tend toward a level such that the desired rate of growth of real reserves (E) equals the actual rate of growth of real reserves (which in these circumstances equals k). It will exceed, equal, or fall short of that level—which may be termed the "dynamic target level" of real reserves by contrast with the "static target level" (R)—according as $j \gtreqless P + k$, or according as the rate of growth of nominal reserves exceeds, equals, or falls short of the sum of the preferred rate of price increase and the rate of growth of basic target real reserves.

3. Whichever of the outcomes, (a) or (b), applies, an increase in the rate of growth of reserves will tend in the long run to increase, leave

unchanged, or reduce the level of real reserves according as abc falls short of, equals, or exceeds unity.

4. If abc is less than unity, normalized real reserves will tend in the long run toward a positive finite equilibrium level only if the rate of reserve growth exceeds a critical value that will be the higher, the higher are the rate of growth of basic target real reserves and the preferred rate of increase of prices.

From the foregoing it appears that all that one can say about the long-term effects of reserve creation within the terms of our model is that, whereas an intensified expansion of money is virtually certain to result ultimately in a decline in real money balances, an intensified expansion of reserves may result in either an increase or a decline in real reserves according as abc falls short of, or exceeds, unity. To go further, a view must be taken as to the probable magnitude of these coefficients, bearing in mind that they are meant to represent the way in which the authorities of a "representative country" would react to the relevant economic stimuli after allowing for lagged effects.

Even with this qualification, the writer considers it probable, though by no means certain, that in the real world abc would fall short of unity. Thus it seems plausible that the government of a representative country might reduce its real reserve target on account of a 2 percent per annum increase in the rate of price inflation by something in the order of 5 percent of its basic target ($c = 2\ 1/2$). Again, it might reduce its desired rate of real reserve increase by, say, $2/3$ percent per annum on account of a decline in its real reserve target amounting to 1 percent of its basic target ($b = 2/3$). In estimating the extent to which it increases its rate of price inflation in response to an increase of the excess of its actual over its desired real reserve increase, we must remember that

$$a = \frac{(1 - w)z}{w(1 - s)}.$$

Now, a representative country might reckon the weight of foreign trade goods to home trade goods in its consumption price level at, say, $1:3$ ($s = 1/4$). And it might reckon that an increment in home demand giving rise to an increment of 1 percent per annum in its domestic price level might result in a decline of 3 percent per annum in its reserves ($z = 3$). Finally, it might attach fifteen times as much importance to a deviation of 1 percent per annum from its preferred rate of price increase as to a deviation of 1 percent per annum from its desired rate of real reserve increase. (With a quadratic welfare function this implies that a 1 percent per annum deviation from its preferred price increase would cause almost as much distress as a 4 percent per annum deviation from its desired real reserve growth.) Hence

$$a = \frac{(1 - w)z}{w(1 - s)} = \frac{1/16 \times 3}{15/16 \times 3/4} = \frac{4}{15}.$$

Putting these numbers together would yield a value for *abc* of only $4/15 \times 2/3 \times 5/2 = 4/9$. The calculation, of course, is purely illustrative, and, in the absence of empirical evidence, anyone is free to assign values to *a*, *b*, and *c* that yield a product exceeding unity.

It has been assumed throughout this paper that the rate of price infla-tion in the representative country is under the control of its government, though the reserve situation may influence the rate of inflation it decides to have and the manner in which firms and residents react to demand pressure may influence the rate of price increase that it "prefers." This implies that the government of the representative country is in a position to offset any undesired or unexpected changes in the foreign demand for its products. It is true that, when world reserve growth is first increased, countries may think that they can curtail this by worsening their trade balance at the cost of a relatively slight increase in the rate of inflation. When they find by experience that exports are rising *pari passu* with imports, they will revise upward their planned rate of price inflation. This, however, has already been allowed for in the explanation of the optimiza-tion process underlying equation (1), and particularly coefficient *a*. It is assumed that countries will not be diverted from the planned rate of demand and price growth by the mechanical repercussions of increased exports.

It is conceivable that repeated experiences of frustration in attempts to alter the balance of trade might lead to a change in the representative country's estimate of the trade-off (*z*) between price inflation and real re-serve growth. This could only be in the direction of reducing *z*, reducing the magnitude of coefficient *a* in equation (1), and thus reducing the inflationary effect of a given acceleration in world reserve growth.

INTEREST ON RESERVES[6]

Since it has been supposed that an acceleration in inflation might reduce the target level of real reserves by reducing the relative attractiveness
of holding reserves as compared with other assets, it is natural to consider
what might be the effects of altering that relative attractiveness by
changing the interest yield on reserves. Insofar as reserves are issued,
as are special drawing rights, by an international authority, it would be
possible to vary the interest paid at least on these reserves, thus acquiring
a new instrument of international policy.

It would be quite easy to introduce the rate of interest on reserves into
our model, for example by adapting equation (3) as follows:

$$R_t = \bar{R}_t \left\{ 1 + c \left(n - \frac{\dot{p}_t}{p_t} \right) \right\} \tag{3}$$

where n is the rate of interest accruing—marginally in any case—to
holders of reserves.[7] Then $\bar{R}_t = \bar{R}_0 e^{kt}$ would be redefined as the level of
target real reserves that prevails when the rate of price inflation equals
the rate of interest paid on reserves.

Now for any given rate of growth of nominal reserves $j = (\dot{r}/r)$, the
higher is the interest paid (n), the higher will be the static target level of
real reserves (R); hence the higher the desired rate of real reserve growth
(E); hence the lower the rate of increase of prices $(\dot{p}/p)$; hence the higher
the rate of real reserve growth $(\dot{r}/r) - (\dot{p}/p)$, provided that $abc > 0$. This
relates to the short-term effects of raising n.

From section VI of the Mathematical Appendix it can be seen that the
higher is the rate of interest paid (n), the more likely it is that normalized
real reserves $(r/p)/\bar{R}$ will tend in the long run toward a finite positive level
and the higher that level will be. This is all irrespective of whether abc
exceeds unity, provided only that it exceeds zero. However, if normalized
real reserves do tend toward a finite level, the size of n will not affect
in the long run the rate at which prices will tend to increase $(j - k)$, nor
the difference between this and the preferred rate of price increase, nor
yet the difference between the actual and the desired rate of increase of

---

[6] This section was added after the discussion at the seminar.

[7] Holders of special drawing rights receive or pay interest according as their holdings
exceed or fall short of their cumulative allocations.

real reserves. In other words, insofar as the relationship between actual and preferred price increase serves as an indicator of the willingness of the representative country to part with reserves, an increase in the interest paid on reserves will reduce that willingness in the short run and leave it unchanged in the long run. By contrast, a rise in the rate of nominal reserve growth (j) will always increase the willingness to part with reserves in the short run and still more in the long run, even in those cases in which the normalized level of real reserves declines.

Now, if willingness to part with reserves is a simple one-dimensional quality in the sense that any change that tends to encourage price inflation also tends to encourage the relaxation of restrictions on international transactions, discourage devaluations, and so on, we may expect that a rise in the interest paid on reserves would encourage restrictions in the short run and leave them unaffected in the long run, despite the rise in real reserves; whereas an increase in the rate of growth of nominal reserves would always encourage liberalization in the short run and even more in the long run, even where it had the effect of reducing the level of real reserves.

Under these conditions, there would seem little point in trying to use the rate of interest on reserves as an instrument of international policy, in addition to the use of deliberate reserve creation.

If, on the other hand, as seems rather plausible, the degree of liberalization of international transactions depends rather more on reserve case, that is, on the stock and rate of growth of real reserves, and rather less on the relative yield on reserves and other assets, than does the rate of increase of prices, it becomes possible to use the two instruments, reserve creation and interest on reserves, in such a way as to approximate more closely than would otherwise be possible world objectives with respect to inflation, on the one hand, and liberalization, on the other.

Thus an increase in the rate of growth of nominal reserves will always lead to higher inflation. This may be attributed to a combination of two factors—a deterioration in the relative yield on money holding, which is inflationary, and a change in reserve ease, which may be positive, and thus inflationary, or negative, and thus deflationary. If the change in reserve ease (in the long run taking the form of a change in the stock of real reserves) is positive, the total effect on trade policy must be to increase liberalization. If the change in reserve ease is negative, the overall effect of the increased rate of growth of nominal reserves may be contractionary owing to the higher weight given to reserve ease in determining trade policy.

Again, an increase in the interest paid on reserves will in the long run have no effect on inflation. This is due to the mutual offsetting of the inflationary effect of greater reserve ease (in the form of higher real reserves) and the deflationary effect of the improvement in the relative yield on reserve holding. Owing to the greater weight assumed to be given to reserve ease in determining trade policy, the net effect of increasing the interest paid on reserves will necessarily be to increase liberalization.

This suggests that changes in the rate of growth of nominal reserves should be directed toward achieving desired effects on demand policy, while changes in the interest paid on reserves should be directed toward achieving desired effects on trade policy. Thus, for example, if the intention were to reduce price inflation while keeping liberalization constant, the procedure would be to reduce the rate of growth of nominal reserves while lowering (raising) the interest paid on reserves to the extent necessary to prevent any decline (increase) in real reserves. Again, if the intention were to increase liberalization while keeping price inflation constant, the procedure would be to raise the interest paid on reserves, while temporarily increasing the rate of growth of nominal reserves, to the extent necessary to prevent a decline in price inflation.

However, the question of varying the rate of interest on such reserves as are created by international action—notably special drawing rights—raises issues regarding effects on the supply of other reserves, effects on the balance of payments adjustment process, effects on the international distribution of income, and so on, which are too complex to be dealt with at the end of an article such as this.

POSTSCRIPT: FEEDBACK EFFECTS
FROM CHANGES IN LIBERALIZATION
AND IN REAL OUTPUT[8]

At this point it is convenient to take account of certain elements in the demand for reserves that have been ignored so far. I refer to the feedback

---

[8] I am indebted to W. White, R. R. Rhomberg, and M. Kemp for various comments that have provoked me into adding this postscript.

effects on target real reserves that may be expected to arise from changes in the volume and variability of international transactions, which in turn result from policy changes evoked by changes in willingness to part with reserves.

Any increase in willingness to part with reserves—in a sense to be defined more precisely later—may be expected to result in (a) an increase in the degree of liberalization of trade insofar as that has been hampered by balance of payments restrictions and (b) a rise in real output associated with a rise in demand and in the rate of increase of prices. Both of these reactions may be expected to raise the levels of trade and international transactions generally, and also to increase the magnitude of potential real payments disequilibria in a way that will enhance the target level of real reserves.

Will these repercussions alter in any way the arguments set forth earlier regarding the effects of increased nominal reserve creation, or of increases in the interest on reserves?

Let us suppose that willingness to part with reserves is one-dimensional, in the sense described in the preceding section, and that liberalization, like inflation, responds to changes in the difference between the actual and the desired rate of growth of real reserves.[9] Changes in real output are in any case assumed to be associated with changes in inflation, and hence with changes in the difference in question, so that the two feedback effects at this point run in parallel.

We can allow for the influence of these on the demand for reserves by yet another adaptation of equations (3) and ($\overline{3}$), namely,

$$\frac{R_t}{\overline{R}_t} = 1 + c\left(n - \frac{\dot{p}_t}{p_t}\right) + d\left(\frac{\dot{r}_t}{r_t} - \frac{\dot{p}_t}{p_t} - E\right). \tag{$\dot{3}$}_1$$

This says that the (normalized) target level of real reserves contains a positive element proportional to the excess of the actual over the desired rate of growth of real reserves.

Then, $\overline{R}_t = \overline{R}_0 e^{kt}$ would be redefined as the static target level of real reserves that prevails when the rate of price inflation is equal to the rate of interest on reserves and the excess rate of growth of real reserves is equal to zero.

---

[9] Strictly speaking, it is the deviation between the actual degree and some desired degree of liberalization that responds in the manner described.

Now the greater is d, the more an increase in excess real reserve growth will tend to raise desired real reserve growth. Owing to this feedback, anything—such as an increase in nominal reserve growth—that tends to increase excess real reserve growth will become less effective in this respect. The greater is d, therefore, the smaller will be the stimulus to part with reserves by way of price inflation and the greater the stimulus to real reserve growth that will result from a given acceleration in the rate of increase in nominal reserves. Not surprisingly, the greater is d, the greater will be the likelihood that an acceleration in the rate of growth of nominal reserves will have a positive rather than a negative influence on the rate of growth of real reserve. The condition of such a positive influence is no longer that $abc < 1$ but that $abc - bd < 1$. By contrast, the tendency of a higher payment of interest on reserves (n) to raise the level of desired reserves, to reduce excess real reserves, and to raise the rate of growth of real reserves will be the weaker, the greater is d.

The long-term effects of the feedbacks under examination are shown in section VII of the Mathematical Appendix. Briefly, the higher is d, the higher will be the long-term equilibrium level of real reserves, if it exists. And the higher is d, the more positive or less negative will be the effect of increasing the nominal rate of reserve growth on the long-term equilibrium level of real reserves—the condition for a positive effect being, as before, that $abc - bd < 1$.

Since, as we have seen, the rate of interest on reserves (n) has no effect in the long run on the excess of actual over desired real reserve growth, and hence no effect on the degree of liberalization or the level of output, the long-term consequences of changes in n on the level of real reserves will be unaffected by changes in d.

Let us now consider the feedback effects of liberalization on the demand for reserves in the more interesting case in which the degree of liberalization and the associated element in the demand for reserves vary, not with the excess of actual over the desired rate of increase in real reserves, but with the degree of reserve ease. Reserve ease is a composite concept comprising both the stock and the rate of change of real reserves. In order to reduce it to a common denominator for the purpose of measurement, one has to assume some rate of equivalence between the two. In equations (1) and (2) it has been assumed, in effect, that a 1 percent per annum increase in the rate of increase in real reserves is equivalent (in its effect on price inflation) to a b percent increase in normalized real reserves. This means that

$$\Delta\left(\frac{\dot{r}_t}{r_t} - \frac{\dot{p}_t}{p_t}\right) \quad \text{is equivalent to} \quad b\Delta\left(\frac{r_t/p_t}{\bar{R}_t}\right).$$

Adopting the same assumption here, we may regard the normalized reserve equivalent (y) of the stock and rate of growth of reserves at any time as

$$y_t = \frac{(r_t/p_t)}{\bar{R}_t} + \frac{1}{b}\left(\frac{\dot{r}_t}{r_t} - \frac{\dot{p}_t}{p_t}\right).$$

Using this, we arrive at still another form of equation (3), namely,

$$\frac{R_t}{\bar{R}_t} = 1 + c\left(n - \frac{\dot{p}_t}{p_t}\right) + f(y_1 - 1)$$

$$= 1 + c\left(n - \frac{\dot{p}_t}{p_t}\right) + f\left\{\frac{r_t/p_t}{\bar{R}_t} + \frac{1}{b}\left(\frac{\dot{r}_t}{r_t} - \frac{\dot{p}_t}{p_t}\right) - 1\right\} \qquad (3)_2$$

where f measures the influence on normalized target real reserves of changes in the normalized reserve equivalent.

Then $\bar{R}_t = \bar{R}_0 e^{kt}$ would be redefined as the static target level of real reserves that prevails when the rate of price inflation is equal to the rate of interest on reserves and the reserve equivalent is equal to the static target level.

It may be presumed that $f < 1$, that is, that an increase in the real reserve equivalent will not, because of the encouragement it gives to liberalization, raise target real reserves by the same or a greater amount.

Any increase that takes place in the rate of growth of nominal reserves, if it leads to an increase in the rate of growth of real reserves, will enhance reserve ease (as measured by the normalized reserve equivalent, z, and hence will provoke an increase in liberalization and in the target level of reserves, the effect of which will be to reduce the rate of price inflation, thus further increasing the rate of growth of real reserves. By contrast, if the increase in the rate of growth of nominal reserves leads to a decline in real reserves, that decline will be reinforced by a decline in the demand for reserves. Therefore, the existence of a positive f, or its increase, will increase the *magnitude*, but will not change the *sign*, of the effect of nominal reserve growth on the rate of growth of real reserves. As before, the sign of that effect will depend on whether $abc \lessgtr 1$.

Again, since any increase in the interest paid on reserves (n) will increase the rate of increase of real reserves, it will trigger an increase in the degree of liberalization, which tends to slow down the rate of price inflation and further raise the rate of real reserve growth. This liberalization effect will, of course, be the greater the greater is f.

In the long run, also (as can be seen from section VIII of the Mathematical Appendix), the condition on which an increase in the rate of increase in nominal reserves will result in an increase in the level of real reserves is unaffected by the level of f, and is that $abc < 1$; furthermore, the higher the level of f, the greater will be the *positive* influence of the rate of reserve increase on the long-term equilibrium level of real reserves, if $abc < 1$, or the greater will be its *negative* influence if $abc > 1$. That is, if real reserves would otherwise be enhanced by an acceleration in the rate of increase of nominal reserves, the enhanced demand for reserves resulting from liberalization will increase them further; and if the level of real reserves would otherwise be decreased by an acceleration in the rate of increase of nominal reserves, a decline in the demand for reserves resulting from deliberalization will reduce them further.

An increase in the rate of interest on reserves (n) will always lead to an increase in the long term in the normalized level of real reserves, and this in turn to a rise in liberalization and demand for reserves. The greater is f, the greater will be this reinforcement of the increase in real reserves.

We have now considered two possibilities regarding the factors that stimulate an increase in liberalization:

1. that liberalization, like price inflation, will be stimulated by an increase in the excess of actual over desired real reserve increase; and
2. that liberalization, unlike price inflation, will be stimulated solely by an increase in reserve ease, that is, by an increase in the stock and/or the rate of growth of real reserves.

The truth probably lies somewhere in between these extreme assumptions, in which case the liberalization feedback effect will enhance any positive effort on real reserves that might otherwise tend to result from an increase in the rate of growth of nominal reserves, but may not detract from any negative effect that would otherwise tend to result from it. It will also enhance the positive effect on real reserves resulting from a rise in the interest paid on reserves.

MATHEMATICAL APPENDIX
I

Let p stand for the price level;

r stand for the stock of reserves (in money terms);

P stand for the preferred proportional rate of increase of the price level;

E stand for the desired proportional rate of increase of real reserves;

R stand for the target level of real reserves;

$\bar{R}$ stand for the target level of real reserves when $(\dot{p}_t/p_t) = 0$; and a, b, and c be constant coefficients.

Now, we may suppose that

$$\frac{\dot{p}_t}{p_t} - P = a\left(\frac{\dot{r}_t}{r_t} - \frac{\dot{p}_t}{p_t} - E_t\right) \tag{1}$$

$$E_t = b\left(\frac{R_t - \dfrac{r_t}{p_t}}{\bar{R}_t}\right) \tag{2}$$

$$R_t = \bar{R}_t\left(1 - c\frac{\dot{p}_t}{p_t}\right) \tag{3}$$

and

$$\bar{R}_t = \bar{R}_0 e^{kt}. \tag{4}$$

From (1), (2), (3), and (4)

$$\frac{\dot{p}_t}{p_t} = \alpha\frac{\dot{r}_t}{r_t} + \beta\bar{R}_0^{-1}e^{-kt}\frac{r_t}{p_t} + \gamma \tag{5}$$

where

$$\alpha \equiv \frac{a}{1 + a - abc}$$

$$\beta \equiv \frac{ab}{1 + a - abc} \equiv b\alpha$$

and

$$\gamma \equiv \frac{P - ab}{1 + a - abc}.$$

In order that the rate of price increase may be in stable equilibrium at each point of time, $(1 + a - abc)$ must be positive.

Now, let the amount of reserves (in money terms) increase exponentially at rate j,

that is,
$$r_t = r_0 e^{jt} \tag{6}$$

Then, from (5) and (6),

$$\dot{p}_t = (\alpha j + \gamma)p_t + \beta \bar{R}_0^{-1} r_0 \exp(j - k)t \tag{7}$$

from which it follows that

$$p_t = \frac{\beta \bar{R}_0^{-1} r_0 \exp(j - k)t}{j - k - \alpha j - \gamma} + \left(p_0 - \frac{\beta \bar{R}_0^{-1} r_0}{j - k - \alpha j - \gamma} \right) \exp(\alpha j + y)t \tag{8}$$

$$\frac{(r_t/p_t)}{\bar{R}_t} = \frac{1}{\dfrac{\beta}{j - k - \alpha j - \gamma} + \left(\dfrac{p_0 \bar{R}_0}{r_0} - \dfrac{\beta}{j - k - \alpha j - \gamma} \right) \exp(\alpha j + \gamma - j + k)t} \tag{9}^{10}$$

$$\frac{\dot{p}_t}{p_t} = \alpha j + \gamma$$

$$+ \frac{1}{(j - k - \alpha j - \gamma)^{-1} + \beta^{-1} \left(\dfrac{p_0 \bar{R}_0}{r_0} - \dfrac{\beta}{j - k - \alpha j - \gamma} \right) \exp(\alpha j + \gamma - j + k)t} \tag{10}$$

and

$$-\frac{\partial \left(\dfrac{r_t/p_t}{\bar{R}_t} \right)}{\partial j}$$

$$= \frac{\dfrac{-\beta(1 - \alpha)}{(j - k - \alpha j - \gamma)^2} - \left(\dfrac{p_0 \bar{R}_0}{r_0} - \dfrac{\beta}{j - k - \alpha j - \gamma} \right) t(1 - \alpha) \exp(\alpha j + \gamma - j + k)t}{\left\{ \dfrac{\beta}{j - k - \alpha j - \gamma} + \left(\dfrac{p_0 \bar{R}_0}{r_0} - \dfrac{\beta}{j - k - \alpha j - \gamma} \right) \exp(\alpha j + \gamma - j + k)t \right\}^2} \tag{11}$$

$$+ \frac{\exp(\alpha j + \gamma - j + k)t \dfrac{\beta(1 - \alpha)}{(j - k - \alpha j - \gamma)^2}}{\left\{ \dfrac{\beta}{j - k - \alpha j - \gamma} + \left(\dfrac{p_0 \bar{R}_0}{r_0} - \dfrac{\beta}{j - k - \alpha j - \gamma} \right) \exp(\alpha j + \gamma - j + k)t \right\}^2}.$$

[10] The expression $(r_t/p_t)/\bar{R}_t$ is hereafter referred to as "normalized" real reserves.

II

Now if, but only if, $j - k - \alpha j - \gamma > 0$, and $a \neq 0$

as $\qquad\qquad t \to \infty$

$$\frac{\dot{p}_t}{p_t} \to j - k \tag{12}$$

$$\frac{(r_t/p_t)}{\bar{R}_t} \to \frac{j - k - \alpha j - \gamma}{\beta} \tag{13}$$

and

$$\frac{\partial \left(\dfrac{r_t/p_t}{\bar{R}_t}\right)}{\partial j} \to \frac{1 - \alpha}{\beta} = \frac{1 - abc}{ab}. \tag{14}$$

If $j - k - \alpha j - \gamma < 0$

$$\frac{\dot{p}_t}{p_t} \to \alpha j + \gamma \qquad [> j - k] \tag{12a}$$

$$\frac{(r_t/p_t)}{\bar{R}_t} \to (+)0 \tag{13a}$$

and

$$\frac{\partial \left(\dfrac{r_t/p_t}{\bar{R}_t}\right)}{\partial j} \to \pm 0 \quad \text{as} \quad \alpha > 1. \tag{14a}$$

III

Now, assuming that $(\dot{p}/p)$ is stable at each point of time and that, therefore, $abc < 1 + a$, then

$$j - k - \alpha j - \gamma \gtreqless 0$$

as

$$(j - k)(1 - abc) \gtreqless P + ak - ab. \tag{15}$$

It can be seen from equation (5) that an increase (decrease) in $(\dot{r}/r)(=j)$ will lead to an instantaneous increase (decrease) smaller than itself in $(\dot{p}/p)$, and hence to an increase (decrease) in the rate of growth of real reserves if, and only if, $\alpha < 1$.

Since, with $abc < 1 + a$, β is positive, it follows from (11) that, whether $j - k - \alpha j - \gamma$ is positive or negative, as $t \to \infty$,

$$\frac{\partial\left(\dfrac{r_t/p_t}{\bar{R}_t}\right)}{\partial j};$$

therefore

$$\frac{\partial\left(\dfrac{r_t}{p_t}\right)}{\partial j}$$

will be positive or negative according as $\alpha \lessgtr 1$; though, if $j - k - \alpha j - \gamma$ is negative, the influence of j on $(r_t/p_t)/\bar{R}_t$, positive or negative, will tend to zero as $t \to \infty$. Now $\alpha \lessgtr 1$ as $abc \lessgtr 1$.

The condition for a positive long-run influence of j on (r_t/p_t) (viz., that $abc < 1$) is somewhat more stringent than the test for the short-term stability of $(\dot{p}/p)$ (viz., that $abc < 1 + \alpha$), so that it is possible, though not necessary, that the system should have short-term stability and yet that increases in j should tend to reduce (r_t/p_t) in the long run.

The question as to whether abc is greater or less than unity is important also for the question as to whether $j - k - \alpha j - \gamma$ is positive or negative, and therefore also for the question whether "normalized" real reserves will converge on a positive finite value or on the contrary tend to zero. If $abc < 1$ (and an increase in j therefore tends to raise real reserves), it follows from (15) that $j - k - \alpha j - \gamma \gtrless 0$ as

$$j - k \gtrless \frac{P + ak - ab}{1 - abc}.$$

For "normalized" real reserves to converge in a positive finite value, rather than dwindle to zero, it is necessary that $j - k$ not fall below a certain critical level, which rises with k. If $abc > 1$ (and an increase in j therefore tends to *reduce* real reserves),

$$j - k - \alpha j - \gamma \gtrless 0$$

as

$$j - k \lessgtr \frac{ab - P - ak}{ab - 1}.$$

For "normalized" real reserves to converge on a positive finite value, it is necessary that j not *rise* above a critical level, given the value of P and k. This critical level falls with k.

IV

In the special cases in which either a or $c = 0$,

$$\frac{\partial \left(\dfrac{r_t/p_t}{\bar{R}_t} \right)}{\partial j},$$

and therefore

$$\frac{\partial \left(\dfrac{r_t}{p_t} \right)}{\partial j},$$

will, of course, be positive as $t \to \infty$. Where $a = 0$, equations (12)–(14) no longer hold, and equations (9)–(11) simplify to

$$\frac{(r_t/p_t)}{\bar{R}_t} = \left(\frac{p_o \bar{R}_o}{r_o} \exp(P - j + k)t \right)^{-1} \tag{9'}$$

$$\frac{\dot{p}_t}{p_t} = P \tag{10'}$$

and

$$\frac{\partial \left(\dfrac{r_t/p_t}{\bar{R}_t} \right)}{\partial j} = \frac{t}{\dfrac{p_o \bar{R}_o}{r_o} \exp(P - j + k)t} \tag{11'}$$

so that, as $t \to \infty$,

$$\frac{\dot{p}_t}{p_t} \to P, \tag{12'}$$

$$\frac{r_t/p_t}{\bar{R}_t} \to \text{or} \begin{matrix} \infty \\ 0 \end{matrix} \qquad \begin{matrix} (13') \\ (13a') \end{matrix}$$

according as $j - k \gtrless P$,
and

$$\frac{\partial \left(\dfrac{r_t/p_t}{\bar{R}_t} \right)}{\partial j} \to \text{or} \begin{matrix} \infty \\ 0 \end{matrix} \qquad \begin{matrix} (14') \\ (14a') \end{matrix}$$

according as $j - k \gtrless P$.

V

In section II above, we saw that if $j - k - \alpha j - \gamma > 0$, and $a \neq 0$

$$\frac{\dot{p}_t}{p_t} \to j - k \text{ as } t \to \infty$$

thus under these conditions, as $t \to \infty$

$$\frac{\dot{p}_t}{p_t} - P \to j - k - P$$

and (from equation (1))

$$\left(\frac{\dot{r}_t}{r_t} - \frac{\dot{p}_t}{p_t}\right) - E_t \to \left(\frac{j - k - P}{a}\right)$$

so that if $j = k + P$

$$\frac{\dot{p}_t}{p_t} \to P$$

and

$$E_t \to \left(\frac{\dot{r}_t}{r_t} - \frac{\dot{p}_t}{p_t}\right) \to (j - P) = k.$$

That is, where $j = k + P$, the actual rate of price growth tends toward the preferred rate, the desired and the actual rates of real reserve growth both tend toward the rate of growth of basic target real reserves, and the desired degree of reserve ease prevails. Moreover,

$$E_t \to \lessgtr \left(\frac{\dot{r}_t}{r_t} - \frac{\dot{p}_t}{p_t}\right) = k$$

as $j \gtrless k + P$.

Again, let $(r/p)_d$, the "desired level of reserves," stand for that level of (r/p) for which

$$E = \frac{\dot{r}}{r} - \frac{\dot{p}}{p}$$

[as distinct from R, which is the level of (r/p) for which $E = 0$].

Then, as $t \to \infty$, from equations (2) and (3),

$$\frac{\left(\frac{r_t}{p_t}\right)_d}{\bar{R}_t} \to 1 - c(j - k) - \frac{k}{b}.$$

Thus as $t \to \infty$

$$\frac{r_t}{p_t} - \left(\frac{r_t}{p_t}\right)_d \gtreqless 0$$

as

$$\frac{j - k - \alpha j - \gamma}{\beta} - \left\{1 - c(j - k) - \frac{k}{b}\right\} \quad 0$$

in other words, as $j \gtreqless k + P$.

VI

Let n stand for the rate of interest paid on the holding of reserves. Then replace equation (3) by the following:

$$R_t = \bar{R}_t\left\{1 + c\left(n - \frac{\dot{p}_t}{p_t}\right)\right\}. \tag{3}$$

Equation (5) will remain as before, except that

$$\gamma \equiv \frac{P - ab - nabc}{1 + a - abc}.$$

In all subsequent equations, γ retains this significance.

For given values of all coefficients, since $abc > 0$ and $1 + a - abc > 0$, from equation (5) redefined as above

$$\frac{\partial\left(\dfrac{\dot{p}_t}{p_t}\right)}{\partial n} = \frac{-abc}{1 + a - abc} < 0$$

and

$$\frac{\partial}{\partial n}\left(\frac{\dot{r}_t}{r_t} - \frac{\dot{p}_t}{p_t}\right) = \frac{abc}{1 + a - abc} > 0.$$

Also,

$$\frac{\partial}{\partial n}(j - k - \alpha j - \gamma) > 0.$$

Therefore, the higher is n, the more probable it is that the condition in which equations (12)–(14) become applicable (viz., that $(j - k - \alpha j - \gamma) > 0$) will be fulfilled.

Moreover,

$$\frac{\partial}{\partial n}\left(\frac{j - k - \alpha j - \gamma}{\beta}\right) = c > 0;$$

hence the level to which $\left(\dfrac{r_t/p_t}{\overline{R}_t}\right)$ tends as $t \to \infty$ will be the higher, the higher is n.

VII

Let us rewrite equations (3) and $(\overline{3})$ to take account of the influence of excess real reserve growth on static target real reserves, thus:

$$\frac{R_t}{\overline{R}_t} = 1 + c\left(n - \frac{\dot{p}_t}{p_t}\right) + d\left(\frac{\dot{r}_t}{r_t} - \frac{\dot{p}_t}{p_t} - E\right). \tag{$\dot{3}$}_1$$

Then equation (5) still stands, with α, β, and γ redefined as follows:

$$\alpha = \frac{a}{1 + a + bd - abc}$$

$$\beta = \frac{ab}{1 + a + bd - abc}$$

$$\gamma = \frac{P(1 + bd) - ab - abcn}{1 + a + bd - abc}$$

$$\frac{\partial \alpha}{\partial d} = \frac{-ab}{(1 + a + bd - abc)^2} < 0$$

$$\frac{\partial \beta}{\partial d} = \frac{-ab^2}{(1 + a + bd - abc)^2} < 0$$

$$\frac{\partial \gamma}{\partial d} = \frac{ab\{P(1 - bc) + b + bcn\}}{(1 + a + bd - abc)^2}.$$

From equation (5), if $j = (\dot{r}/r)$ increases by 1 percent, $(\dot{p}/p)$ will increase in the short run by α percent. The higher is d, the lower will be the increase in $(\dot{p}/p)$ and the greater the increase in $(\dot{r}/r) - (\dot{p}/p)$.

Again

$$\frac{\partial(\dot{p}_t/p_t)}{\partial n} = \frac{\partial \gamma}{\partial n} = \frac{-abc}{1 + a + bd - abc} < 0,$$

and

$$\frac{\partial^2 \gamma}{\partial n \partial d} = \frac{ab^2 c}{(1 + a + bd - abc)^2} > 0,$$

that is, an increase in d tends to reduce the negative effect on $(\dot{p}/p)$ [and the positive effect on $(\dot{r}/r) - (\dot{p}/p)$] of an increase in n.

If $j - k - \alpha j - \gamma > 0$, as $t \to \infty$

$$\frac{\partial \left(\dfrac{r_t/p_t}{\overline{R}_t} \right)}{\partial j} \to \frac{1 - \alpha}{\beta} = \frac{1 + bd - abc}{ab} \gtrless 0 \quad \text{as} \quad abc - bd \gtrless 1,$$

and

$$\frac{\partial^2 \left(\dfrac{r_t/p_t}{\overline{R}_t} \right)}{\partial j \partial d} \to \frac{1}{a} > 0.$$

Again,

$$\frac{\partial \left(\dfrac{r_t/p_t}{\overline{R}_t} \right)}{\partial n} \to \frac{\partial}{\partial n} \left(\frac{j - k - \alpha j - \gamma}{\beta} \right) = c > 0,$$

Therefore

$$\frac{\partial^2 \left(\dfrac{r_t/p_t}{\overline{R}_t} \right)}{\partial n \partial d} \to 0.$$

VIII

Let us rewrite equations (3) and (5) to take account of the influence of reserve ease on static target real reserves, thus:

$$\frac{R_t}{\overline{R}_t} = 1 + c \left(n - \frac{\dot{p}_t}{p_t} \right) + f \left\{ \frac{r_t/p_t}{\overline{R}_t} + \frac{1}{b} \left(\frac{\dot{r}_t}{r_t} - \frac{\dot{p}_t}{p_t} \right) - 1 \right\}. \tag{$3)_2$}$$

Then equation (5) will remain as before, except that

$$\alpha = \frac{a(1 - f)}{1 + a(1 - f) - abc}$$

$$\beta = \frac{ab(1 - f)}{1 + a(1 - f) - abc}$$

$$\gamma = \frac{P - ab(1 - f) - abcn}{1 + a(1 - f) - abc}.$$

Now, from equation (5),

$$\frac{\partial^2 \left(\frac{\dot{p}_t}{p_t}\right)}{\partial j \partial f} = \frac{\partial \alpha}{\partial f} = \frac{a(abc - 1)}{(1 + a(1 - f) - abc)^2} \gtreqless 0 \quad \text{as} \quad abc \gtreqless 1,$$

$$\therefore \frac{\partial^2 \left(\frac{\dot{r}_t}{r_t} - \frac{\dot{p}_t}{p_t}\right)}{\partial j \partial f} \lesseqgtr 0 \quad \text{as} \quad abc \lesseqgtr 1.$$

Again, if $j - k - \alpha j - \gamma > 0$, as $t \to \infty$

$$\frac{\partial \left(\frac{r_t/p_t}{\bar{R}_t}\right)}{\partial j} \to \frac{1 - \alpha}{\beta} = \frac{1 - abc}{ab(1 - f)} \gtreqless 0 \quad \text{as} \quad abc \lesseqgtr 1,$$

and

$$\frac{\partial \left(\frac{r_t/p_t}{\bar{R}_t}\right)}{\partial j \partial f} \to \frac{(1 - abc)}{ab(1 - f)^2} \gtreqless 0 \quad \text{as} \quad abc \gtreqless 1.$$

Again,

$$\frac{\partial \left(\frac{r_t/p_t}{\bar{R}_t}\right)}{\partial n} \to \frac{\partial}{\partial n}\left(\frac{j - k - \alpha j - \gamma}{\beta}\right) = \frac{c}{1 - f}$$

$$\frac{\partial^2 \left(\frac{r_t/p_t}{\bar{R}_t}\right)}{\partial n \partial f} = \frac{c}{(1 - f)^2} > 0.$$

12

SPECIAL DRAWING RIGHTS: SOME PROBLEMS AND POSSIBILITIES

THE SPECIAL DRAWING RIGHT

THE YEAR 1969 witnessed a potentially important development in the international monetary system in the form of an amendment to the Articles of Agreement of the IMF, authorizing the IMF to issue a new fiduciary international reserve asset, as and when required, to supplement the supply of traditional reserve assets for the purpose of meeting the world's estimated need for reserves. The first allocation of the new reserve assets, called special drawing rights (SDRs), was made very shortly thereafter—at the beginning of 1970. The IMF had already for many years been generating reserve assets in the form of gold tranche drawing rights and liquid loan claims, a by-product of the extension of medium-term credit to countries in payments difficulty, undertaken on the initiative of the latter. Other fiduciary reserve claims on the Bank for International Settlements or on individual countries had also been created as a by-product of the extension of short-term credit under various arrangements. The supply of these credit-related reserves, however, was determined, at least proximately, by individual countries' need to borrow rather than by the general need for reserves. The SDR is the first reserve

First published in International Monetary Fund, *Staff Papers*, March 1961. This paper was also presented at a seminar for Scandinavian economists and officials held under the auspices of the International Monetary Fund at Store Kro, Fredensborg, Denmark, in September 1975.

asset to be supplied on the basis of a deliberate assessment of the global need for reserves and reserve growth.

Before going on to consider some of the problems that have arisen and may arise in connection with the SDR, let us recall some of the salient features of both the asset itself and the manner in which it is issued to the world.

In the first place, the SDR is essentially an entry in the IMF books. All operations and transactions in SDRs are conducted through a special drawing account, financially quite separate from the general account of the IMF, which conducts all other IMF's business. Special drawing rights can be held at present only by such national monetary authorities as are members of the IMF and elect to participate in the scheme, or by the general account of the IMF, although there is a provision whereby the right to hold them may be extended to other international monetary institutions. Possession of SDRs entitles a country to obtain a defined equivalent amount of currency from other participating countries and enables it to discharge certain obligations toward the general account of the IMF.

The right to obtain currency from other countries is based ultimately on the legal obligation undertaken by all participants, when designated by the IMF, to provide convertible currency to participants using their SDRs at prescribed rates of exchange. This obligation is not unlimited but extends only to the point at which the designee is holding three times its net cumulative allocation of SDRs. Moreover, the principles on which participants are designated by the Fund to receive SDRs are such as to ensure that no country is required to hold more than its fair share of SDRs. A country is required to receive SDRs only if its balance of payments and reserve position is deemed sufficiently strong, and designations are distributed so as to promote approximate equality among participants in the ratios of their SDR holdings in excess of net cumulative allocations to their reserves in other forms, or to restore this equality if it has been disturbed.

Special drawing rights may be transferred between any two participants by agreement without recourse to the designation system of the IMF, where the purpose is to redeem currency liabilities of the transferor to the transferee. This facility is particularly useful to the United States and the United Kingdom, to whom it offers a substitute for conversions of their currencies into gold or dollars, respectively. It is possible that the scope for transfers without designation may be extended later to other types of case.

Transfers among participants, whether with or without designation of the transferee, should be made only to the extent required to enable the transferor to avoid a declining trend in its gold and foreign exchange reserves. Use of SDRs is not subject to challenge, but if it does not fulfil the requirement of need it may be offset by designation of the transferor. The rules governing the need to use SDRs and designation, although not entirely symmetrical, are broadly intended to bring about a balanced relationship between the use and holdings of SDRs, on the one hand, and of other reserves, on the other.

Participants exchange SDRs among themselves for convertible currency at prescribed rates of exchange. The rate for the U.S. dollar is the par value of the dollar in terms of gold. The rate for any other currency is determined by the current market value of that currency in terms of U.S. dollars. This is to ensure that a participant using special drawing rights will receive the same market value, whichever currencies are provided in exchange and whichever participant provides the currency.

Participants are permitted to transfer SDRs to the general account of the IMF for certain purposes, namely, to pay charges and to repay drawings from the IMF. The general account, on its side, is entitled to require participants to provide their currencies in exchange for SDRs if it requires to replenish its holdings of such currencies, and may use SDRs in other transactions, such as drawings, by agreement with the participant in question.

Although participants may use their SDR balances up to the hilt if they need to do so to meet payments deficits, they are required to maintain, over any five-year period, an average balance equal to 30 percent of their net cumulative allocations. In order to ensure, as far as possible, the observance of this requirement, the IMF will give priority in designation to those countries that need to reconstitute their SDR holdings in order to fulfill this requirement, and will designate them whether or not their balance of payments and reserve position is strong. Participants in this position may also obtain SDRs for convertible currency from the general account or from specified other participants, who may be released for this specific purpose from the normal requirement of need to use SDRs. These provisions are necessary because there is no general right of participants to obtain SDRs from other participants or even to require other participants to convert their own currencies into SDRs.

Unless participants are continuously in too weak a balance of payments and reserve position, their SDR holdings, even if they fall to less than 30 percent of the net cumulative allocation, are likely to be restored by the ordinary processes of designation in advance of their becoming subject to special designation for the purpose of reconstitution, and more completely than would be necessary to enable them to meet the legal reconstitution requirement.

Participants are given an incentive to hold or accumulate SDRs not only by the assurance that they can use them to meet payments deficits, and by the fact that they benefit from an absolute gold value guarantee—even in the event of a general devaluation of currencies—but also because a small interest (presently $1\frac{1}{2}$ percent) is paid on any excess of a country's holdings of SDRs over its net cumulative allocation, and the same interest is charged on any shortfall.

Now, a word about how SDRs are brought into existence. Most of the important features of this process are referred to in Article XXIV, Section 1(a):

> In all its decisions with respect to the allocation and cancellation of special drawing rights the Fund shall seek to meet the long-term global need, as and when it arises, to supplement existing reserve assets in such manner as will promote the attainment of its purposes and will avoid economic stagnation and deflation as well as excess demand and inflation in the world.

In the first place, SDRs are created by a decision of the IMF. More precisely, a decision to allocate has to be based on a proposal by the Managing Director, concurred in by the Executive Directors, and has to be voted by IMF governors representing an 85 percent majority of the voting power of all participants.

Second, the IMF's general objective when it creates SDRs must be to meet a *global need* to supplement reserves, that is, the need of the membership as a whole and not merely of particular countries that happen to be short of reserves.

Third, the need in question is a need *to supplement existing reserve assets.* This does not necessarily imply that there must always be types of reserve asset other than SDRs, but it does imply that if such other types of asset do exist account must be taken of their existing and prospective supply.

Fourth, the need in question has to be a *long-term need.* This concept finds expression in the provision that decisions to allocate or cancel SDRs shall be made for basic periods that will normally be five years in duration, though they may be of some other duration: in fact, the first decision to allocate related to a basic period of only three years. Moreover, there is a provision whereby the rates of allocation during a basic period may be changed in the event of "unexpected major developments."

In the fifth place, the manner of supplementing reserve assets is to be such as to avoid inflation and deflation in the world and to promote IMF purposes. This supplies, in effect, the criterion of global need. In the Managing Director's proposal relating to the first decision to allocate SDRs it was explained that the relevant purposes of the IMF could be be grouped as follows:

1. expansion of international trade, economic activity and development;
2. promotion of multilateral payments and elimination of restrictions;
3. promotion of exchange stability and orderly exchange-rate adjustments; and
4. correction of payments maladjustments and reduction in payments disequilibria without resort to measures destructive of national or international prosperity.

A further important feature of the allocation of SDRs remains to be mentioned, namely, that SDRs are to be distributed among participants in proportion to their IMF quotas but any participant that did not vote in favor of the decision may choose not to receive an allocation.

EXPERIENCE THUS FAR

We have now had some 13 months' experience with SDRs.[1] This is a very short time for an asset designed for the long run. However, the

---

[1] This paragraph has been updated since the paper was originally presented in 1972.

system is already working with surprising smoothness. Only seven members of the IMF, comprising 1.7 percent of IMF quotas, have failed to become participants in the special drawing account. The first decision to allocate was made for a basic period of three years, in such a way as to distribute the equivalent of approximately $3.5 billion of SDRs at the beginning of 1970 and $3 billion each at the beginning of 1971 and 1972. The issuance of SDRs, combined with certain other favorable developments, has had a good effect on the degree of confidence felt in currencies. Some $1.1 billion of SDRs has been used thus far—about 17 percent of the amount allocated—showing that most countries have not been unduly eager to part with the new fiduciary instrument. Special drawing rights have, however, been used, to a rather greater extent than was generally expected, for the repayment of drawings from the general account, particularly by some less developed countries. Use of SDRs for such repayments is not subject to the requirement of need—an arrangement that can be rationalized to some extent by the fact that, from the standpoint of the general account, SDRs are more useful assets than any particular creditor currency that might otherwise have been used for such repayment. A wide range of countries has been designated to receive SDRs—wider than the range of currencies normally used by the general account. Practical working criteria for the need to use, and the fitness to receive, SDRs are being developed through experience. One of the minor problems here is an asymmetry between the criteria for using and for receiving, which makes possible the economically rather meaningless situation in which the same country is both receiving and legitimately using SDRs. The precise system of designation is being gradually developed in the light of experience and up to now has been working quite satisfactorily.

PROBLEMS AND POSSIBILITIES

In turning now to some of the questions that have arisen and possibilities that have been envisaged, in academic literature and elsewhere, in connection with the SDRs, I will reverse the order in which the broad classes of topics were dealt with at the beginning of this paper. The general character of the SDR is for the time being fixed, and to change its characteristics would in many cases involve amending the articles. But the process of deciding on allocations is relatively fluid and discretionary and has already thrown up a number of issues.

Estimation of Need for Total Reserve Growth

First of all, there is the problem of how to estimate the need to supplement global reserves. This can be broken down into two subproblems, namely, (a) how big the need is for total reserve expansion and (2) how much of this need will be met by an expansion in other types of reserves.

We in the IMF have tried to estimate the need for total reserve increase in the world, mainly by guessing at the sort of effects that different rates of reserve growth might have on national policies, and hence on various target variables. But the trouble is that international economic policymakers are faced with a multiplicity of targets and a paucity of effective instruments. One is interested in the effects on national policies for demand management, trade and capital flows, exchange rates, and the financing of payments surpluses and deficits, and even on the willingness of donor countries to provide aid to developing countries. But, of course, it is impossible to optimize all of these policies simply by manipulating the rate of reserve expansion. The particular dilemma encountered on the occasion of the first decision to allocate SDRs was how far one could go in bringing about the expansion in liquidity required to prevent the seizing up of international trade without giving undue encouragement to world inflation. Of course, some instruments other than reserve creation are at the disposal of international policymakers. For example, there is some scope for controlling the supply of types of liquidity—such as IMF drawing facilities in the credit tranches—the use of which is subject to policy conditions. Again, the IMF has a possibility of direct influence over countries' exchange-rate behavior and demand management. The Bank for International Settlements can do something to coordinate certain aspects of monetary policy. The Organization for Economic Cooperation and Development attempts to improve balance of payments adjustment among major countries by a method of direct confrontation and discussion of national forecasts and intentions. But these instruments are all rather weak in themselves and are exercised from different centers at different times.

Another type of problem in the determination of international reserve needs arises from ignorance about the relevant empirical relationships.

Owing to the novelty of deliberate reserve creation, relatively little work has been done in estimating the policy effects of reserve levels and reserve changes. If lack of research were the only trouble, it might at length be remedied. But there are more fundamental difficulties. In view of the small number of economic agents involved, namely national governments, one can hardly hope to establish clear statistical uniformities. Then again, the existence of two-way causal relationships between reserves and national policies and the probability that the influence of reserves on policies may depend considerably on the manner in which these reserves accrue to the country in question make it difficult to gauge the strength of the influences in which one is interested without setting up models of formidable complexity.

There is no escape from these difficulties by having resort to rough-and-ready methods such as those that the IMF had to employ in preparing the first decision to allocate SDRs. On that occasion we started from the proposition that the degree of reserve ease over the period 1954–68 was about right—though possibly more than adequate at the beginning and less than adequate at the end—and we sought to extrapolate into the future the relationships between reserves and other economic variables that had prevailed in that period. But which relationships? Reserves over that period rose much more slowly than international trade, international transactions, balance of payments disequilibria, or money supply (although the last-mentioned criterion was not used). Did that mean that reserves could safely continue to rise more slowly than these other magnitudes, or was the decline in the ratio of reserves to other economic magnitudes rendered tolerable only by the special circumstances that reserves at the beginning of the period had been very high and, moreover, had been redistributed during the period from high-reserve countries to low-reserve countries? If so, one might conclude that reserves in future, to avoid stringency, would have to rise more rapidly than before. This question of the relative importance to be attributed to reserve stocks and to reserve growth is still unsolved.

In view of all these uncertainties it is not surprising that in the Managing Director's proposal for the allocation of SDRs for the first basic period the trend growth of the need for reserves over the ensuing five-year period was estimated rather broadly (at $4–5 billion per annum).

Estimation of Supply of Other Reserves

The need for reserve creation in the form of SDRs depends not only on the prospective need for reserve growth in general but also on the prospective supply of other reserves, such as gold, foreign exchange holdings, and reserve positions in the IMF. Over the period 1956–65, inclusive, reserves in these forms rose at an average rate of $1.5 billion per annum.

Now, to some extent the supply of these other reserves arises out of international credit operations. These may be called credit-related, or credit-induced, reserves. Such, for example, are reserve positions in the IMF other than those resulting from gold transactions, creditor balances arising out of mutual credit arrangements, and dollar balances that accrue when the United States provides balance of payments assistance to other countries. To some extent the supply of these reserves varies directly with the global need for reserves, and inversely with the supply of other reserves—presumably including SDRs. If this responsiveness were complete, there would be little point in issuing SDRs. However, the responsiveness of the supply of credit-related reserves to global need is very imperfect, especially in the long run, since it is geared to a disproportionate extent to the payments deficits of particular countries, and since, as far as they arise from bilateral credit arrangements, the quality of the reserves created may not be all that could be desired. Again, the tendency for the supply of credit-related reserves to offset the supply of others may be expected to be only partial. For these reasons it remains both possible and desirable to attempt to optimize the supply of total reserves through the issuance of SDRs. In estimating the need for the latter, however, the prospective supply of credit-related reserves has to be regarded as a function of the supply of other reserves as well as of the total demand for reserves and not as a fixed datum.

The supply of foreign exchange reserves in both dollars and sterling is also influenced by the payments deficits (or surpluses) of the reserve centers in question, and by the distribution of reserves among third countries. The former factor is the more important for dollars, the latter for sterling; both are difficult to predict. The growth of both gold and foreign exchange reserves may also be influenced by speculative and confidence factors that are in no way responsive to the need for reserves. The influence of speculation in gold has, of course, been dampened by the introduction of the two-tier market, and that of speculation in sterling by the introduction of the exchange guarantees for sterling balances and by improvement in the balance of payments of the United Kingdom, but this factor may still be troublesome.

In view of its dependence on factors that are highly uncertain, such as the balance-of-payments disequilibria of particular countries and the emergence or appeasement of speculative flurries, it is extremely difficult to predict the development of the supply of "other reserves" for a number of years ahead. By the same token, it is difficult to estimate the need for reserve supplementation through the issuance of SDRs over any such period. This suggests that the number of years ahead for which the articles consider it normal that a decision to allocate SDRs should provide— namely, five years—may be too long, and that the three-year life span of the first basic period might in practice become the norm. Not that it is so much to predict the expansion of other reserves over a three-year than over a five-year period, but the shorter the period, the easier it is to correct, to the extent that this may be desirable, for any past deviations in actual compared with planned reserve growth. The rationale for the five-year basic period was that in view of the uncertain, but presumably long, time lags characterizing the causal linkage between reserve creation and its economic effects, there was no point in trying to gear reserve creation to short-term variations in the need for reserves. The best that could be hoped for was to get the trend growth approximately right. But such a view, though consistent with a long basic period, does not require it, any more than a Friedmanite view about the aims of monetary policy requires that decisions about the growth of the money stock should be taken only at lengthy intervals. Thus it would be possible to determine an annual rate of allocation over a relatively short period on the basis of trend projections relating to a longer period.

However, a mere shortening of the basic period will not solve the problem, either. It would be highly unsatisfactory that the amount of SDRs created, which are distributed in proportion to quota, should have to fluctuate to offset unexpected developments in the growth of other reserves, which are distributed in quite a different way. It seems to follow that something ought to be done to stabilize the growth of gold, foreign exchange, and other types of reserves, but how this is to be accomplished is far from clear. I revert to this question in the penultimate section of this paper.

Rate of Interest on SDRs

The relatively high level of world interest rates, including rates paid on foreign exchange reserves, that has prevailed, and the rather rapid changes that have occurred over the last few years raise the question whether the rate of interest presently paid on SDRs (viz., $1\frac{1}{2}$ percent) is not too low, and whether the provisions governing rate changes are not too rigid. Under the present articles, any increase in the rate beyond 2 percent can take place only if the remuneration payable to net creditors of the IMF is likewise raised above 2 percent, a decision that executive directors can make only by a 75 percent majority of the total voting power. The question is the more acute in that the possibility of a rise in the dollar price of monetary gold has receded, and the fixed equivalence of the SDR in terms of gold has thereby been robbed of much of its importance.

Too low a rate of interest on SDRs can have consequences that, although limited in various ways, are inconvenient. The lower the rate of interest on SDRs, the more inclined countries in deficit will be to use their SDRs, in preference to other reserve assets, to finance their deficits, and the more likely it is that SDRs will be accumulated by surplus countries, or countries with a balance of payments and reserve position strong enough to qualify them to be designated. The lower this rate of interest, too, the less eager will be the surplus countries to accumulate SDRs. Both of these consequences may lead the surplus countries to be more grudging and negative than they would otherwise be in their estimate of global needs to supplement reserve assets on the occasion of future decisions to allocate SDRs.

The lower the interest rate on SDRs, the more inclined countries will be to repay drawings from the IMF in SDRs rather than in currency or gold. This, however, need have no international consequences, since the IMF can use the SDRs to replenish its stock of currencies and would probably be able to induce members to draw SDRs rather than currencies.

It might be thought that, given the passive role generally played by the United States in foreign exchange markets, too low an interest rate on SDRs would lead to a net transfer of SDRs to the United States and—to the extent that this was in exchange for dollars rather than for gold—to an increase in official dollar holdings, and hence in total world reserves. This tendency, however, could not go very far. It is true that a low interest rate on SDRs might make it more difficult for the United States, when it is in deficit, to induce countries to convert dollar accumulations into SDRs. The issue, however, is more likely to arise with respect to SDR conversions that are a substitute for gold conversions than to those that affect the amount of dollar reserves in the world. Moreover, it is always open to the United States, as to other countries, to use the designation mechanism to acquire the currencies it needs to finance its deficit and to reduce dollar accumulations. If, on the other hand, the United States was in a strong balance of payments and reserve position and was subject to designation, the general rules of designation would make it impossible for other countries to unload onto the United States a stock of SDRs out of proportion to its other reserves.

Indirectly, however, the low interest rate on SDRs might influence the supply of dollar reserves by affecting the choice of reserve-holding countries between gold and dollars. For example, a low rate of interest on SDR reserves might make monetary authorities want to sell more gold to the United States for dollars or to convert fewer dollars into gold in order to keep up the income from their reserve holdings.

At a more fundamental level, a lower rate of interest on SDRs, by lowering the average interest yield of reserves, might lead in the long run to a decline in the real volume of reserves that countries would wish to hold for any given rate of increase in nominal reserves. This is so because the lower the yield on reserves compared with other assets that countries might expect to be able to acquire by running less favorable balances of payments, the higher, in the short run, may be the rate of inflation that the authorities are prepared to tolerate, and although this effect will be only temporary it may bring about a permanent reduction in the amount of real reserves. The long-term effects on trade and exchange policy will be mixed, since the influence of reduced real reserves on balance of payments policies will be offset by the reduced yield on reserve holdings, but it is at least possible that the net effect may be to lead to more severe and widespread balance of payments restrictions and to more frequent devaluations.

While the quantitative importance of some of these interactions is uncertain, it would seem that the question of the interest to be paid on SDRs is one that deserves further thought. We cannot, however, overlook the distributional aspect of the problem, since an increase in interest on SDRs would induce a transfer of income from countries with a debtor position to countries with a creditor position in SDRs: the former might often, although by no means always, be relatively poor and the latter, relatively rich.

A Link between SDRs and Economic Development? .

Domestic money is created as the counterpart of bank credit. Newly created money is not distributed among the population by a rationing procedure but accrues initially to those who receive bank credit, presumed to be those who can use it most productively. A single instrument, the national banking system, is used to serve a double purpose—that of supplying the optimal amount of liquidity and that of promoting the best use of the national capital.

In the sphere of international reserve creation, a different course has been adopted. Newly created reserves are rationed out among countries virtually as a gift in predetermined proportions. Some people have been surprised at this solution, since they had always imagined that international reserves would have to be created by a process analogous to that adopted for domestic money creation. Others have regretted it as the loss of an opportunity to kill two birds with one stone. For international liquidity, the second bird would be the promotion of an optimal distribution of world capital, not, however, in a purely commercial or economic sense but rather in a social sense, taking account of the desirability of richer countries assisting poorer ones. In other words, they would like to use SDR creation to help to finance the development of poorer countries.

A typical scheme would be one in which some proportion, fixed or variable, of newly issued SDRs would be allocated to the International Development Association and other institutions for financing development. The acceptance obligations associated with the amounts allocated for development would be assumed by all participating countries in proportion to quotas. The development institutions could sell the SDRs allocated to them to the countries receiving individual allocations in exchange for convertible currency, which could then be used as and when required to finance projects in the developing countries.

The allocation of SDRs to development institutions would, of course, require an amendment of the Articles of Agreement.

The strongest arguments in favor of a scheme of this kind are the following:

1. It would probably increase the total amount of development aid accruing to the poorer countries. While there might well be some offsetting decline in the amount of aid provided directly by individual donor countries, the fact that the aid provided under the scheme would appear to governments and legislatures as a deduction from an allocation received by the country as a quasigift from heaven, together with considerations of prestige, humanitarianism, and special interest that would speak against too great a reduction of national aid, makes it likely that some net increase in the quantity of aid would result.

2. Almost certainly there would also be some net increase in aid provided (a) through international institutions, (b) for well-considered projects, and (c) in a form that did not require the proceeds to be spent on the products of particular countries. In other words, there would be some improvement in the quality of aid.

The strongest arguments against any compulsory linking of the provision of aid with the receipt of SDRs appear to be the following:

1. If the link is in fact likely to result in a net addition to the amount of development aid provided by the richer countries, it can only be because one or another of the national authorities involved in decisions to grant aid—the civil servants, the ministers, the parliament, or the electorate—is being tricked into greater generosity by the fact that aid giving and reserve receiving come in a single "package." Of course, the whole process of representative democracy is riddled with "package deals" of all kinds. Nevertheless, many may feel that there is some constitutional impropriety about this one.

2. Insofar as the amount of SDRs created varies from basic period to basic period, the amount of aid provided for less developed countries may tend to vary also, in a way that has nothing to do with variations in the need for such aid. The force of this objection is

reduced by the fact that the timing of the actual provision of aid associated with the SDRs will not coincide with that of the SDR creation itself, and may perhaps be made to vary somewhat less. Moreover, variations in the amount of SDRs created are likely to decline in importance as the SDR gradually comes to account for a larger and larger proportion of both total reserves and reserve changes.

3. The fact that a proportion of any SDRs received in allocation would involve the provision of aid and would, therefore, have to be earned through additional exports might well have an adverse effect on the willingness of important creditor countries to vote for adequate proposals to allocate SDRs, or even to accept allocations when voted. This might be particularly so for countries that, because of the structure of their trade or because of temporarily inadequate competitive power, appeared unlikely to be able to secure additional exports (despite the increase in imports in the developing countries) in an amount equal to the additional aid that they would be financing. This danger might be particularly great in the early years of a link arrangement, before its *modus operandi* had become familiar.

4. It has been argued that the link would be a particularly inflationary way of putting SDRs into circulation, since the SDRs would, in effect, have to be earned through additional exports, and that therefore it would be inappropriate to introduce such a link in a world environment that is already too inflationary. This might be questioned on the grounds that under modern methods of demand management any additional exports arising from this cause in industrial countries would be taken into account, in the same way as any other factors affecting the current account balance of payments, in determining the fiscal and monetary policies to be pursued. From an institutional standpoint, however, it seems likely that the additional taxation required to offset the inflationary pressure arising from aid would be more easily obtained if the aid in question did than if it did not appear as public expenditure in the budget. Against this possibility that the link might increase inflationary pressure, one may set the possibility that it would improve its timing. For, insofar as the degree of world inflation was taken into account in determining the amount of SDRs to be created, there would be some tendency to countercyclical variation in the amount of aid financing carried out via the SDRs.

It would probably be difficult at this time for advocates of the link to secure the acceptance of an amendment to the Articles of Agreement authorizing the allocation of SDRs for the purpose of development financing. Such an amendment is unlikely to be attempted until ministers and civil servants in industrial countries become more generally convinced that some way must be found of increasing aid above the levels for which they can secure direct parliamentary authorization.

Should SDRs Users Have the Right to Transfer Them Freely without Designation and without Meeting A Requirement of Need?

The IMF is empowered to prescribe certain transactions in which transfers of SDRs may be made, by agreement between the participants, without designation, and also to prescribe certain transactions that may be made without meeting the requirement of need. In both cases this power can be exercised for transactions that would help participants to meet the reconstitution requirement, or that would offset a misuse of SDRs, or that would bring the holdings of both participants closer to their net cumulative allocations.

If use of SDRs were completely free from the requirement of need, countries that wished to reduce the proportion of their reserves held in the form of SDRs could do so irrespective of their balance-of-payments positions, provided that other participants refrained from reversing the transaction. If participants in general desired to hold a lower proportion of SDRs in reserves than that borne by total SDRs to total reserves, the velocity of circulation of SDRs might rise very high.

Relaxation of the system of designation or guidance of SDR transfers could take place along a number of different routes. The scope for voluntary transactions (i.e., transfers to a willing transferee) might be extended, even indefinitely, while retaining in the background the right of users to transfer SDRs willy-nilly to designated participants. The only danger in this course would be that if SDRs became a coveted reserve asset some participants with good connections might be able to attract to themselves an undue proportion of these assets while others, who might need them more urgently, for instance, to fulfill their reconstitution obligations, were unable to obtain them.

To abolish the system of designation entirely, and with it the obligation to accept transfers of SDRs, would be a much more radical course and would risk undermining altogether an asset whose value is derived mainly from the fact that it is accepted at a fixed rate in exchange for currency.

A third possibility would be to extend the obligation to accept transfer of SDRs to undesignated participants. This, while somewhat less radical than the second course, would mean that countries in a strong reserve and balance-of-payments position could never be sure that they might not be called upon to acquire a disproportionate share of total SDRs up to the limits of their holding obligations—a fact that might make them reluctant to increase those obligations by voting in favor of new allocations of SDRs. Again, countries in a weak payments position might find themselves unwillingly acquiring SDRs that they would then be obliged, on pain of exhausting their stocks of intervention currency, to pass on immediately to other participants.

It seems clear that it would be unwise to venture any distance down the second or even the third of the paths described above. Just how far the IMF should go in freeing transactions between a willing transferor and a willing transferee from the requirements of designation and of need is a matter on which sound judges may differ. Doubtless, as the SDR becomes established, greater freedom in its use can be envisaged. Adoption of adequate and flexible interest rates for SDRs might facilitate greater liberalization in this respect. I am personally very skeptical, however, that any substantially freer use of SDRs under conditions in which their price in terms of currencies is fixed would produce a distribution of SDRs as acceptable as that resulting from observance of the requirement of need combined with a predominance of designated transactions.

Should Currencies be Convertible into SDRs?

At present, participants are entitled to demand SDRs in exchange for currency only if they are in danger of being unable unable to fulfill their obligation to maintain an average balance of SDRs equal to 30 percent of their net cumulative allocations. In that event they have a right to purchase SDRs, either from the general account of the IMF or from another participant whom the IMF shall specify.

It might be thought to be advantageous if a more general right to convert currencies into SDRs were extended to countries in payments surplus. Such countries are not presently able to convert currencies in general into gold, but their ability to convert U.S. dollars into gold is an important element in their willingness to accumulate dollars to whatever extent is required to prevent their rates of exchange from appreciating beyond the prescribed margins above par value. If SDRs are to become an increasingly important element in reserves, relative to gold, it might be argued that countries should be able to convert currencies generally, or at least their intervention currency, into SDRs.

Such a right of conversion into SDRs, however, even if confined to conversion of intervention currency, would appear to be neither necessary nor desirable. A right to convert U.S. dollars into SDRs is unnecessary, since surplus countries can always, if they wish, convert into gold, and since the normal method of designating the recipients of transfers of SDRs will ensure that a proportion of their reserve accumulation will over time accrue to them in the form of SDRs. Again, an unconditional right to convert dollars into SDRs would be impracticable as long as the SDRs constitute only a small part of the total reserves of the United States as of other countries. If, on the other hand, countries were merely given a right to convert dollars into gold or SDRs *at the choice of the United States*, it is difficult to see that they would be any better off than they are at present. On the one hand, they would no doubt gain a possibility, which they do not have at present, of obtaining SDRs for dollars, provided that the United States agreed, even when the latter was accumulating reserves. On the other hand, they would lose the right, which they have at present, to obtain gold (rather than SDRs) for dollars, when the United States is losing reserves.[2]

Any right to secure conversion into SDRs, whether confined to U.S. dollars or of a more general character, would tend to run counter to the mechanism for distributing SDRs through the designation of transferees, unless the right to convert were confined to cases where the converting country was deemed to have an unduly low holding of SDRs, and unless the countries required to convert were selected by a system of designation analogous (in reverse) to that used for transferees. It was in part because of the complications involved in such dual arrangements that

---

[2] This statement requires some qualification, since countries' right to obtain gold, rather than SDRs, for dollars is affected, even at present, by the right of the United States, when losing reserves, to compel these countries, if designated, to accept SDRs for dollars.

no general system of conversion was provided for in the initial design of the SDR.

Should SDRs Become the Standard for Par Values?

At the present time the par values of currencies are measured essentially in terms of gold weight, either in ounces of gold or in U.S. dollars of a fixed gold weight, that is, in effect, in thirty-fifths of an ounce of gold. The same is true of SDRs. In other words, gold is the standard, or numeraire, for par values.

Now anything real or imaginary can serve as a numeraire for par values. Pounds of cheese or angels' wings would do just as well as gold. This is so because all that matters is the *relative* par values of currencies and of any other things whose par values are measured in terms of the numeraire.

The only significance of choosing some real asset as numeraire is to fix the par value of *that asset itself*, at least in certain contexts, at unity. Just how significant this is depends on the circumstances in which that par value is applicable. For gold it is applicable if the monetary authority of any country wishes to buy or sell gold. This is particularly important for a country, such as the United States, that maintains the exchange value of its currency by buying and selling gold for that currency but also for other countries that may wish to increase or reduce their stocks of intervention currency by buying and selling gold from and to the United States or each other. It is also important for certain transactions between the general account of the IMF and its members. The fact that gold has a fixed par value is important to all countries that hold gold in their reserves.

It is sometimes suggested that gold should be replaced by SDRs as the standard for par values. It is not entirely clear how much would be accomplished by this. To be sure, the par value of the SDR itself would thereby be implicitly fixed at unity. But this would alter nothing, since the value of the SDR is already explicitly fixed in terms of gold, which is the present standard. To be sure, the par value of gold would cease to be implicitly fixed, but it would immediately become necessary—in view of the importance of monetary gold as a reserve medium—to give it an explicit par value; and if this were fixed, again nothing would be changed.

Some of those who advocate making SDRs the standard believe that to displace gold from this particular "throne" would facilitate par value changes on the part of the U.S. dollar, which might otherwise be inhibited by a fear that the increase in the dollar price of gold that would be involved might weaken confidence in the dollar as a reserve currency and lead to conversions of dollars into gold. This, however, would be avoided only if it were agreed that the "par value" of gold should always change *pari passu* with that of the U.S. dollar. While it is not inconceivable that the par value of gold might be made subject to change by a procedure less cumbersome than that presently provided for a "uniform change in par values," it seems unlikely that countries with substantial gold reserves would readily agree that its value should always vary with that of the U.S. dollar. Only, perhaps, if the countries in question became convinced that the dollar would never be adjusted relative to gold but could be adjusted relative to SDRs alone might they prefer the latter arrangement to one in which they themselves had to do all the exchange rate adjustment vis-à-vis both dollars and gold.

Pooling of Other Reserve Assets in Exchange for SDRs

It is sometimes suggested that the SDR should become in effect the only reserve medium except for working balances of intervention currency. The following appears to me the simplest way of achieving this. All participants would surrender to the IMF their holdings of gold and currency in excess of agreed working balances and would receive SDRs in exchange. The IMF would hold the reserve currencies thus acquired indefinitely or over a long period of amortization. However, any new accumulation of reserve currencies in the hands of any country in excess of the limit of its working balance would be surrendered to the IMF for SDRs, and any country running short of working balances could obtain them from the IMF in exchange for SDRs. If as a result of these transactions the IMF were accumulating reserve currencies, it would present them to the issuer in exchange for SDRs: similarly, if the IMF were losing reserve currencies, it would buy them from the issuer with SDRs.

Developments of this kind would, of course, require substantial amendment of the IMF articles, to which it would be extremely difficult, for many years to come, to obtain agreement. However, they would carry with them very important advantages. At one stroke would be eliminated (a) the possibility of a crisis in the monetary system, arising out of the widespread conversion of reserve currencies into gold or other reserve currencies, (b) the possibility of unplanned increase or reduction in the amount of world reserve assets, arising out of either the deficits or surpluses of reserve center countries or official conversions of reserve assets, and (c) the necessity to restrict the use and to control the transfer of SDRs. The system of guidance of SDR transfers would, in effect, be replaced by the obligation to sell excess currency balances to, and the right to buy working balances of currencies from, the IMF in exchange for SDRs. Indeed, the whole system of intercountry transfers of SDRs might well be replaced by transactions with the IMF.

Should Private Individuals be Allowed to Hold and Use SDRs?

The holding of SDRs by private individuals is sometimes advocated on no very clear grounds—as if SDRs would somehow lack credibility as a "real" asset until they were bought and sold on private markets.

Clearly, to permit SDR transactions with private individuals would make it very difficult to retain the present system of limiting the use of SDRs by monetary authorities to the financing of payments deficits and of controlling the distribution of SDRs by designating transferees. Even if steps were taken to ensure that transactions in SDRs between monetary authorities and private individuals took place only at prices in the vicinity of parity, countries that wanted to get rid of SDRs could force down the dollar value of their currencies by buying dollars and thus make it profitable for the market to purchase SDRs from them (unless, indeed, sales to the market as well as to other authorities were made subject to the requirement of need). Again, countries that wanted to accumulate more than their normal share of SDRs might sell dollars against their own currency, thus pushing up their exchange rate to the point at which it would pay the market to sell them SDRs. Such a competition for SDRs might be as disturbing to exchange markets as the opposite tendency.

Those who advocate private holding of SDRs probably envisage that the whole apparatus of control and guidance over the use and transfer of SDRs would be abolished and that the SDR would, to a greater or lesser extent, take the place of the dollar as a means of market intervention to keep exchange rates in the vicinity of relative par values. This would amount to the institution of an SDR standard of the type of the pre-World War I gold standard (although with provision for IMF authorization of par value changes). To make this possible, a sufficient number of important countries would have to be prepared to buy and sell SDRs without limit in the vicinity of par for private as well as for official transactions. There would, moreover, probably have to be a wide private market in SDRs. (This might not be entirely impossible, when the total issue of SDRs becomes sufficiently large, in view of its stability of value and the fact that it bears interest.)

There are undoubtedly many who would prefer an international to a national intervention currency. For one thing, such an arrangement (like that discussed on p. 217 would compel the United States to finance any payments deficit out of its reserves. However, it has at least one serious drawback—namely, the danger that variations in the private holdings of SDRs, inspired possibly by anticipations of par value changes, might give rise, from time to time, to drains on official reserve stocks. It would seem strange if countries, having combined to segregate private and official holdings of gold primarily in order to prevent private hoarding from depleting reserves, were to set up a new mechanism that would permit similar depletion to occur through another channel.

13

ON EXCHANGE-RATE
UNIFICATION

IN THIS ESSAY it is debated whether a group of countries, each of which has previously possessed its own currency and has adhered to the par value system of the IMF, should or should not unify their exchange rates, in the sense that their relative par values would thereafter be irrevocably fixed, while their absolute par values when changed at all would change in the same proportion.

The question has a certain current actuality in that in December 1969, a summit conference of the EEC meeting at the Hague decided that the Community should evolve, by stages, into a monetary and economic union, characterized either by a common currency or at least by an irrevocable fixing of the relative exchange rates of member currencies. Countries desiring to join the EEC are expected to subscribe to this objective.

The considerations advanced here have much in common with those debated in the literature in relation to the concept of an "optimum currency area." I would prefer, however, to formulate the problem more narrowly. Thus, the question is not how to determine the best possible frontiers for an area within which a common currency shall prevail but rather how to determine the desirability of unifying the exchange rates of a given set of countries. Moreover, the alternative to a unified exchange

First published in *The Economic Journal* (September 1971), 81:467–88. Reprinted by permission of Cambridge University Press.

rate is here taken to be continued adherence to the par value system as we know it rather than, as is often assumed in discussions of the "optimum currency area," freely floating exchange rates, or else a vaguely defined exchange-rate flexibility.

In general, in what follows, it will be assumed, unless specific mention is made to the contrary, that trade and capital flows between members of the group are free from restrictions imposed on balance of payments grounds. Such restrictions would frustrate some of the avowed objectives of currency or exchange-rate unification, as these are envisaged, for example, in the EEC.

THE PROBLEM OF
FUNDAMENTAL DISEQUILIBRIA

The principal danger involved in participating in a fixed exchange-rate area arises from the certainty, in the absence of perfect competition in product and factor markets, that developments would occur from time to time that pushed the relative cost levels of the participating countries out of line, and even some that tended to push them progressively further and further out of line.[1] Such developments would be bound to arise even if—as is quite improbable—relative cost levels were initially in perfect alignment when relative rates were fixed. Cases of the first, or static, type of disequilibrium might result from temporary bouts of wage inflation in particular participating countries not shared by other participants, or from once-and-for-all changes in world demand favouring the products exported by some participants as against those exported by others. The second, or dynamic, type of disequilibrium might arise because differences between participants in the strength of trade unionism, in national attitudes to full employment or inflation, or in the rates of productivity growth, led to differences in the rates at which wage costs tend to rise at the nationally preferred levels of unemployment.

---

[1] The *relative* cost levels of countries in a group may be said to be "out of line" if there is no uniform change in these cost levels (relative to countries outside the group) that would permit each of the countries in the group to combine, over a period of years, the level of real output that is domestically desirable (from the standpoint of its effect on employment and price inflation) with a reasonable overall balance of international payments.

If the participating countries remained free to meet incipient disequilibria by altering their exchange rates relative to each other and to outside countries, they would be able, by nonrecurrent or repeated adjustments of par values, to maintain or restore payments equilibrium while preserving levels of aggregate demand compatible with the nationally preferred compromises between full employment and price stability. If, however, such adjustments were precluded by adherence to a group with fixed relative exchange rates, then, if the external payments and receipts of the group as a whole were kept in balance through suitable adjustments of the uniform exchange rates, participants in a relatively weak payments position would tend to be in overall payments deficit, and those in a relatively strong position would tend to be in overall surplus. The former, after they had exhausted their ability to run down reserves or to borrow, would be forced to tolerate, either temporarily or even (in the case of dynamic disequilibrium) indefinitely, a level of unemployment that was higher, and a rate of inflation that was lower, than would correspond to their preferred compromise between the two. The latter, on the other hand, might be compelled, through a technical inability to offset the effect of their surpluses on money stocks or flows, or through unwillingness to go on financing the accumulation of reserves by government borrowing from the private sector, to permit a rate of price inflation greater, and a level of unemployment lower, than would correspond to their preferred compromise between the two.

Where tendencies towards progressive relative disequilibrium existed within a unified exchange-rate area because some of the participating countries had more favorable unemployment/inflation relationships than others, the following situation would tend to emerge and persist. Much the same rate of price inflation would prevail over the area as a whole, a rate somewhat higher than that preferred by the surplus members. The deficit members would be able to keep their rates of inflation down to the common level only by tolerating indefinitely a level of unemployment higher than they would prefer if they were free to change their exchange rates and adopt their preferred positions on the unemployment/inflation curve.

The argument in the foregoing paragraph assumes the existence in each country of an inverse long-term relationship (given the rate of productivity growth and the rate of change in the terms of trade) between the rate of unemployment on the one hand and the rate of price inflation on the other. In the short run this relationship will be affected by such dynamic factors as past rates of change of prices and the rate of change of unemployment, but this does not preclude the existence of steady-state relationships linking levels of unemployment with the corresponding long-term equilibrium rates of price increase.

In discussing, above, the effects of *relative* cost disequilibria among countries belonging to a unified exchange rate area it has been assumed that the exchange rates of all participants would be adjusted uniformly, though discontinuously, vis-à-vis outside countries in such a way as to permit the union as a whole to remain in payments balance over the medium to long run. It has been argued that the fact that the exchange rates of the group would necessarily move together at the decision of a single authority might make it possible to secure prompter and more continuous adjustment of these rates to developments in the external balance of the group as a whole than if changes in rates were a matter for decision by individual members of the group, since the latter might hesitate to alter their own rates for fear of altering their competitive positions vis-à-vis other members. On the other hand, the institutions of the union might be such as to make it difficult to secure the required measure of agreement on such uniform changes in exchange rates since such changes, even when generally desirable, would usually be against the interests of some members.

Even if it proved possible to secure sufficient flexibility in the exchange rates of members of the group vis-à-vis the outside world, there would be a tendency for the relationship between unemployment and price inflation for the union as a whole to be less favorable than if the members had retained their right to adjust their relative exchange rates.[2]

The basic reason for this is that the inverse relationships between unemployment and price inflation, which we have assumed to prevail in the various member countries, are typically curvilinear, at least in the

[2] Certain countertendencies are discussed on p. 226 below. See on this point G. C. Archibald, "The Phillips Curve and the Distribution of Unemployment," *American Economic Review* (May 1969), 59:124–34; and Richard G. Lipsey, "The Relation between Unemployment and the Rate of Change of Money Wage Rates in the United Kingdom, 1862–1957: A Further Analysis," *Economica* (February 1960), 27:1–31.

vicinity of full employment. As unemployment approaches zero successive percentage point declines in unemployment must impart increasingly powerful stimuli to inflation. We have seen that fundamental balance of payments disequilibria are likely to be more prevalent in a group of countries that maintain fixed relative exchange rates than in one where countries are free to alter their relative rates.[3] Consider, now, the effect of three types of disequilibrium on the aggregate unemployment/inflation relationship, given the curvilinearity of that relationship in each country.

1. Among countries having the same rate of inflation at their preferred positions on the unemployment/inflation curve, disequilibria are equally likely to occur in either direction. If the countries have similarly sloping unemployment/inflation curves at the preferred points the emergence of disequilibria, if unemployment in the group as a whole were kept constant, would result in an increase in the average rate of price inflation. For it the responses to disequilibria were such as to keep unemployment constant, this would involve a transfer of unemployment from surplus to deficit countries, and while the rate of price inflation would fall in the latter as it rose in the former, the average rate of inflation (weighted in each country by the size of the labor force) would clearly rise. (See Graphical Appendix, Figure 1.) To prevent this net acceleration in inflation it would be necessary—as is indeed quite likely—that unemployment should rise more in the deficit country than it declined in the surplus one. In other words, there would have to be some increase in aggregate unemployment. Whichever of these outcomes occurred, one could speak of a deterioration in the relationship between unemployment and inflation in the union as a whole. If the slopes of the unemployment/inflation curves were somewhat dissimilar in the different countries, the above conclusion might not hold for specific disequilibria, but would hold even more strongly for the (equally likely) reverse disequilibria, so that it would hold on the average for disequilibria of this type.

2. Among countries in the group whose rates of price inflation differ, those with the lower rates of inflation are more likely to develop payments

---

[3] Overt payments disequilibria may be suppressed by domestically undesired unemployment or inflation. Fundamental disequilibria are defined so as to include such suppressed disequilibria.

surpluses under conditions of fixed exchange rates and those with higher rates of inflation, deficits. Consider two typical cases:

a. The more inflationary countries have less favorable unemployment/inflation relationships than the less inflationary ones, but the slope of the curves is the same for all countries at the preferred positions. In this case, as in case 1, payments disequilibria would tend to bring about a higher average rate of inflation in the group as a whole for a given aggregate amount of employment. (See Graphical Appendix, Figure 2.)

b. Countries have similar unemployment/inflation curves but some are more inflationary because they (i.e., their authorities) have more aversion to unemployment and less to inflation than have others. In this case the consequential payments disequilibria would tend to *reduce* the average rate of inflation for a given aggregate amount of unemployment in the group as a whole. (See Graphical Appendix, Figure 3.)

There seems little doubt but that disequilibria of types 1 and 2(a) would tend to predominate over disequilibria of type 2(b), and that the fixation of exchange rates among any group of countries, by increasing the number and severity of disequilibria existing at all times, would on balance worsen the unemployment/inflation relationship for the group as a whole.

FACTORS AFFECTING THE IMPORTANCE OF BASIC RELATIVE DISEQUILIBRIA

The difficulties confronting a unified exchange-rate area owing to the propensity for relative disequilibria, sometimes of the progressive type, to arise between members has been generally, if sometimes only tacitly, acknowledged by economists. Much of the discussion relating to the criteria of an optimum currency area has been concerned with pointing out the factors that may determine whether this loss will be so great as to outweigh any possible advantages of forming such a union or, on the contrary, small enough to be outweighed by those advantages.

Wage and Price Flexibility

One of these factors has already been mentioned, namely, the flexibility of wages and prices, that is, the degree of their responsiveness to situations of excess demand and excess supply. If prices and wages were both entirely flexible, the need for relative exchange-rate adjustments within the union would not arise. As we know, however, the growing importance of collective bargaining in the labour market and of monopoly, natural or state-induced in product markets has been progressively reducing, in almost all economies,[4] the extent to which wages and prices are in this sense flexible. It is this development, together with the greater importance attached to stability of output and employment, that has been largely responsible for the increasing emphasis placed, in the course of the inter-war period and again in the later years of the postwar period, on the necessity for countries to be in a position to promote the harmonisation of their relative cost levels and the correction of their payments disequilibria through the adjustment of their exchange rates vis-à-vis the rest of the world. The same tendencies must be seriously taken into account in assessing the probable need for exchange-rate adjustment within any sizeable group of countries.

Factor Mobility

Labor. In the pioneering article[5] that introduced the concept of an "optimum currency area," Professor Mundell presented as the principal criterion of such an area the existence within it of a high degree of factor mobility. Some years earlier Professor Meade had pointed to the importance of such mobility for the mitigation of disequilibria within a "free trade area."[6] We might expect, therefore, that the greater the mobility of labor and capital between the members of a group of countries the less

---

[4] The formation of the European Common Market might have been expected to increase the degree of flexibility, at least in product prices within the area of the EEC, but the results thus far have been disappointing.

[5] R. A. Mundell, "A Theory of Optimum Currency Areas," *American Economic Review* (September 1961), 51:657–65.

[6] J. E. Meade, "The Balance of Payments Problems of a European Free-Trade Area," *Economic Journal* (September 1957), 67:379–96.

would be the need for alterations in their relative exchange rates and the less the harm done by their participation in a fixed exchange rate union.

In fact, however, an important distinction has to be drawn. The mitigating effect of factor mobility is much more certain in the case of labor-mobility than in that of capital-mobility. Particularly if any unemployment that may arise tends to be concentrated on individual workers rather than spread thinly in the form of short time, and so forth, tendencies toward the emergence of unemployment in some of the countries in the union and of excess demand in others will be likely to evoke a transfer of workers from the former to the latter. The greater the mobility of labor, the greater will be the extent of the transfer and the less the amount of unemployment and of inflation that will persist in the respective countries. The effect of this mobility will be reduced but not eliminated by the fact that it is likely to be associated with a change in the location of workers' expenditure from the countries of emigration to the countries of immigration.

It should be noted, however, that a transfer of labor provoked by unemployment, while it mitigates the more obvious signs of disequilibrium, is not necessarily justifiable from a structural point of view, and may later have to be reversed.

Capital. Whether a high mobility of capital will mitigate or accentuate the hardships resulting from exchange-rate fixity within a group of countries, in the event of payments disequilibria between the members of the group, is much more doubtful than in the case of labor mobility, and depends on the nature of the disequilibria, the sensitivity of investment to the level of economic activity, and the time period one has in mind. By a high mobility of capital is meant a high elasticity of substitution, for holders, between assets in one country and assets in another, and, for debtors, between liabilities in one country and liabilities in another.

Suppose that the relative cost levels of different members of the group are out of equilibrium for reasons connected with the current account balance of payments, whether because of a shift in relative demand for their products, or from differential cost-push factors, and that payments equilibrium in the medium term is restored partly by contraction of demand (involving unemployment) in the countries with relatively high costs, and partly by expansion of demand in the countries with relatively low costs.

On the assumption that these demand adjustments are not brought about through budgetary improvement in the high-cost countries and deterioration in the low-cost countries, there will be some decline in saving in the former and rise in saving in the latter countries. Everything— as regards the role of capital mobility—now depends on the extent to which the incentive to invest in the high- and low-cost countries respectively responds to the decline of activity and profits in the former and the increase in activity and profits in the latter. If the incentive to invest declines less than savings in the high-cost countries, and rises less than savings in the low-cost countries, interest rates will rise in the former and fall in the latter, and capital flows will shift in favor of the former and against the latter in such a way as to enable the high-cost countries to maintain a higher level of employment and activity and the low-cost a lower degree of inflationary pressure than would otherwise be compatible with payments equilibrium. If, however, the incentive to invest changes in both types of countries *more* than the level of savings, capital flows will shift against the former and in favor of the latter so that payments equilibrium will be attainable only with more unemployment in high-cost countries and more inflation in low-cost countries.

The higher the degree of capital mobility the greater will be the shift in capital flows, whether of an equilibrating or of a disequilibrating kind.[7] From this standpoint capital mobility is Janus-faced.

In the very short run one would expect investment to be very unresponsive to changes in economic activity, that interest rates would tend to rise in the high-cost and fall in the low-cost countries, and that capital flows would therefore play an equilibrating role, the more powerful the greater the degree of capital mobility.

Casual observation of cyclical behavior, however, suggests that in the medium term there may be a range of output variation over which, if interest rates are kept constant, changes, positive or negative, in output tend to generate bigger changes, positive or negative, in investment than in savings—that is, a range, over which demand expansion or contraction is explosive. If and when output in the high-cost or low-cost countries

---

[7] Changes in capital flows are here termed "equilibrating" if they make it possible to achieve payments equilibrium with less undesired unemployment, on the one hand, and less undesired inflation, on the other, and "disequilibrating" in the opposite case.

lies within this range of instability, mobility of capital will play a dis-equilibrating role. The importance of this case may be disputed. The likelihood that capital mobility will be disequilibrating, however, becomes greater if the assumption that high- and low-cost countries alike conduct their monetary policies with a view to payments equilibrium is dropped in favor of the assumption that the low-cost countries aim their monetary policies at securing internal stability (i.e., attaining their preferred compromise between unemployment and inflation), leaving the burden of adjusting the balance of payments to the high-cost countries. In this case, the low-cost countries will raise their interest rates to prevent undesired inflation, and even if the high-cost countries are in a position to raise interest rates without causing investment to fall more than savings this may not suffice to prevent a disequilibrating flow of funds to the low-cost countries.

Thus far we have discussed only disturbances directly affecting the current account. Consider now another kind of disturbance, an exog-enous change in the incentive to invest in some countries relative to other countries in the unified exchange-rate area. In the absence of capital mobility this change could be offset by changes in relative interest rates as between the countries in the area, thus retaining both full employment and balance of payments equilibrium. With capital mobile, however, the changes in rates would evoke a flow of funds from the countries where investment incentives have declined to those where they have risen, and the countries with relatively low incentives to invest will either have to contract investment and suffer unemployment or will have to practice an expansionary budget policy and reduce saving, as well as investment. Here mobility of capital would have less favorable consequences in the short run in a unified exchange-rate system than in one in which countries with low investment incentives could devalue their exchange rates.

Altogether, it will be seen that mobility of capital among the members of the group is as likely to aggravate as to mitigate the losses and frictions that would otherwise result from the inability to adjust par values in the face of disequilibria arising among members of the area.

What is said above about the bearing of capital mobility on the rela-tionship between exchange-rate unification and payments disequilibria is based on the assumption that within the unified exchange-rate area there are no official measures tending to restrict or distort capital flows. Admittedly, capital mobility increases the effectiveness of certain measures to divert capital flows such as official intervention on the forward exchange market, interest-equalization taxes, taxes and subsidies on investment expenditure, and variations in interest rates rendered possible by variations in public saving. For example, the greater is capital mobility, the easier it will be for the deficit countries in the group to finance their deficits, and the surplus countries their surpluses, by capital flows evoked by raising and lowering interest rates, respectively, meanwhile offsetting the effects of such interest changes on investment expenditure, as well as any expenditure effects associated with the payments disequilibria themselves, by budgetary expansion and contraction. However, most such measures tend, like outright restrictions on capital movements, to involve distortions in the geographical distribution of investment, while the last involves distortions in the levels of national saving.

Product Similarity

Mundell's argument[8] implies that similarity, or substitutability in demand, as between the products of member countries of a group should serve, along with factor mobility, to mitigate the disadvantages of adopting a common currency (or fixing their relative exchange rates). This view again calls for qualification. It is true that where such substitutability is high, payments disequilibria resulting from switches in demand as between the products of the different member countries can be corrected by moderate changes in relative national cost levels, such as might be attained without the necessity for exchange rate adjustment through fiscal and monetary policy measures at relatively low cost in terms of unemployment and of output foregone. On the other hand, where disequilibria result from divergent movements in national cost levels due to cost-push factors, the extent of the offsetting adjustment in costs that is required will be equally great whether product substitutability is high or low, and failure to make such adjustment, for example, by changes in relative par values, will have more severe consequences on

---

[8] R. A. Mundell, "A Theory of Optimum Currency Areas," pp. 659–60.

the balance of payments and on employment in the high-cost countries where such substitutability is high than where it is low.

Degree of Trade Interpenetration

Another factor that has a bearing on the costs of participation in a fixed exchange rate group is the extent to which the potential members trade with each other, that is, the ratio to national income of each member's trade with the rest of the group.

Consider first the proportion of national income that is derived from exports to the group. The higher is this proportion the greater are likely to be the balance of payments disequilibria among members arising from demand shifts, technological changes, and so on. However, in these circumstances, the elasticity of substitution in demand between the products of each member and those of the rest of the group is also likely to be relatively high, and this reduces the extent to which relative cost levels have to change to correct a given disequilibrium. Moreover, labor may be more mobile between members of the group the more they are integrated economically. On balance, therefore, the greater the integration, the less relative cost levels may have to shift because of structural shifts.

Consider next the proportion of national consumption (absorption) derived from imports from other members of the area. This is the aspect on which McKinnon, in an important article on the optimum currency area,[9] has laid a particular emphasis. It has two principal aspects. First, the higher the marginal propensity to import, the less will be the amount of unemployment that will be required over time to correct a given deficit in the balance of payments, or the amount of excess demand required to correct a given surplus. Although the disequilibria may themselves be the larger the greater the degree of trade integration, this probably means that the real cost of such disequilibria, when corrected by demand policy alone rather than by a combination of demand policy and exchange-rate adjustment, will be the less the greater is the degree of trade interpenetration among the members of the area.

---

[9] Ronald I. McKinnon, "Optimum Currency Areas," *American Economic Review* (September 1963), 53:717–25.

Second, the higher the propensity to import from other members of the area, the greater will be the influence of the cost of imports from other group members on the overall cost of living of each member. Cost disequilibria between members, however arising, will therefore lead to rather slight disequilibria in relative consumption price levels, and their correction will therefore involve rather large real income changes for wage earners in member countries that are out of line with the rest. Where such disequilibria arise from demand shifts, this may argue for making the necessary real income changes somewhat gradually, through changes in relative nominal wages, rather than abruptly through par value changes. However, where the disequilibria arise from an uneven degree of wagepush in the member countries, which itself involves a change in relative real incomes, it is difficult to see why both the real income change and the associated disequilibrium should not be offset or prevented by exchangerate adjustment. The most important aspects of the degree of intertrade, however, are probably those considered below under the headings of "money illusion," "effects on capital flows," and "effects on trade." In these aspects a high degree of intertrade constitutes an important argument for exchange-rate unification.

Similarity in Rates of Inflation

At least as important as any of the factors so far discussed, though occupying a much less prominent place in the literature on optimal currency areas, is the extent to which costs in the various parts of the fixed exchange rate area tend to rise at similar or at different speeds when employment is at nationally acceptable levels. Circumstances favoring similarity in rates of inflation are (a) similarity in national employment goals, (b) similarity in rates of productivity growth, and (c) similarity in the degree of trade union aggressiveness. It is not necessary that similarity prevail in all of these respects; it will suffice if differences in one respect are offset by differences in another. Thus, inferiority in productivity growth could be compensated by a political willingness to tolerate higher unemployment, or by cautious unaggressive trade unionism.

Particular importance attaches to the degree of coordination or unification that exists among the trade union and employers' organizations that are active in the various countries of the fixed exchange-rate area. So long as these bodies are organized on a purely national basis, and so long as moods and motivations affecting the workers are different and change differently in different countries, there will probably arise shifts and divergencies in relative labor costs that will require for their correction adjustments in relative exchange rates.

While unification of collective bargaining organizations across national frontiers on a group-wide basis would tend to mitigate these difficulties, it might bring difficulties of its own by encouraging tendencies toward uniformity in levels or rates of change of wage rates—probably first of all uniformity in rates of change, with some effort at "catching up" in the countries whose wages are relatively low. This would probably lead to disparities in the levels or growth rates of wage–costs among countries with disparate levels or growth rates of productivity.

Money Illusion in Wage Determination

The less willing are workers and owners in a country to maintain unchanged the prices in domestic currency of what they sell in the face of changes in the prices of what they buy, the more difficult it will be to control relative national price levels by means of changes in exchange rates. Willingness of bargainers under conditions of imperfect competition to allow their real rewards to be altered by changes in the prices of what they buy, whether or not these in turn are caused by changes in exchange rates, is often referred to as "money illusion," but it may be due less to illusion than to lethargy or to agreements or understandings that fix wages or prices, at least for a time, in terms of the national money.

This fact is of primary importance to the consideration of any proposal to break up an existing currency area into a number of national or regional areas. It is often argued that Wales in the interwar period or West Virginia today would have been much better off with a separate currency of its own that could be devalued vis-à-vis the pound sterling or the dollar respectively. This may well be true, were it not for the probability that Welsh or West Virginian workers would have continued to make wage contracts in pounds or dollars respectively, rather than in terms of any regional currency that might have been devised. It requires all the patriotism attending the setting up of a new state, *plus* the exercise of the power of that state to prevent the use of a former currency as a means of exchange and standard of contract.

It follows that the point often made an favor of unification of existing national currencies that "no one would dream" of setting up a number of separate currencies inside the United States is ill-taken. The fact that the regions of an existing country could not hope to have separate exchange rates because of the impossibility of creating a regional money illusion does not imply that countries of a similar size, where national money illusion persists, should not retain separate exchange rates. National currencies, unless thoroughly abused by inflation, have shown great powers of retaining their functions as means of exchange and standards of value for all domestic transactions, particularly the payment of wages. And while cost-of-living clauses in wage agreements are quite widespread, they seldom operate instantaneously or more than partially to offset the effect of exchange-rate adjustments.

The true lesson to be learned here is that any exchange rate unification of national currencies that involves the setting up of a common currency may be difficult to revoke at a later time if it turns out to be a mistake.

Degree of Economic Policy Integration

Certain types of coordination, centralization, or harmonization of the economic policies of the member countries of a unified exchange-rate area can help to mitigate basic payments disequilibria among them and thus reduce the costs of rate rigidity; others cannot.

For example, in the field of fiscal policy, no advantage for the mitigation of payments disequilibria within the area is to be drawn from the harmonization of fiscal arrangements (adoption of the same type of taxes, or the same rates of tax) whatever the advantages of such harmonization may be from other points of view. Again, little advantage for such mitigation is to be drawn from a mere centralization of public services except insofar as they are financed by taxes so levied that more tends to be paid by countries when they are prosperous and less when they are depressed. Still more advantage is to be drawn from the centralization of social security arrangements where payments are well as receipts are affected by incomes, so that net transfers will tend to flow from prosperous to depressed countries.[10] Most helpful of all would be any centrally financed schemes designed specifically to assist member countries, or regions within countries, that are economically depressed.

However, such arrangements as they would be helpful in mitigating disequilibria only to the extent that relative prosperity among the countries of the area was correlated with relative payments strength. This would be the case where payments disequilibria within the area resulted from shifts in relative demand for the products of different members, or or from differences in productivity growth. It might not be the case where such disequilibria arose from changes in the relative strength of cost pressures among members, for then those whose costs had risen most and whose currencies had become relatively overvalued might have to bear an increased share of the common taxation. It should also be noted that transfers between member countries dependent on the relative economic situation of particular economic sectors (e.g., agriculture) would be unlikely to be at all closely correlated with intermember payments disequilibria.

In the field of monetary and banking policy, arrangements such as those that have recently been set up within the EEC, whereby the central banks of countries in a relatively strong payments position lend on short or medium term to the central banks of countries in a relatively weak payments position are, of course, specifically designed to mitigate intermember payments disequilibria. It is not clear that any advance in this respect would be achieved by further measures of centralization, such as the setting up of a supercentral bank for the area, and the issuing of a common currency. While the volume of resources available for compensatory official financing within the area would doubtless be increased, the policy pursued might not be so strongly compensatory. The tendency of a supercentral bank, especially when the establishment of a common currency had rendered the maintenance of fixed intermember exchange rates quite irrevocable, would probably favor the equalization of short-term interest rates

[10] Cf. Marina v.N. Whitman, *International and Interregional Payments Adjustment: A Synthetic View*, Princeton Series in International Finance, no. 19; and Peter B. Kenen, "The Theory of Optimum Currency Areas: An Eclectic View," in Robert A. Mundell and Alexander Swoboda, eds., *Monetary Problems of the International Economy* (Chicago: University of Chicago Press, 1969).

throughout the area. In other words, it would tend, at least so far as short-term funds are concerned, not so much to finance disequilibria as to promote the development of perfect mobility of capital among participating countries—a mobility that, as we have seen, is by no means always helpful in mitigating intermember disequilibria.

The centralization of fiscal and monetary policy in a fixed exchange-rate—or common currency—area could conceivably go so far that the central authorities began to assume at least part of the responsibility for aggregate demand in the area as a whole. Or quite possibly a centralized monetary authority, administering a common currency, might feel a responsibility for influencing the level of aggregate demand in the area as a whole (as well as defending its balance of payments) while national governments still tried to influence, through fiscal policy, the level of demand in their own countries. As will be indicated, this centralization of responsibility for demand management might well lead to a higher level of demand within the area than if the responsibility had remained purely national; whether this aggravates or alleviates the costs of internal disequilibria is debatable.

To the extent that the factors considered earlier in this section tend to mitigate the immediate internal effects (in the form of unemployment or inflation) of relative payments disequilibria within the area, they will tend to reduce the speed of adjustment and slow down the process of correcting the disequilibria. By contrast, the tendency described in the foregoing paragraph would quicken the pace of such adjustment.

Another form of joint action which, if it were practicable, would both mitigate the problem of relative basic payments disequilibria in a unified exchange-rate union and speed up the process of adjustment, would be the harmonization of incomes policies. This would, of course, have special importance for the prevention of the progressive type of disequilibria described above.

EFFECTS ON EXCHANGE-RATE SPECULATION
AND CAPITAL FLOWS

The considerations mentioned up to this point have a bearing on the magnitude of the disadvantages involved in forfeiting the possibility of correcting disequilibria in relative national price levels by exchange-rate adjustments. Under certain circumstances these disadvantages will be great and under others, negligible. If this were all that was to be said, however, there would never be any outright advantage in throwing away the possibility of exchange-rate adjustment, though the possibility might not be worth much.

In what follows, however, we discuss ways in which the formation of a unified exchange-rate area may possibly, though not necessarily, yield positive advantages.

Some of these ways relate to capital flows. Establishment of a fixed exchange-rate area will do away with any possibility of exchange profits or losses from capital flows between participating countries. Moreover, once participants have unified their rates, changes in exchange rates even between participants and nonparticipants will probably become less frequent and smaller, so that exchange profits and losses on capital flows between participants and nonparticipants also may become less important.[11] For both of these reasons, especially the former, there should be a decline in the exchange-speculative element in capital flows.

This conclusion may require some modification for reasons discussed earlier, so far as capital flows between the fixed exchange-rate area and the outside world are concerned. If the authorities of the area for political reasons should be more reluctant to alter the exchange rate when required than the national authorities would have been, speculation across the frontiers of the area might increase as a result of unification. If, on the other hand, as Triffin believes likely, they were to adopt a more flexible policy, speculation might be reduced even more than we have assumed.

The elimination or reduction of the speculative element in capital flows is to be reckoned an advantage of the unified exchange-rate area. Speculative flows may lead (through effects on expenditure in the countries concerned) to short-term transfers of real capital not justified in terms of the relative productivity of capital in the countries concerned. Still more important, they may lead to deflation and unemployment in the countries where exchange rates are expected to fall and to inflationary price effects

---

[11] For example, in situations where in the absence of unification one participant might have unvalued and another devalued its currency, no change may be required in the unified rate.

in the countries where rates are expected to rise. These effects will, of course, be mitigated to the extent that arrangements exist for offsetting reserve movements or other forms of official compensatory financing between the countries concerned. Moreover, to the extent that speculative capital flows speed up exchange-rate adjustments under the par value system, it may be argued that they enhance the superiority of the latter over the fixed exchange-rate area from the standpoint of promptly correcting fundamental disequilibria. As an offset to this last argument, however, such flows presumably tend to make the exchange-rate adjustments unduly large when they do occur. On balance, the elimination of speculative capital flows should be counted as a gain. The greater the mobility of capital within the fixed exchange rate area, the greater this gain will be.

A second favorable consequence of the establishment of a fixed exchange-rate area would be that of increasing the mobility of capital within the area in the sense of increasing its responsiveness to differences among participating countries with respect to interest rates and profit rates in national currency. This is clearly an advantage when, as is generally the case, no particularly severe cost disequilibria have arisen as between participating countries. As we have seen, however, capital mobility may be a very mixed blessing in circumstances where such disequilibria have arisen and cannot, because of the fixity of the exchange rates, be speedily corrected.

The increase in capital mobility is, of course, much more likely to arise, to a significant extent, among the countries of the unified exchange rate area than between that area and the outer world. Indeed, if the formation of the area should lead to undue rigidity in the unified rate, this could result in the imposition of restrictions on outflows, or inflows, of capital as a means of reducing payments deficits or surpluses of the area as a whole.

EFFECTS ON PRICE INFLATION

As has been argued above, the fixation of exchange rates among a group of countries will probably worsen the unemployment/inflation relationship for the area as a whole. That is, it will increase the amount of unemployment required to hold inflation at any given rate and will increase the rate of inflation corresponding to any given level of unemployment. It does not follow that both inflation and unemployment must necessarily rise. In any arrangement in which the maintenance of a fixed exchange rate is given overriding priority, the countries in payments surplus can usually maintain the rate by accumulating reserves, while those in payments deficit may lack the reserves to spend in maintaining the rate. So long as demand management remains a national responsibility, and any balance of payments assistance among members is held to modest proportions, therefore, the deficit rather than the surplus countries are likely to have to assume the greater part of the burden of removing the payments disequilibria by adapting the level of demand. The surplus countries may be able to stay fairly close to the preferred point on their employment inflation curves while the deficit countries may have to depart considerably from theirs in a deflationary direction. In this event, the entire worsening in the unemployment–inflation relationship in the area as a whole may take the form of increased unemployment, and the average rate of inflation in the area may decline. There may, moreover, be a secondary disinflationary effect on demand management. The fact that payments deficits are liable to involve the necessity for substantial deflation and unemployment may well have the result of making participating countries more cautious about embarking on expansionary policies even when they are in balance or in surplus in order to avoid falling into deficit later. How these tendencies are evaluated depends, of course, on whether the policies of most governments are, or are not, considered to be "too inflationary" after account is taken of the effect on employment as well as on prices.

What has been said above about the disinflationary effects to be expected from adherence to a fixed exchange-rate area is true only so long as it operates in a decentralized fashion without too generous arrangements for financial assistance from surplus to deficit countries and without effective centralization of monetary and budgetary policies. Should such centralization prevail, the anti-inflationary tendencies inherent in fixed parities may be offset or even outweighed by expansionary action on the part of the central authorities. Mere fixity of exchange rates, as we have seen, would be likely to force the deficit countries within the area to pursue policies involving more unemployment and less inflation (or more deflation) than they would voluntarily have adopted in the absence of payments difficulties. In these circumstances it would not be unreasonable for any central monetary or financial authority to expand demand to a point at which the "surplus" countries were suffering as much from unwanted inflation as the deficit countries from unwanted unemployment.

Apart from this uncertainty about where the precise balance between inflation and unemployment will be struck in a fixed exchange-rate area, it may be argued that the fixation of exchange rates within the area may have favorable effects on the unemployment/inflation relationships within participating countries, which would offset, at least in part, the tendency for this relationship to deteriorate in the area as a whole.

In the first place—and this is the most clearly beneficial type of disinflationary effect—employers in each country might feel that if they raised their profit margins or failed to keep down their costs they could no longer reckon on maintaining their competitive position vis-à-vis the outside world by exchange-rate devaluation. And trade unions might feel that they could no longer be saved by devaluation from the curtailment of employment that would otherwise follow excessive wage increases. Both of these effects, to the extent that they obtain, would tend to improve the Phillips curves of participating countries. Such reactions, however, would probably be important only in countries where wages or price margins were determined by centralized agreements, each covering a large proportion of the economy, or at least of its foreign-trade sector. Only in these circumstances would the parties involved be likely to take into account the effects their actions might have on national exchange rates.

It is also possible that the establishment of a fixed exchange-rate area by increasing the penalties of falling into payments deficit may give a greater incentive to some member governments to improve their unemployment–inflation relationships directly by intervening, through more effective incomes policies, in the process of wage and price formation.

EFFECTS ON AREA INTERTRADE

It is sometimes argued that the unification of exchange rates would reduce risks of international trade at least among the participating countries themselves. This, however, seems rather debatable. What matters is not the risk involved in individual trade transactions—which can be hedged in a variety of ways—but rather the risk involved in investment in foreign-trade industries. The speculative flurries that occur under the par value system at times when exchange rates are believed to be imminent add somewhat to the risks of such investment, but these are likely to be outweighed by the fact that under that system variations in competitiveness due to a variation in relative national cost levels are likely to be sooner corrected than under a system of unified rates.

EFFECTS ON THE CENTRALIZATION OF GOVERNMENTAL FUNCTIONS

Much of the support for the establishment of fixed exchange-rate areas is based on the consideration that it would further the transfer of responsibility for the exercise of various governmental functions in the economic sphere from national to area authorities.

Thus, avoidance of the sudden changes in relative nominal incomes of participating countries that are associated with changes in par values should make it easier to arrange fiscal transfers between governments, to levy federal taxes, or pay federal bounties on a stable and equitable basis. Fixity of exchange rates, or the existence of a common currency, should also facilitate the payment of area civil servants, the issuing of area debt and the centralized price fixing of agricultural or other products. It should be borne in mind, however, that sudden changes in the relative nominal incomes of countries that are associated with changes in exchange rates often represent a sudden reversal of distortions in relative nominal incomes that had been developing more gradually over a period. Such distortion among members of a fixed exchange-rate area, if uncorrected, would themselves put area arrangements under increasing strain.

Another way in which unified exchange rates might foster the development of area institutions is by giving rise to situations that, unless such institutions are developed, are calculated to give rise to serious hardships. Thus it might be argued that the emergence of depressed conditions in participating countries that have become uncompetitive would force the development of compensatory fiscal and credit arrangements of a centralized type or even the creating of a centralized money-creating authority. In any event, of course, fixity of exchange rates is a technical prerequisite for the emergence of a common currency. As against this, the possibility has to be borne in mind that if adherence to a unified exchange-rate area were found to lead to excessive hardships, reactions might ensue leading not only to the abandonment of exchange-rate unification but even to a rejection of other forms of economic integration among participating countries.

The weight attached to the arguments set forth above will, of course, depend on the extent to which a transfer of responsibility from national to supranational authorities in the spheres in question is believed to be advantageous to the countries concerned.

THE CASE OF THE EUROPEAN ECONOMIC COMMUNITY

The considerations set forth in this paper have considerable relevance to the question whether or not it is advisable to set up a unified exchange-rate area, with or without a common currency, within the EEC with its present or with an enlarged membership, and it may be appropriate to conclude with certain reflections on this matter. For this purpose we again ignore any special problems that might arise if at the time of the unification one or more of the exchange rates concerned were imperfectly aligned.

In considering this question it is convenient to compare the circumstances of such a unified exchange-rate area with those of the United States. As is well known, the United States has had a higher "average" level of unemployment in the 1960s than any of the other industrial countries (except Canada). Indeed, the long-term relationship between unemployment and inflation appears to have been highly unfavorable in the United States, which has therefore found it particulary difficult to reconcile high employment and reasonable price stability. This remains true even when due allowance is made for differences between countries in the manner in which they measure unemployment.[12] A plausible explanation for this lies in maladjustments in the distribution of labour demand and supply, respectively, among different areas, occupations, and types of labor. To

---

[12] See *Measuring Employment and Unemployment* (Washington: U.S. President's Committee to Appraise Employment and Unemployment Statistics, 1962), ch. 10.

some extent this may be due to the persistence over much of the period of a fairly low degree of demand pressure in the U.S. economy: such a situation, as was illustrated by the U.K. experience in the interwar period, makes for the persistence of maladjustments. Some importance may also be attributed to frictional unemployment arising from a greater readiness of U.S. employers to fire employees when demand is slack, and a willingness on the part of workers to remain unemployed for a longer period between jobs.

However, in the light of the foregoing discussion, it should not be surprising that a relatively high unemployment level and a relatively unfavorable unemployment/inflation relationship are found in an exchange-rate area with a large labor force, where labor mobility is reduced by the dispersion of that force over a wide territory and by its heterogeneity in skill and education, and where the division of governmental responsibility between federal and subordinate governments makes it more difficult for the central authority to pursue effective demand management policies, labor market policies, or income policies.

In any uniform exchange rate area based on the EEC with its present, or with an expanded membership, it is difficult to escape the conclusion that the propensity to develop internal disequilibria and the difficulty of reconciling high employment with reasonable price stability would be even greater than in the United States. This would appear to be true not only if economic integration and centralization were carried as far as it is reasonable to expect in the foreseeable future. The area, even with its present membership, would be a large one. Labor mobility, though aided by a greater density of population and a less heterogeneous labor force than in the United States, would be adversely influenced for some time to come by language difficulties. Wage and price flexibility in highly unionized and monopoly-minded Europe would probably remain lower than in the United States. Partly, once more, for language reasons, it would be difficult to attain the degree of centralization of trade-union organization and coordination of collective bargaining that obtains in the United States. While a centralized control over money creation might conceivably be achieved in such a European area, it is difficult to imagine a centralization of taxing and spending powers within the EEC and, therefore, an effectiveness of centralized demand management approaching that of the United States. Demand management would be likely to suffer for a very long time from the difficulties inherent in a division of responsibilities between central and national authorities.

It may well be that an accentuation of structural difficulties and a normal level of unemployment higher than prevails in the United States and substantially higher than has prevailed in general in Western Europe in the last decade is a price worth paying for an arrangement calculated to promote the unification of the European capital market, to eliminate internal currency speculation, and (with some reservations) to foster economic and political integration in Europe. The "pros and cons" are to some extent incommensurable and a precise quantification is in any case impracticable. But it is at least desirable that the costs as well as the benefits be soberly weighed.

GRAPHICAL APPENDIX

Let A and B be two countries with the same size of labor force, and identical unemployment/inflation curves. Percentage rates of price increase are measured along the N-axis and percentage rates of unemployment along the U-axis.

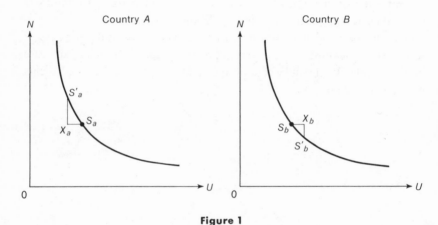

Figure 1

In the initial situation (S_a, S_b) the slope of the unemployment–inflation curves (the S-curves) is the same in both countries, and the rates of inflation and unemployment are likewise the same.

Suppose that a payments disequilibrium occurs that necessitates a shift from S_a to S_a' and S_b to S_b', and that this involves a decline in unemployment in A equal to the increase in unemployment in B, that is,

$$S_a X_a = X_b S_b$$

Since both in A and B the S-curves are concave to the origin, and the curves have the same slope at S_a and S_b respectively,

$$\text{angle } S_a' S_a X_a > \text{angle } S_b' S_b X_b$$

and since

$$S_a X_a = X_b S_b$$
$$S_a' X_a > X_b S_b'$$

that is the increase in the rate of inflation in *A* exceeds the decline in inflation in *B*, and the (unweighted) average rate of inflation in the two countries increases.

It is clear that if the payments disequilibrium had resulted in a shift of unemployment from *B* to *A* rather than from *A* to *B*, the effect on the average rate of inflation would have been the same.

In this case, country *B* has a less favorable unemployment–inflation curve than country *A*. The slope of the *S*-curve is the same in both countries in the initial (i.e., the preferred) position.

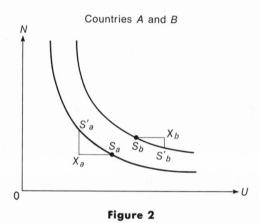

Figure 2

Suppose that, since price inflation in *B* at S_b is greater than in *A* at S_a, *B* develops a deficit against *A* and to correct this disequilibrium unemployment in *B* increases by the same amount as it declines in *A*:

$$S_a X_a = X_b S_b$$

Since the slope of the *S*-curves is the same at S_a as at S_b, and the curves are concave to the origin,

$$\text{angle } S'_a S_a X_a > \text{angle } S'_b S_b X_b$$

and

$$S'_a X_a > X_b S'_b$$

that is the unweighted average rate of inflation in *A* and *B* rises.

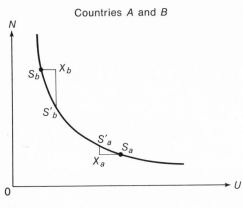

Figure 3

In this case countries A and B have identical S-curves, here represented by a single curve.

In the initial position (the preferred position), country B (at S_b) has a higher rate of inflation and a lower rate of unemployment than country A (at S_a) because of a difference in relative preferences as between unemployment and inflation. Because its rate of inflation is higher, it develops a deficit vis-à-vis A, and has to move to S_b' while A moves S_a'. As before, suppose that $S_a X_a = X_b S_b$. But since the slope of the S-curve is steeper at S_b than at S_a,

$$\text{angle } S_b' S_b X_b > \text{angle } S_a' S_a X_a$$

and

$$X_b S_b' > S_a' X_a$$

In this case the average (unweighted) rate of inflation in the two countries declines.

14

TOWARD A NEW REGIME FOR INTERNATIONAL PAYMENTS

WHEN CONSIDERING a thoroughgoing reformation of the international payments system, it is logical to begin, as did the founding fathers of the IMF, by formulating some basic objectives that such a system should fulfill.

My suggestions would be as follows:

1. It should permit governments to maintain a level of demand for national output that represents their preferred compromise between full employment and price stability;
2. It should promote maximum freedom of international trade;
3. It should foster, over time, balances of payments on current account that correspond—with due allowance for reserve growth—to an optimal international movement of capital.
4. It should promote reasonable stability in external economic relationships.

There is a certain conflict between these objectives. Objectives (1) and (2), which require, respectively, that demand policy, while accommodating any changes in the foreign balance, should ultimately be oriented to domestic objectives, and that freedom of trade be preserved, imply heavy reliance on the adjustment of relative price levels as the means of keeping international payments in balance. If it were required, in addition, that the current balance be continuously adjusted so as to implement a free international movement of capital, or even an optimal international

First published in the *Journal of International Economics*, (September 1972), 2:345–73. Reprinted by permission of North Holland.

movement of capital, however that might be determined, competitive conditions among countries would be so variable as to be unduly disturbing to the foreign trade sector of national economies, and this would offend against objective (4). No doubt a certain flexibility is permissible in applying objective (2) and even objective (1). But in the main it is objective (3) that has to give way in the short run, though it is important that equilibrium be so interpreted as to implement it over the longer run.

The main instruments at the disposal of governments for the achievement of these four objectives are demand policies (in the sense of policies affecting aggregate domestic expenditure), commercial policy, exchange-rate policy, capital control policy, and international official financing. My view as to how, ideally, these instruments would be employed within the context of the international monetary-cumcommercial policy system defined by the Bretton Woods (IMF) and GATT agreements have been set forth in detail elsewhere.[1] Broadly speaking, demand policy should be aimed primarily at objective (1), though slight departures from the domestic optimum in the interest of the balance of payments objectives may be reasonable. Commercial policy, of course, aims at objective (2). This leaves to be considered exchange-rate policy, on the one hand, and the policies involved in controlling and financing private capital flows, on the other: these have to be combined in such a way as to strike the best compromise between objectives (3) and (4), given the necessity that each country's external payments and receipts should balance.

These very general propositions hold true not only for the Bretton Woods system but also for any conceivable reform thereof. Under the Bretton Woods system, policies affecting net capital flows—including reserve movements—supply in the very short run the residual influence required to keep payments and receipts in balance; under a floating exchange-rate system exchange policy would supply this residual element. Any reform of the international monetary system is bound to be concerned primarily with the relative roles to be played by these two sets of policies and with the institutional framework affecting their application by countries.

---

[1] Guidelines for balance-of-payments adjustment under the par value system. In *Essays in International Economics* (Cambridge, Mass: Harvard University Press; London: Allen and Unwin, 1971).

In what follows I assume that the reader has a general knowledge of the main features of the system governing international trade and payments, exchange rates, and reserves that has prevailed and developed over the postwar period, and of the difficulties that have increasingly beset it, at least to the time of the Smithsonian Agreement of December 1971.

I. EXCHANGE-RATE REGIME

In considering possible improvements of the international monetary system it is appropriate to begin with exchange rates. The exchange rate is the principal instrument whereby each country, consistently with the basic objectives outlined above, can maintain its price level in an appropriate competitive relationship with those of other countries in the face of tendencies for national price levels to diverge at preferred levels of aggregate demand for national output. In some cases it may be justifiable to permit the demand for domestic output to vary somewhat for the sake of external equilibrium; any variation in domestic *output*, however, should only be slight and temporary. However, domestic *expenditure* must of course be adapted to accommodate any changes in the foreign balance that may be brought about by other means. At some future time it may prove possible to moderate the divergent tendencies in price levels through appropriate incomes policy, but this is not yet a reliable instrument in any country. Therefore, for a long time to come exchange rates will continue to be an indispensable instrument of international adjustment.

In addition to offsetting divergent movements in national price levels, exchange rates should also be such as to bring about any changes in relative price levels that may be required to accommodate fundamental changes in real demand and supply conditions, including any trend changes—but not cyclical or other temporary variations—in capital flows.

As a rule, the changes in relative exchange rates ideally required on these criteria will be smooth and continuous, rather than abrupt, though occasionally surges of demand or cost inflation in a country will call for a substantial rate adjustment in a short time period.

In practice, a continuous smooth adjustment of exchange rates such as has been described is difficult to achieve under the par value system established at Bretton Woods. Under that system countries are obliged to establish par values for their currencies in terms of gold, and to maintain their exchange rates within a relatively narrow margin of the parities (relative par values) of the currencies concerned. Countries may not change their par values except to correct a "fundamental disequilibrium" and with the concurrence of the IMF. But the IMF cannot compel a country to change its par value even if a fundamental disequilibrium exists.

"Fundamental disequilibrium" has nowhere been defined, but may, perhaps, be thought of as a situation in which a chronic payments imbalance would tend to exist at levels of employment and capital control practices customary in the countries conerned. Small disequilibria of this kind are difficult to identify and still more difficult to measure. It is sometimes hard for a country to know how much of any disequilibrium it should seek to remove by changing its own par value, and how much can and should be left to the actions of other countries. Moreover, governments are apt to fear the effects of revaluation on employment more than they welcome its disinflationary effects, and to fear the inflationary effects of devaluation, and the loss of prestige involved in it, more than they welcome its effects on employment. Finally, in order to avoid the disturbing and self-fulfilling effects of speculation, they deny to the last the need for exchange-rate adjustment, and sometimes deceive themselves in the process.

For all of these reasons, par values, and with them exchange rates, have long been unduly rigid, with the result that trade and production have been diverted from appropriate channels, international reserve flows maldistributed, and even employment sometimes affected. Speculative capital flows have, from time to time, built up to a point at which abrupt and disturbing movements in exchange rates have become inevitable. If in recent years exchange-rate rigidity has been broken and adjustments have become more frequent, it is primarily because of the vastly enhanced strength of these speculative forces, and adjustments forced by these means have not always been those required to correct true basic disequilibria.

What can be done to make exchange rates in general more responsive to the continuous changes in long-term equilibrium rates? (The special difficulties involved in "flexing" the U.S. dollar are considered in section II. An approach favored by many economists is for countries to discard any commitments to maintain fixed parities, and to allow their exchange rates to "float" on the market, subject, possibly, to limited market intervention to smooth out rate fluctuations. This would certainly permit desirable exchange rate adjustments to take place inconspicuously and with minimal repercussions on prestige. This solution, however, has its own difficulties and defects. If intervention is slight, exchange rates may vary excessively in response to cyclical and other temporary variations in capital flows and other elements in the balance of payments, with excessive resource shifts and frictional unemployment in the international sector of the world economy and possible ratchet effects on prices and wages. Alternatively, monetary policy, though no longer under pressure from reserve movements, may be excessively oriented toward the stabilization of the rate, with repercussions on internal demand.

Where, as is more commonly the case, market intervention is considerable, the problem arises of ensuring that such intervention takes place with due regard to the interest of the international community, and is not directed, for example, to obtaining a competitive advantage for the intervening country. Ideally, a country with a floating exchange rate should accept a measure of international surveillance over its intervention policy designed to ensure, for example, that it does not force the rate to move in a direction contrary to the pressures of the market except when this is agreed by the IMF to be desirable in the interest of longer-term equilibrium. Up to now, countries with floating rates have shown no great disposition to welcome international surveillance over their exchange market policies, but if the growth of speculative international capital flows were to lead to a move widespread adoption of the floating system, acceptance of such surveillance would become a matter of crucial importance. Whatever the potential merits of internationally supervised floating as a way of approaching the objectives listed earlier, however, it is clear that the great majority of countries, including particularly the less developed countries, are still attached to a system in which they can maintain a parity relationship between their own currency and as many as possible of the currencies of their trading partners. Account has to be taken of this preference in any practical proposal for the reform of the exchange system.

This does not mean that countries fail to recognize, in varying degrees, the need for greater flexibility in exchange rates. The principal forms in which such flexibility may be sought are: (a) prompter and more frequent adjustment of par values, (b) a widening of the margins within which exchange rates may deviate from parity, and (c) the authorization in certain circumstances of temporary floating as a way of moving from one parity, or set of parities, to another.[2]

One technique for achieving gradual and smooth exchange-rate adjustment that is favored by many economists but is unlikely, in the writer's opinion, to have much of a future is known as the "crawl." Under this system exchange parities would be adjusted automatically at very short intervals (daily, weekly, or monthly) in response to the behavior, over some preceding period (e.g., a year), of indicators of short term payments disequilibria (e.g., the level of exchange rates or the rate of increase or decrease of reserves) in such a way that the annual rate of change in parities would not exceed 2 or 3 percent. While this arrangement would certainly have a tendency to reduce fundamental disequilibria insofar as these were manifested in the indicators and not suppressed in various possible ways, it could have unfortunate consequences in relation to temporary or cyclical imbalances. Given the time lag between the appearance of imbalances and the response of parities (a lag intensified by the slowness of the "crawl") and the lag between any change in parities and the effect on current account balances, it is quite possible that the result would be to intensify rather than to moderate cyclical imbalances. In any event, the short-run effect of anticipated movements in rates could be to intensify disequilibrating capital flows and to intensify the need for capital controls. Although governments might at times be tempted by a system that offered to relieve them of the responsibility for deciding on necessary exchange-rate movements, in practice they would be unlikely to sign away their powers in this field, and likely to insist on the right to veto small changes in rates of which they disapproved, and more particularly on the right, subject to IMF concurrence, to make large discrete rate changes when these appeared necessary to restore confidence in their currencies.

---

[2] In the report entitled "The Role of Exchange Rates in the Adjustment of International Payments," presented in 1970 by the Executive Directors of the IMF, the first of these reforms is advocated; the second and third, if subject to adequate safeguards, are treated as deserving of further study.

A "crawl" that depended on official assent, however, would be far less effective than an automatic one, and would soon break down. Governments would fear that their acquiescence would be taken as evidence that they acknowledged the existence of a fundamental disequilibrium to which the crawl itself might be an inadequate response, and that it would therefore give rise to strong anticipations of a continued crawl or even of a larger adjustment. Fearing this, they would be likely to withhold assent to microchanges and to refuse to allow the "crawl" to operate in the manner for which it was designed.

From what has been said above it would seem that any greater flexibility in par values will, for the most part,[3] have to take the form of more flexible discretionary adjustments. How can one hope to alter the conditions governing such adjustments so as to make them prompter and more frequent than they have been in the past?

In the past the IMF has had only a negative voice in par value changes. It has been authorized to withhold assent from such changes if it disapproves of them, but not to initiate them. In practice, the IMF has been forced increasingly to play, albeit informally, a more active role, notably in the case of the recent general realignment of currencies, and the time may have come when this role should be exercised in a more systematic way.[4] For example, the IMF might adopt the practice of conducting, in private, regular reviews of the manner in which the equilibrium structure of relative exchange rates among the principal currencies appeared to be developing and of the extent to which actual rates diverged from this structure. Such divergencies cannot, in the writer's view, be estimated from current statistical indicators whether these relate to market exchange rates, reserve movements, or price developments, but only on the basis of a complex analytical appraisal and forecast that takes into account all of the relevant data. If experience with this exercise should indicate that it is possible to arrive at a reasonable measure of agreement in estimating

---

[3] See, however, the discussion of wider margins and temporary "floats" at the end of this section.

[4] The suggestions that follow are similar to ideas that have been advanced by Fred Hirsch in "The Exchange Rate Regime: An Analysis and a Possible Scheme," International Monetary Fund, *Staff Papers*, July 1972. Mr. Hirsch, however, is not responsible for the particular form in which they are advanced here.

an equilibrium structure of exchange rates, the IMF might be authorized to recommend appropriate adjustments in par values in cases in which substantial deviations appeared to be developing. It might be authorized in extreme cases to declare publicly that the par values in question were inappropriate, and if no steps were taken to correct the situation, to apply such remedies as appeared likely to be effective.

One cannot translate deviations from optimal relative exchange rates into appropriate par value changes without taking a view as to the desirable balance between devaluations. At a time when changes in the value of the U.S. dollar were regarded as out of the question it was important that the balance of devaluations and revaluations should, if possible, be such as to permit the United States to remain in equilibrium. Now that it is accepted that the par value of the dollar itself can be changed, this consideration is less important, and more weight can be given to the desirability of maintaining, or even increasing over time,[5] the currency value of the primary reserve assets, SDRs and gold, in terms of which par values are reckoned. This does not mean that over each short period of time there should be an attempt to balance devaluations and revaluations, for account has to be taken of the degree of dispersion of disequilibria and of the undesirability of multiplying small changes in par value if the same result can be achieved by a few larger changes; but over the longer run there should be a reasonable balance.

The question of the kinds of sanctions that might be applied by the IMF in cases where a country refuses to alter an exchange rate which the IMF has ruled to be excessively out of line, or changes it in the wrong direction, has to be approached with circumspection. Countries have a way of reacting perversely to weak sanctions, especially if they are imposed conspicuously. It is better to seek to persuade countries that adherence to the established rules is in the general interest. As is well known, the sanctions available are not strong and apply mainly to deficit countries. Up to now withholding of the resources of the General Account, in accordance with the rules applicable to drawings in the credit tranches,

---

[5] Acceptance of SDRs is a matter of legal obligation. Nevertheless, if SDRs are to constitute an increasing proportion of reserve assets they should not be much less attractive to hold than reserve currencies. Since, however, the latter will probably always bear a higher rate of interest than SDRs, it would be convenient if the SDR had some slight tendency to rise in relative value.

has been the only sanction applied in practice. To this could conceivably be added withholding of SDR allocations or even a freezing of the use of SDR balances, though these sanctions may be pre-empted by the need to ensure observance of the rules of the Special Drawing Account itself. If, as is suggested in section VII, the IMF were entrusted with the control over the supply of very short-term credit, of the type now produced under bilateral credit arrangements, such credits also might be withheld from a country that stubbornly refused to devalue. As for persistent surplus countries that refuse to revalue, the only penalties—apart from the withholding of SDR allocations—that might theoretically be applicable are those that would involve concerted discrimination on the part of other countries, such as restrictions on imports from them, discriminatory treatment with respect to their capital transactions, or the withholding of convertibility or even transferability from currency balances which they accumulate. It might, however, be difficult to induce countries to cooperate in applying some of these sanctions because of their punitive character, but an indirect pressure might, be exercised on surplus countries through a generous financing of countries whose deficits correspond to their surpluses.

Action undertaken to promote the liberalization of international transactions may also indirectly foster appropriate exchange-rate adjustments. For example, if the IMF withholds consent to a continuation of restrictions on current payments, or the GATT to a continuation of import restrictions, these actions, which directly promote one of the basic objectives of these organizations, indirectly promote adjustment of overvalued currencies. Again, if, as is suggested in section VII, a code of good behavior were established in the field of international capital flows, one element in such a code might be—as in the case of trade restrictions—that the maintenance of effective restrictions on capital outflows or inflows for balance of payments reasons would be permitted for no more than limited periods, and that countries with persistent restrictions would be asked to show cause why they should not dismantle them. Any success the IMF might have in actions of this kind would promote exchange adjustment on the part of surplus as well as of deficit countries.

Another approach to improving the operation of the par value system relies not on the exercise of international pressure but on the removal of obstacles to national action in this field. I am not referring to suggestions for removing the necessity for IMF consent to small changes in par value, since this necessity has never presented a serious obstacle to any desirable change in par values. The reference is rather to proposals for facilitating prompt adjustments in par values by permitting greater flexibility in the movement of actual exchange rates in relation to parities. The main proposal of this kind concerns the widening of the margins within which the exchange rates of any two currencies are permitted to deviate from parity. In 1959 these margins were widened from 1–2 percent by an IMF decision, provided that each of the countries concerned maintained a margin not exceeding 1 percent vis-à-vis some particular currency, (i.e., normally its intervention currency). At the realignment of December 1971 a further widening of these margins to $2\frac{1}{4}$ percent from the intervention currency and $4\frac{1}{2}$ percent from other currencies was informally authorized for countries that desired to avail themselves of it. It would seem desirable that margins of this order (4 percent or more vis-à-vis the generality of other currencies) should be made a permanent feature of the international exchange-rate system.

To a considerable extent—as is indicated in the ensuing section— wider margins are desired in order to enable countries to retain control over their monetary policies in the face of enhanced capital mobility and speculative capital flows. But they have also an important role to play in facilitating adjustment to basic disequilibria.[6] If the monetary authorities of a country believe a fairly small change in par value to be desirable, they can prepare for it by allowing or even forcing the exchange rate to move at least a part of the way within the margins. The wider the margins and the greater this preparatory movement in rates, the smaller is likely to be the further change in exchange rates as a result of a given par value change. By this means the authorities can forestall speculation and reduce the necessity for denying any intention to change the par value—denials that add to the loss of prestige involved when the par value is finally changed. Moreover, industry has an opportunity to begin adapting to a new exchange rate before the change in par value occurs. For all these reasons the widening of margins may be expected to make changes in par values less important and thus less traumatic.

---

[6] A detailed discussion of the case for substantially wider margins in both of these aspects is contained in chapter 13 of *Essays in International Economics.*

Proposals whereby the benefits of substantial margins could be more fully extended to the ultimate intervention currency (the U.S. dollar) are made in section IV.[7]

Wider margins are primarily useful in facilitating small par value changes. Where larger changes are required there is a good case for granting legal authorization for temporary "floats," that is, temporary deviations of exchange rates from parity by more than the permitted margins. Such "floats" might sometimes be required solely to deal with disruptive capital flows but would normally be transitional toward a new par value. Countries may wish to "float" in preference to attempting from the outset to determine a new parity partly to discern by trial and error what new rate is sustainable, at least in the short run, partly to invoke the "judgment of the market" in support of the new rate, and partly to accustom people by degrees to the magnitude of the adjustment that is required. It is, in my view, desirable to give legal authorization to such a course, in order to (a) avert worse solutions such as the adoption of restrictions on current transactions, (b) prevent countries from abusing the "float" for competitive purposes, and (c) encourage them to allow the rate to converge on an appropriate new parity. To ensure that these advantages are effectively reaped, such departures from par values should be authorized only for limited periods subject to renewal, and only for countries that are willing to accept a measure of IMF supervision and guidance in their exchange market intervention policies. In some cases, conditions might also be imposed on internal policies in the interest of stabilization.

II. THE U.S. ADJUSTMENT PROBLEM AND THE SUPPLY OF WORLD RESERVES

A special rigidity has long characterized the exchange relationships of the U.S. dollar as the currency of the country that bulks largest in the world economy, the principal reserve currency, the ultimate intervention currency to which others are directly or indirectly linked, and the currency in terms of which exchange margins are generally expressed.

---

[7] If margins vis-à-vis the U.S. dollar, or those obtaining among the currencies of the EEC, remain at half the normal margin, the latter might have to be considerably wider than 4 percent to obtain the benefits described above.

In the first place, the fact that the dollar has been for the main industrial countries, the principal—until recently the sole—intervention currency and the currency in terms of which their margins of exchange variation were fixed has deprived the United States of that exchange flexibility "in the small," which other countries derive from such margins. The very nature of the arrangement has prevented the U.S. dollar from deviating from parity in terms of other currencies by more than half the potential deviation of the latter from parity relative to one another. In addition, since the United States, to avoid confusion and cross purposes, has itself abstained from intervening on exchange markets, it has not been in a position to control the variation of its exchange rate even within its relatively narrow margins; this has been determined by the actions of other countries. Now, the need of the United States for the latitude afforded by wider margins, whether to pave the way for par value changes or to cope with disturbing capital flows, is no less than that of any other country.

As regards par value changes the position has been less one-sided. Par values are measured in terms of gold, not U.S. dollars, but though it has always been legally possible to change the par value of the dollar, such a step has until recently been considered as practically out of the question. First, the usual prestige motives for resisting devaluation were in this case particularly strong. Moreover, the importance to other countries of transactions with the United States, the consideration that U.S. dollars made up so large a part of their monetary reserves, and the fact that any change in the par value of the dollar could affect its exchange value only through the action of other countries in shifting their intervention points made it probable that any devaluation of the dollar would be largely offset by devaluations of other currencies. Finally, the United States was rendered relatively immune to pressures that elsewhere forced devaluations by the high reserves with which it started on the period of payments deficits and—up to a point—by its ability to finance deficits through the expansion of reserve liabilities.

An important aspect of the relative exchange-rate rigidity of the U.S. dollar has been its inability to float freely in the market even when the U.S. authorities would have liked it to do so. This, of course, is closely related to its role as an intervention currency. Since other countries have defended their parities by pegging on the dollar and since in most cases they have not wanted their currencies to float upward relative to the dollar and independently of each other—as well as for the other reasons described above—they have been loath to stop buying dollars and holding the dollar rate even when their reserve accumulation became excessive and when they could no longer convert dollars into any preferred form of reserves. In effect, the United States and the countries holding dollars became at a certain point each other's prisoners. On the one hand, the United States could not, without intervening on the exchange market in a disorderly way, force other countries to allow the dollar to depreciate, and therefore lacked an important last-resort sanction against currency undervaluation by competing countries. On the other hand, the other countries through their unwillingness to "let go" of the dollar rate, were forced to choose between a vast and unwanted influx of dollar reserves and the imposition of ever more stringent controls over capital inflows— controls which, if perpetuated, could not fail to have harmful effects.

This situation had unfortunate consequences for the supply of world reserves. The Special Drawing Account of the IMF was instituted in 1969 for the purpose of subjecting the world's supply of reserves to conscious collective control. Such a result, however, can be achieved through allocations of SDRs only if the supply (amount) of other types of reserves changes predictably and rises, if at all, only moderately. This condition has not been fulfilled, partly because the amount of certain types of reserves varies with the amount of short- and medium-term international credit outstanding, partly because of changes in official holdings of certain minor reserve currencies, but mainly and overwhelmingly because the United States has increasingly financed its occasional massive surpluses and its even more massive deficits by varying the amount of its reserve liabilities rather than the amount of its reserves.

What can be done to remove the special factors that impede or discourage adequate exchange rate flexibility of the U.S. dollar, and frustrate all efforts to bring the world supply of reserves under adequate international control? Some progress has been made by the establishment of a precedent, in the realignment of December 1971, for an agreed par value change of the U.S. dollar, which was not only not offset but was instead reinforced, by action with respect to other currencies. Further progress could be made along the lines suggested in section I. In addition, certain changes tending to reduce the asymmetries in the present international system would contribute toward the desired result.

In the first place, the United States like any other country, should finance its deficits by the loss of reserves or by drawing on negotiated credits, rather than by the increase of ordinary reserve liabilities, and should correspondingly earn reserves when in surplus. Such a system would be preferable, from the standpoint of maintaining international control over the financing of payments imbalances and the growth of world reserves, to the complete dollar inconvertibility that now prevails, and preferable from the standpoint of minimizing imbalances themselves to any attempt to restore complete convertibility, including the convertibility of outstanding balances. Cooperative arrangements to achieve such an asset settlement system are discussed in section III. These, so long as they were observed, would provide the United States, like any other country, with an incentive to control disruptive capital flows and limit temporary imbalances when its deficits exceed the normal means of financing, and, when appropriate, to adjust its par value. Similar arrangements would apply to other reserve centers.

Second, the principal countries other than the United States should cease to maintain their relative exchange rates within the permitted margins of deviation around parity by pegging on the U.S. dollar. Together with the United States they should keep their relative exchange rates within the permitted bands either by direct intervention in each other's currencies or by pegging on some international reserve asset such as SDRs. Methods of symmetrical intervention and pegging are considered in section IV. These methods would permit the United States to enjoy the same margin of exchange rate variation around par as other countries, and the same possibility as is afforded other countries of determining to what extent the margin would be used. A second consequence would be to backstop the asset settlement of payments imbalances by enabling countries to refrain from increasing or reducing, through market intervention, their holdings of any currency, even if it were the U.S. dollar, if the currency in question should cease to be convertible (to the required extent and in the required mode) into other reserve assets, or if it should cease to be obtainable through the official transfer of reserve assets. They would be enabled to do this because, thanks to the symmetrical intervention arrangements, they could cease to peg their currencies vis-à-vis the currency for which official settlements were no longer possible while continuing to maintain exchange parities among themselves.

A third device for adding to the exchange flexibility of the dollar is that of replacing dollars to some extent in official reserves by an international asset such as the SDR, additional amounts of which would be created for the purpose. As will be shown in the following sections, a facility for such replacement would be virtually indispensable in connection with asset settlement arrangments for the U.S. dollar and other reserve currencies, and would facilitate the operation of symmetrical intervention systems, while any actual substitution of SDRs for dollars in substantial amounts would directly promote the exchange flexibility of the dollar.

III. SETTLEMENT OF IMBALANCES

The object of establishing an asset settlement system would be to ensure that all countries, including reserve centers, financed their payments surpluses and deficits by the transfer of reserve assets, nonreserve assets, or liabilities arising from the use of negotiable credit arrangements (e.g., IMF drawing facilities and possibly bilateral swap arrangements), rather than through variations in reserve liabilities.

There are a great many possible arrangements for achieving this. Some of them involve considerable interference with the freedom of countries to determine the composition of their reserves—a freedom that, save in the case of poor countries, is probably not very important from a welfare standpoint but is much prized by monetary authorities. The following scheme, which relies almost exclusively on the cooperation of reserve centers, seeks to reconcile asset settlement of their imbalances with the maximum satisfaction of national preferences regarding reserve composition. It is conceived of as operating in the context of the present type of exchange market intervention centered on the U.S. dollar.

This scheme would call for the establishment of a new account in the IMF, the Reserve Substitution Account (described in section V), which could create SDRs ad hoc and exchange them with monetary authorities for reserve currencies which it would hold. The SDRs in question would be indistinguishable in use from those created and allocated by the Special Drawing Account. Any country holding currencies in its reserves would be free to sell them for SDRs to the Reserve Substitution Account. This account could be used to assure asset settlement as follows.

If national official holdings of any currency plus the holding of that currency in the Reserve Substitution Account should decline in any period—showing that the issuing country was running a payments surplus in excess of any net increase in reserve assets—that country would be entitled to obtain SDRs to the amount of the excess from the Reserve Substitution Account in exchange for its own currency. Conversely, if the combined national and Reserve Substitution Account holdings of a currency should increase—showing that the issuer was running a payments deficit in excess of any net decline in reserve assets—the latter would be entitled and obliged to redeem its currency from the account with SDRs, gold, or the currencies of other countries. In this way, reserve centers would settle both surpluses and deficits by the transfer of reserve assets vis-à-vis countries or the Reserve Substitution Account. However, if the decline in national official holdings of a currency should exceed the amount of that currency held by the Reserve Substitution Account, the issuing country would settle its remaining deficit through a transfer of reserve assets—gold, SDRs, reserve positions in the IMF, or currencies of other countries—to countries designated by the IMF.

The main weakness of the scheme described above is that it makes no provision for the contingency that the reserve center might find itself unable or be unwilling to continue to finance its deficits by the use of reserve assets (or negotiated credits). In these circumstances it is desirable, for reasons explained in the preceding section, that the currency in question, like any nonreserve currency in a similar case, should be allowed to depreciate. This might be a little more likely to happen, even in the case of the U.S. dollar, if, in addition to the arrangement described above, the principal industrial countries were to undertake (a) not to allow their holdings of any reserve currency to rise above the levels attained at the initiation of the scheme, *less* any sales of the respective currencies to the Reserve Substitution Account, and (b) to present any accruals of these currencies above the permitted levels to the issuing countries for conversion into the latter's reserve assets. Such conversions would not in any way add to the burdens of the reserve center, which would automatically recoup any reserve losses from the Reserve Substitution Account. But the obligation to limit reserve currency holdings and the habit of limiting them might be useful if asset settlement and convertibility were suspended. However, any such provisions and undertakings would probably be somewhat fragile in the absence of symmetrical intervention arrangements as discussed in the following section.

IV. ESTABLISHMENT OF A SYMMETRICAL INTERVENTION SYSTEM

Symmetry in intervention may take the form either of multicurrency intervention on exchange markets or of intervention on a market for an international asset, such as the SDR. In either case, it is probable that participation in the symmetrical arrangements would be confined to major trading countries; other countries would prefer to implement their exchange-rate obligations by pegging, as at present, on a single currency. It is assumed that the basic obligation of each country would continue to be that of preventing the exchange rate of its currency in terms of each other currency from differing from parity by more than a fixed percentage (say, 4 percent), but this obligation would be deemed to be fulfilled for any currency whose issuer was fulfilling the requirements of a symmetrical intervention scheme or which was narrowly pegged to such a currency.

There are many possible forms of multicurrency intervention. One possible system would be as follows:

1. Each country participating in the multicurrency intervention scheme would have a *notional* exchange margin which could not exceed 2 percent on either side of par value, but might, at the discretion of the country in question, be fixed at some lesser percentage. These notional margins could be thought of as relating to the value of the currency in terms of gold and SDRs, but this is in some respects misleading since their sole operational significance would be in the calculation of actual exchange margins under condition (2).

2. Each participating country would stand ready to buy or sell the currency of each other participating country on the exchange market with or for its own currency at prices respectively falling short of

and exceeding parity by a margin equal to the sum of the "notional" margins of the two countries concerned. Thus, two countries with "notional" margins of ±1 percent and ±2 percent respectively, would maintain their relative exchange rates within margins of ±3 percent from parity.

3. All purchases or sales of currency on the foreign-exchange markets by participants in the scheme would be settled at frequent periodic intervals by transfers of reserve assets between monetary authorities. Any country whose currency was at the lower limit vis-à-vis that of another participating country would borrow the currency of the latter from its central bank, use it to support its own currency on the exchange market, and subsequently settle the debt by the transfer of reserve assets. Similarly, any country whose currency was at the upper limit vis-à-vis that of any other participating country would buy the currency of the latter on the exchange market and subsequently present its balance to the central bank for conversion into reserve assets. It has been assumed that both "floor" and "ceiling" intervention would be obligatory, but strictly speaking either would suffice alone.

4. The assets used in settlement would consist of gold, SDRs, reserve positions in the IMF, or national currencies *other than the currencies of the two countries involved in the transfer*, in proportions determined by the reserve composition of the country transferring the assets. Except for these settlement transfers, and for any sales of currency to the Reserve Substitution Account (see section V) in exchange for SDRs, participants would not be allowed to vary their holdings of the currencies of other participants.

5. Currencies used in settlement would be valued at market price. Gold, SDRs, and IMF positions used in settlement would be valued at par with a selected "representative basket" of principal trading currencies; the "basket" would, however, exclude currencies whose exchange rates were, at the time, floating outside internationally permitted margins.

6. No participating country would be obliged to buy or sell on the exchange market any currency whose the issuer was not fulfilling the settlement requirements, and all participants would indeed be expected to refrain from so doing.

7. In general, it would be simpler, and probably from the standpoint of exchange rate flexibility preferable, if no intervention were allowed within the nationally determined margins. However, it would

presumably be necessary to allow subgroups among the participating countries (e.g., members of the EEC) to intervene in each other's currencies in such a way as to maintain narrower exchange margins with each other than would correspond to the sum of their "notional" margins. Also, *ad hoc* intramarginal intervention might be permitted subject to rules designed to minimize conflicting intervention on the part of different countries.

An alternative, and conceptually simpler, approach to symmetrical intervention is one whereby participating countries keep their relative exchange rates in line by intervening on private markets with gold or, alternatively, with SDRs. The latter alternative is preferable. In view of the scarcity of gold as a commodity which will tend, sooner or later, to draw it out of the reserves of monetary authorities, a restored gold standard system could survive only by repeated revaluations of gold in terms of currencies, which would be both wasteful and disturbing.

A system of pegging on SDRs would, of course, call for the creation of a private market in these assets. If private institutions and firms were allowed to hold SDRs, and if the currency value of the SDR had a tendency to rise owing to a preponderance of devaluations over revaluations, and especially if international banking operations in SDRs were favored by national regulations somewhat after the fashion in which European-currency operations are so favored at present, it is quite possible that a substantial private market in SDRs could, over time, be created. Even if the market remained thin, however, countries could always rely on being able to prevent their relative exchange rates from diverging from parity by more than the internationally authorized margin (say, 4 percent) by standing ready to buy SDRs at not more than 2 percent below par, and to sell SDRs at not more than 2 percent above par. More generally, the spread or range of variation of the relative exchange rates of the currencies of any two countries could never exceed the sum of the spreads between their buying and selling rates for SDRs. It would be preferable that countries undertaking to intervene in SDRs abstain entirely from currency intervention within the margins, but it might be difficult to insist on this.

Even if the principal trading countries adopted schemes of multi-currency intervention or SDR intervention, it would be desirable to retain arrangements of the type described in section III to ensure asset settlement of residual variations in reserve currency holdings resulting from currency intervention by nonparticipants or intramarginal intervention by participants in these schemes.

Market intervention in SDRs has several advantages over multicurrency intervention. Countries' obligations would be simpler, being confined to buying and selling SDRs within a certain range of prices; by doing this they would discharge their obligations regarding exchange rate margins. Intramarginal intervention, though possibly discouraged by the thinness of the market, would be much simpler than under the multicurrency system, and need be encumbered by no rules; the market would automatically direct and SDRs sold to the proper purchasers and extract any SDRs bought from their appropriate sellers. Since there would always be a market price for SDRs in terms of currencies, there would be no need to adopt a convention as to the price at which purchases and sales of SDRs should be carried out by countries not participating in the scheme and using a reserve currency as their intervention medium. On the other hand, market intervention in SDRs has the same weakness as the gold standard in that private speculation in SDRs might reinforce the disturbing effects of exchange-rate speculation on the reserves of particular countries. Most primary producing countries would probably prefer to peg on currencies rather than on SDRs; moreover, any group such as the EEC that wished to maintain narrow margins inter se would probably find it convenient to do so by mutual currency intervention rather than by coordinated intervention in SDRs, though if the systems were combined they could also, presumably, maintain outer margins in SDRs. For the next few years, at any rate, multicurrency intervention would seem to offer a more acceptable alternative to the asymmetrical system focusing on the U.S. dollar than SDR intervention.

V. REPLACEMENT OF CURRENCY RESERVES
BY SDRs

As indicated in section III, the establishment of a reserve substitution account is of crucial importance to any arrangement for the asset settlement of the imbalances of reserve centers under the existing intervention system. For a reserve center to acquire reserves to the full extent of its surpluses, it is virtually indispensable that there be such an account from which it can buy SDRs in exchange for its own currency. And for that center to utilize reserves to pay for its deficits with the least possible encroachment on the reserve asset preferences of other countries, it is useful that there be such an account to which the latter can sell the reserve currency for SDRs and from which the former can redeem its currency in exchange for reserve assets.

The establishment of a symmetrical intervention system as described in section IV might increase still further the need for a reserve substitution account. Even the system of multicurrency intervention, which would permit partial settlement in third currencies, would increase the role of primary reserve assets in settlements, and would thus create a need for participating countries to transfer some of their holdings of reserve currency to the account in exchange for SDRs. Under a system of market intervention in SDRs, there would, of course, be a need to acquire SDRs in exchange for reserve currencies for intervention purposes, and if currency intervention were entirely prohibited among the main countries the amounts requiring to be substituted in this way would be very substantial.

Apart from the contribution that a reserve substitution account would make to the achievement of asset financing by reserve centers and to any system of symmetrical intervention, the substitution of SDRs for currencies in reserves would also directly reduce countries' incentive to continue to peg on reserve currencies and follow them in any par value adjustments for the sake of preserving the domestic currency value of their reserves. For this purpose it is important not merely that there should be an option to substitute SDRs for currencies in reserves, but that the option should to a substantial extent be exercised.

To ensure that the replacement of reserve currencies by SDRs is indeed considerable, a number of techniques could be employed. One of these, already mentioned, would be to make the substitution of SDRs for currencies a one-way operation so that countries can obtain SDRs for currencies from the account, but not currencies for SDRs. Over time this should ensure a gradual reduction in currency holdings. Another would be to adopt methods of settlement or intervention that tend to extend the use of SDRs at the expense of currencies. A third (very dubious) device would be to set a time limit to access to the reserve substitution facility. This might encourage a faster substitution of SDRs for currencies, but not necessarily a larger one in the long run. A fourth approach would be to make SDRs more attractive as assets by paying an interest rate on SDRs higher than the present $1\frac{1}{2}$ percent, and also by ensuring a rising currency value of SDRs through a preponderance of devaluations over revaluations of currencies. A final possibility would be to attempt to secure through international agreement, at least among the main countries, a concerted substitution of SDRs for currencies.

Currencies accumulated by the Reserve Substitution Account would bear a gold or SDR value guarantee, and might therefore carry a somewhat lower interest rate than that previously paid on such balances when held in national reserves. The interest accruing to the account should, however, exceed that paid by the account on the additional SDRs created and sold for currency, and this excess would be available for general purposes such as the financing of development. Any amortization paid by the issuing countries might also be made available for such purposes.

VI. THE ROLE OF MONETARY GOLD

The objectives of international policy with respect to monetary gold should be (a) to gradually turn monetary gold over to commodity use, (b) to prevent any movement of this kind from impairing reserve adequacy, and in the meantime (c) to maintain the usefulness of monetary gold both to countries and to the general account of the IMF, and (d) to prevent the premium on gold in the free market from hampering the operation of the international monetary system by making countries reluctant to use gold in settlement of deficits or in payment of subscriptions to the general account of the IMF.

To these ends the following measures are suggested:

1. Special drawing rights should replace gold as the standard of par values, but the value of monetary gold should be fixed in terms of SDRs.

2. The two-tier market should be retained. National monetary authorities should abstain from buying or selling monetary gold from or to the market at any price above par.

3. Countries should be entitled to use monetary gold in the compulsory settlement of deficits in the manner described in section III and IV.

4. Countries should be entitled and encouraged to sell monetary gold to the Reserve Substitution Account in exchange for newly

created SDRs in amounts not exceeding in the aggregate what the account can currently sell to the market at prices above par. Any shortfall in national gold sales to the substitution account below what the latter can currently dispose of should be made up by sales from the general account to the substitution account.

5. The proceeds of market sales by the substitution account should be invested to yield an income at least sufficient to cover the interest cost on the additional SDRs.

6. The general account of the IMF should continue to be entitled to sell gold to replenish its stocks of reserve currencies, and to purchase gold in exchange for currencies from countries that wish to sell. It should also be entitled to sell gold on the market so long as the price is above par.

VII. MEASURES FOR DEALING WITH TEMPORARY PAYMENTS DISEQUILIBRIA

The reforms envisaged thus far in this paper have mostly been aimed directly or indirectly at improving adjustment to basic disequilibria in international payments. It is difficult to suggest comparable improvements in the ways of handling temporary imbalances such as those resulting from exchange-rate speculation or its cessation, from cyclical factors acting on current or capital account, or from basic disequilibria that persist for a time even though the exchange-rate adjustments that will ultimately correct them have already been undertaken.

It is almost a definition of such imbalances that they are not such as can appropriately be corrected by par value adjustments. The problem is to contain them so that they will not exercise disruptive effects on countries' monetary systems, domestic economies, or foreign trade. The instruments available are: (a) use of reserves (combined with offsetting of domestic monetary effects), (b) use of international credit (combined with similar offsetting where required), (c) temporary import restrictions, (d) controls over capital flows (in a very broad sense that includes not only payments restrictions and regulations affecting the net foreign position of banks, etc., but also such arrangements as dual-exchange markets for current and capital transactions, forward-exchange market intervention, fiscal measures affecting capital flows, and even interest-rate policy, insofar as that is divorced from domestic objectives), and (e) wider margins of exchange-rate variation around par value, or temporary floating rates.

Under the system of SDR allocations, it is intended that the supply of world reserves be brought under international control, and some of the reforms previously considered have been designed to make that control effective. The growing importance of temporary payments imbalances should undoubtedly be taken into account in determining the magnitude of planned world reserve increases. However, payments imbalances, fueled as they often are by speculative capital flows, are so erratic and variable over time that reserves sufficient to finance these disequilibria in stormy times would be excessive—and likely to encourage inflationary pressures—in periods of calm.

Official facilities for short- or medium-term international borrowing have the advantage over reserves that the need to reconstitute them *plus*, in the case of IMF drawing facilities, the fact that their availability is subject to policy conditions provide an incentive to borrowing countries to use the breathing space accorded them to correct their deficits if the latter are not in themselves temporary and self-correcting. Since, however, the use of such credits generally involves for the creditor countries a mere substitution of one form of reserves for another, the effect is asymmetrical. Borrowers' reserves no longer contract, but lenders' reserves continue to expand. The supply of world reserves varies with the use or repayment of credit facilities, just as it does in the case of liability financing by reserve centers, in a way that is not necessarily desirable. Moreover, intercentral bank credit arrangements are often improvised *ad hoc* and, as in the case of the successive rescue operations for sterling in the 1960s, may be available in unduly generous amounts. Medium-term credit facilities may be adequately organized through the IMF, but the problem of achieving a centralized organization of short-term credit available in appropriate circumstances and amounts and on appropriate conditions (e.g., regarding interest) is still unsolved. Another unsolved problem, in connection with both medium- and short-term financing, is to contrive means whereby a higher proportion of the creditor claims arising out of the use of such facilities would be held in nonreserve form and, if possible, outside the banking system.

Import restrictions are regarded under the GATT as a permissible temporary expedient for dealing with balance-of-payments difficulties. In recent years also temporary import surcharges have been used for the same purpose on the ground, for which there is some justification, that they are economically preferable to quantitative restrictions. However, the truth is that both types of restriction are liable to cause distortions in production and trade, and neither should be used in dealing with temporary disequilibria, though they may perhaps be legitimately employed as sanctions in dealing with surplus countries unwilling to carry out recommended currency revaluations.

The free floating of exchange rates is the most effective of all measures for suppressing payments imbalances and buffering external pressures on domestic monetary systems. However, when the imbalances are temporary and reversible, the buffering effect may not extend to prices and demand conditions generally and may be bought too dearly in terms of instability of demand and employment in the foreign-trade goods sector. When applied in the modified form of wider margins of exchange-rate variation around parities, the trade-off between insulating and disturbing effects may be better than with freely floating rates because of the encouragement to equilibrating speculation given by the existence of limits on exchange fluctuation. However, the case for wider margins rests more securely, in my view, on their role in facilitating prompter par value changes (mentioned earlier) than on their role in dealing with temporary imbalances, for which other instruments are available.

The most controversial question that arises in connection with measures to deal with short-term payments imbalances is whether the present almost complete freedom of national governments to control or not to control capital outflows and inflows on balance of payments grounds should continue or whether some degree of international coordination or regulation of capital controls is required.[8] Such regulation would take a purely negative form. Provided that international official financing were properly organized so that it was neither too plentiful nor too scarce, there would be no reason why countries should be *required* to deflect, promote or restrict private capital flows beyond what their own interest would dictate. One could, however, imagine an international code of liberation for capital flows under which any positive national action to deflect, promote or restrict such flows would have to be justified on one or other of a limited number of grounds, of which the need to preserve

[8] Even the selective liberalization of capital flows practiced within the EEC and the Organization for Economic Cooperation and Development can be set aside in circumstances of balance-of-payments difficulty.

balance of payments equilibrium would be one.[9] Under this part of the code, for which it would be natural to make the Fund the administering authority, capital control measures would generally be approved on a temporary basis subject to renewal provided (a) that they were so operated as to promote payments balance rather than payments imbalance for the country concerned, and (b) that they were not calculated to perpetuate exchange parities that had been judged to be inappropriate under the arrangements governing par values discussed in section I.[10] Since, as already indicated, the chronic maintenance on payments grounds of measures unduly promoting or restricting capital flows would be one of the criteria of the overvaluation or undervaluation of a currency, condition (b) above would be tantamount to a requirement that such measures be of limited duration. Although there is much to be said in favor of a code such as that described above, I must confess that agreement on such a plan seems unlikely to be obtainable in the foreseeable future.

VIII. CURRENCY BLOCS AND "ONE WORLD"

The foregoing suggestions for the reform of the international monetary system have assumed the desirability of a "one-world" solution in the sense of the maintenance of a single legal framework conferring uniform rights and imposing uniform obligations on all countries. It has even been sought to mitigate the organizational differences and asymmetries that can arise as a result, for example, of the use of particular currencies as reserve and intervention media, within a legal regime which, like the Bretton Woods system, is formally the same for all.

Since, however, the circumstances of countries differ greatly, it is certain that they would wish to make a very varied use of the freedom of action that would be assured to them within such a uniform legal framework.

---

[9] Clearly, it would not be possible to regulate all the forms of capital control listed, including indirect measures such as interest rate policy, and forward-exchange market intervention. But exchange restrictions, banking regulations affecting external positions, dual-exchange markets, and the more direct forms of fiscal intervention would be covered.

[10] It would probably not be feasible for such a code to draw distinctions of merit between the different kinds of capital control. However, the writer has made clear elsewhere his view that the dual-exchange market for current and capital transactions is potentially superior, from the standpoint of allocative efficiency and balance-of-payments effectiveness, to other types of control.

Some countries would certainly wish to make fuller use than others of the possibilities of exchange rate flexibility or of capital restriction open to them within the system. Some might prefer to peg their exchange rates, through multicurrency intervention, in terms of a number of currencies, while others, in terms of a single currency.

To some extent this variety of behavior might involve applying different rules to categories of countries that had chosen different options open to them under the uniform system of law. For example, countries choosing to have wider exchange-rate margins might have to conform to intervention rules from which those preferring narrower margins would be free. Or the rules governing the transfer of SDRs might differ as between countries operating on a symmetrical intervention system and those pegging on a single currency.

Somewhat more difficult—though not perhaps impossible—to accommodate within a one-world system are arrangements such as those being established within the EEC in which a group of countries, which others are not free to join at their option, establishes a special system of rules to govern the relative exchange rates of its members, and separate and discriminatory arrangements governing intermember trade and capital flows, and aspires to establish a separate fiduciary reserve asset and ultimately a separate currency.

In considering preferential trade groups it has long been concluded that they will be compatible with the liberal objectives of a worldwide trade organization only if intragroup trade is sufficiently free and barriers to trade with the outside world sufficiently low to ensure that the trade-creating effects outweigh the trade-diverting effects. Similarly, discriminatory monetary groupings or areas can serve the purpose of the international monetary system only if on balance they contribute to the smooth adjustment of payments disequilibria, whether internal or external to the group, by reducing the disturbance that such adjustment involves to production, employment, trade, and capital flows everywhere.

The financial arrangements now applied or under contemplation for the EEC may well serve to promote a smoother and more effective adjustment process as between European countries, on the one hand, and the United States, on the other, by making it easier for European currencies as a group to vary vis-à-vis the dollar. In particular, arrangements such as have recently been introduced for the pegging of mutual exchange rates within the group within relatively narrow margins may have some of the advantages in this respect which have been claimed earlier for more widely generalized systems of symmetrical intervention, as compared with a system in which the dollar is the predominant and ultimate intervention currency. The establishment of an EEC-centered multicurrency intervention system may already have the effect of confining intervention in U.S. dollars by participating countries to intervention at the margin, that is, of discouraging intramarginal intervention.

The principal dangers to the adjustment process arising from the present program of the EEC in the financial field arise with respect to the internal rather than to the external relations of the EEC–a community that will comprise a majority of the main industrial countries. Admittedly, certain aspects of the EEC arrangements—the common market as such, and the promotion of free movement of labor, and, within limits, the extension of mutual credit facilities—are favorable to the smooth adjustment of internal disequilibria. The same cannot be said, however, of the officially sanctioned objectives and plans of the EEC in the direction of monetary unification. So long as the factors making for disparate movements in the relative cost levels of the constituent countries of the EEC persist, and indeed so long as factors making for the adjustment of domestic cost levels to the requirements of balance of payments equilibrium are insufficiently strong—and there is little sign as yet of any increase in flexibility in this regard—the adjustment of relative exchange rates within the EEC will from time to time be required.[11] Any movement in the direction of exchange rate rigidity among the major currencies— and a common currency is the very acme of exchange rigidity—must be regarded as a flouting of the experience of the postwar period. So long as the members of the EEC retain the right to alter their par values, and monetary unification is confined to the maintenance of somewhat narrower exchange margins among members than between members and other countries, no great harm will have been done. However, the considerations that have motivated the writer in recommending a widening of exchange margins for countries in general as a means both of facilitating a smooth and prompt adjustment of par values and of mitigating the

---

[11] The sort of considerations that are relevant to a judgment of this kind are set forth in some detail in my article "On Exchange Rate Unification" *The Economic Journal* (September 1971), 81:467–88.

monetary consequences of disequilibrating capital flows apply with equal validity within the EEC as in the world at large. It should be added that just as a measure of exchange flexibility is recommended to the world at large to make it possible to maintain, at one and the same time, desirable demand conditions and liberal international trade and investment relationships, so it is recommended to the members of the EEC to promote the larger objectives of that body in the matter of economic integration.

If the manifestations of EEC cooperation in the monetary sphere can be steered in the direction of mutual multicurrency intervention and mutual balance-of-payments assistance rather than mutual exchange-rate rigidity, there is no reason why its members should not continue to play a constructive role in a one-world international monetary system. If it should develop in the direction of a common currency or fixed exchange-rate area, it could again play a constructive role as a single unit in a world system even though many of its balance-of-payments problems would have been "internalized" rather than solved. However, there is a school of thought, both in Europe and in the United States, which, basing itself on the latter assumption, is already beginning to conceive of the international monetary system as a loose association of monetary blocs centered, respectively, on the United States, Europe, and perhaps Japan, in which each bloc would be unified by internal arrangements of a more or less formal character while relationships between blocs would be regulated by informal ad hoc understandings. Such a solution, even if it did not lead to the raising of economic barriers and acts of economic hostility between the blocs, would set back international organization by almost forty years to the time of the Tripartite Agreement. It would leave dissatisfied many countries who would be loath to tie themselves down to an exclusive relationship with any single bloc. And it would spell defeat to the efforts that have been made to regulate the growth of international liquidity in a rational manner through the development of a single fiduciary reserve asset—the SDR—and a single main source of conditional liquidity, the drawing facilities of the General Account of the IMF. Both of these require for their operation and development a firm adhesion to a truly worldwide system of international law.

15

DUAL-EXCHANGE MARKETS AND OTHER REMEDIES FOR DISRUPTIVE CAPITAL FLOWS

IT HAS BECOME a commonplace observation that one of the principal factors undermining the international monetary order that was set up at Bretton Woods has been the ever-growing magnitude of payments disequilibria caused by temporary and often reversible capital flows. Doubtless the regime of fixed though adjustable par values that was the centerpiece of the Bretton Woods system has been subjected to considerable stress by other factors also, notably the increasing importance of the cost-push element in inflation, with its differential impact on national competitive positions; but it is the extreme volatility of international capital flows, in response to interest differences or speculative incentives, that has compounded these difficulties to such a point that the feasibility of restoring the par value system itself can be called in question.

These disruptive capital flows have the effect of reducing not only the stability of exchange rates but also the independence of monetary policies and the internal financial stability of countries. Indeed, in the case of the countries receiving such flows, the desire to avoid losing control of the domestic money situation has been the primary motive for allowing exchange rates to rise.

Countries that have been exposed to disruptive capital flows and do not wish their exchange rates to be determined entirely by market forces have generally sought to cope with such flows, at least in part, either by

First published in International Monetary Fund, *Staff Papers*, March 1974.

controlling or by financing them. "Financing," which includes not only official borrowing and lending abroad but also the rise and fall of reserves, is generally accompanied by policies to offset the disturbing effects of the flows on domestic monetary conditions and on interest rates. "Controlling" is used in a very wide sense to cover not only restrictions on individual capital transactions and quantitative regulations governing the external assets or liabilities of banks and other residents, but also more indirect methods of influencing capital flows, such as interest rate-policies, fiscal measures, official intervention on the forward-exchange market, and various arrangements affecting spot exchange rates.

This paper is particularly concerned with a technique for influencing capital flows that has attracted increasing attention in recent years both in official circles and among economists. This method involves the setting up of separate exchange markets, with separate exchange rates for current and capital transactions, respectively. A dual exchange market of a fairly full-fledged character has been established for many years in Belgium, although it is only since 1971 that the Belgian financial franc has been free to rise to a premium as well as fall to a discount. Similar—though not identical—dual markets were set up in France in 1971 and in Italy in 1973. Partial exchange markets applicable to particular types of capital transactions have existed for many years in the United Kingdom, France, and the Netherlands, and segregated exchange markets covering various types of both capital and current transactions have been common in several developing countries, particularly in Latin America.

The aim of the present paper is to assess the relative merits of dual markets as a means of dealing with disequilibrating capital flows (or more precisely, with the temporary and reversible payments imbalances that are frequently associated with such flows), as compared with each of the other main techniques available for this purpose. Through such a serial comparison it is hoped to achieve an overall evaluation of the dual market device and, by using it as a standard of comparison, to bring out the special characteristics of the other approaches.

For these evaluations, though taking into account the lessons of experience, this paper considers the various techniques as they might be applied rather than as they have been applied. This is particularly necessary in the case of dual markets, since this technique is a relatively recent one and its potentialities have not yet been fully explored.

In general, the paper deals with arrangements that provide for only two exchange markets—one comprising (as far as possible) all capital transactions and the other (with the same qualification), all current transactions. And for the most part it is assumed that the exchange rate for current transactions is pegged by official intervention in the vicinity of parity, as has indeed generally been true of the Belgian and French (though not of the Italian) dual market.

MAIN FEATURES OF THE DUAL MARKET

The operation of a dual-exchange market has been described in some detail in a previous article.[1] It calls for the segregation of exchange transactions into two categories, connected respectively with current and with capital payments and receipts. As explained in that article,[2] such segregation necessitates a close control over at least one of the categories of underlying transactions (usually the current items), as well as over actual payments and receipts, and it involves the establishment of two kinds of nonresident balances in domestic currency and, at least on the part of the foreign exchange banks, two kinds of resident balances in foreign currency.

It is sometimes thought to be of the essence of the dual-exchange market that the rate for capital transactions is allowed to float freely without official intervention. This is a misunderstanding of the possibilities of the system. There is no reason why the authorities should not buy or sell foreign currency for domestic currency on the capital-exchange market. Indeed, if they wish that market to make its maximum contribution to the equilibrium of the balance of payments as a whole, they *must* so intervene, selling in the capital transactions market the foreign

---

[1] J. Marcus Fleming, "Dual Exchange Rates for Current and Capital Transactions: A Theoretical Examination," in *Essays in International Economics* (Cambridge, Mass.: Harvard University Press, 1971), pp. 296–325. See also Vittorio Barattieri and Giorgio Ragazzi, "An Analysis of the Two-Tier Foreign Exchange Market," Banca Nazionale del Lavoro, *Quarterly Review*, no. 99 (December 1971); Pascal Salin, "Un double marché des changes est-il justifié?" *Revue d'Economie Politique*, no. 6 (November-December 1971), pp. 959–74; and Anthony M. Lanyi, "Separate Exchange Markets for Capital and Current Transactions" (unpublished, International Monetary Fund, 1973).

[2] Fleming, "Dual Exchange Rates," pp. 298 ff.

exchange they are acquiring in the current transactions market and buying in the former the foreign exchange they are selling in the latter.[3] This will give them a profit (or a loss) as they bring the "capital" rate closer to (or pry it apart from) the "current" rate.

There are two mechanisms whereby movements in the "capital" exchange rate affect capital flows, both inward and outward.[4] (1) A change in the actual rate associated with an equal change in expected future rates results in a proportionate change in the yield of domestic capital invested abroad or foreign capital invested in the country, provided that interest in both directions is transferred as a current item through the official market. (2) A change in the actual rate unaccompanied by a corresponding change in the expected future rate—for example, a change in the actual rate that is expected to be reversed—*in addition* creates the prospect of a corresponding capital gain on any temporary investment in one direction and of a capital loss on any investment in the other direction.

Of the two mechanisms, the second offers a much more powerful incentive for short-term placements. For example, a 10 percent rise in a country's "capital" rate that was expected to be permanent might reduce the yield on foreign investment in that country only from 5 percent to about $4\frac{1}{2}$ percent, and increase the yield of investment abroad from 5 percent to $5\frac{1}{2}$ percent. But a 10 percent rise in the "capital" rate that was expected to be reversed in six months would give, in addition, a 10 percent capital gain over that period. Owing to this speculative element, a temporary change in the relationship of the "capital" rate to the "current" rate might be strong enough to counteract expectations of a

---

[3] If the system is to make its maximum contribution to buffering external influences on the domestic monetary system, a slightly different criterion must be followed—that of buying or selling as much domestic currency on the capital market as is sold or bought on the official market. This involves some reserve changes, corresponding to net profits or losses.

[4] Compare Barattieri and Ragazzi, "An Analysis of the Two-Tier Foreign Exchange Market."

Herman C. Verwilst (doctoral candidate, Johns Hopkins University) has drawn my attention to a third possible mechanism whereby movements in the "capital" rate might affect capital flows; namely, through a change in the degree of uncertainty of investors regarding the future level of that rate. A rise in uncertainty such as might occur when the "capital" rate diverged from its normal relation to the "current" rate would presumably discourage capital flows, both inward and outward, and also reduce the net capital flow corresponding to any given level of the capital rate.

change in the latter rate, if the "capital" rate was expected to revert to a normal relationship to the "current" rate.

When the "capital" exchange rate is at a discount from the "current" rate, the operation of the first mechanism described above is likely to be weakened by the difficulty of ensuring that interest and dividend receipts from the foreign investments of residents are in fact transferred through the market for current transactions. It may be partly for this reason that, under the Belgian system, such receipts can be transferred through whichever channel yields the most profit. By contrast, the purchase of foreign investments by British residents under the investment currency scheme is controlled, and earnings have to be repatriated through the regular exchange market.

The first mechanism, however, is more reliable than the second, which depends on the existence of a negative elasticity of expectations. This, in turn, is probably dependent on a variety of factors—such as an expectation (a) that a change in the "current" rate or other adjustment measures will remove the speculative motive for capital flows and allow a narrowing of the spread between the two rates, (b) that evasion of controls will occur whereby current transactions pass for capital ones (or vice versa), or (c) that a shift will occur in official intervention on the exchange market for capital transactions that will be designed to draw the rates closer together. The last two expectations assume that the authorities will tolerate a widening of the overall imbalance in their external transactions.

To the extent that the second mechanism is operative, movements in the "capital" rate, as has been seen, operate with special force on short-term capital flows—which may be what the situation requires, if the expectations of temporariness on which this mechanism depends are warranted.

In any realistic appraisal of the dual-exchange market, it must be noted that it is not administratively practicable to achieve a full segregation of capital and current transactions. As long as some flexibility is allowed in the timing of current payments, variations cannot be prevented in the amount of trade credit given and received that passes through the official (i.e., the current) market. Again, there may be variations in the amount of working balances arising out of, or to be used for, current transactions held in domestic currency by nonresidents or in foreign currencies by residents, including the banks and dealers in foreign exchange. In addition to working balances proper, the banks may be allowed some variability in their spot positions to enable them to provide a reasonably stable market in forward exchange for their commercial customers. Some types of current transactions, notably those financed by travelers checks or banknotes, are usually put through the financial market, because if they were admitted to the official market they would serve as a cover for illicit capital transactions. On the other hand, it is difficult to prevent evasions under which certain types of current transactions—for example, border trade, trade in diamonds, emigrants' or immigrants' remittances, interest and dividend payments, and other current invisibles—are paid for through the "capital" exchange market, when the rate there is more profitable than the rate in the "current" market. It would be particularly difficult to ensure that foreign firms paid the appropriate tax on retained and reinvested earnings when the "capital" rate was at a premium, or that national firms paid this tax on their retained earnings of their foreign branches when the "capital" rate was at a discount. There may also be inhibitions about applying an adverse rate to the repatriation of capital, both resident and especially nonresident. All of these difficulties also apply to capital control systems of all kinds, not merely to the dual market.

The general effect of these loopholes and imperfections in the segregation of capital and current transactions for the operation of the dual market depends on the intervention policy of the authorities.[5] If in the absence of evasion the existence of the dual market would be a factor making for equilibrium in the balance of payments, any increase in evasion by reducing the discrepancy between the "current" and the "capital" exchange rates would tend to promote a payments imbalance. If, however, the authorities altered their intervention on the capital market in such a way as to restore the original rate discrepancy, they would—despite the incentive given to further evasion—reduce the overall payments imbalance to approximately the original, evasion-free level.[6]

---

[5] Lanyi, "Separate Exchange Markets."

[6] The reason why maintenance of the original rate discrepancy does not maintain precisely the original payments balance is that the evaders make profits—in reserves or in domestic currencies—at the expense of the authorities. Maintenance of the original payments balance in the face of evasion thus calls for some widening of the original rate discrepancy when the domestic currency is at a discount in the "capital" exchange market, but is compatible with some narrowing of the discrepancy when the domestic currency is at a premium in that market.

Insofar as property income transfers are allowed to pass through the capital exchange market or insofar as they do so illicitly, one of the basic mechanisms of the dual market—the effect of the rate discrepancy on the yield of capital—will be crippled. It will operate only where it continues to be profitable for investment and investment income to pass through separate exchange markets—that is, only for foreign capital where the domestic currency is at a discount in the capital exchange market or only for domestic capital where the "capital" rate is at a premium. If, as in France, the foreign investment income of nationals has to be repatriated at the "capital" rate, even the latter effect may be precluded. However, as has been seen, the speculative or "capital gain" effect of the dual market is probably more important than the "yield" effect.

As was shown in the author's previously cited article and as is seen later in this paper, some of the most interesting characteristics of the dual-exchange market system arise when it is applied simultaneously by a number of countries—on a national basis, not collectively. In this case capital flows between these countries will be influenced in a direction and to an extent determined by the *relative* premiums or discounts on their "capital," as compared with their "current" rates. Thus, flows from a country where the "capital" rate is at a premium of 10 percent to a country where it is at a premium of 5 percent will benefit from a subsidy of approximately 5 percent.

EVALUATION OF DUAL-EXCHANGE MARKET

The alternative techniques for dealing with temporary and reversible payments imbalances, with which the dual-exchange market is compared, are: (a) quantitative or administrative restrictions on capital transactions or balance sheet positions, (b) taxes or subsidies affecting capital transactions or income from capital, (c) official intervention in forward-exchange markets, (d) monetary or interest-rate policies, (e) official financing or use of reserves, and (f) floating exchange rates or wider margins.

No consideration has been given in this paper to systems of par value adjustment or nonadjustment—such as absolutely fixed parities or parities which cannot alter by more than a small percentage in a given year. Although proponents of these systems have claimed great merits for the avoidance or mitigation of disequilibrating capital flows, their examination would be long and the author is skeptical of both their feasibility and of their power to fulfill the primary function of a par value system—namely, the correction of fundamental disequilibria.[7]

Dual-Exchange Markets versus Capital Restrictions

The dual-exchange market, when compared with quantitative or administrative capital restrictions as a means of influencing net capital flows, has two major advantages and a single disadvantage. To the extent that it is effective, it is likely to be preferable from the standpoint of economic welfare to any type of quantitative or administrative restrictions; it is likely to achieve a higher degree of effectiveness against evasion for a given cost of administration than any form of restriction that relies on the screening of individual transactions. It may, however, have a stronger disequilibrating effect on exchange-rate speculation.

The superiority of the dual-exchange market from the welfare standpoint arises from its use of the coordinating mechanism of the market. Over the wide range of transactions that it covers, it is equivalent to a uniform, though not constant, percentage tax (subsidy) on purchases of securities by domestic residents from foreign residents, combined with an equal subsidy (tax) on sales of securities by domestic to foreign residents (all taxes or subsidies being measured as a percentage of the price in the domestic market). Quantitative or administrative restrictions, on the other hand, are inevitably uneven in their incidence because of their piecemeal character and because they operate by determining quantities of assets or liabilities traded (or held vis-à-vis the outside world) rather than by price differences. In most cases they operate in the same manner as taxes to restrict transactions in one direction without operating (as subsidies do) to encourage transactions in the opposite sense.

Let us assume that the price of a security in any country represents its true marginal utility to the holders in that country. Then the following can be shown. If country A has placed on the importation of two types of securities from country B restrictions that are unequal (in the sense

---

[7] See, however, John H. Williamson, *The Crawling Peg*, Essays in International Finance, no. 50 (Princeton, N.J.: Princeton University Press, December 1965).

that they are equivalent to unequal ad valorem import taxes)—then if the import of the lower-taxed security were increased and that of the higher-taxed security were reduced—as would tend to happen if the two rates of tax were brought closer together—in such a way as to leave the balance of payments between the two countries unaffected, while any repercussions on the prices of the securities traded between the two countries were compensated by unilateral transfers, any such adjustment would be beneficial to some of the residents of both countries and harmful to none. Such adjustments could continue with advantage until the rate of tax became equal on all imports of securities from B to A.

It can also be shown that, on the same assumption with respect to the payment of compensatory transfers from B to A, country A could with advantage promote the exportation of securities to country B by means of a uniform subsidy on all securities and that the subsidy on exportation should equal the tax on importation of securities when measured in the percentage of the prices of the taxed or subsidized securities in country B (see Appendix, section B). Now, this is precisely the effect that would be achieved if country A applied a uniform exchange premium on its currency in capital transactions with country B. Since price repercussions would not, in reality, be compensated by unilateral transfers, the optimal relationship between taxes and subsidies on capital flows would be somewhat more complicated than that described above.[8] The latter situation, however, probably represents the approximation to

---

[8] More precisely, as can be seen from the Appendix, section A, optimization requires that

$$\frac{\mu(\varepsilon + 1)}{\varepsilon(\mu - 1)} = \frac{U_B - U_A(1 + t)}{U_B - U_A(1 + s)}$$

where
    ε = elasticity of net supply of B securities to A;
    μ = elasticity of net demand for A securities in B;
U_A, U_B = marginal utility of money in A, B;
    t = the tax in A on the import of securities from B as a proportion of the price in B;
    s = the subsidy in A on the export of securities to B as a proportion of the price in B.

This formula will permit equality between t and s, that is, a uniform capital exchange rate, only if either (a) the elasticity of net demand for A's securities in B and the elasticity of net supply of B's securities to A are both infinite or (b) the marginal utility of money in A relative to that in B happens to be precisely equal to the exchange rate for B's currency in terms of A's currency for capital transactions. In this case both numerator and denominator on the right-hand side of the equation would be zero.

the optimal situation most suitable for adoption as a convention to govern international relationships.[9]

By analogous reasoning it can be shown that restrictions and incentives affecting capital transactions among any group of countries may be assumed to be optimal if they result from application by *each* country of a uniform exchange premium or discount on capital transactions with *all* other countries. This implies that capital transactions between any two countries would be affected by the premium or discount, as the case may be, in *both* countries, so that, for example, a capital transaction between two countries having equal premiums on their capital exchange rates would in effect be free from taxation or subsidization.

The discussion here involves the choice between one method of capital control and another, and it is assumed that "current" exchange rates, price levels, and the balance of payments on current account remain approximately unaffected by this choice. Therefore, the welfare superiority of the dual-exchange rate technique relates not to its effect on the flow of real resources nor on the geographical distribution of physical capital *among* countries, but mainly to its effect on changes in the composition of portfolios and on the distribution of real investment among industries and types of firms *within* countries. The general effect of substituting dual-exchange rates for quantitative controls would be to foster (a) the international diversification of portfolios and (b) multinational business. There may be some social disadvantages in doing this, but if it is desired, for example, to keep domestic industry in domestic hands, this should be promoted by suitably adapted measures of a permanent nature rather than by methods that vary in their effectiveness with the balance-of-payments situation.

A second advantage of the dual-exchange market over direct administrative restrictions on capital flows is that, with an equal degree of severity in penalizing evasion, it is likely to achieve either a given balance-of-payments effect with less administrative effort than the direct restrictions

---

[9] The foregoing argument calls for some qualification to take account of the possibility that, given the uncertainty of the future "capital" rates in any dual-exchange market system, such a system may create greater uncertainty regarding the profitability of capital flows both inward and outward than would a system of administrative restraints on such flows (cf. footnote 4). To the extent that this is the case, there is a possibility that the dual-exchange market system may unduly restrict gross capital flows in a way that the system of administrative restraints would not, though the effect on net flows might be welcome.

on capital flows or a greater balance of payments effect with the same administrative effort. The reason is that, if a set of administrative restrictions is compared with a particular level of the capital-exchange rate (relative to the exchange rate on current transactions) both of which, *in the absence of evasion*, would have an equal effect on the balance of payments, the capital rate would be likely to give a smaller incentive to evasion than would the quantitative measures.

Administrative interference with capital flows generally operates by inhibiting or restricting rather than by promoting such flows. Moreover, as has been seen, it restricts very unevenly.[10] Some transactions that are barely profitable may get through the controls, while others that would be very profitable are inhibited. A uniform tax on such flows (with an effect, in the absence of evasion, equal to that of the restrictions) would be likely to promote less evasion, since the transactions inhibited by the tax would all be of a less profitable sort; while some of those inhibited by administrative interference would be of a more profitable sort where the incentive to evade would be greater. A dual-exchange rate that has an equivalent evasion-free effect offers an even smaller incentive to evasion than the uniform tax. Since part of its effect is achieved through promoting transactions by subsidization, the inhibiting exchange premium or discount is lower than a uniform tax of equivalent effect, and the transactions inhibited by it are of lower average profitability. It is true that the effect of the dual market in subsidizing capital flows in one direction may enhance the profitability of illicit capital flows through the current exchange market in the contrary direction, but this is likely to be a second-order effect.

Since evasion would be less profitable under a dual market than under a regime of direct administrative restrictions over capital flows, it may be assumed that there would be less of it for a given degree of severity in the policing of the controls or that the policing itself would be less severe. There is reason to think that some of the countries that have applied dual rates, notably Belgium, have taken advantage of this to apply less onerous surveillance and enforcement measures than they would have

---

[10] Apart from the unevenness, inseparable quantitative controls, and licensing arrangements, countries are often loath to apply such restrictions to the outflow of nonresident funds or the inflow of national funds held abroad. Inhibitions about applying the "capital" rate to such transactions may be less marked.

done had they relied instead on quantitative restrictions. It is sometimes asserted that "experience" has shown that the dual-market system is undermined by evasion as soon as the premium or discount on the capital exchange market widens beyond a moderate level—at least for any considerable period of time. It seems possible, however, that this is true only where the authorities have been unwilling to police and enforce the segregation of capital and current transactions with the same energy that they would have had to use to enforce capital restrictions of a more familiar type.

An indication of this is seen in the very substantial discounts prevailing over periods of years in markets such as the market for security sterling, in which nonresidents bought and sold currency usable for transactions in domestic securities—or in markets such as the U.K. market for investment currency, in which residents buy and sell foreign currency derived from and usable for transactions in foreign securities. Facilities for arbitrage between two such markets are all that is necessary to create an exchange market for capital transactions, and it is difficult to believe that the addition of this element of arbitrage need fatally weaken the barriers to evasion.

The incentive to evade restrictions depends not only on the profitability of such evasion, but also on the ease with which it can be carried out. There is no reason why controls over capital flows such as those operating through the licensing of actual transactions or payments should have any advantage over the controls required for implementation of the dual market in regard to evasion or to the ease of preventing it. The situation may be otherwise, however, when capital flows are controlled indirectly through quantitative regulation of the external positions or through foreign exchange parities of banks or other enterprises. Such regulations, although they have the other defects of quantitative restrictions described above, probably have the merit of being easier to enforce with a given degree of effectiveness than the regulations underlying dual-exchange markets. However, they can provide an alternative to direct controls over capital transactions or to dual-exchange markets over only a part of the field.

Evasion is undesirable in that: it (a) produces allocative inefficiencies among different types of capital flows and different types of current transactions, (b) absorbs productive resources in the actual process of evasion and in the prevention thereof, (c) involves a loss of income to the authorities, and (d) either weakens the desired equilibrating effect in the balance of payments or, if this is countered by intensifying restrictions, intensifies the other evils mentioned. The superiority of dual markets over direct administrative restrictions in the matter of evasion therefore yields advantages in all of these respects.

As regards the cost of administering the controls, a distinction has to be drawn between direct controls over capital transactions and controls over external positions. The former are probably more costly to operate than dual markets for equal effectiveness, not only because of the greater incentive to evasion but for other reasons as well. Not only do they require government decisions as to the quantities of the different categories of external assets or liabilities to be held or transacted by residents; they also require that the different types of transactions be not only identified, as in the case of dual markets, but also regulated as to quantity. In the case of dual markets the first requirement does not exist; the second stops at identification. Where quantitative controls are exercised with respect to amounts *held* rather than *transacted*, however, the costs of ensuring that external positions are what they should be are probably quite small for large holders such as banks and financial institutions.

The main disadvantage of dual markets as compared to quantitative capital restrictions lies in the visibility of the exchange premia and discounts on the capital exchange market and in the speculative repercussions that may arise therefrom on the current exchange market. By creating an expectation that the official rate will move in the direction of the "capital" rate, such repercussions may reduce the extent to which the "capital" rate is expected to revert to its original norm, may increase the spread between the two rates that is required to keep capital flows under control, and may strengthen the incentive to evasion.

The question arises as to whether dual-exchange markets, by their very effectiveness in maintaining temporary payments balance when it is inadvisable to adjust the current account balance of payments, might become an obstacle to adjustment of the current balance when appropriate. In this context, however, the greater visibility of market premia and discounts as compared with quantitative barriers, which was a disadvantage in dealing with temporary disequilibria, may be advantageous in that such premia and discounts, if continued over a long period, can be taken as indicative of the need for fundamental adjustment.

What has been said thus far about administrative and quantitative restrictions relates to restrictions on capital transactions not directly linked to current transactions. However, some of these restrictions have to do with types of capital flows directly related to current transactions, such as changes in foreign trade credit outstanding, in the temporary holding by residents of working balances in foreign currency derived from export receipts or to be used for purchase of imports, or in analogous working balances held by nonresidents in domestic currency. Variations in trade credit and in such working balances can give rise to significant net capital flows ("leads and lags") in response to changes in relative national interest rates and to very large net flows in response to changes in expectations about exchange rates.

To prevent such flows from taking place through the "current" exchange market, as would be required for a complete segregation of current and capital transactions, it would be necessary to synchronize current payments with the corresponding current transactions and also with the associated exchange transactions, so that any trade credit extended would have to be carried out as a separate transaction on the capital-exchange market. To enact a real synchronization would be inconvenient and possibly seriously discouraging to trade. It may therefore be preferable to tolerate such flows through the "current" exchange market or to limit them by a looser type of regulation governing the timing of payments if relation to the underlying transactions, the amounts of residents' and nonresidents' working balances, or the time elapsing between credits and debits to such balances. Such regulations should not be regarded as alternatives to the use of a capital exchange market but as "imperfect" complements to such use.

Dual-Exchange Markets versus Fiscal Interventions

Fiscal interventions affecting capital flows may take the form of taxes or subsidies on capital transactions, on the external assets or liabilities of residents, or on income receipts and payments derived from such external assets or liabilities. They may also take the form of taxes or subsidies on domestic capital outlays that will permit domestic interest rates to be higher or lower than they would otherwise be, thus attracting or repelling capital flows.

Taxes and subsidies on capital transactions, if enforced by exchange controls, would resemble dual markets in potential effectiveness and susceptibility of evasion. They would, however, be far less flexible than dual markets and would therefore be less effective in arresting short-term fluctuations in payments imbalances. Also, since such interventions are generally applied without the enforcement aid of exchange control, they are likely to be far more open to evasion and far less effective than dual markets. Certain types of taxes or subsidies on external positions may be enforceable without the aid of controls over transactions, but they are likely to cover only a limited range of potential capital flows. Taxes and subsidies on domestic capital outlays, with the associated variations in interest rates, might well be the most effective and comprehensive fiscal instrument for influencing capital flows, but they suffer from the same lack of flexibility as other fiscal instruments.

Dual-Exchange Markets versus Forward-Exchange Market Intervention

If a country is in temporary payments surplus, its authorities may seek to check the inflow by acquiring foreign exchange on the forward-exchange market or by "swapping out" reserves to its commercial banks; if it is in temporary deficit, they may seek to check the outflow by supporting the national currency on the forward-exchange market. Such forward market intervention is likely to evoke private countertransactions of a speculative or hedging character, since it will make such transactions cheaper; occasionally, however, if the movement in forward rates affects expectations about future spot rates, it may have the opposite effect. In any event, the greater part (if not the whole) of the amount of official intervention is likely to be matched by a shift in private balances covered forward, and it is this shift that produces the effect on reserves desired by the authorities.

Forward market intervention, like the dual market, is a very flexible technique, affecting both inward and outward movements of funds and both resident and nonresident capital. Moreover, it has the great merit of being able to influence to some extent just those types of capital flow—leads and lags connected with current transactions, and shifts in working balances—which the dual market cannot reach. On the other hand, it is more limited in scope, being confined to short-term funds of those (banks, traders, etc.) who wish to avoid exchange risk and therefore cover their foreign exchange positions on the forward market or of those who can be induced to shift their speculative positions from the spot market to the future market.

Again, forward market intervention may be expensive, if, for example, it is applied to resist an interest-motivated flow of funds or a speculative flow that is followed by a change in the spot exchange rate in the expected direction. In the first case the authorities are likely to have to buy forward exchange at a premium or sell it at a discount; in the second case, although the opposite is true, they may have to take a loss on outstanding contracts when the spot rate is adjusted. With dual markets, on the other hand, the authorities can usually obtain some relief from the undesired influx or efflux of reserves without intervening in the capital exchange market, and thus avoid losses; only if they have to intervene to push the forward and official rates still further apart will they begin to create losses.

Because of the difference in their range of influence, dual-exchange markets and intervention on the forward market for current transactions may be used with advantage as complementary instruments of policy.

Dual Markets versus Fiscal–Monetary Policy

When countries are affected by balance-of-payments deficits or surpluses that are believed to be temporary, the response traditionally recommended by conservative economists and bankers is for the deficit countries to raise interest rates and contract credit and for the surplus countries to lower interest rates and expand credit in the attempt to evoke equilibrating capital flows or to stem disequilibrating ones. Today it is generally recognized that such a policy carries with it dangers to domestic stabilization policy, and it is customary to recommend its application in conjunction with fiscal policies designed to counteract any undesired inflationary or deflationary effects of the monetary policies. This fiscal–monetary mix, with its mélange of Keynesian and pre-Keynesian elements, is popular among those who are reassured by the familiar and market-respecting character of the instruments employed. In reality, however, of all the policies for coping with disruptive capital flows, it is one that is most likely to generate diseconomies and distortions.

In comparing reliance on the fiscal-monetary mix with the dual-exchange market system, it is necessary to draw a distinction between a mix in which the fiscal element is confined to measures affecting capital outlay and a mix in which it is confined to measures affecting consumption. As an example of the former case, a country in temporary deficit might raise its interest rate by a restrictive monetary policy and offset the effect on domestic capital outlay or investment expenditure by subsidizing the latter. Such a policy would in principle operate in a manner similar to a dual-exchange market in which the financial rate was allowed—or made—to fall. There are, however, certain differences. The fiscal–monetary mix would affect all sorts of capital flows, including those (such as leads and lags) that normally bypass the financial exchange market; to this extent it is superior to the dual market system. On the other hand, certain (relatively unimportant) diseconomies would result from the separation of the interest rates applicable to domestic savings and investment, but these would not occur under the dual market system. The real inferiority of the fiscal–monetary mix, however, lies in the area of practical application. It would not be feasible in practice to apply taxes or subsidies to all forms of capital outlay in a country, and it would be still less feasible to vary them flexibly in harmony with interest rates so as to bring about the desired level of net capital flows—a result that the market can bring about automatically through variations in the financial exchange rate.

By extending fiscal manipulation beyond the area of capital expenditure to forms of public expenditures and taxation that presumably affect consumption, it would become technically somewhat more feasible to offset the aggregate demand effects of internal rate variations designed to bring about the appropriate capital flows. Even in this case, however, it would hardly be feasible to vary budgetary surpluses and deficits to the extent that would be required to offset the very large variations in interest rates needed to restrain disequilibrating capital flows of the speculative sort (as distinct from interest-motivated flows resulting from differential phasing of cyclical situations in different countries). In principle it should be technically possible to deal with exogenous demand variations associated with the business cycle while keeping interest rates at levels that, in the absence of exchange speculation, would evoke the required inflows or outflows of capital. Such a result, however, is one that governments are understandably reluctant to attempt, since it involves considerable diseconomies and sectoral maladjustments.

The diseconomies in question arise from the fact that if budgetary surpluses or deficits are used to stabilize aggregate demand by expanding or contracting consumption, they are likely to cause the level of national savings to diverge from the level corresponding to the true preferences of individuals and public authorities.[11] If the circumstances that give rise to this necessity are temporary and reversible, no permanent harm will have been done. Considerable harm may be done, however, if under-saving or oversaving persists for a long period of years and is not recognized for what it is—a symptom of basic disequilibrium in the balance of payments.

Sectoral maladjustments are likely to arise from the fiscal–monetary mix where this is used as a way of dealing with payments disequilibrium evoked by speculative flows or by interest arbitrage associated with cyclical discrepancies in the incentive to invest. Variations in demand induced by interest rate variations affect primarily the construction industries and secondarily (partly through the effect on the stock market) investment goods industries. Compensating variations in budgets primarily affect consumer goods industries. Such compensation is therefore imperfect and is likely to result in a patchy situation combining unemployment and scarcity in different sectors. Admittedly, where the payments disequilibria are due to temporary export variations, the inevitable sectoral maladjustments may be more easily mitigated by using fiscal policy for internal stabilization and by using monetary policy to equilibrate external payments and receipts than they could be by attempting to use monetary policy for stabilization purposes. Even in the last-mentioned case, however, a still better result might be attained by using intervention on a capital exchange market to equilibrate the balance of payments without disturbing the domestic interest rate and by using selective budgetary policy to offset the effects of export variation on sectoral and total demand.

In summary, the dual-exchange market offers a far more flexible technique of equilibration than the fiscal–monetary mix, and it is free from the deleterious effects of the latter on savings and sectoral adjustment.

---

[11] This is true whether the variation in investment demand that has to be compensated for is due to a change in interest rates undertaken for balance-of-payments reasons or to a change in the incentive to invest to which monetary policy, for balance-of-payments reasons, fails to respond.

Despite the gaps in its coverage of capital flows (e.g., leads and lags), it is far superior to the mix in dealing with violent speculative movements of funds; its advantage may be somewhat less marked in dealing with more moderate flows of a cyclical nature, though in this case the gaps in coverage may be less important. In this case a combination of the two techniques may be advantageous, especially if the dual market is applied in such a way as to permit substantial evasion.

Dual-Exchange Market versus Official Financing

There are two methods whereby governments or monetary authorities can finance balance-of-payments deficits (surpluses) namely: (a) by using (accumulating) reserves and (b) by borrowing abroad (repaying foreign loans).

There are two great disadvantages of official financing, particularly in the form of reserve movements, from which dual-exchange markets (like other devices for preserving payments balance) are free and two others that they share.

Reserve losses tend to bring about a contraction of money supply and bank credit along with a decline in security prices and expenditures, while reserve increases tend to have the opposite effects. These effects, which are likely to be unwelcome to the authorities from the standpoint of demand management, can in principle be prevented by a combination of high marginal bank reserve requirements, variable reserve requirements, official purchases and sales of securities, quantitative credit controls, and so on. However, particularly in the case of reserve inflows, some authorities are not equipped to carry these measures as far as would be necessary for complete offsetting and others are unwilling to do so, either because they impair the profits or liquidity of particular banks or because open market sales are expensive for the authorities themselves. From a national standpoint, also, it is costly for a country to permit foreigners to acquire assets carrying a substantial yield in exchange for reserves yielding a low return or none at all.

The financing of payments imbalances through official lending or borrowing gives rise to much the same difficulties for monetary management as do reserve movements. Increases or reductions in official lending act like reserve changes and indeed usually *are* reserve changes; increases or reductions in official liabilities do not help to offset the domestic effects of payments surpluses or deficits. Insofar as the sterilization of payments imbalances is concerned, one country can help another only by borrowing or lending in the other's private credit or capital markets.

Given the technical and psychological limitations of official offsetting policies, reliance on reserve movements or on liability financing to meet external disequilibria carries the danger that the countries concerned will be exposed to inflationary pressures when in payments surplus and to deflationary pressures and unemployment when in payments deficit.

Access to certain forms of official financing, if available to countries generally on a scale that would suffice to meet possible deficits caused by temporary capital flows, would be likely to impart an inflationary bias to the world economy. This would not apply to IMF drawing facilities in the credit tranches, because these can be utilized by countries only on condition that they adopt prudent noninflationary policies. However, it would constitute an objection to the provision of reserves, including currency holdings and SDRs on the scale that would be required for this purpose, since the yield on such reserves (in the form of interest and possible capital appreciation) is generally considerably lower than that of assets that the holding country could acquire at home or abroad if its authorities chose to adopt a more expansionary policy that would use up reserves. Although a separate exchange market for capital transactions, on the other hand, could also be manipulated to finance the payments deficits entailed by an inflationary policy, it would not offer the same temptation to the authorities, since the funds it would attract would have to be remunerated at the current rates on international markets. Moreover, if the authorities were to attract such funds by depreciating the "capital" rate, they would themselves eventually incur increasing financial losses.

On the other hand, official financing is likely to have certain advantages over the dual-exchange market in that (a) it may involve less distortion and disturbance between different sectors of national capital markets and (b) by reason of its very limitations in dealing with short-term disequilibria, it may offer less resistance to fundamental adjustment in the face of persistent disequilibria.

First, the inevitable evasion and bypassing of the obstacles to capital flow set up by a "capital" exchange rate that diverges from the "current" rate might lead to certain distortions in the relative prices of different types of assets in countries applying the dual market, which a skillful policy of stabilization and offsetting of reserve movements would have avoided. This, however, is not likely to be of great quantitative importance.

Second, it seems evident that, however clearly a persistent premium or discount on the financial exchange market would signal the existence of a fundamental disequilibrium, a persistent reserve flow or even a persistent resort to borrowing by monetary authorities would signal it even more clearly. Moreover, owing to the necessarily limited availability of official financing, persistent losses of reserves are almost bound to enforce adjustment on the part of deficit countries, although the same is not equally true of reserve gains by surplus countries, until such gains grow to massive dimensions.

Dual-Exchange Markets versus Flexible Unitary Rates

Flexible rates here mean rates that float, subject only to intervention sufficient to smooth out minor short-term fluctuations. Such floating may have no definite limits or may occur within rather wide margins on either side of a central rate fixed against an intervention currency. It is convenient to begin by comparing dual-exchange rates to flexible unified rates that are unhampered by formal or informal margins.

Flexible unified spot-exchange rates tend to make capital flows more equilibrating or less disequilibrating to the extent that, as the rate falls, the expectation that it will fall (rise) further is reduced and the expectation that it will rise (fall) again is increased. Given such a negative elasticity of exchange-rate expectations, disequilibrating elements affecting the balance of payments will tend to produce rate movements that bring equilibrating capital flows into play and thus limit the movement in the rate. The probability that, after half a year or so, changes in the exchange rate are likely to begin to produce an equilibrating effect on the current account items in the balance of payments—an effect that will grow more powerful as time passes—may be a good reason why rate expectations beyond the short run should behave in the manner described above. Many of those who move funds in response to exchange-rate changes, however, are influenced by short-term considerations; therefore, it is unfortunate that the early effects of rate changes on the current account are likely to be perverse. In these circumstances, even if rate changes are at first checked by expectations of early reversal, these expectations may well be disappointed and hence revised so that rates in a "clean" float may move far from the level toward which they might reasonably be expected to move in the longer run. This is a weakness in uniform floating exchange rates that is not shared to the same extent by the floating "capital" rates in a dual-rate system.

Experience with floating rates has been very diverse. When they have been in operation over a considerable period with reasonably stable internal conditions and no large structural disequilibria in the balance of payments, flexible rates have shown considerable stability in the face of random shocks. This is especially true where the authorities have intervened to smooth out day-to-day variations and have striven, if only indirectly through financial policies, to keep longer-term variations within a normal range. However, where floating has occurred in circumstances of basic disequilibrium or where demand management has been inadequate, wide fluctuations in rates have taken place.

The disadvantages of flexible unified spot rates, as compared with dual markets, are that they are disturbing to trade and to the foreign trade industries.[12] While the exchange risks of particular trade transactions can usually be covered chiefly in the forward-exchange market, the risks of production and especially of investment in the foreign-trade industries cannot be so covered. Such investment may thus be misdirected or unduly curtailed.

Again, a system of flexible rates may be more open to the abuse of competitive exchange depreciation than would a dual market, because such depreciation could in the former case be achieved through market intervention, whereas in the latter it would require a par value change.

On the other hand, since flexible rates exercise their equilibrating effects on *all* forms of capital flow (including leads and lags and variations in convertible balances) and since they are not subject to evasion, they are free from distortions between different types of capital flow and from the waste of resources in the evasion and enforcement of controls to which dual rates are subject. For the same reason they are far more certain of achieving the required equilibrating effect on the balance of payments.

[12] Both flexible unitary rates and dual markets are open to objection because of the unduly discouraging effect which their uncertainty may exercise on gross capital flows, especially in the medium term, and because of their tendency to discourage net capital flows, whether or not this is called for in the interests of short-term equilibrium. Neither appears to have a differential advantage over the other in this respect.

This consideration may in practice make floating rates inevitable where really massive speculative capital flows are concerned, even when in principle other solutions might be preferred.

Finally, flexible rates have the important advantage that if (as very often happens) an apparently temporary payments disequilibrium masks a basic disequilibrium or is accompanied by one, the consequent movement in the spot rate would initiate the required basic adjustment, while a dual market would simply bottle up the disequilibrium until a persistent—or persistently growing—premium or discount in the "capital" rate showed it to be basic in character.

There are two ways in which the variations in floating rates may be limited by official intervention. The first is the adoption of rigid, publicly announced, but widely spaced margins of exchange rate variation around an announced though adjustable central rate. The second is a much more informal arrangement, under which there is no announced margin or central rate but where the authorities in fact take action, either through direction intervention on the exchange market or through the adoption of the sort of equilibrating short-term balance of payments policies that have been discussed in earlier sections of this paper.[13] Thus, they prevent rates from diverging too far from whatever rate would seem at the time to be most likely, if maintained, to bring about payments equilibrium over the next several years. This second type of limitation would seem to be a *sine qua non* if the flexible rate system is to operate with a reasonable degree of stability. Such limits would greatly enhance the equilibrating effects of exchange-rate changes, since the market is more likely to anticipate a return to a normal rate if it feels that the authorities themselves have such a norm in mind and are prepared to enfore it. A readiness on the part of the authorities to intervene in this way would thus strengthen the case for using floating rates (within the limits) as an instrument to deal with temporary and reversible disequilibria, in preference to other instruments, such as dual rates.

A system of announced central rates with wide but rigid margins within which exchange rates could float freely might exercise an even stronger equilibrating effect on capital flows than the system of informally limited floating just discussed—not to mention a system of unlimited floating—

---

[13] The use of the dual-exchange market as an instrument to limit the range of variation of a unified floating rate is discussed below.

if there is confidence that the central rate and the margins are likely to be held. If, however, there is a fear of devaluation or revaluation of the central rates, the opposite may be true, since under the informal intervention system there is no clear target to speculate against and those speculating in such a way as to exaggerate exchange-rate fluctuations can never be sure when they may encounter aggressive official opposition on the exchange market. Moreover, if there is a basic payments disequilibrium, the fixed central rates and margins may inhibit or delay the necessary adjustments in the same way as the fixed "current" exchange rates under the dual-market system.

CONCLUSIONS

From what has been said, it would seem that dual-exchange markets, supplemented as necessary by controls over the timing of current payments and by controls or incentives affecting changes in nonresident holdings of convertible balances, have considerable advantages over most of the other methods of dealing with temporary and reversible payments disequilibria—with the possible exception of unified rates that (within reasonable limits) are allowed to float freely, subject to day-to-day smoothing operations. They are, at least potentially, more effective and more economic in their incidence than quantitative restrictions on capital transactions, more flexible than fiscal measures, more flexible and less disturbing to production and saving than the fiscal–monetary mix, of wider scope than forward-market intervention, less inflationary than some forms of compensatory official financing, and less disturbing to trade—though also less effective—than floating unitary rates. Where persistent disequilibria are present, however, adjustment in the spot-exchange rates is clearly indicated, and this can be most smoothly and easily attained by the use of floating rates.

Possibility of a Hybrid System

This suggests the possibility of a hybrid system under which (a) capital and current transactions would be segregated in separate exchange markets, (b) both the "current" and the "capital" rates would be allowed to float, (c) official sales of foreign exchange on one market would be balanced by official sales on the other, so that there would be no net reserve change or at least any net reserve change would be confined to amounts deemed internationally appropriate, and (d) the gross amount of intervention would be such as to keep rates on the two markets together, except when the rate thus unified tended to diverge too far from its presumed longer-term norm, in which event the "current" rate would be prevented by intervention from diverging further from its normal level, while the "capital" rate would find its level subject to the operation of rule (c).[14]

For example, if the two rates were equal but were tending to fall too far below the "norm," the authorities could intervene on both markets in such a way as to produce a discount of the "capital" rate compared with the "current" rate. This would raise the "current" rate or prevent it from falling as far as it otherwise would. However, if the discount on the "capital" rate persisted too long, it would be a sign that the "norm" for the "current" rate might have been set too high.[15]

Under a system of this kind it would not be necessary for large long-lasting divergences between the two rates to emerge. It might, therefore, be unnecessary to take any very drastic steps to interfere with capital flows through the "current" market in the form of leads and lags, and so on.

Principles for Operation of
Dual-Market System

It may be well to conclude by reiterating two principles that should govern the operation of a dual-market system, whether of the simple or of the "hybrid" type:

1 The capital-exchange market, and in particular official intervention on that market, should be conducted so as to promote short-term equilibrium in the overall balance of payments of the country concerned. This should be interpreted as compatible with aiming to achieve a rate of reserve growth that is internationally appropriate in relation to world reserve growth and to the need to achieve a gradual improvement in the international distribution of reserves.

[14] Some of the features of this arrangement are approximated in Italy's present dual float.
[15] It is vital to the operation of such a system that official intervention on the two exchange markets follow rules (c) and (d) above. Any attempt to operate the system without official intervention could be saved from disaster only by leakages from one market to the other, since a completely segregated current exchange market would be highly unstable as the impact effect of exchange-rate changes on the current account would naturally be perverse.

2. The persistence of chronic premia (discounts) in the "capital" exchange rate as compared with the "current" exchange rate should be recognized as one indication of the need to raise (lower) the par value of the country concerned or (in a floating exchange-rate system) the range within which the exchange rate for current transactions is expected to move in the medium term.

APPENDIX

Optimal Relationship Between Taxes and Subsidies on Capital Flows

Let there be only two countries, A and B.

U, U^A, and $U^B \equiv$ utility in general, in A, and in B

$q_x \equiv$ amount of securities (capital account items) exported from A to B

$q_m \equiv$ amount of securities imported from B to A

P_{xA} and $P_{xB} \equiv$ price of A's securities in A and B

P_{mA} and $P_{mB} \equiv$ price of B's securities in A and B

$t \equiv$ proportionate tax in A on import of securities from B

$$\equiv \frac{P_{mA} - P_{mB}}{P_{mB}}$$

$s \equiv$ proportionate subsidy in A on export of securities to B

$$\equiv \frac{P_{xA} - P_{xB}}{P_{xB}}$$

$\varepsilon \equiv$ elasticity of net supply of B-securities to A

$$\equiv \frac{dq_m}{dP_{mB}} \cdot \frac{P_{mB}}{q_m}$$

$\mu \equiv$ (negative) elasticity of net demand for A-securities in B

$$\equiv -\frac{dq_x}{dP_{xB}} \cdot \frac{P_{xB}}{q_x}$$

U_A and $U_B \equiv$ marginal utility of money in A and in B.

Then

$$U = U^A(q_m, q_x \cdots) + U^B(q_m, q_x \cdots)$$

where

$$\frac{\partial U^A}{\partial q_m} > 0, \qquad \frac{\partial U^A}{\partial q_x} < 0.$$

$$\frac{\partial U^B}{\partial q_m} < 0, \qquad \frac{\partial U^B}{\partial q_x} > 0.$$

A. Constant Payments Imbalance

Let t and s vary in such a way as to leave unchanged the balance of payments between A and B. Since the exchange rate and level of money income in A and B are kept constant, it is assumed that the current account items in the balance of payments remain constant also, with only the flow of securities being affected. The balance of payments constraint is, therefore, as follows:

$$\delta(q_x P_{xB}) = \delta(q_m P_{mB}) \tag{1}$$

where δ signifies a total differential.

As t and s vary, subject to this constraint, the effects on U^A, U^B, and U are:

$$\delta U^A = \delta q_x \frac{\partial U^A}{\partial q_x} + \delta q_m \frac{\partial U^A}{\partial q_m}, \, \delta U^B = \delta q_x \frac{\partial U^B}{\partial q_x} + \delta q_m \frac{\partial U^B}{\partial q_m}$$

$$\delta U = \delta q_x \left(\frac{\partial U^A}{\partial q_x} + \frac{\partial U^B}{\partial q_x} \right) + \delta q_m \left(\frac{\partial U^A}{\partial q_m} + \frac{\partial U^B}{\partial q_m} \right).$$

Since competitive conditions are assumed to prevail in security markets in both A and B, and since the marginal utility of money is assumed to be the same for all residents of each country, though different as between countries, therefore:

$$\frac{\partial U^A}{\partial q_x} = -U_A P_{xA}, \frac{\partial U^A}{\partial q_m} = U_A P_{mA}, \frac{\partial U^B}{\partial q_x} = U_B P_{xB}, \text{ and } \frac{\partial U^B}{\partial q_m} = -U_B P_{mB}.$$

Thus,

$$\delta U^A = U_A(P_{mA} \delta q_m - P_{xA} \delta q_x), \, \delta U^B = U_B(P_{xB} \delta q_x - P_{mB} \delta q_m)$$

and

$$\delta U = P_{xB} \delta q_x \{U_B - U_A(1 + s)\} + P_{mB} \delta q_m \{U_A(1 + t) - U_B\} \cdots \tag{2}$$

From equation (1),

$$\frac{P_{xB}\delta q_x}{P_{mB}\delta q_m} = \frac{\mu}{\varepsilon} \cdot \frac{(\varepsilon + 1)}{(\mu - 1)}.$$

Substituting in equation (2),

$$\delta U = P_{mB}\,\delta q_m \left[\frac{\mu(\varepsilon + 1)}{\varepsilon(\mu - 1)} \{U_B - U_A(1 + s)\} + \{U_A(1 + t) - U_B\} \right].$$

When t and s are at their optimal levels, subject to the balance of payments constraint, $\delta U = 0$, that is:

$$\frac{\mu(\varepsilon + 1)}{\varepsilon(\mu - 1)} = \frac{U_B - U_A(1 + t)}{U_B - U_A(1 + s)}.$$

The foregoing analysis assumes independent demand curves for A's securities and B's securities in B and ignores cross-elasticities linking changes in demand for A's securities to changes in the price of B's securities and changes in demand for B's securities to changes in the price of A's securities. In the case of securities, one would expect such cross-elasticities to be high. The broad effect of taking cross-elasticities into account, when s and t are brought closer together, would be similar to that of a higher level of μ and ε.

B. Compensatory Payments Between Countries

If the variations in t and s had been accompanied by compensatory payments (positive or negative) from A to B, sufficient to prevent any changes in U_B, then, by hypothesis:

$$\delta U^B = U_B(P_{xB}\,\delta q_x - P_{mB}\,\delta q_m) = 0$$

or

$$P_{xB}\,\delta q_x = P_{mB}\,\delta q_m. \tag{1'}$$

Equation (1') now takes the place of the balance of payments constraint (1). Then

$$\delta U = \delta U^A = U_A(P_{mA}\,\delta q_m - P_{xA}\,\delta q_x)$$
$$= U_A\{P_{mB}(1 + t)\delta q_m - P_{xB}(1 + s)\delta q_x\}$$

which, from equation (1),

$$= P_{mB}\,\delta q_m U_A(t - s).$$

At the optimum point,

$$\delta U = \delta U^A = 0$$

or

$$t = s.$$

16

REFLECTIONS ON THE INTERNATIONAL MONETARY REFORM

It is, I feel, a great honor to have been asked to follow so many distinguished economists who have given this Frank D. Graham Memorial Lecture. I think of Frank Graham as one of the first to initiate me, through his writings, into the mysteries and preversities of floating exchange rates—which were as actual in the 1920s as they are today. I also remember him with affection, as a person who could not have been kinder to me when I spent a few months in Princeton as a Rockefeller fellow some thirty-five years ago.

O NE OF THE most ambitious attempts ever made to achieve a synchronized and many-sided reconstruction of the international monetary system by an orderly process of multilateral consultation and agreement is now grinding to a halt. Its place will be taken, on the most optimistic assumption, by a series of piecemeal reforms, strung out over time at moments that appear opportune in the light of current developments on the international scene. It is not yet clear how much of the original effort can be salvaged in the form of an initial installment of reform. The whole episode is one that is instructive not only to the economist but also to the student of international affairs.

What was to be reformed, of course, was the international monetary system set up at Bretton Woods and administered by the IMF, as that

First published in *Essays in International Finance*, December 1974. Reprinted by permission of the International Finance Section, Department of Economics, Princeton University, copyright © 1974. This essay contains the text of the Frank D. Graham Memorial Lecture delivered at Princeton University on April 18, 1974.

system had evolved up to, say, 1968. The most important features of the system, or at least those most prominent in the reform discussions, were the following:

1. the exchange-rate system, that is, the manner of regulating exchange rates;
2. the intervention system, that is, the manner in which these regulations are implemented by exchange-market intervention;
3. the settlement system, that is, the manner in which currencies acquired in intervention can be used to obtain other reserve assets and in which the currencies required for intervention can be obtained in exchange for these assets; and
4. the international reserve system, that is, the manner in which the aggregate supply of reserves and its composition are determined.

BACKGROUND

The first part of the international system to be reformed was the reserve system. In the latter half of the 1960s, it became clear that reserves were not increasing rapidly enough to keep pace with the expansion in the need and demand for them called for by the growth of international transactions. This was particularly true of the gold component of those reserves, but it was also true of reserves as a whole, despite the steep rise in the dollar holdings of central banks made possible by recurrent U.S. payments deficits and by the willingness of other countries to hold the proceeds of the corresponding payments surpluses in U.S. dollars. It came to be recognized, thanks in large part to the work of Professors Triffin and Kenen, that the method of meeting the world's reserve needs through an expansion in currency liabilities convertible into gold or other currencies was an inherently unstable one, that it tended to bring about maladjustments as well as instability in the payments balances of the countries issuing these currencies, and that it should, if possible, to be replaced by something better.

The first step toward a solution of this problem was the creation of a new type of international fiduciary reserve asset, the SDR, issued by the IMF and distributed among countries on the basis of IMF quotas. This solution, adopted in 1969, took years to prepare. By way of comparison with the procedures adopted later for the main reform, it is interesting to note that the first stages of preparation of the SDR scheme took place primarily in the Group of Ten, an exclusive club consisting of the main industrial countries, and the final stages primarily in the IMF itself.

It soon became obvious that, while the SDR provided a technique for relieving any shortage of reserves, merely to add a new type of reserve asset gave no assurance that the total volume of international liquidity would be kept under international control if autonomous forces were to create an excessive amount of reserves in other forms—in the form, for example, of currency balances.

Moreover, the feeling had been growing throughout the 1960s, first among academicians and then among officials, that the Bretton Woods arrangements might require amendment, not only with respect to liquidity supply but also with respect to the adjustment process in general and the exchange-rate regime in particular. During the 1950s and early 1960s, the process of balance-of-payments adjustment worked remarkably smoothly. In a world in which, outside the United States, gentle demand inflation prevailed and capital movements were limited, most countries tending to run into payments deficit could get back into line, without too much sacrifice of domestic prosperity, by temporarily checking the expansion of demand. Progressively during the 1960s, however, these conditions changed. The increasing importance of cost-push elements made for differential rates of inflation as between countries and created basic disequilibria that were difficult to correct without altering exchange rates. Although the rapid growth in the international mobility of capital (previously marked only as between the United States and Canada) sometimes helped to tide over payments imbalances, more frequently it tended to accentuate them, especially when doubts grew as to the possibility of defending existing exchange parities. The long siege of the pound sterling ending in the devaluation of the pound in 1967, the upward pressure on the deutsche mark and the *événements* in France ending in the devaluation of the franc and revaluation of the deutsche mark in 1969, followed by the upward float of the Canadian dollar in 1970, persuaded officials to take somewhat more seriously some of the suggestions for flexible exchange rates that had been made by academic economists in the early and mid-1960s.

An examination of these problems was conducted by the executive directors of the IMF in 1969–70 and eventuated in a report on *The Role of Exchange Rates in the Adjustment of International Payments*. This 1970 report, it must be said, was cautious and tentative in its conclusions. Its authors were still much influenced by the long years during which the Bretton

Woods arrangements had worked very well. Floating exchange rates as a permanent regime, substantially wider margins of fluctuation around parity, and automatic crawling pegs were all rejected. Par values should be retained but should be changed more promptly after the emergence of a fundamental disequilibrium, not—as too often had been the case—belatedly, as a last resort. Further consideration should be given to two more radical innovations; namely: (a) a slight widening in the margins around parity to dampen down short-term capital flows and help smooth the transition from one parity to another and (b) the authorization of strictly temporary periods of floating, but only in exceptional circumstances and under safeguards adequate to protect the interests of the international community.

These cautiously forward-looking proposals were soon to be swamped and lost to sight in a torrent of events that revealed the necessity for much more fundamental changes in the system. In the latter part of 1970 and in 1971, speculation against the dollar set in and official dollar reserves multiplied threefold from end-1969 to the third quarter of 1971. When one or two countries began to demand the conversion of their dollar balances, the United States was compelled, in August 1971, to abandon convertibility and the sale of gold.

The flood of dollars, and particularly the removal of what had been considered to be the linchpin of the par value system, caused a tremendous shock to confidence. Many, and finally most, of the principal currencies began to float; the United States kept urging Japan and the Europeans to float up and to revalue; these countries, in turn, considered that the United States should devalue. In the end, a temporary compromise was arrived at in the Smithsonian Agreement of December 1971 with a mixture of devaluation by the United States and revaluation by others, and with a widening of the margins of fluctuation around parities from ± 1 percent to $\pm 2\frac{1}{4}$ percent.

SUGGESTIONS FOR REFORM BY THE IMF EXECUTIVE BOARD

These developments suggested that a much more thoroughgoing reform of the international monetary system was required, and at the IMF Annual Meeting of Governors in September 1971 the executive directors were asked to report on the measures necessary for this reform. They duly reported in August of the following year. In this report (Executive Directors to the Board of Governors of the IMF, *Reform of the International Monetary System*, Washington, International Monetary Fund, 1972), most of the themes that dominated the later phases of the reform discussions were introduced. Some of the new ideas, particularly those of asset settlement and substitution, received a fairly elaborate treatment.

Asset settlement was put forward as a possible substitute for convertibility. Under the system of Bretton Woods, most countries settled their payments surpluses and deficits, apart from the use of special credits, by variations in their reserve holdings. Countries whose currencies were used in intervention and held in reserves, however, and particularly the United States as the issuer of the central intervention currency and principal reserve currency, might settle their payments imbalances through variations in their liabilities to foreign central banks. The extent to which the United States settled in assets or in liabilities depended, at least in theory, on the decisions of the foreign holders as to whether they would or would not exercise their right to convert their dollar balances into gold. It was therefore conceivable that the United States could gain reserves when in deficit and lose them when in surplus. In practice, holders of dollars were expected to show some restraint in using their conversion rights, and the United States, particularly from 1970 on, financed its deficits in the main by increasing its liabilities.

The idea behind asset settlement was to put reserve centers and others on the same footing—to regulate conversion in such a way that reserve centers, like other countries, settled their deficits and surpluses through the transfer of reserve assets, except insofar as they, like other countries, might obtain negotiated credits. One of the main advantages seen in this arrangement was that it would complete the work, begun by the creation of the SDR, of bringing the world's supply of reserves under international control; SDRs would ensure that there were enough reserves, asset settlement that there were not too many. A second advantage was that it would subject reserve centers to the same sorts of pressure for adjustment when in deficit that other countries in that position had to bear, although this was not seen as an advantage by everyone. Finally, this arrangement would protect the reserve centers against the possible conversion of the overhang of liabilities to central banks that had accumulated in earlier years.

I will not describe in detail the mechanisms whereby asset settlement was to be assured. Broadly speaking, two main techniques could be employed, alternatively or in combination. Under the first approach, all countries, or at least the principal ones, would undertake to prevent their stocks of each reserve currency from rising by converting accruing balances into primary reserve assets, and possibly prevent them from falling by selling primary assets to the issuer. Under the second, or collective, approach, reserve centers would regularly settle any net increases or decreases in outstanding reserve liabilities either by exchanging SDRs and their currencies with other countries designated by the IMF or by exchanging SDRs and currencies directly with the IMF. This collective approach to asset settlement, which certainly seemed the simpler of the two so far as the traditional reserve currencies are concerned, led naturally into another suggestion, which constituted the second of the two new ideas advanced in the 1972 report, namely the idea of a substitution account.

The substitution account or substitution facility, as suggested in the 1972 report, was to be an account in the IMF that could exchange currencies and SDRs with central banks. It would have two main features. First, it would enable countries to alter the composition of their reserves by selling to them—or standing ready to sell to them—newly created SDRs in exchange for their holdings of reserve currency, and possibly (though this feature was subsequently dropped) by selling reserve currency to them in exchange for SDRs. Second, it would ensure that reserve centers were able to earn reserves through their surpluses by standing ready to buy their currencies from them in exchange for newly created SDRs to the extent that other countries' holdings of their currencies declined. And it would ensure asset settlement by the reserve centers, if this were not otherwise provided for, by requiring them to redeem their currencies from the account with SDRs to the extent that other countries' holdings of their currencies increased. In its first aspect, its transactions with non-reserve-currency countries, the substitution facility would have the effect of increasing the role of the SDR in reserves and reducing that of currencies, thus weakening the temptation for these countries to devalue their own currencies whenever their reserve currency was devalued and paving the way for systems in which the SDR would be the principal means of settlement. In its second aspect, its transactions with reserve centers, which came to predominate as the reform discussions proceeded, the facility would be an instrument for implementing asset settlement.

These two main innovative suggestions of the 1972 report, the idea of asset settlement and the substitution facility, were not received with unalloyed enthusiasm by all countries, and especially not by the United States. It is easy to see why. Asset settlement, while it might protect the principal reserve center against the conversion of outstanding balances of its currency, takes away from it a valuable source of liquidity, the ability to finance deficits by the expansion of its liabilities rather than the loss of its reserves. In other words, the reserve center when in deficit would be under the same pressures to deflate, restrict, and devalue as other countries in deficit normally are. Moreover, the United States, being not only the principal reserve center but also having the ultimate intervention currency, and being accustomed to playing a passive role in exchange markets, might well feel that other countries were in a position to put her into deficit and keep her there. Other countries when in deficit were at least free to devalue their exchange rates or float their rates downward. The United States, as the intervention center, was not able to float its currency and might not be allowed to devalue effectively. Asset settlement, unaccompanied by other reforms in the adjustment and intervention system, might weaken the incentive for industrial surplus countries either to adjust upward themselves or to allow the United States to adjust downward through the rate of exchange.

As for substitution, it might add to the freedom of action of the reserve-currency countries, but questions would arise as to the terms on which the substitution would be carried out and as to the form in which the claims of the substitution account on the reserve center would be held.

For the United States, certain other aspects of the reform program had a greater attractiveness, namely, proposals for increasing the pressure on other countries to adjust when in surplus, and perhaps also proposals for changing the intervention system to give greater freedom to the United States to alter its own exchange rate.

The 1972 report considered adjustment mainly from the standpoint of the exchange-rate regime. In addition to repeating the suggestions of the 1970 report regarding prompter par value adjustments, slightly wider margins, and temporary floats, the later report put emphasis on the need to allow the United States greater initiative in changing its own rate without being exposed to retaliatory measures, and on the positive expectation that countries would change their rates whenever they fell into fundamental disequilibrium rather than merely abstain from changing their rates when not in fundamental disequilibrium. Bearing in mind the experience of the year 1971, the report emphasized the need for simultaneous joint consideration of the relative exchange rates of all the principal currencies and for the initiation of a process of continuous assessment that would make this possible. Ideas were also tentatively put forward, with pros and cons, for granting greater initiative to the IMF to suggest the need for changes, for using quantitative statistical indicators to create a presumption of the need for change, and even for providing pressures and penalties that could be applied to countries that did not alter their rates when change was found to be necessary. All this constituted a line of thought that received further development in the later stages of the reform discussions.

Another idea that got a first airing in the 1972 report was that of shifting from an intervention system in which all currencies were directly or indirectly pegged to the dollar to one in which intervention was somehow made much more symmetrical. This notion, which I have personally regarded as of crucial importance, comes in two modes; namely: (a) SDR intervention and (b) multicurrency intervention. Under SDR intervention, central banks buy and sell their domestic currencies in exchange for SDRs at a fixed margin around par in transactions with private parties, who are free to transfer the SDRs between central banks. Under multicurrency intervention, the central banks buy and sell each other's currencies in transactions with the foreign-exchange markets at fixed margins around their bilateral parities. Only multicurrency intervention is mentioned in the 1972 report. There it is seen as a way in which the U.S. dollar could have the same effective margins of exchange-rate variation as other currencies; a way in which asset settlement could be reinforced—assuming that all accumulating balances under such a system would be settled promptly in primary assets or third currencies, and a way in which the dollar could float, if the United States were unable to maintain its convertibility, without other currencies also having to float. This scheme had some attractions both for the United States and for the Europeans, who, indeed, were already operating something similar within the EEC.

The elements of the reform program I have outlined so far were not too attractive to the less developed countries. Of course, they stood to gain indirectly from anything that would improve the adjustment process for industrial countries and enable the latter to avoid balance-of-payments difficulties which they might be tempted to relieve by applying restrictions to imports, capital exports, or aid. But the particular techniques suggested were not generally to the less developed countries' taste. Whatever they might do about their own exchange rates, the primary producers did not welcome variability in the relative exchange rates of the principal currencies. Such variability might make it difficult for them to stick to their practice of pegging narrowly on a particular intervention currency and might involve them in competitive uncertainties *vis-à-vis* primary producers pegging on other currencies. Asset settlement threatened to rob the reserve-management system of an expansionary bias to which these countries, quite rationally, had no objection. Schemes for substituting low-yield SDRs for high-yielding currency reserves had no great charm for them either. Consequently, their tendency was to look for some compensating feature of the monetary reform that would be decidedly to their benefit and to make that a condition for their cooperation.

The nature of this compensation was not far to seek. It had to have something to do with improving the flow of real resources from developed to less developed countries, a flow that had for some years been declining as a percentage of world real income. Ever since Stamp mooted the idea in the 1950s, schemes had been current under which international reserve assets, created to meet the world's liquidity needs, could be used for the benefit of less developed countries, thus diverting to the latter the seigniorage which under the gold-exchange standard accrued mainly to the benefit of the United States. Two main forms of a "link" between SDR creation and economic development were mentioned in the 1972 report. Under one of these, SDRs would be allocated to development-finance institutions and used to finance development expenditures on concessionary terms. Under the other, the SDRs that would normally have been allocated to developed countries would be diverted to less developed countries. This began as a highly controversial proposal and was to remain so.

DELIBERATIONS OF THE COMMITTEE OF TWENTY

All of the suggestions contained in the 1972 report were advanced in the most tentative way and garnished with "pros" and "cons." It was clearly necessary, if a reform as many-sided as that under contemplation were to be agreed upon, that the financial authorities of the IMF's member countries, both ministers and senior permanent officials, should first familiarize themselves with the complex and rather esoteric subject under discussion and then make the necessary choices among the various possible arrangements. The reform process therefore moved into a new phase. In July 1972 the governors of the IMF appointed a committee at ministerial level, containing one member and two associates for each of the twenty constituencies that choose an executive director of the IMF, and charged this Committee of Twenty (C-XX) to advise and report on all aspects of reform of the international monetary system. They also set up a committee at deputy level to formulate proposals for approval by the Ministerial Committee. Finally, the chairman and four vice-chairmen of the deputies, sometimes described as the "bureau," formed a high-powered secretariat to draft these proposals for approval by the deputies.

The method of work adopted by the deputies and bureau was one that has seldom been applied in international affairs to such complex and highly technical issues. It was extremely democratic, extremely thorough in its educative effect on the participants, and extremely demanding on the time and energies of all concerned. When the Articles of Agreement of the IMF were hammered out, at and prior to Bretton Woods, it was on the basis of two or three alternative drafts, each elaborated in considerable detail and in self-consistent form by the experts of a major country. On the present occasion, a much more Socratic procedure was adopted. On the basis of general discussion, couched in terms appropriate to the degree of understanding achieved at the time by the senior officials involved, the bureau sought to elicit points of agreement and clarify points of difference on all the manifold and interrelated issues, and to resubmit the results for further general discussion. Very few of the major countries established coherent national positions over the entire range of these issues, and only one of them, the United States, brought out a fairly comprehensive statement of its position. Even that was not comparable in clarity and precision to the Keynes and White plans of former days. The Europeans handicapped themselves by trying to agree issue by issue on a joint EEC position. The less developed countries made great efforts to agree on a common program of reform through the Group of Twenty-Four, but this agreement was inevitably confined to a few isolated matters of common interest, such as the nature of the link between SDR creation and development finance.

Initially, it was hoped that an outline of reform could be presented within a year. This was an unrealistic goal based on a radical underestimate of the complexities of the problem. In fact, it has taken much longer than that, despite the labors of several working groups, for the technical issues to be fully clarified, if indeed they have been fully clarified. This long-drawn-out educational process is not to be regretted. In the first place, it was necessary if countries were to understand what they were getting into. And, secondly, changes that were taking place at breakneck speed in the real world were such as to throw doubt on some of the features of the reform as originally conceived.

The first fruits of these deliberations under the C-XX's auspices were set forth in the first *Outline of Reform* presented to the IMF governors in Nairobi in September 1973. This *Outline*, though prepared by the bureau—the chairman and vice-chairmen of the deputies—without commitment on the part of any government, reflected the stage then reached in the C-XX's discussions. Although the *Outline* did not, save in few particulars, show any great substantive advance on the 1972 report of the executive directors, it gave rather fuller expression to the American point of view, which had by that time been more fully worked out. It also took some account (though less, perhaps, than one might have expected) of the fact that, in the meantime, the provisional Smithsonian system of parities and central rates had broken down; most European currencies, though tied together in the EEC "snake," were floating free of the U.S. dollar; and the pound, the lira, and the yen were floating on their own.

As regards the adjustment process, the main innovations of the outline were as follows. Surveillance of the adjustment process, at least so far as imbalances of international importance are concerned, should be carried out at special meetings of a high-level body in the IMF. In that process, considerable importance would be attached to automatic reserve in-dicators: They would play a role coordinate with the initiative of the Managing Director of the IMF in triggering consultations about a case of imbalance; they would have a major—the North Americans said a presumptive—role in determining the need for adjustment; they might also operate presumptively, or even automatically, in triggering financial pressures on surplus countries in the form of negative interest rates on their excess balances. Despite a certain amount of verbal obscurity, it could be discerned that the type of indicator favored for these purposes related to reserve levels rather than reserve flows. Thus, Robert Triffin's "fork" proposal for relating adjustment action to reserve levels, which, of course, reproduces one aspect of Keynes's clearing union proposal, finds a certain echo here.

Actually, the case for using reserve levels to trigger financial sanctions is much better than the case for using them to indicate the need for adjustment. The imbalances to which they point are past rather than present ones, and to use them to trigger adjustment might set up an oscillatory process. As signals for sanctions, on the other hand, they might cast their shadows before and evoke corrective action at an earlier stage.

The outline is rather vague as to what is meant by adjustment and, indeed, as to what kinds of imbalance adjustment is supposed to correct. The old distinction between fundamental and other disequilibria is nowhere mentioned. The IMF is not given the formal right to recommend a change in exchange rates or, indeed, any specific type of adjustment measure—which may be a genuflexion to national sovereignty but seems to me a backward step. In the sphere of exchange rates proper, the principal innovation of the outline is that, while the par value system is retained, floating rates are now regarded as a legitimate and useful technique "in particular situations" and no longer merely as a temporary or transitional device. Floating rates are, however, to be subject to IMF authorization and surveillance—a subject to which I revert later on.

On the mode of settling payments deficits and surpluses, American attitudes hardened, during the discussions under C-XX auspices, against mandatory asset settlement and in favor of something more like the old system of "on demand" convertibility. The new version differed from the old in that countries of intervention currency could obtain protection, if they wished, against any net conversion of outstanding balances, and countries that had accumulated excessive holdings of primary reserve assets would be denied the right to convert further accruals of reserves. The general tendency of these proposals, as of the proposals about objective reserve indicators, was to bring more adjustment pressure on surplus countries and to leave to the issuers of intervention currencies possibilities of financing their deficits in an informal way through the growth of reserve liabilities over and above any recourse to formal credit facilities. In justice, it should be added that, under multicurrency-intervention arrangements, such flexibility in external financing would be available not merely to traditional reserve centers but to all participants in the multicurrency-intervention scheme, constituting, perhaps, some ten to twenty countries.

By contrast with these views, industrial countries outside North America tended to favor tight asset settlement relieved only by formal credit arrangements under international supervision. Putting it very broadly, one might say that the Europeans favored symmetry of settlement arrangements as betweem reserve centers and others, while the Americans favored symmetry of adjustment pressures as between surplus and deficit countries.

On the matters just discussed, it cannot be said that great progress toward agreement has thus far been made under C-XX auspices. A more hopeful development has been the tendency toward a convergence of view in favor of a more symmetrical intervention system. This was still treated somewhat tentatively in the 1973 *Outline*, but since then a good deal of work has been done on it. Multicurrency intervention is still the preferred technique for achieving symmetry and is generally considered to be feasible technically for the ten to twenty countries that would be likely to participate in it. Other countries would defend their margins around parity by intervening in one or several of the currencies of the multicurrency intervenors. Rules have been suggested to govern the trickier aspects, such as intramarginal intervention and the assets to be used in settlement. I feel that, if par values are ever restored, an attempt will probably be made to go over to such a system.

One of the surprises of recent discussions, however, is the amount of support that has built up among a few European central bankers and the great mass of developing countries in favor of the alternative system of symmetrical intervention, namely, intervention in SDRs. This does not now mean a system in which SDRs are owned and traded by private persons. Central banks would sell for domestic currency, at a fixed margin, promises to deliver SDRs to other central banks, and would buy rights to receive SDRs from other central banks, in deals arranged for a profit through the private market. The arbitrage operations of the market would then keep exchange rates within limits determined by the SDR margins. This scheme charms the central bank technicians because of its resemblance to the gold standard, and attracts the less developed countries because they could participate if they wished on an equal footing with the main industrial countries, which is not the case with multicurrency intervention.

While the idea of using the SDR as an intervention medium is still somewhat new and strange, there has been an encouraging degree of unanimity, at least in theory, that it should become the principal asset of settlement between central banks and, in time, the principal reserve asset of the system. These roles are interconnected. If, as many advocate, the SDR is to be the only mandatory settlement asset, it must be available in large amounts in reserves. The logic of this has helped to reduce the resistance of many to the idea of a substitution facility in which SDRs could be obtained by monetary authorities in exchange for currency reserves.

UNRESOLVED ISSUES

Such progress toward consensus, however, has been slight. Not only are the big issues of asset settlement and automaticity in the adjustment process still unresolved, but there are some problematic areas of crucial importance in the international monetary system where little or no progress has been made in finding solutions. One of these areas concerns the role of gold in reserves. If the SDR is to become the principal reserve asset in the monetary system, gold must be gradually eliminated from it. But, in practice, all the methods for dealing with gold in the *Outline* would involve increasing its value share in world reserves. Even the proposal least favorable to gold would allow central banks to sell it on the market at market prices, thus in present conditions quadrupling the value of gold reserves as compared with the present monetary price. This proposal at least leaves open the possibility that such market sales would bring down the price. Alternative proposals, which would allow central banks to sell gold to each other at market prices, or even buy from the market, would ensure that this did not happen and would make it much more likely that gold, rather than SDRs, would be the growing element in world reserves.

But the real Achilles' heel of the reform discussions lies in yet another area, the failure to generate a sufficiently convincing international program for handling the ever-growing problem of disruptive capital flows or, more generally, of short-term instability in balances of payments under a par value system. This problem was rather thoroughly examined in a working party, and the whole armory of national techniques for dealing with payments imbalances—including capital controls, domestic financial policies, exchange-market techniques, and official financing—was passed in review and evaluated. Some rather novel and interesting techniques, such as dual-exchange markets, were discussed. The usual recommendations about international harmonization of monetary policies, prompt adjustment of par values, and international financing were repeated. But it is difficult to feel that anything short of heroic measures of recycling could make the par value system viable in the presence of such flows, or that anything short of floating rates could check or canalize the flows and thus protect countries' monetary systems from external shocks.

Oddly enough, it was something lying entirely outside the sphere of the international monetary discussions, a sudden and catastrophic change in the price of a major primary commodity, crude oil, that led to an equally sudden decision to bring to a quick conclusion the efforts at achieving international monetary reform under the auspices of the C-XX. Even before the reduction of Arab oil exports and the hoisting of oil prices in December 1973, doubts had been growing regarding the prospects of reaching simultaneous agreement on all of the international aspects of a comprehensive reform, and regarding the realism of an agreement based on the restoration of a par value system in a situation where not even all the EEC countries seemed able to maintain par values among themselves. The inability of the pound sterling and then the lira to stay with or return to the "snake"—an inability, incidentally, in part attributable to steep increases in the prices of foodstuffs and raw materials—tended to intensify these doubts. The shock of oil-price increases that caused current-account shifts of the order of $60–80 billion made it inevitable that floating rates would become still more widespread and would persist for some time to come.

The decision of the C-XX, at its Rome meeting in January 1974, to wind up its operations by the middle of the year did not mean that international monetary reform was to be abandoned, but only that it should be accomplished on a gradual and piecemeal basis and that it should be worked out in a somewhat different forum. The ministerial committee would, in effect, be perpetuated under different names, as the Interim Council and the Council of Governors, with functions no longer confined to reform. But the Committee of Deputies, together with its Bureau of Chairman and Vice-Chairmen, would lapse, and their function in preparing the work of the ministerial body would, in effect, be taken over by the executive directors of the IMF.

It is hoped that the C-XX may be able to agree on certain elements in the ultimate reform by the middle of the year, but it seems doubtful whether consensus can be achieved at this time on anything beyond broad generalities. It may be possible, however, and indeed it is urgently necessary, to make certain practical arrangements—some of them involving legal changes—to deal with the problems of the interim period.[1] One such arrangement has already been authorized in principle by the C-XX and is being worked out by the executive directors, namely, an arrangement for valuing the SDR in terms of a combination of currencies rather than of a single currency, the U.S. dollar. This should give the SDR, and with it the value of positions in the General Account of the IMF, a higher degree of stability than belongs to any single currency in a floating world and should therefore facilitate the use and receipt of SDRs, the use of the resources of the General Account, and possibly the creation of new types of international credit facilities, which are so much required in present circumstances.[2]

The big question now, however, is whether it is going to be possible to work out a way of living with floating rates that would be compatible with the maintenance of international harmony and that, without sacrificing internal prosperity, would preserve a measure of exchange stability and stability in the conditions of international trade and investment. An answer to this question is necessary whether the present state of generalized floating is perpetuated or a par value system of sorts is reestablished, for the latter is likely to mean the establishment of a revolving core of countries maintaining reciprocal parities from which individual countries would float off from time to time as their currencies came under heavy pressure.

The question of guidelines for floating is under consideration both in the C-XX and in the Executive Board. The main issue is whether market intervention should be confined to smoothing of day-to-day and week-to-week fluctuations in exchange rates, and possibly to the moderation of movements lasting over a period of months, or whether intervention designed to resist undue deviations in the rate from a reasonable estimate

[1] The *Outline of Reform*, as adopted in June 1974, indicated, in Part I, the general direction in which the C-XX believed the system might evolve; set forth, in Part II, a number of steps, mostly of an institutional and procedural nature, that the Committee agreed should be taken immediately or on which work should be done; and suggested, in the Annexes, illustrative schemes in various areas of the reform (see "Outline of Reform Supplement," *IMF Survey*, June 17, 1974).

[2] For the precise mode of valuation of the SDR as ultimately adopted, see IMF Press Release No. 73/34 of July 1, 1974, as reproduced in *IMF Survey* for July 8, 1974.

of its medium-term norm should be permitted and even encouraged. A second question concerns the extent to which reserve levels should be used to provide an indicator of the need for the latter type of intervention. A third question concerns the extent to which measures designed to influence capital flows—including fiscal-market intervention, capital restrictions, dual rates, and even monetary policies, insofar as they diverge from those required for internal stability—should be subjected to rules similar to those applying to spot intervention. All this is clearly a very sensitive area in which governments will be loath to tolerate effective surveillance by international organizations; yet, without it, chaotic conditions leading to accusations of antisocial behavior may well arise.[3]

Still further problems loom up behind. Market intervention is carried out entirely in currency. Such intervention affects the value of the intervention currency as well as of the currency of the intervening country. The extension of floating to many members of the EEC has led to a narrowing of the sphere of organized multicurrency intervention and a restoration or intensification of the situation in which the great bulk of the intervention is carried out in dollars. This threatens to perpetuate the asymmetries and the limitations on the freedom of action of the United States, which it was one of the main objects of the reform to remove. Should there be rules of the game relating to which currencies can be bought and which sold in intervention, or should this be left to bilateral haggling? Can there be any rules of this kind without a fairly massive prior substitution of newly created SDRs for existing currency balances?

Then there is the question of world reserve management. If countries can buy any currency they want and sell any currency they have, or even if such intervention is negotiated bilaterally, there can be multiplied expansions and contractions of world reserves beyond international control. Would it be possible to check this by introducing arrangements for asset settlement even under floating? Clearly, this would not be possible if countries were free to buy whichever currencies they desired. Might it become possible if the choice of currencies were regulated?

---

[3] "The Guidelines for the Management of Floating Exchange Rates," as adopted by the Executive Directors of the Fund on June 13, 1974, and endorsed by the C-XX as an arrangement for the present period of widespread floating, are set forth in the *IMF Survey* for June 17, 1974.

It might be objected that all this no longer matters; that under floating rates the world supply of reserves will no longer have to be regulated but will regulate itself; and that, if there are too few reserves, countries will bid up the currency value of existing reserves by buying them and, if there are too many, will reduce their currency value by selling them. But such a system would work satisfactorily only if all reserves consisted of primary reserves—gold or SDRs—that were bought and sold in the market. Otherwise, the supply of real reserves would adjust to demand only at the cost of creating disequilibria between reserve-currency countries and other countries.

CONCLUSION

From what I have said, it should be clear that general resort to floating rates is far from solving all the problems of the international monetary system. The question is whether all of these problems can be solved *ambulando*, one by one, or whether it is still going to be necessary, not only for political reasons but for reasons of economic consistency, to put together at some point a package of mutually complementary reforms? Only the future will tell, but obviously no package can be put together until experience with floating has convinced most people either that a tolerable international order can be worked out on a floating basis or that it is desirable as well as feasible to resume the effort to create a central system of par values, though one containing greater pressures for adjustment and more safety valves for floating than existed under the former system.

In any event, we shall have to wait until the turbulence in the international monetary system dies down somewhat. The attempt to work out a complicated trapeze act while simultaneously shooting Niagara has not proved successful. At every stage in the discussion, reform proposals have lagged behind events and have been quickly outmoded by new events. Perhaps, in time, the pace of change will slacken and it will become possible for thought to catch up with fact and for the experts to devise and the politicians to accept a new order suitable to the new conditions.

17

FLOATING EXCHANGE RATES, ASYMMETRICAL INTERVENTION, AND THE MANAGEMENT OF INTERNATIONAL LIQUIDITY

ECONOMISTS and financial journalists, particularly in the United States and in the United Kingdom, often write as though they believed that the general abandonment of exchange-rate pegging by the major countries in favor of independent floating had solved at a single stroke the difficulties besetting the international monetary system under the par value system.

In truth, however, while some of these difficulties have been overcome or greatly attenuated by the advent of floating, others persist in aggravated form. For example, the complex of problems arising out of asymmetries in the intervention system (involving asymmetries in the adjustment process and difficulties in the management of the world reserve supply)—problems to which the recent effort at international monetary reform[1] was largely addressed—has been rendered in some respects more intractable than ever. It is the contention of this paper that, if these problems are to be solved, some of the proposals for reform of the par value

First published in International Monetary Fund, *Staff Papers*, July 1975.
[1] Meetings of the Committee on Reform of the International Monetary System and Related Issues (Committee of Twenty), a committee of the Board of Governors of the International Monetary Fund, in 1973–74. See the report, *International Monetary Reform: Documents of the Committee of Twenty* (Washington: International Monetary Fund, 1974).

system may have to be resurrected and adapted to the circumstances of floating.[2]

FLOATING AND ADJUSTMENT AMONG NONRESERVE CENTERS

Before embarking on the main theme of this paper, it may be well to consider briefly the bearing of floating exchange rates on the adjustment process as it applies to countries that are not issuers of intervention and reserve currencies.

The exchange rate between any two currencies may be said to be floating if it is not fairly narrowly pegged by market intervention on the part of one or other of the issuers of the currencies involved. A currency may be said to be floating if its value is not pegged to that of any other currency, reserve asset, or composite of currencies. Currencies, like those of countries in the European common margins agreement (the so-called European "snake"), that are pegged reciprocally and exclusively to each other but not to currencies outside the group, may be said to be floating jointly vis-à-vis outside currencies. The type of floating under discussion in this paper is not, however, "clean" or "free" floating, but "managed" floating, in which the value of the currency, though not closely pegged, is, nevertheless, influenced in one direction or another by market intervention on the part of the issuing country and/or by other policies of the country directed toward that end. At the present time all floating currencies are managed to a greater or lesser extent, though in some cases (e.g., that of the U.S. dollar and the European "snake" currencies regarded collectively) the degree of management is very slight.

The replacement of a regime of par values by one of managed floating in this sense tends to improve the adjustment process by making it easier for a country to move its exchange rate if it wishes (or permit it to move) in such a way as to maintain medium-term equilibrium in its balance of payments since the country is not hampered by prestige-involving expectations that it will maintain fixity in the rate. It also enables a country to cope with temporary and reversible capital flows, which might other-

---

[2] The present paper represents in certain respects a development of some of the ideas referred to in John Williamson, "Increased Flexibility and International Liquidity" (not yet published).

wise endanger its control over its domestic money supply, by allowing the exchange rate to fluctuate over a relatively wide range.

On the other hand, floating puts no greater pressure than does the par value system on countries that are reluctant to make desirable adjustments, and it removes one safeguard that the par value system offered against inappropriate changes in exchange rates, brought about by the authorities of the country in question—namely, the necessity of obtaining IMF concurrence in any devaluation or revaluation. Moreover, there is a possibility that floating exchange rates—even, and perhaps especially, if they are allowed to vary freely in response to market forces—may fluctuate to an extent that is unduly damaging to stability in the foreign trade industries and possibly also unduly inflationary in its net effect on prices.

It is with these weaknesses in the regime of floating rates that the Guidelines for the Management of Floating Exchange Rates, recently adopted by the IMF,[3] are intended to deal. These guidelines are reproduced, for convenience of reference, in the Appendix to this paper.

The intention of guideline (2), in conjunction with guideline (3)(a), is to prevent countries from actively moving their exchange rate—as distinct from resisting market tendencies—except in the direction of the medium-term norm. The intent of guideline (3)(b) is to encourage countries to yield to market pressures that tend to move the rate in the direction of the norm and to resist tendencies that cause the rate to diverge unduly from it. The intention of guideline (4) is to urge countries to take account in their intervention policies of the level of their reserves, so as to discourage undue reserve accumulation or reduction.

These guidelines, taken together, should help to prevent competitive depreciation or appreciation and to promote—though they do not ensure—appropriate adjustments of exchange rates. Guideline (3)(b) should also do something to prevent excessive swings in rates. Appropriate exchange adjustment can be further promoted, under floating rates as under par values, by rules prohibiting the use of measures that tend to bring about maladjustment or inappropriate types of adjustment. An

---

[3] The guidelines were adopted by Executive Board Decision No. 4232–(74/67), June 13, 1974. See *Selected Decisions of the International Monetary Fund and Selected Documents, Seventh Issue* (Washington: International Monetary Fund, January 1, 1975), pp. 21–26. Also see *IMF Survey*, vol. 3, no. 12, June 17, 1974, pp. 181–83; *Annual Report of the Executive Directors for the Fiscal Year Ended April 30, 1974*, Appendix II, J, pp. 112–16; and *International Monetary Reform*, pp. 34–36.

example of this is provided by guideline (5), which is directed against the use of restrictions on current transactions or payments.

ASYMMETRY AND RESERVE CONTROL UNDER THE PAR VALUE SYSTEM

Some of the principal problems of the par value system as it existed up to 1971 arose out of the degree of asymmetry with which it operated between the issuer of the principal reserve and intervention currency and other countries. On the one hand, the United States was hampered in dealing with short-term and cyclical fluctuations in its balance of payments by the fact that the potential range of fluctuation of the dollar around parity vis-à-vis other currencies was only half the range open to other countries. It was also hampered in adjusting to fundamental disequilibrium by the likelihood that, even if it were to suspend convertibility, intervention by other countries would limit the freedom of the dollar to float in search of a new and viable parity. On the other hand, as a byproduct of the intervention system even under convertibility, U.S. deficits tended to be financed in large part through an accumulation of official dollar claims, and this relieved the United States of the pressure, to which any other country would have been subjected, to devalue its currency, or otherwise adjust, when in balance of payments deficit. Moreover, to an extent that is a matter of dispute, the role of the U.S. dollar as the central intervention and reserve currency may have made it more difficult for the United States to change its par value without provoking corresponding changes by other countries.

Finally, the asymmetrical character of the intervention system, taken in conjunction with the system of currency convertibility at the discretion of the holder, made the supply of foreign-exchange reserves in the world a function of the payments imbalance of the principal reserve center and may have made it more difficult to attain the objective for which the special drawing account of the IMF had been set up (that of achieving a rational control over the world's reserve supply). However, the main responsibility for this lay with the practice of holding foreign exchange in reserves as such and with the irregularity of conversion and settlement arrangements; if asymmetry made matters worse, it was probably through its tendency to accentuate the payments imbalances of reserve centers.

A very large part of the effort from 1972 onward to reform the international monetary system was devoted to this complex of problems. Two main solutions were advanced, but the reform effort ended without agreement on these:[4]

1. The adoption by the principal countries of a multicurrency intervention system under which the U.S. dollar would have the same margin of fluctuation as other currencies, and from which, if the United States were forced to suspend convertibility, the U.S. dollar, like other currencies, would be free to float without being hampered by intervention on the part of countries other than the issuer.
2. The adoption of a system of settlement under which reserve centers like other countries, would settle deficits and surpluses in the main through variations in their reserve asset holdings and not through variations in their liabilities, thus preventing unplanned variations in the aggregate supply of foreign exchange reserves.

In addition, it was suggested that a substitution facility be created in the IMF, from which countries could obtain newly created SDRs in exchange for foreign currency, and to which reserve centers could in certain circumstances sell and from which they could redeem their own liabilities against SDRs. (This was advocated as essential to the implementation of these solutions.)

The question arises as to whether problems of asymmetry and reserve control persist under conditions of generalized floating and, if so, whether they can be solved without resort to devices analogous to those described above.

ASYMMETRY UNDER FLOATING RATES

As floating has spread, there has been little, if any, decline in the asymmetry of intervention arrangements in the world. The abandonment of convertibility by the United States, which signaled a desire that the dollar should float and stimulated floating by other countries, at first strengthened multicurrency intervention in Europe, but the victories of independent floating in 1972 and 1973 involved the abandonment of these

[4] For a description and analysis of these proposals, see J. Marcus Fleming, *Reflections on the International Monetary Reform*, Essays in International Finance, no. 107 (Princeton, N.J.: Princeton University Press, December 1974).

arrangements by one participant after another and led to a recrudescence of dollar intervention by the floating countries. Although some of the countries customarily pegging their currencies to the U.S. dollar may have been induced by the events of 1971–74 to diversify their reserves and intervention practices, this effect has been offset by a shift into dollars on the part of sterling-area countries.

This persistent asymmetry is likely to be at least as damaging to the exchange-rate autonomy of the United States under floating rates as it was under par values. Admittedly, the fact that the issuers of the other main currencies do not in practice intervene as promptly to limit fluctuations in their own dollar-exchange rates as they would have done under par values gives somewhat greater freedom for the dollar to move in the direction indicated by market forces. However, it is no longer possible, as it was under the par value system, for the United States to achieve a change in its effective exchange rates by formal devaluation. Moreover, the value of the dollar is much more responsive than under that system to the balance of purchases and sales of dollars by other monetary authorities undertaken in the light of their own situations. Thus, if countries that peg closely to the dollar happen to have deficits (surpluses) while other countries allow their currencies to float more freely, the value of the dollar may fall (rise) for reasons that have nothing to do with the U.S. balance of payments as such. Again, if important countries, for reasons of anti-inflationary policy, welcome the appreciation of their currencies, the dollar may be allowed to decline too much in the market. But if changing domestic conditions in these countries should make competitive depreciation appear advantageous, the dollar might be forced into an overvalued position very much more quickly and easily than would have been the case under par values.

It is possible, however, to exaggerate the problems arising out of this asymmetry. In the first place, these problems arise only to the extent that countries seek to influence their exchange rates through market intervention. If a country intervenes on the exchange market in order to raise or lower the value of its currency, it may alter the value of the intervention currency vis-a-vis third currencies, whereas if it uses a capital-flow-deflecting policy (such as monetary policy or capital restrictions) for the same purpose the effect is diffused over a much wider range of currencies and the value of the intervention currency vis-à-vis third currencies need not be affected. Moreover, the United States itself can use such policies to influence the value of the dollar.

Guidelines for floating may also help to mitigate the effects of asymmetry of intervention. As a general rule, the more that other countries conform to the guidelines in conducting their intervention policies, the more appropriate the movements in the value of the currencies of intervention will tend to be. Indeed, if only one intervention currency existed, and if the effective exchange rates of all the other currencies were appropriately adjusted to consistent balance of payments targets, the effective rate of the single intervention currency would likewise be entirely appropriate.

From some points of view, the fact that the U.S. dollar—the principal intervention currency—is no longer officially convertible into primary reserve assets may be regarded as yet another factor making asymmetry more tolerable. Dollar inconvertibility may somewhat reduce the temptation for other countries to buy dollars in intervention and thus bid up its value. And even when it does not have this effect and the dollar experiences some overvaluation, at least the United States does not suffer a loss of reserves. On the other hand, as is seen later, this very inconvertibility may have unfortunate consequences for the world supply of reserves.

MEANS OF DEALING WITH ASYMMETRY UNDER FLOATING RATES

Three ways of dealing with the problem of asymmetry are considered below: unilateral intervention by the reserve center, bilateral agreements on intervention, and multilateral regulation of the choice of intervention currencies.

Intervention by the United States

Thus far, it has been assumed, as an expository device, that the United States, as issuer of the main intervention currency, would not itself intervene on exchange markets. But, of course, the United States is as much entitled to intervene as any other country, and indeed has done so. Such intervention, however—unlike that of the issuers of secondary intervention currencies, such as the United Kingdom and France, which intervene on a substantial scale in dollars—has thus far been on a relatively small scale. Moreover, it has been of a very short term and—insofar as it has been conducted with currencies obtained under swap arrangements—of a quickly reversible character. Intervention by the United States, to a much greater extent than that of subsidiary reserve centers, has been of a bilaterally coordinated type, but in this section we consider the possibilities (and difficulties) of unilateral intervention.

Intervention by the issuer of intervention currencies is subject, like that of other countries, to the guidelines for floating. In this connection a preliminary question of definition arises as to whether intervention should be measured in terms of the movement of gross or of net reserves.

The case for guideline (2) rests on the theory that intervention should neither exaggerate nor thwart the influence of market forces on the rate of exchange. If variations in official holdings of foreign currencies are regarded as outside the concept of market forces—and, indeed, as primarily compensatory to such forces—there is a logical case for defining intervention by a country in terms of the change in its reserves net of liabilities to foreign monetary authorities. In that case, it would be compatible with guideline (2) for the United States to acquire gross reserves (for dollars) even when the dollar was falling in value, if other countries were simultaneously buying dollars in larger amounts, or for the United States to use reserves to buy dollars even when the dollar was rising, if other countries were selling dollars in larger amounts. However, this process would have the disadvantage that, in order to comply with guideline (2), when the dollar was falling, the United States would have to buy at least as many dollars as other countries were selling, and when the dollar was rising, it would have to sell at least as many dollars as other countries were buying. Since it would clearly be burdensome on the United States to be obliged to offset the dollar interventions of other countries, it would seem preferable to define intervention for reserve centers as for other countries, in terms of gross reserve changes adjusted for compensatory official transactions—thus treating movements of other countries' holdings of a country's currency, other than those attributable to official borrowing, as analogous, from the standpoint of the latter country, to movements of private capital.

Even with this definition of intervention, it is still possible for the United States, conformably with guidelines (2) and (3), to resist, to a greater or lesser extent, movements in the dollar's effective rate, including movements that result from the intervention of other countries, particularly if these are carrying the rate away from any reasonable estimate of the medium-term norm. In that event it would also be free to overcompensate market tendencies and the effects of intervention by others by action that brings the rate closer to the norm.

There are, however, considerable difficulties in large-scale intervention by the United States, some of which apply to intervention by subsidiary reserve centers, while some do not.

1. Insofar as reserve centers tend to buy (sell) other currencies in intervention when their own currencies are bought (sold) in intervention, variations will take place in the supply of reserves. This problem, which concerns intervention by all reserve centers, large or small, are considered in a later section.

2. While subsidiary reserve centers, such as the United Kingdom, for the most part conduct their intervention in dollars, for which a very broad exchange market exists, the United States, if it has to intervene, must do so in currencies for which the market is much narrower, so that any U.S. intervention would be likely to have a greater effect on the value of the currency used than on that of the dollar, relative to currencies in general. This means, at least, that any substantial U.S. intervention, unless it happens to be in a direction welcome to the issuer of the currency used, would have to be divided among a number of currencies. Even if this were done, the countries affected might not welcome such an intervention whenever it appeared desirable to the United States from the standpoint of dollar management, especially as some of these countries are not accustomed to having their currencies used for intervention purposes.

3. While subsidiary reserve centers intervene in currencies other than those of the countries that normally intervene in their currencies, the United States would have to intervene in the currencies of countries accustomed to intervene in dollars. Such mutual intervention, unless somehow regulated, is likely to give rise to frictions. Even in the most favorable conditions, when both parties wish to intervene in the same direction—that is, both wish to buy dollars for the other currency or to buy the other currency for dollars—differences of opinion might arise as to how large the total intervention should be

or as to how it should be shared between the countries. Much more unfortunate would be a situation in which the two parties intervened at cross purposes, in a mutually offsetting way. This situation could occur without malice on the part of either country if both the United States and the other country considered its own currency to be undervalued or overvalued, as the case might be, if the other country regularly intervened in the dollar, and if the United States had no criterion but convenience of choice of its currencies for counter-intervention. Even so, there would clearly be a danger that disputes would arise.

Bilateral Agreement

One approach to the solution of these problems is to require that intervening countries arrive at agreements with the issuers of intervention currencies regarding the use of these currencies in intervention. The Ministers of the Group of Ten came close to adopting this approach in their meeting of March 16, 1973, at which each nation stated that it would be prepared to intervene at its own initiative in its own market in close consultation with the countries whose currencies were being traded. The United States appears to have followed this practice in the fairly moderate interventions which it has undertaken from time to time. Guideline (6) goes a little further by suggesting, though not prescribing, that mutually satisfactory arrangements be agreed between the issuers and users of intervention currencies with respect to the use of such currencies in intervention.

The problem is, however, how such arrangements are to be made mutually satisfactory. In particular, how can customary reserve centers be protected against interventions that lead to undesirable movements in their rates without depriving customary users of their currency of the ability to stabilize their own rates, when issuers of other currencies either do not wish them to be used or wish to be in a position to control each use? Guideline (6) says that such arrangements should be compatible with the purposes of the other guidelines. This protects the right of customary users of the main intervention currencies but might not do much to protect the interests of the reserve centers even if the latter were to seek to act as judges and enforcers of the observance of guidelines (1) to (4) by other countries, an attitude bound to lead to disputes.

All intervenors are adjured in guideline (6) to bear in mind the interests of the countries issuing reserve currencies—interests that, in the commentary to the guidelines, are stated to include their need for reasonable freedom of exchange-rate movement. The question is how the intervenors are to do this without impairing their rights of intervention in circumstances where countries other than reserve centers are reluctant to allow their own currencies to be used for this purpose. A system in which all countries had the right to control the use of their currencies in intervention, and exercised that right with respect to each use, would clearly be unduly restrictive of desirable intervention.

Guideline (6) envisages that the IMF would assist in resolving disputes in connection with arrangements between users and issuers of intervention currencies, and the commentary suggests that such disputes may arise with respect to intervention in noncustomary reserve currencies, interventions that move the value of an intervention currency in an undesirable direction, and mutually offsetting interventions. This comment represents an implicit acknowledgment that such difficulties and problems are un-unlikely to be entirely resolved on the basis of purely bilateral arrangements without the working out of more general principles to which such arrangements would conform.

Guidelines for the Choice of Intervention Currencies

At this moment there is neither an accepted doctrine governing the choice of currencies to be bought and sold in intervention nor a mechanism for making that choice effective. In Annex 4 of the *Outline of Reform*,[5] which was based on the assumption that par values would be the rule and floating the exception, it was proposed that (*a*) a floating country should normally buy the "weakest" and sell the "strongest" of the currencies among which it had an effective choice and (*b*) other countries should not normally intervene in a floating currency without the agreement of the issuer.[5] As regards "effective choice," there is some ambiguity in the *Outline* as to the extent to which countries other than members of a multicurrency intervention system would be entitled to choose, among

---

[5] The *Outline of Reform* was prepared by the Committee of the Board of Governors on Reform of the International Monetary System and Related Issues (Committee of Twenty) and was made public on June 14, 1974. It appears in *International Monetary Reform*, pp. 7–48. Annex 4 appears on pages 33–37.

nonfloating currencies, their preferred intervention currency; they must consult the issuer about this choice, but they are entitled to have appropriate intervention facilities made available to them.[6] Since intervention would normally be carried out in currencies with a par value, there is no ambiguity as to what is meant by the "strongest" and by the "weakest" of the available currencies—strength and weakness would be measured by the position of market rates relative to parities. Since it is assumed that many countries whose currencies could serve as intervention currencies would be observing par values, countries whose currencies happened to be currently floating would be entitled to deny the use of their currencies for this purpose, except possibly to countries that "regularly" intervene in their currencies, in which case some suitable arrangement should be worked out.[7]

When all the principal currencies are floating, the provision of the *Outline* according to which floating currencies can be used only for intervention with the consent of the issuer cannot apply without qualification; as already noted, guideline (6) does not attempt so to apply it. It would seem desirable in these circumstances to establish under guideline (6) a set of arrangements that would enable each country to intervene in a variety of currencies, provided that in choosing the currency to use on each occasion the country would follow some generally accepted principles or rules. Is it possible to devise a system governing the appropriate choice of intervention currencies that would be applicable in such circumstances? Prima facie, the principle governing such choice of currencies should be that of reinforcing the action that the issuers of the currencies should themselves be taking under the guidelines. The elaboration of this principle, however, is not without difficulties. Guidelines (2) to (4) attempt to blend in a particular way three separate criteria: the "moderation" criterion of guideline (2), the "normal rate" criterion of guideline (3), and the "normal reserve" criterion of guideline (4). In certain circumstances, as described in guideline (4), the moderating intervention of guideline (2), modified by the reserve criterion, is supposed to operate; in other circumstances, the normal rate criterion of guideline (3), again modified by the reserve criterion, takes over.

---

[6] *International Monetary Reform*, Annex 3, pars. 7–8, p. 32.
[7] *International Monetary Reform*, Annex 4, Section C, p. 37.

Now, it is difficult to conceive of choosing intervention currencies on the basis of guideline (2), even as modified by guideline (4). This would require the intervening country to buy on the market currencies whose market value was falling (unless their issuers had abnormally low reserves) and to sell on the market currencies whose market value was rising (unless their issuers had abnormally high reserves). Moderating intervention ("leaning against the wind") may be a costly business, and countries can hardly be expected to share in the cost of moderating the movements in other countries' currencies, as they would presumably have to do in the absence of immediate asset settlement (see below). Any system governing the choice of intervention currencies would therefore probably be based on the normal rate principle of guideline (3) as modified by reserve considerations of guideline (4). In other words, intervening countries would be permitted and encouraged to buy, in exchange for their own, currencies that were considered to be undervalued and to sell those considered to be overvalued relative to their medium-term norms.[8]

Even this criterion raises problems of implementation, only some of which can be mentioned here. There is a general resemblance between the overvaluation–undervaluation criterion offered here and the strong-currency–weak-currency criterion suggested in the *Outline* and referred to above. In the *Outline*, where the assumption is that intervention currencies are observing par values, it is understood that the "strength" or "weakness" of a currency relates to its market value relative to parity—a rather precisely defined concept. Here, however, where the intervention currencies are assumed to be floating, overvaluation or undervaluation relates to the much vaguer concept of market value relative to a "normal zone," the width of which may vary from country to country and that may not be universally recognized as such. There is the question of who is to be the judge of overvaluation and undervaluation: the issuing country, the intervening country, or the IMF; and the question of how such judgments would be arrived at. It would clearly simplify matters if countries generally followed the procedure of guideline (3)(a) and agreed at all times with the IMF on a target or normal zone for their effective exchange rates. Failing this, any such judgments would have to be implicit in any guidance

---

[8] Both the market value and the norm of a currency are expressed in terms of its effective exchange rate, that is, some average of its exchange rates.

that might be given by the IMF, under guideline (6) or otherwise, as to which currencies would be appropriate to use for intervention.

Apart from the problem of identifying the most overvalued and the most undervalued currencies, there is the problem of ensuring that the amount of intervention that takes place in particular currencies is adapted to the capacity of the market and does not lead to excessive rate movements. This requires that the flow of net intervention be proportioned to the capacities of different markets and that large interventions by particular countries be divided among different currencies. For the IMF to carry out successfully the function of guiding the countries' choices of intervention currencies would require that it maintain close consultation with the issuers of the currencies to be recommended for use. Issuing countries might sometimes desire that their currencies be bought or sold in intervention, thus supporting or depressing their exchange rates, without wishing to intervene themselves, and their wishes could be taken into account by the IMF in its recommendations to intervening countries.

Thus far it has been assumed that a country can always obtain the currency or currencies appropriate for it to sell on the market when it wishes to support its own currency. But, of course, a country in this position may not currently possess the currency it is supposed to sell, and the problem then is how to obtain this currency. If the country were to buy it on the market by selling, say, a currency held in its reserves, it would, in effect, be bringing downward pressure on the market value of the reserve currency, and not on that of the appropriate intervention currency. What is required is some technique whereby supplies of appropriate intervention currencies can be obtained otherwise than through the market. One way might be through the use of swaps that are subsequently settled in primary reserve assets (gold or SDRs); another might be through direct purchase with primary reserve assets. But there is at present no obligation on countries to provide currency in exchange for gold (even at market price), and while countries are obliged to accept SDRs in designation, they are free to provide any currency convertible in fact and are not obliged to provide the particular currency required for intervention, even if it should be their own currency. Moreover, the criteria presently used in designating countries to receive SDRs pay no regard to the overvaluation or undervaluation of their currencies. There might, therefore, be a need for a new or additional system of designation geared to the needs of the intervention problem, operating under rules that differ from those set forth in Article XXV, Section 5(*b*) and Schedule F.[9]

A system of guided intervention of the type described above would require countries to be willing to acquire in intervention reserve currencies that are unfamiliar and that possibly cannot be appropriately sold when the time comes for the country to support its own currency. Again, in order that countries may be able to sell the appropriate currencies in intervention, it is necessary that they possess or have access to a sufficient supply of primary reserve assets to enable them to obtain these currencies through designation. For both of these reasons it would probably be necessary to the success of the system that any currencies that countries hold or acquire should be convertible into SDRs. In order to avoid undue pressure on the reserves of traditional reserve centers, such conversion would have to be carried out by, or with the aid of, a substitution account of the type mentioned in paragraph 22 and described in Annex 7 of the *Outline of Reform*.[10] Such an account would have to be prepared to acquire, in exchange for SDRs created for the purpose, not only traditional reserve currencies but also other currencies used in intervention. The problems which convertibility raises for the issuing countries are considered more fully in the following section.

The system of guidance described here has the advantage over un-trammeled intervention by the reserve center of avoiding any danger of countries intervening at cross purposes in each other's currencies. It has the advantage over intervention under bilateral agreement of ensuring that countries are not frustrated in their desire to stabilize their own exchange rates. And it probably has the advantage over both of these alternatives in the extent to which it achieves the purposes of the guidelines for floating exchange rates. It does, however, have some tendency to increase the amount of stabilizing intervention that takes place in any currency beyond what the issuer might have desired; those who wish to intervene can always do so, but those who do not wish their currencies to be used for intervention may be unable to prevent it. It might, however, prove possible to counteract this bias to some extent through requirements to consult issuing countries and other procedural guidance.

[9] *Articles of Agreement of the International Monetary Fund* (Washington, D.C., International Monetary Fund, n.d.), pp. 60 and 84.
[10] *International Monetary Reform*, pp. 14 and 41–42.

ASSET SETTLEMENT AND THE MANAGEMENT OF INTERNATIONAL LIQUIDITY

One of the main weaknesses of the par value system as it operated in the past, with official reserves held in large part in the form of foreign exchange convertible on demand, was that it made the supply of world reserves a by-product of (a) disequilibria in the balance of payments between reserve countries and nonreserve countries, and between countries with different marginal propensities to hold foreign exchange in reserves and (b) variations in the relative attractiveness of holding reserves in the form of foreign exchange and gold, respectively.

Under a system of managed floating without convertibility, variations in the holding of foreign exchange reserves as a result of (b) would be reduced if not completely eliminated. As regards (a), such reduction is more doubtful. If the issuers of intervention and reserve currencies themselves refrained from intervention, and if exchange rates were allowed to respond more flexibly to short-term balance of payments disequilibria than they could under the par value system, the volume of intervention by countries with independently floating currencies would probably be reduced. However, as Williamson has pointed out,[11] the extent of such reduction may not be great and the volume of intervention by countries whose currencies are pegged to particular floating currencies might well increase. This has implications not only for the demand and need for reserves but also for the stability of their supply. The greater the use of reserves—presently almost exclusively a use of foreign exchange reserves—the greater are likely to be the variations in the net aggregate official purchases or sales of currency and hence in the world reserve stock. Moreover, if countries with floating currencies were to make use of their ability to intervene on the exchange market to bring about a chronic undervaluation of their currencies relative to the U.S. dollar (and this was argued above to be a potential danger), they might accumulate at least as many reserves as under a par value system.[12]

---

[11] John Williamson, "Exchange Rate Flexibility and Reserve Use" (unpublished, International Monetary Fund, August 29, 1974).

[12] Effective world reserves may rise or fall on a massive scale as a result of the accumulation of surpluses by the oil-producing countries, but these appear to be invariant with respect to the exchange-rate system.

To the extent that competitive depreciation was reduced by the observance of guidelines for floating, the chronic accumulation of reserves in the form of foreign exchange would likewise be diminished. However, if the same result were achieved through counterintervention by the reserve centers, the *gross* accumulation of currency holdings might be even further increased. Moreover, temporary inequalities between the accumulation of reserve currency holdings by countries with a strong payments position and their reduction by countries with a weak one would tend to evoke a corresponding accumulation or reduction of other currencies by the reserve countries, and thus lead to magnified variations in total holdings of foreign exchange. This magnification both of chronic reserve accumulation and of reserve variation through counterintervention could be avoided by the adoption of a system governing the choice of intervention currencies, such as has been described toward the end of the preceding section. In general, the observance of guidelines for floating, including those for the choice of intervention currencies, would minimize the amount of uncontrolled variation in the supply of reserves; however, it would not eliminate such variation.

In the reform discussions, the most effective remedy advanced for the purpose of preventing undesired variations in the supply of foreign exchange reserves and of ensuring effective management of the global reserve supply was some form of systematic and regular asset settlement, whether applied through bilateral presentation of currency accruals by the holders to the issuers for conversion or, preferably, through collective settlements between the issuers and a substitution account in the IMF.[13] Under managed floating also, asset settlement remains the only device through which any precise international control over the supply of reserves could be achieved.[14]

It is often assumed that asset settlement and floating are mutually exclusive, but this is a mistake. While readiness on the part of the issuer of a currency to convert it into some primary reserve asset or other currency *at a fixed rate of exchange* might well suffice to peg the value of the

[13] For the modus operandi of an asset settlement, see the *Outline of Reform*, Annex 5, Section A, in *International Monetary Reform*, p. 38.

[14] The possibility that under a system of generalized floating the autonomous variations in the supply of reserves would be of so benign a character that no international control over their supply would be necessary is considered in the following section.

former even without active intervention on the exchange market, convertibility *at rates determined by the conventional value of the primary reserve asset and the market value of the currency* would not, of itself, interfere with floating. It is this second type of convertibility that is in question here, and asset settlement of deficits and surpluses at market-determined rates is all that is required to prevent variations in the supply of currency reserves and to permit international control through SDR allocation over the supply of reserves.

Asset settlement calls for a regulated amount of conversion by the issuing country. Given a strict asset-settlement system, it makes no difference either to the reserve position of the issuing country or to the amount, as distinct from the composition, of the reserves of other countries whether or not holders of currency reserves can convert them into primary reserves at will, even if such conversion is carried out by presentation to the issuers rather than to a substitution account. Any variations in the primary reserves of the issuer resulting from variations in the amounts converted by holding countries will be made good to the issuer through its settlements with the substitution account. In view of this, and since, as indicated above, it would facilitate the choice of appropriate intervention currencies, it would seem desirable that asset settlement be accompanied by freedom for countries to convert their currency holdings at will.

There would be obvious difficulties about introducing asset settlement in a situation of generalized floating so long as counterintervention by issuers of reserve currencies was not regarded as normal and no effective rules governed the choice of intervention currencies. The harm done to the issuer of an intervention currency that was bid up to an overvalued level by the intervention of others would be greater and more difficult to endure if that country were not merely forced to accumulate indebtedness and possibly suffer unemployment through foreign competition but were actually drained of its reserves, thus losing its power to protect itself against a subsequent possible depreciation. Asset settlement might be less unwelcome to a reserve center that practiced counterintervention since, as it accumulated claims against other countries to balance other countries' claims against it, the former would be canceled against the latter, thus reducing or eliminating any net loss of reserves. However, the dangers of conflict associated with the acquisition of mutual claims might be intensified if the claims so acquired had to be mutually canceled, however desirable such action might be from the standpoint of world reserve management.

The conditions under which asset settlement would be least burdensome for issuers of intervention currency would probably be those in which intervention was subject to international guidance of the type described in the preceding section. The issuers could be assured that their currencies would be bought by other countries only when they were considered to be undervalued, at which time they might themselves be contemplating intervention in support of their currencies. One should not, however, underrate the difficulties of inducing countries to accept asset settlement under conditions of floating. A country that is obliged to spend reserves to redeem its currency that other countries have bought in intervention is, in effect, being forced to intervene in support of its own currency; similarly, a country that is designated to receive SDRs in exchange for its own currency, which is then sold on the market is, in effect, being forced to intervene to hold down the value of its currency. There is, of course, a natural limit to the extent to which asset settlement can be carried; if a country did not have sufficient reserves to finance the asset settlement of the deficits that would be imposed upon it if other countries purchased its currency, it would be entitled to refuse settlement—and, if it did refuse, its currency might be removed from the list of those suitable for purchase in intervention, although the currency might still be undervalued.

SELF-REGULATION OF RESERVE SUPPLY UNDER CONDITIONS OF GENERALIZED FLOATING

Granted that floating, even if managed on acceptable lines, is likely to involve substantial variation in holdings of currency reserves, which, in turn, could impede the successful control of the quantity of world reserves through SDR allocation, the question arises as to whether the supply of reserves resulting from the operation of the floating system would not automatically adapt itself to the need for reserves, thus making SDR allocation unnecessary. Quite a strong case can be made for this thesis.

If all countries had floating currencies, if all exercised their rights to intervene on exchange markets, and if the level of reserves were the only criterion determining the amount and direction of their intervention, then each would soon attain its desired level of reserves in the form of foreign currency. This would mean clearly that reserves were acquired either for their own sake or for the income they might yield, but in fact they are also acquired for potential use, which involves intervention for purposes other than attaining or retaining a desired level of reserves. Even under floating rates, exchange market intervention in the short to medium term is governed by considerations relating to the stability and level of exchange rates, including attitudes toward competitive undervaluation and disinflationary overvaluation. These considerations not only dominate intervention in the short run but also may impede or delay progress toward the attainment of the level or trend-path of reserves around which countries would wish their reserves to fluctuate.

Adherence to guidelines (1) to (3), with their concern about exchange-rate tendencies and levels, might impose a slight further obstacle to the rapid attainment of countries' desired reserve targets, although guideline (4) might actually facilitate such attainment.

A system of complete freedom in the choice of intervention currencies would probably impede the attainment of desired reserve levels since, as has been pointed out above, concern about exchange rates could lead in the short run to multiplied expansions and contractions in reserve holdings, including substantial variation in the mutual holding of balances by pairs of countries. In such a situation countries would tend to lose sight of reserve targets or become uncertain about them. A system in which the use of intervention currencies was tightly controlled by the issuing countries would tend to hamper intervention and thus the attainment of desired reserve levels in another way. Probably international guidance of the choice of intervention currency would be most favorable of all to the attainment of desired reserve levels.

After all of the qualifications have been noted, it must be admitted that in a regime of generalized floating, even of a highly managed variety, the amount of reserves held would probably tend to approximate much more closely and continuously the amount that countries desired to hold than it would in a par value system. Some would conclude that this would make the reserve system more nearly self-regulating and would make the need for SDR allocations less. However, it should be borne in mind, as the author has argued in previous publications,[15] that the optimal level of world reserves is not necessarily identical with the sum of the reserves demanded by countries.

Finally, lest the argument be misapplied to the present situation, it should be noted that the currencies of the great majority of countries are not floating independently but are pegged to other currencies and that the reserves of such countries are no more under their control than they were in the heyday of the par value system.

CONCLUSIONS

The foregoing argument has followed a somewhat meandering course with many feedbacks and interrelationships among its phases. Let us try to set it forth in broad outline. It has been argued that in a system of widespread managed floating, as in a par value system with occasional floating, there is a problem of asymmetry of adjustment between the issuers of the principal intervention currencies and other countries, as well as a problem of ensuring an effective international management of reserves. If the latter problem is less acute under a floating system, the former problem is potentially more acute than it would be under a par value system.

It is argued that under floating rates as under par values, the best solutions for these problems involve a combination of three elements: organized multicurrency intervention, asset settlement, and an SDR substitution account. A development of the system of SDR designation would also be required.

Although widespread floating would appear to offer no particular obstacle to the operation of a substitution account, its effect on the acceptability of asset settlement is debatable, and it would add considerably to the difficulties of organizing multicurrency intervention. Insofar as the arrangements for floating, including observance by other countries of the existing guidelines for the management of floating rates and the proposed guidance for the choice of intervention currencies, gave assurance to

---

[15] See, for example, J. Marcus Fleming, *Essays in International Economics* (London: Allen and Unwin, 1971), pp. 95–101 and 190–91.

reserve centers that they were unlikely to be in payments deficit unless their currencies were genuinely undervalued, asset settlement should be easier to accept under floating than under fixed rates; but the fact that these deficits were to some extent imposed by the intervention decisions of other countries might work in the opposite direction.

The peculiar difficulty of organizing multicurrency intervention under a floating rate system arises from the absence of clear, precise, and agreed criteria as to which currencies should be bought and sold in intervention and in what quantities they should be bought and sold. Under a par value system, these criteria are supplied by the fixed margins around known exchange-rate parities; under floating rates they would necessarily involve some exercise of judgment by an international body in consultation with the countries concerned.

If it is politically acceptable, a system of guided intervention oriented to an established system of normal exchange-rate zones would probably be superior to any other arrangement under floating for the purpose of promoting symmetry in adjustment while permitting an adequate degree of exchange-rate management and avoiding the anomaly of mutually offsetting intervention. It could be achieved, if at all, only as a result of a gradual evolution, which is unlikely to get seriously under way as long as countries nurse the hope of returning, someday, to a par value system.

APPENDIX

Guidelines for the Management of Floating Exchange Rates

(1) A member with a floating exchange rate should intervene on the foreign exchange market as necessary to prevent or moderate sharp and disruptive fluctuations from day to day and from week to week in the exchange value of its currency.

(2) Subject to (3) (b), a member with a floating rate may act, through intervention or otherwise, to moderate movements in the exchange value of its currency from month to month and quarter to quarter, and is encouraged to do so, if necessary, where factors recognized to be temporary are at work. Subject to (1) and (3)(a), the member should not normally act aggressively with respect to the exchange value of its currency (i.e., should not so act as to depress that value when it is falling, or to enhance that value when it is rising).

(3) (a) If a member with a floating rate should desire to act otherwise than in accordance with (1) and (2) above in order to bring its exchange rate within, or closer to, some target zone of rates, it should consult with the Fund about this target and its adaptation to changing circumstances. If the Fund considers the target to be within the range of reasonable estimates of the medium-term norm for the exchange rate in question, the member would be free, subject to (5), to act aggressively to move its rate toward the target zone, though within that zone (2) would continue to apply.

(b) If the exchange rate of a member with a floating rate has moved outside what the Fund considers to be the range of reasonable estimates of the medium-term norm for that exchange rate to an extent the Fund considers likely to be harmful to the interests of members, the Fund will consult with the member, and in the light of such consultation may encourage the member, despite (2) above, (i) not to act to moderate movements toward this range or (ii) to take action to moderate further divergence from the range. A member would not be asked to hold any particular rate against strong market pressure.

(4) A member with a floating exchange rate would be encouraged to indicate to the Fund its broad objective for the development of its reserves over a period ahead and to discuss this objective with the Fund. If the Fund, taking account of the world reserve situation, considered this objective to be reasonable and if the member's reserves were relatively low by this standard, the member would be encouraged to intervene more strongly to moderate a movement in its rate when the rate was falling than when it was rising. In considering target exchange rate zones under (3), also, the Fund would pay due regard to the desirability of avoiding an increase over the medium term of reserves that were recognized by this standard to be relatively high, and the reduction of reserves that were recognized to be relatively low.

(5) A member with a floating rate, like other members, should refrain from introducing restrictions for balance of payments purposes on current account transactions or payments and should endeavor progressively to remove such restrictions of this kind as may exist.

(6) Members with a floating rate will bear in mind, in intervention, the interests of other members including those of the issuing countries in whose currencies they intervene. Mutually satisfactory arrangements

might usefully be agreed between the issuers and users of intervention currencies, with respect to the use of such currencies in intervention. Any such arrangements should be compatible with the purposes of the foregoing guidelines. The Fund will stand ready to assist members in dealing with any problems that may arise in connection with them.

Executive Board Decision No. 4232-(74/67)
June 13, 1974

18

MERCANTILISM AND
FREE TRADE TODAY

WHEN MERCANTILISM is spoken of in a modern context it is commonly treated as embracing almost any departure from freedom of international trade. Piety, as well as prudence, suggest that I give the concept a somewhat narrower interpretation. The father of political economy, in whose honor we are convened here, traced the various manifestations of mercantilist policy, which admittedly embraced most of the breaches of free trade practice of which he disapproved, to a single root in the fallacious ideas that the mercantilists entertained about money and the balance of payments. This is perhaps fortunate for me since the limitations of my own professional experience suggest that I should focus most of my remarks about modern mercantilism on those aspects of commercial policy most closely related to a balance-of-payments rationale.

Adam Smith treated mercantilism as a *system* of political economy.[1] Those who have researched in depth the economic policy prescriptions of merchants and others in the period of preindustrial capitalism have naturally discerned numerous strands of thought, not all of which can be woven together into anything as unified as a system. To me, however, it appears that Smith isolated, quite successfully, the dominant feature of the ideology underlying the practices he wished to attack. For, of course, he was quite aware that mercantilist doctrine was a way of rationalizing,

Originally prepared by Mr. Fleming as his contribution to the bicentennial of the publication of Adam Smith's *The Wealth of Nations*, held in Glasgow, Scotland, April 2–5, 1976. The paper was delivered by J. J. Polak. It will also be published in Andrew S. Skinner and Thomas Wilson, eds., *The State and the Market* (Oxford: Clarendon Press).

[1] Book IV of *The Wealth of Nations*, in which mercantilism is discussed, is headed "Of Systems of Political Economy."

as being in the general interest, policies whose main motivation lay in special interest, notably desire of merchants and manufacturers to monopolize the home market. The core of the doctrine, as presented by Smith, was that a country could only enrich itself by acquiring the monetary metals, and that the way to acquire these—for a country without gold and silver reserves—was by measures of commercial policy, such as tariffs, export bounties, colonial preferences, and the like, designed to achieve a favorable balance of trade. Heckscher has tried to find an additional reason for the advocacy of a favorable balance of trade in what he calls the "fear of goods," but where it is an exchange of goods and money that is in question it is not altogether easy to distinguish the desire to import fewer goods from a desire to import more money.[2] Perhaps the writers Heckscher had in mind thought of a favorable balance of trade as contributing to increased production, employment, and profits in the country without thinking of its influence being mediated through its effects on the money stock. If so, it prefigures a distinction that later became important in Keynesian theory between the direct influence of the foreign balance on the income flow and its indirect influence via the supply of liquidity.

Smith has been accused with some justice of exaggerating the extent to which the mercantilists identified money and wealth, though he is explicitly aware that they do not always do this, and mentions at least one other reason for which they recommend the accumulation of bullion, namely, to serve as a means of paying for foreign wars. Schumpeter goes so far as to say that the mercantilists never equated money and wealth,[3] but in the next breath he admits that they very often do imply that the export surplus or deficit is the only source of gain or loss for a nation, which comes to very much the same thing. However, it is probably true that Smith does not adequately explain the reasons why the acquisition of money or bullion appeared so desirable to mercantilists. Viner[4] gives a much fuller explanation, citing not only the role of bullion as a symbol of wealth, an emergency reserve, and a store of wealth, but also as a means to bringing about lower interest rates, more active trade, greater output, and higher employment in a country. In what follows I lean a good deal on these particular elements in mercantilist thought.

[2] See E. Heckscher, *Mercantilism* (London: Allen and Unwin, 1935), part IV, ch. 1.
[3] J. A. Schumpeter, *History of Economic Analysis* (London: Allen and Unwin, 1954), p. 361.
[4] J. Viner, *Studies in the Theory of International Trade* (New York: Harper and Row, 1937), ch. 1.

To the practices of interventionism in commercial policy, practices that he treated under the rubric of the mercantile system, Adam Smith opposed his own philosophy of free trade. Several aspects of Smith's presentation of this doctrine are worth mentioning:

1. Free trade is advocated in its unilateral form. Apart from consideration of defense it is assumed to serve the national interest as well as that of the international community.
2. While Smith paid due regard to the virtues of free trade in bringing about the most advantageous distribution of labor and capital among alternative uses or employments, his special contribution was his emphasis on the role played by international trade in promoting a more intensive division of labor and a consequent rise in productivity through the opening up of new or wider markets.
3. While very sensitive to the importance of giving employment, Smith regards the level of employment as determined by the supply and distribution of capital and is not responsive to mercantilist views as to the importance of monetary demand generated by a favorable balance of trade.
4. Smith does not examine the question of freedom of capital movement, as distinct from freedom of trade. Had he done so he would doubtless have supported it from a cosmopolitan standpoint, but his own reasoning about the link between capital and employment would have made it difficult for him to support it in all circumstances from a national standpoint.

I do not propose to dwell on the triumph of free trade in Britain in the first half of the 19th century or what Viner called the intermission in the reign of mercantilism from 1846 to 1916.[5] Classical economics from David Hume onward triumphed over the grosser fallacies of the mercantilists and revealed the attempt to accumulate money and treasure through a favorable balance of trade as a self-frustrating exercise, detracting from, rather than contributing to, the national wealth. Moreover, free trade chimed in with the interests of Britain as the pioneer industrial country, while the success of British industry conferred prestige abroad on the free-trade ideas associated with that success.

When protectionism outside Britain revived in the form of higher tariffs later on in the 19th century, it was at least ostensibly on the basis of arguments that were far from absurd in the light of economic theory—

[5] *Ibid.*, ch. 2, p. 118.

industrial protectionism based on Friedrich List's elaboration of the infant-industry argument, and agrarian protectionism evoked by the rapid cheapening of ocean transport and justified on social or on military grounds that Adam Smith might not have rejected entirely out of hand.

Today, only a few disparate strands of the true mercantilist ideology survive. Gold still retains its role as a store of value for monetary authorities: less, however, as a war chest, or even as a means of securing essential supplies for a country in an emergency, than as a form of asset that is expected to rise in value in the long run relative to currencies. It remains to be seen whether its attractiveness will persist if its value is no longer steadied by the action of central banks but fluctuates according to demand and supply on the market.

Favorable balances of payments and trade continue to be regarded as desirable, but this desire is no longer based on any confusion of money and wealth. It is, however, connected, if somewhat loosely, with one of the objectives entertained by some of the mercantilists, namely, that of securing a sufficiently expansive development of money demand.

BALANCE-OF-PAYMENTS RESTRICTIONS

This brings me to the particular manifestation of modern economic policy that is most strongly reminiscent of mercantilist ideas and to which I largely confine my attention in this paper, namely, the use of restrictions on trade and payments for what are called balance-of-payments reasons. Such restrictions have usually taken a quantitative form—import licensing, quotas, exchange restrictions, tourist allowances, and the like—but sometimes also the form of advance import deposits, multiple exchange rates, or even of import duties. The essence of the balance-of-payments motivation for such measures is the desire to avoid running out of reserves, so as not to be placed before a choice of evils, the choice, namely, between curtailing demand, output, employment, and profits and allowing the exchange rate to depreciate. The first horn of this dilemma entered into the thinking of some of the true mercantilists, the second scarcely at all, since the option of depreciation was open to countries in the days of a metallic monetary system only through the cumbersome mechanism of a debasement of the coinage. Such debasements came to an end in England after the Tudor period. The option became much easier and more tempting after paper had replaced metal as a circulating medium and the monetary metals had been collected into central bank vaults.

It should be added that, though even in modern times the balance-of-payments justification has sometimes served as a screen for other motivations—protection of special interests, or social or developmental policies—this is much less true than during the mercantilist period proper. Special interests have found other rationalizations for the policies they advocate, and it is not so much from merchants and manufacturers as from politicians, bureaucrats, and occasionally economists that the pressure to apply such restrictions has come.

THE INTERWAR PERIOD[6]

Balance-of-payments restrictions came to the fore during the interwar period for two main reasons: (a) highly disturbed conditions of international trade and capital movement and (b) the growth of rigidities in the internal cost structure impeding the correction of international disequilibria.

In the early 1920s, balances of payments in eastern, central, and part of western continental Europe were subjected to tremendous strains as a result of the carving up of new states out of old empires, the strongly resisted attempt to exact high reparations, and above all the development of hyper-inflation in many countries where public finances had broken down. For the most part, however, these strains were taken, not by trade and capital restrictions, but by exchange depreciations. The exenemy countries were limited in their freedom to raise tariffs and the techniques of exchange control had not then been perfected. Nevertheless, in Germany and other countries of central and eastern Europe, import restrictions set up during World War I were retained in order to slow down the depreciation of currencies and thus to avoid the extra fillip to inflation and the deterioration in the terms of trade that were found to result from exchange depreciation.

---

[6] On balance-of-payments restrictions in the interwar period, see various League of Nations publications, particularly *Report on Exchange Control* (1938); *Quantitative Trade Controls: Their Cause and Nature* (1943); *International Currency Experience* (1944). See also Margaret S. Gordon, *Barriers to World Trade* (New York: Macmillan, 1941); H. Ellis, *Exchange Control in Central Europe* (Cambridge, Mass.: Harvard University Press, 1941); and J. Viner, *Trade Relations between Free-Market and Controlled Economies* (Geneva: League of Nations, 1943).

Another factor making for balance-of-payments disequilibria during the 1920s was, of course, the determination of the United Kingdom and one or two other countries to restore their currencies to their prewar parities with gold and the dollar. The difficulties resulting from the overvaluation of sterling were mitigated by the ability of the United Kingdom, as a reserve center, to finance part of its deficits by accumulating reserve liabilities and by attracting private short-term funds from abroad through a tight interest-rate policy. Nevertheless, the high resulting level of unemployment created a climate in which Britain's free-trade tradition was bound to be undermined and protectionist sentiment was bound to grow. Under the circumstances, it is a tribute to the strength of the tradition that the sentiment grew so slowly and manifested itself at first in such comparatively trivial forms as the McKenna duties, safeguarding duties, and the like.

A more general international factor tending to intensify payments difficulties in the 1920s was the scarcity of real reserves in the world. This was attributable in part to an increase in the demand for reserves, associated with enhanced instability in balances of payments and in part to a decline in their rate of growth due to a rise in the prices of other goods and services relative to gold. The scarcity was lessened by the spread of the practice of holding reserves in the form of dollars and sterling, but this afforded only partial relief. Through the pervasive influence that it exercised in favor of monetary restraint, reserve stringency contributed to keeping unemployment relatively high and exercised a downward pressure on primary product prices even during the so-called boom of the late 1920s. It is not surprising, therefore, that tariff protectionism, particularly in the agricultural sphere, should have tended to become more severe at this time.

It was in the 1930s, with the advent of the Great Depression, that balance-of-payments restrictions first appeared on a massive scale and in a variety of forms. With the collapse of primary product prices and the heavy unemployment that developed everywhere, countries became strongly desirous to have more favorable balances of payments on overall, and especially on current, account. Keynesian thinking reflected and encouraged a tendency to think of a favorable current account as a means to higher employment, and Keynes himself advocated revenue import duties prior to the devaluation of 1931.[7] Naturally enough, depression

---

[7] See the Report of the MacMillan Committee (Committee on Finance and Industry, Addendum 1, 1931).

conditions also stimulated protectionism in the field both of industry and, particularly, agriculture.

As in the early 1920s, severe payments disequilibria developed, intensified by "hot money" movements of funds out of countries where bank failures or currency devaluations were feared. The healthful flow of capital that had taken place from the United States to Europe in the later 1920s ceased and was reversed.

An interesting correlation—though not a perfect one—is observable between the extent to which countries subjected to balance-of-payments pressures resorted to restrictions and the nature of the currency experience they had gone through a decade before. By and large, countries like Germany that had experienced hyperinflations were so impressed by the past association of exchange depreciation with inflation that they clung to an overvalued exchange rate despite the severity of their depression and had resort to the severest type of exchange restriction. France and other gold bloc countries, most of which had had milder inflations in the 1920s, adhered for a number of years to a fixed rate before they devalued; they mostly used import restrictions but not exchange controls.[8] And countries such as Britain and the Scandinavians that, though they had experienced free floating had not experienced inflation, relied predominantly on exchange depreciation or devaluation, or pegging on a depreciated currency, together with the use of tariff measures, with but little in the way of quantitative restrictions. Cutting across this classification, however, many primary producing countries, in Latin America and elsewhere, were obliged by the collapse of their export prices to have resort both to exchange depreciation and exchange control.

The difference among countries in their attitudes toward exchange depreciation and the differences in the timing of their resort to it contributed greatly to the payments disequilibria that developed during the 1930s and particularly to the volume of disequilibrating hot money flows. The depreciation of one set of currencies made things more difficult for the countries left stranded with overvalued currencies. Nevertheless, the newfound flexibility of exchange rates probably helped to set the world as a whole on the path to recovery from the depression in two ways, first because the

---

[8] Switzerland and the Netherlands were also members of this group, though they had no inflationary experience of their own. However, as close neighbors of countries that had suffered greatly from inflation they may have been particularly open to a "demonstration effect."

floaters and devaluers felt freer in adopting expansionary policies, and second because the rise in the currency and commodity value of gold helped to relieve the reserve stringency from which the world had been suffering.

As indicated, the spectrum of mercantilist devices more or less related to a balance-of-payments rationale was wide indeed. They ranged from general tariffs and Ottawa Agreements in Britain—belated manifestations of protectionism and economic imperialism for which the basic excuse of cost rigidity no longer existed after 1931—through import quotas in the gold bloc countries to exchange control in central Europe and Latin America.

Exchange control—the restriction of international payments, exchange transactions, and transfers of domestic balances among nonresidents and the enforced surrender of exporters' earnings of foreign exchange—constituted the big contribution of the 1930s to the techniques of intervention. It had two special characteristics. It enabled governments to influence not merely trade flows but also, and indeed especially, capital flows. And it supplied a financial ambiance that provided an incentive for discrimination and for the balancing of international transactions on a bilateral basis. By this method residents could be prevented from exporting, and foreigners from withdrawing, capital. Moreover, by applying to import payments restrictions more stringent than were applied to imports themselves, foreign suppliers might even be induced to provide financing. Sometimes, in order to obtain transfer of debt service, even countries like Britain that did not in general apply exchange controls applied them to exchange-control countries like Germany. Clearing agreements sprang up among exchange-control countries or between exchange-control and nonexchange-control countries in which currently accruing mutual claims were offset, though one side or the other would usually have to queue up to await payment.

As time passed, blocking of export proceeds and even queuing up of exporters for settlement tended to disappear and be replaced by bilateral arrangements under which any balances accumulating in the hands of the bilateral surplus country were held by the monetary authorities of that country. Such an arrangement gave an incentive to each country, particularly the surplus country, to exempt the other from any import restrictions it might have. In this way countries with overvalued currencies could avoid some of the curtailment of trade that would otherwise have taken place, though on a distorted and discriminatory basis. True, both sides, particularly the surplus country, also had an incentive to restrict exports to the other if alternative hard currency markets were available, but the net effect was probably liberalizing. The protection against capital outflows by exchange control and the stimulus to exports afforded by bilateral balancing arrangements enabled some exchange control countries, such as Germany, to restore employment and output, despite extreme overvaluation, in a way that countries relying on trade controls were unable to do and to an extent that few of the flexible exchange-rate countries could equal.

The practice of bilateral bargaining, facilitated by the existence of quantitative restrictions and exchange controls, gave to the larger countries such as Germany and Britain that directly or indirectly were able to exploit it, the advantages of discriminating monopsony. This bargaining power was used by both countries mainly to improve the terms of trade, but in the German case also to achieve a shift in its markets and sources of supply to nearby countries. Britain had a particularly successful fling in the 1930s. Having large import surpluses with most of the exchange control countries, she was able to force them, through the threat of imposing clearings or import restrictions, to discriminate strongly in her favor in their own import policies. Moreover, she derived additional bargaining power from her transition from virtual free trade to tariff protection, and from the expansion of her currency area resulting from the desire of many countries to peg their currencies to a depreciated pound. One of the manifestations of this success was the intensification of imperial tariff preference, which took place under the Ottawa Agreement.

THE POSTWAR PERIOD[9]

The lessons of the interwar period regarding the appropriate role of balance-of-payments restrictions, as assessed by the best contemporary opinion, were reflected after the war in the Articles of Agreement of the

[9] On balance-of-payments restrictions in the post-World War II period, see the Exchange Restrictions Reports of the International Monetary Fund, *The International Monetary Fund, 1945–1965*, J. K. Horsefield, ed. (Washington, D.C.: International Monetary Fund, 1969), chs. 6 and 10 by M. G. de Vries. See also J. H. C. de Looper, "Current Usage of Payments Agreements" and "Recent Latin American Experience with Bilateral Trade and Payments Agreements," both in International Monetary Fund, *Staff Papers*, vol. 4; and M. G. de Vries, "Multiple Exchange Rates: Expectations and Experiences," International Monetary Fund, *Staff Papers*, vol. 12.

IMF and the provisions of the GATT. Controls over capital movements, deemed indispensable for dealing with hot money flows, were regarded as legitimate, and indeed encouraged. Restrictions on current payments and trade were tolerated as temporary devices only, in the absence of adequate financing, pending corrective action through exchange-rate adjustment or other means, and subject to the agreement of the IMF and GATT. Exchange-rate adjustment, though preferred to restriction, was itself subject to IMF consent in order to prevent the competitive exchange depreciation, inspired by mercantilist motives, that had marked the 1930s. This was the long-term regime envisaged at Bretton Woods, but it was recognized that the balance-of-payments situation as it existed at the end of the war would permit only a gradual dismantling of restrictions, and this was provided for in the transitional period arrangements.

The years immediately following World War II were marked by a severe balance-of-payments disequilibria between: (a) the United States and one or two other Western Hemisphere countries and (b) the other industrial countries and most less developed countries. The war and its aftermath led to a severe undervaluation of the dollar and a situation of more or less suppressed inflation in Europe and elsewhere. Suppressed inflation and the associated shortages for a time made exchange-rate adjustment seem unlikely to be effective. Moreover, balance-of-payments assistance on an enormous scale from the United States, though not sufficient to eliminate the disequilibrium, provided in its way a further incentive to postpone adjustment.

In such a situation some restriction of imports and capital exports was inevitable for the great majority of countries. The appropriate financial framework for this was provided by a network of bilateral payments arrangements between countries and currency areas far more extensive than anything that had existed in the 1930s. Within this framework, trade was regulated by quantitative restrictions, undertakings to supply, state trading, and so on. The bilateral payments arrangements, which usually provided for limited swing credits, provided a financial incentive for a mutual relaxation of restrictions. The degree of strict bilateral balancing involved in the system was tempered in the case of the United Kingdom by the practice of freely permitting transfers of sterling earnings between soft-currency countries and the individual members of the sterling area and, after 1947, by the gradual extension of such transferability on a selective basis between soft-currency holders outside the sterling area. The unfortunate attempt made by the United Kingdom in 1947, on the strength of a large loan, to restore the convertibility of sterling into dollars, thus exposing its exports to nondiscriminatory treatment—and to do this without devaluation, without tying up the accumulated sterling balances, and without contracting the money supply—was one that was bound to fail, and Britain returned quickly to the bilateral fold. The events of 1947 do not, as Dr. Balogh has recently alleged, mark the early collapse of the Bretton Woods arrangements, but merely reflect a premature abandonment of the transitional period safeguards.

There is no doubt that the trade discrimination inherent in the system described had the advantage, at least in the short run, of enabling useful trade to flow that might otherwise have been suppressed. The objection to it was that it might blunt the incentive for the soft-currency countries to take the necessary steps to achieve the sort of adjustment of their price levels and balances of payments that would enable them to get rid of restrictions altogether.

These fears were quite natural and logical, but they were not fulfilled. For this there were a number of reasons. In the first place, sterling was forced into devaluation in 1949, and with it went the other sterling-area currencies and most of the European currencies as well. An overvalued currency is always in a precarious position, no matter how strong a bastion of controls may be built around it. There is always a possibility that adverse developments in world markets and speculative capital outflows may bring it tumbling down. In this case, the U.S. business recession of 1948 was enough to do the trick. Many types of outflow from Britain could be prevented by capital controls and inconvertibility, but with a trade turnover as large as that of the sterling area a relatively slight shift in the timing of trade payments was enough to bring about the exhaustion of Britain's reserves.

These devaluations were very large. Indeed, from a longer-term point of view they were probably excessive. Once brought to the point of devaluation it seemed prudent to the authorities concerned to include a safety margin. This was an early example of how the system of adjustable par values, incorporated in the Bretton Woods Agreement of 1944, was likely to work, and how difficult it was to prevent competitive depreciation. However, a good foundation was laid for the correction of the dollar shortage and the elimination of restrictions and controls.

Other factors came in to reinforce the effect of the exchange-rate adjustment. First came the rapid recovery of European productivity in the 1950s and 1960s from the low levels to which it had sunk in the immediate postwar period—a recovery that was given a powerful impetus by the capital investment made possible by Marshall Aid. And finally governments did gradually learn to control excess demand and give up the cheap-money ideology that had prevailed in the Dalton era. In this way it became possible to prevent the gains of devaluation and productivity growth from being swallowed up by inflation. In this some countries, such as Germany and Belgium, which had had monetary reforms involving the radical curtailment of their money stocks, led the way, and Belgium, in particular, became a relatively hard-currency member of the soft-currency bloc—a fact that gave rise to some trade discrimination against it within the European area.

The semibilateralist phase in European recovery was followed by a phase of resolute liberalization and multilateralization on a regional basis. The improvement of the balance-of-payments position of the European countries, the continuance of Marshall Aid, and the paternal encouragement of the ECA emboldened the members of the OEEC in 1950 to take the leap of adopting multilateral settlement of their bilateral imbalances, leaving settlement to be made between regional surplus and regional deficit countries. This leap would have been impossible at the time without the setting up of the European Payments Union (EPU), which enabled these settlements to be made partly in credit (which pleased the deficit countries), partly in gold or dollars (which pleased the surplus countries). The multilateralization of settlements removed the incentive for discrimination in trade policy as among the members of the EPU. Nondiscrimination, however, might conceivably have led to some restriction of trade among the softer-currency countries. That this did not happen is due, first, to the buffer of EPU credit and, second, to the organized effort to remove import restrictions within the OEEC, which went by the name of the liberalization program. This effort took the form, primarily, of removal of restrictions on prescribed percentages of imports, increasing through time, in different categories.[10] Individual OEEC countries in-

---

[10] There was also a liberalization program for invisibles.

creasingly extended OEEC liberalization also to specified soft-currency countries outside the OEEC area. However, this liberalization was not at first extended in equal measure to imports from the dollar area, so that the result that the founding fathers of Bretton Woods had intended to achieve by the famous "scarce currency clause" of the Articles of Agreement of the IMF was achieved in a very indirect way through the extension of liberalization within the nondollar world. This result, which, of course, involved a discrimination against the United States, was carried out with the backing and approval of the U.S. authorities themselves— something that appears rather remarkable in these more contentious days.

Of course, there were some, including some within the IMF, who felt misgivings lest tolerance of discrimination against the United States might prove an obstacle to the balance-of-payments adjustment that would permit an all-around liberalization of quantitative restrictions. But the truth was that the actions necessary for this adjustment had already taken place, and in the course of the 1950s would work out their effects.

The 1950s witnessed the crumbling of inconvertibility in the world and the dwindling of restrictions in industrial countries on imports from the dollar area. Transferability of nondollar currencies was not extended to the dollar area, nor were nondollar currencies generally made convertible, through exchange markets, into dollars until 1958, but before that dollar settlements within the EPU had been increasing in importance and a sort of indirect convertibility had sprung up through the transit trade and the London commodity markets. Moreover, from 1955 on, the Bank of England had been intervening in the market in support of transferable sterling. All of this tended to erode the distinction between "hard" and "soft" currencies. At the same time, both in the OEEC and in the IMF, increasing pressure was brought to bear on countries to reduce differential restrictions on dollar imports. More importantly, the "dollar shortage," the basic disequilibrium between the United States and other industrial countries, was disappearing—though some economists in Britain found that difficult to believe, possibly because the United Kingdom with its relatively low savings and productivity growth and its high employment objectives was having recurrent difficulties in balancing its own accounts with the rest of the world. Some remnants of balance-of-payments restriction on dollar imports lingered on in Europe for a few years after the restoration of convertibility, but these had virtually disappeared by the end of the decade.

RESTRICTIONS IN LESS DEVELOPED COUNTRIES

The removal or even reduction of balance-of-payments restrictions proved much more difficult in less developed than in industrial countries. Just after the war many of the former were in a strong balance-of-payments position because of the balances of foreign exchange that they had accumulated and been unable to spend during the war. However, they had also accumulated a backlog of import requirements, and within a few years most of them were getting very short of foreign exchange.

A number of factors combined to bring this about. In many cases, particularly in Latin America, governments pursued lax fiscal and monetary policies, partly because they were weak in the face of special interests and partly because of the urgency of expanding development expenditure. But while pursuing this inflationary course most of these countries were unwilling to maintain their competitiveness by an adequate depreciation of their currencies. Many of them had to resort to multiple exchange rates. Others resorted to severe import restrictions which, in extreme cases, extended to the importation of materials and the throttling of the economy.

The reluctance to devalue sometimes reflected financial conservatism and a fear that depreciation would worsen the terms of trade and aggravate inflation, but it was also motivated by the desire to have a balance-of-payments excuse for policies that facilitated the raising of revenue, the protection of import-competing industry, the diversification of exports, or the cheapening of imports of capital goods and wage goods, and thus were deemed to promote economic development and social peace. In some countries, which developed an ideology of planning and interventionism as the royal road to development, quantitative import restriction was welcomed as a technique for controlling imports and the flow of materials and thus the direction of economic activity. In such cases we can say that rather than restrictions being the consequence of balance-of-payments difficulties, the payments difficulties were a means to the enjoyment of restrictions.

In ECLA in the 1950s and UNCTAD in the 1960s a rather sophisticated doctrine was developed according to which less developed countries were deemed to suffer from balance-of-payments difficulties of a structural sort that could not easily be relieved by devaluation.[11] This doctrine, not without foundation in fact, postulated that, owing to the relatively low income elasticity of demand for primary products as compared with manufactures and to the substitution of natural by synthetic products, there is a tendency for primary producers, particularly the less developed ones, to experience persistently deteriorating terms of trade and persistent balance-of-payments difficulties. Moreover, owing to price inelasticity in the demand for their products, primary producers as a group could not relieve these difficulties by devaluation or price adjustment without an unconscionable further deterioration in their terms of trade. Initially, the conclusion drawn from this argument, the validity of which has been a matter of some controversy, was that the developing primary producers should ration foreign exchange and encourage import-competing industries through suitably devised protective measures. Later, in the 1960s, the conclusion was rather that the advanced industrial countries should relieve the balance-of-payments constraint of the less developed countries through the provision of aid and the preferential treatment of imports from the latter.

Whatever advantages currency overvaluation may have for the terms of trade of primary exporting countries taken collectively—and this is rather doubtful considering the supply conditions governing many primary products—there can be little doubt that it has proved an unfortunate policy for the countries adopting it, taken individually. Indeed, when it has resulted in multiple exchange rates and still more, when it has resulted in quantitative import restriction, it has distorted the economies and hampered the development of the countries concerned, discouraging the production of exports and of essential goods for the home market and encouraging the costly and inefficient production of less essential manufactures. There has indeed been, over the postwar period, a marked correlation among less developed countries in the rate of growth of per capita output and the degree of reliance on market mechanisms in preference to controls.

[11] See "The Economic Development of Latin America and its Principal Problems," *Economic Commission for Latin America* (New York: United Nations, 1950): R. Prebisch, "Towards a New Trade Policy for Development," (New York: United Nations, 1964): M. J. Flanders, "Prebisch on Protectionism: An Evaluation," *The Economic Journal* (June 1964), 74:305–26.

In the case of developing countries, a major role in the struggle against inflation, overvaluation, and balance-of-payments difficulties has been played by the IMF, particularly in the 1950s and 1960s. Not only was the IMF itself in a position to offer relatively cheap financial assistance in the form of three-to-five-year loans and stand-by credits as a bait to the adoption of appropriate adjustment policies, but commercial bank lenders, particularly in New York, fell into the habit of making their own financial assistance to these countries contingent on the obtaining of a stand-by credit from the IMF, which added considerably to the latter's "clout."

Policies insisted on by the IMF as a condition for stand-bys and drawings in the higher credit tranches have generally included the imposition of quantitative limitations on the expansion of central bank credit and particularly credit to the public sector; in addition, there have usually been conditions regarding the reduction or elimination of multiple exchange rates, and the devaluation of or, frequently, the floating of exchange rates. In advocating these somewhat monetarist policies, the IMF generally found itself in alliance with the central banks and the finance ministries of the countries concerned, but not always with other parts of the government.

Progress in overcoming inflation and reducing payments restrictions in developing countries was slow at first but gained speed later. The second half of the 1950s and first half of the 1960s witnessed a widespread decline in the use of bilateralism and multiple exchange rates. Bilateralism, of course, lost much of its *raison d'être*, even for less developed countries, as the currencies of trading partners became convertible; however, it revived somewhat with the growth of trading connections with Communist countries. The less developed world found it harder to dispense with import restrictions; the quantitative kind were on the whole relaxed in the 1960s, but were in part replaced by more refined techniques, such as import surcharges and import deposit requirements. In some important countries in Latin America, liberalization was fostered in the 1960s by the adoption of a system of sliding parities under which exchange rates were frequently adjusted to keep pace with relative inflation. On the other hand, the emergence, in Africa, of a large number of newly independent states was followed by the appearance of balance-of-payments difficulties and the adoption of restrictions in areas where trade had previously been relatively free.

DOLLAR DEFICIT

While the 1950s witnessed the dwindling of the dollar shortage, the extrapolation of that movement into the 1960s, reinforced by the expansionism of the Kennedy and Johnson administrations, tended to increase the payments deficits of the United States to a point which gave rise to a certain mild anxiety in that country and evoked somewhat petulant reproaches about the exportation of inflation in one or two of the surplus European countries. That the anxiety felt in the United States was mild was due to the fact that, as the ultimate reserve center, it could rely on financing a sizable proportion of any deficits through the dollar accumulations of other countries, besides which it was still sitting on a sizable fraction of the world's gold. This anxiety therefore did not find expression for a long time in any sort of commercial restriction. Indeed, in the Kennedy round the United States took the lead in promoting a notable reduction of tariff barriers. The principal form in which it expressed itself was the imposition of restrictions on the outflow of capital through such measures as the Interest Equalization Tax, the restrictions on direct investment financed from the United States, and the voluntary program restricting the outflow of banking funds. These restrictions, though mercantilist on one interpretation, were entirely in accordance with the ideology of Bretton Woods, and since they exempted the developing countries and Canada from their scope, were offensive to nobody except certain groups in the United States itself. An additional manifestation of balance-of-payments anxiety in the United States in the 1960s is found in the moral pressure exerted on official holders of dollars to refrain from converting them into gold, and in the decision in 1968 to terminate the gold pool and allow the value of gold in the private market to rise far above its official value. These developments had sinister implications for the future of the Bretton Woods arrangements.

To most countries outside the United States, the U.S. deficit in the 1960s provided a welcome, if somewhat inadequate, stimulus to world reserves of foreign exchange and contributed to the prolongation of the period of economic euphoria beginning in the 1950s. However, as I said, there were one or two countries, such as Switzerland and Germany, which felt, even in the early 1960s, that they were being subjected to inflationary pressures from an undue influx of reserves. These countries adopted various techniques to restrict the inflow of capital. Whether one regards this policy as antimercantilistic or mercantilistic depends on whether he regards the mercantilistic preoccupation with the balance of payments as relating to the overall balance or the current account balance. By preventing capital imports, these policies reduced the need for an exchange appreciation or rise in the price level that, had they occurred, would have entailed a deterioration in the balance of trade.

In the early 1970s the overvaluation of the U.S. dollar, masked in 1969 by inflows of funds of a cyclical character, became indisputable and apparently progressive to a point that alarmed the U.S. authorities, first because of its effect on the balance of trade and second because it threatened to overstrain the gentlemen's agreement of central banks not to convert their dollar accumulations and thus to exhaust U.S. gold reserves. This situation, it will be recalled, drove the United States into putting an end to convertibility in August 1971 and effectively devaluing in December 1971 and again in February 1973. It also led them to the imposition of a temporary import surcharge on balance-of-payments grounds in August 1971. The primary motive of all these actions was to improve the balance of payments of the United States either directly or by inducing other industrial countries to allow their dollar exchange rates to appreciate. The reluctance shown by some of these countries, particularly in 1971, to revalue their currencies, or allow them to appreciate, probably reflected, in part, a desire to avoid a deterioration in the current account balance at a time when business was not too brisk.

The period of rather widely generalized floating of exchange rates among industrial countries, which began in February 1973, is still very young and it is uncertain how long it will last. The primary producing countries generally continue to peg their currencies to one of the principal currencies or to a composite of currencies, but even for them exchange-rate flexibility has greatly increased. In the 1930s resort to exchange depreciation by one group of countries had led to the imposition of restrictions of increasing severity on the part of other countries. The more generalized application of exchange flexibility in the 1970s, however, has had a very different effect, despite the fact that the system has been exposed to one of the biggest exogenous balance-of-payments shocks of all time in the form of the oil-price increase of December 1973. It is true that, for non-oilproducing countries *as a group*, the so-called oil deficit on current account was matched by a corresponding surplus on capital account, as the OPEC countries invested their profits abroad or accumulated reserves in currency form. Nevertheless, there was plenty of scope for massive disequilibria within the group of non-oilproducing countries themselves and such did indeed tend to arise. The less developed countries, in particular, though initially protected from the impact of the oil price increases by high prices for their export products, suffered in 1975 a sharp deterioration in their terms of trade *vis-à-vis* industrial countries, and this coming on top of the oil-price increase has put many of them into a very difficult position.

In spite of these disturbances there has thus far been remarkably little resort to restrictionism by industrial or even by primary producing countries. This has been due to a combination of circumstances. Some of the credit must go to the much-abused European-currency market, together with the willingness of countries to borrow where necessary from the private market. Some of it must go to the system of managed exchange-rate floating which, at some cost to exchange stability in the short term, has succeeded in containing disequilibrating capital flows, and has also permitted exchange rates to adjust in the longer run to differential rates of inflation. A good deal of credit also must go to international bodies, such as the IMF, the OECD, the GATT, and the EEC, which in their various ways have cooperated to resist a spread of restrictions. The Committee of Twenty of the IMF, in January 1974, called upon countries to refrain from responding to the oil deficit by escalating trade restrictions or by competitive depreciation,[12] and the OECD ministers of the principal countries have, in two successive years, adopted a pledge to this effect.[13] Special facilities were set up, inside and outside the IMF to help countries finance the payments deficits arising out of the oil-price increases, and in the administration of its oil facility, both in 1974 and 1975, the IMF has been very firm in requiring borrowers to refrain from introducing import restrictions (quantitative or otherwise) or, where this seemed unavoidable, to apply them on a strictly temporary basis.

These influences have not been able entirely to prevent a recrudescence of restrictionism, but they have succeeded in keeping it within bounds.

[12] See communiqué of the January 1974 meeting of the Committee of Twenty in Rome.
[13] See communiqués of OECD ministerial meetings (OECD press releases of May 30, 1974 and May 29, 1975).

In general the new or intensified restrictions on imports have been selective rather than general in their application, and in only a few cases have they been used as a major instrument of adjustment. There has been a noticeable increase in the use of advance import deposit requirements, notably in the case of Italy; these are intended to affect domestic liquidity as well as the balance of payments. And many countries, notably the United Kingdom, have applied restrictions on imports competing with particular industries; these are in part protective in character. Only in a few cases have restrictions been used as a major instrument of balance-of-payments adjustment, and then their use has avowedly been temporary. Such restrictions, if of the quantitative type, can sometimes be justified as a means of avoiding the cost-inflationary effects of a too rapid exchange depreciation.

CONCLUSION

Many of you will probably be thinking I have a tendency to look at the world through rose-colored spectacles. Economists usually prefer the part of Cassandra to that of Pollyanna, but I appear to have reversed that preference. I have argued that the neo-mercantilism that arose in the interwar period and culminated immediately after the second world war, in the form of trade and payments restrictions undertaken on balance-of-payments grounds, has been whittled down in the course of time into a phenomenon of relatively minor and temporary importance. Let me summarize the main reasons for this. The spread of international organization and consultation has given increased leverage to the academic arguments against restriction by making it an issue of reciprocal rather than unilateral action. The fact that the largest payments deficits have fallen on countries in an exceptionally good position to finance them has made the avoidance of restrictions somewhat easier. But the principal factor has been the increasing flexibility of exchange rates, necessitated first by the existence of national price rigidities and secondly by the phenomenal increase in the international mobility of short-term capital, which restrictions were clearly unable to control. Once floating rates had been adopted as the sovereign means of keeping overall payments in balance, the retention of restrictions for the purpose of influencing the balance of current account payments as such became more difficult to justify.

Lest I be accused of exaggerating my thesis, I would say there has been a certain disassociation of mercantilist means or measures from mercantilist ends or motivations, though each taken by itself has, in some measure, continued to flourish. As we have seen, there have been times when countries have sought to improve the balance of payments in general, not by import restriction, but by overdevaluation (or nonrevaluation) or to improve the balance of trade in particular by restricting capital inflows and thus holding down the exchange rate. And, of course, there have been many cases in which trade restrictions have been applied with a protectionist rather than a balance-of-payments motivation.

Consciousness of my limitations has prevented me from extending my review over the field of commercial policy and protectionism in general. If I had done so I might have come to conclusions almost as optimistic on that subject. Progress towards trade liberalization in that broader area may owe rather more to deliberate international cooperative action and rather less to developments in the economic environment than in the narrower sphere of balance-of-payments restrictions. However that may be, I believe that it would be a mistake for economists today to direct too much of their attention to the question of freedom of international transactions as a means to economic welfare. The present-day world is full of evils and horrors, even in the purely economic sphere. But they lie in the areas of excessive population growth, persistent poverty in underdeveloped countries, and the conjunction of inflation and unemployment in countries in general rather than in that of impediments to international economic integration.